THE HUMAN RIGHTS OF COMPANIES

The Human Rights of Companies

Exploring the Structure of ECHR Protection

MARIUS EMBERLAND

OXFORD
UNIVERSITY PRESS

This book has been printed digitally and produced in a standard specification in order to ensure its continuing availability

OXFORD
UNIVERSITY PRESS

Great Clarendon Street, Oxford OX2 6DP

Oxford University Press is a department of the University of Oxford.
It furthers the University's objective of excellence in research, scholarship,
and education by publishing worldwide in

Oxford New York

Auckland Cape Town Dar es Salaam Hong Kong Karachi
Kuala Lumpur Madrid Melbourne Mexico City Nairobi
New Delhi Shanghai Taipei Toronto

With offices in

Argentina Austria Brazil Chile Czech Republic France Greece
Guatemala Hungary Italy Japan South Korea Poland Portugal
Singapore Switzerland Thailand Turkey Ukraine Vietnam

Published in the United States
by Oxford University Press Inc., New York

Reprinted 2008

ISBN 978-0-19-928983-7

Le secret d'ennuyer est celui de tout dire

Voltaire

Preface

This is a study of the European Court of Human Rights' doctrinal response to complaints for protection under the Convention for the Protection of Human Rights and Fundamental Freedoms (the European Human Rights Convention) (Rome, 4 November 1950; TS 71 (1953); cmd 8969) submitted by or on behalf of companies. Companies indisputably enjoy Convention protection in principle yet the protection of persons closely tied with for-profit and corporate business enterprise is sometimes doctrinally problematic. The book analyses the Court's reasoning in three groups of cases in which corporate human rights litigation has presented particular problems of treaty interpretation. The case law is streamlined in a minimalist fashion, which often obscures the Court's rationale. The book construes the structural framework within which the Court operates, and seeks to explain how the relevant case law is largely coherent when considered on these grounds. The Court's response is used for highlighting crucial aspects of the Convention system that are aptly revealed but which extend beyond the company context. These are the Convention as a European liberal project, a characteristic that makes it stand out from the bulk of international human rights law; the complex nature of the Convention's object and purpose, and, consequently, the Court's teleology; and finally, the collective and economic aspects of the Convention's civil and political rights. Ultimately I have wanted to show that human rights law can be a many-sided thing.

The book is based on my thesis submitted to the Faculty of Law at the University of Oxford for the degree of D.Phil. It is the result of three and a half years of work in Oxford, in New York, and in Oslo. A number of people and institutions deserves acknowledgement. In particular I wish to thank my supervisor, Professor Christopher McCrudden of Lincoln College. I have benefited from his brilliance and been encouraged by his geniality.

Thanks also to my first year assessors, Professor Paul Craig of St John's College and Professor Vaughan Lowe of All Souls College; to my examiners, Professor Colin Warbrick of Durham University and Dr Mads Andenæs, then Director of the British Institute of International and Comparative Law; and to Professor Peter Muchlinski of the University of Kent, the Press's reviewer. I am indebted to Sir Nicolas Bratza and Professors Lucius Caflisch and Matti Pellonpää, judges of the European Court of Human Rights, who found time to read parts of my thesis and discuss some problems with me in Strasbourg in between their work at an overburdened Court. I also thank Associate Professor Jan E. Helgesen of the Norwegian Centre for Human Rights, University of Oslo; Professor Ola Mestad of the Centre for European Law at the University of Oslo; Professor Jørgen Aall of the University of Bergen; and Professor Francesca Klug of the Centre for the Study of Human Rights, London School of Economics. Professor Joseph H. H. Weiler of the New York University School of Law I thank for his general advice that good research is characterized less by finding answers and more by discovering new problems that need further studies. Dr Gwen Booth deserves a particular thank-you for her kind and properly demanding editorship at the Press.

Thanks to the staff of the Bodleian Law Library; the Lincoln College Library; the library of the Centre for Socio-Legal Studies in Oxford; the New York University School of Law Library; and the library of the Norwegian Centre for Human Rights; to Mr Chris Saunders for his proof-reading and improvement of a rather un-English manuscript; to Mr Fredrik Anspach for his diligent check of sources; and to Associate Professor Solveig Schult Ulriksen at the Institute of Classical and Roman Studies at the University of Oslo in finding the original version of a proverb of Voltaire, which has been rendered in countless ways in various sources.

The work has largely been financed by the Research Council of Norway, but I have also benefited from stipends from the Otto Løvenskiold Foundation for my stay in Oxford; and Ruhrgas stipends from the Deutsch-Norwegisches Stipendienprogramm that enabled me to browse the impressive library holdings of the Max-Planck-Institut für ausländisches öffentliches Recht und Völkerrecht in Heidelberg. I was very fortunate to work in the proximity of Professor Joseph H. H. Weiler as an Émile Noël Fellow at the Jean Monnet Center for Regional and International Law & Justice at the New York University School of Law in the academic year 2002/2003. I have been affiliated throughout with the Norwegian Centre for Human Rights at the Faculty of Law, University of Oslo, and therefore thank Directors Nils Butenschøn and Geir Ulfstein for their institutional support. I have also been affiliated with the Centre for Socio-Legal Studies at the University of Oxford during my doctorate period.

Le secret d'ennuyer est celui de tout dire can roughly be translated thus: the best way to bore people is to tell them everything. It epitomizes my thesis approach in the sense that it has not been my intention to reveal all aspects of the status of companies' rights under the European Convention on Human Rights, but rather to focus on some problematic fields for the purpose of generating insight of the Convention as a whole.

Writing a doctoral thesis is a daunting experience. Since it also is fun, it inevitably distracts you from other aspects of life. Lill and Filip have constantly pulled me back to daily life and thereby kept me sane during the last three and a half years. It may be sentimental to say so, but nonetheless it is true. When all comes to all, nothing but them really matters.

The materials consulted have been updated as of 1 September 2005.

M.E.

Table of Contents

Table of Cases

This table lists all judicial decisions referred to in the dissertation.

EUROPEAN COURT OF HUMAN RIGHTS—JUDGMENTS

EUROPEAN COURT OF HUMAN RIGHTS—ADMISSIBILITY DECISIONS

EUROPEAN COMMISSION OF HUMAN RIGHTS—ADMISSIBILITY DECISIONS

EUROPEAN COMMISSION OF HUMAN RIGHTS—REPORTS

COMMITTEE OF MINISTERS OF THE COUNCIL OF EUROPE—RESOLUTIONS

INTERNATIONAL COURT OF JUSTICE

PERMANENT COURT OF INTERNATIONAL JUSTICE

INTER-AMERICAN COURT OF HUMAN RIGHTS

INTER-AMERICAN COMMISSION OF HUMAN RIGHTS

UNITED NATIONS HUMAN RIGHTS COMMITTEE

EUROPEAN COURT OF JUSTICE AND THE COURT OF FIRST INSTANCE

IRAN–UNITED STATES OF AMERICA CLAIMS TRIBUNAL

ICSID DECISIONS

BUNDESVERFASSUNGSGERICHT

SUPREME COURT OF THE UNITED STATES

HOUSE OF LORDS

Table of Legal Instruments

List of Abbreviations

JOURNALS AND OTHER ACADEMIC PERIODICALS

AEL	Collected Courses of the Academy of European Law
AfP	Archiv für Presserecht
Am Bus L J	American Business Law Journal
Am J Comp L	American Journal of Comparative Law
AöR	Archiv des öffentlichen Rechts
Asian Ybk Intl L	Asian Yearbook of International Law
Austrian Rev Intl & Eur L	Austrian Review of International and European Law
BYIL	British Year Book of International Law
Cambridge Ybk Eur Leg Stud	Cambridge Yearbook of European Legal Studies
CDE	Cahiers de droit européen
CLJ	Cambridge Law Journal
Cornell Intl L J	Cornell International Law Journal
Cornell L Rev	Cornell Law Review
Delaware J Corp L	Delaware Journal of Corporate Law
DöV	Die öffentliche Verwaltung
EHRLR	European Human Rights Law Review
EJIL	European Journal of International Law
ELR	European Law Review
EuGRZ	Europäische Grundrechte-Zeitschrift
Eur Comp L Rev	European Competition Law Review
Eur J Intl Relations	European Journal of International Relations
Finnish Ybk Intl L	Finnish Yearbook of International Law
Ga L Rev	Georgia Law Review
Geo Wash L Rev	George Washington Law Review
German L J	German Law Journal
Hague Ybk Intl L	Hague Yearbook of International Law
Harv HRJ	Harvard Human Rights Journal
Harv L Rev	Harvard Law Review
Hastings L J	Hastings Law Journal
HRJ	Human Rights Journal
HRLJ	Human Rights Law Journal

HRLR	Human Rights Law Review
HRQ	Human Rights Quarterly
ICCLR	International Company and Commercial Law Review
ICLQ	International and Comparative Law Quarterly
ICSID Rev	ICSID Review
Intl Bus Lawyer	International Business Lawyer
ILM	International Legal Materials
IO	International Organization
Israel Ybk HR	Israel Yearbook on Human Rights
It Ybk Intl L	Italian Yearbook of International Law
JIEL	Journal of International Economic Law
JdT	Journal des Tribunaux: Droit européen
JMWP	Jean Monnet Working Paper
L & Contemp Probs	Law and Contemporary Problems
L & Phil	Law and Philosophy
LQR	Law Quarterly Review
Mich J Intl L	Michigan Journal of International Law
MLR	Modern Law Review
Notre Dame L Rev	Notre Dame Law Review
OJLS	Oxford Journal of Legal Studies
Phil Intl L J	Philippine International Law Journal
Phil & Pub Aff	Philosophy and Public Affairs
PL	Public Law
RDISDPS	Revue de droit international, de sciences diplomatiques, politiques, et socials
RGDIP	Revue générale de droit international public
RZaiP	Rabels Zeitschrift für ausländisches und internationales Privatrecht
Receuil des Cours	Receuil de Cours de l'Académie de Droit International
S Ct Rev	Supreme Court Review
SMU L Rev	South Methodist University Law Review
Va L Rev	Virginia Law Review
VJIL	Virginia Journal of International Law

YEL	Yearbook of European Law
YLJ	Yale Law Journal
ZaöRV	Zeitschrift für ausländisches öffentliches Recht und Völkerrecht

MISCELLANEOUS

ACHR	American Convention on Human Rights
App	Application No
BverfGE	Entscheidungen des Bundesverfassungsgerichts
CD	Collection of Decisions of the European Commission of Human Rights
DR	European Commission of Human Rights: Decisions and Reports
ECJ	European Court of Justice
ECHR	European Convention for the Protection of Human Rights and Fundamental Freedoms
ECR	European Case Reports
ETS	European Treaty Series
GC	Grand Chamber
ICCA Ybk	ICCA Yearbook Commercial Arbitration
ICCPR	International Covenant on Civil and Political Rights
ICSID	International Centre for Settlement of Investment Disputes
ICJ	International Court of Justice
ICJ Rep	ICJ Reports
ILC	International Law Commission
Iran–US CTR	Iran–US Claims Tribunal Reports
OJ	Official Journal of the European Communities
PC	Plenary Court
PCIJ	Permanent Court of International Justice
PCIJ Series	Permanent Court of International Justice: Series A: Collection of Decisions
Reports	European Court of Human Rights: Reports of Judgments and Decisions
Rules of Court	Rules of Court of the European Court of Human Rights

Series A	European Court of Human Rights: Series A: Judgments and Decisions
UDHR	Universal Declaration of Human Rights
UNTS	United Nations Treaty Series
US	United States Supreme Court Reports
Vienna Convention	Vienna Convention on the Law of Treaties
Yearbook	Yearbook of the European Convention on Human Rights

1

Introduction

A. Object and Purpose

1 The Coupling of Business and Fundamental Rights and Freedoms

In various legal systems business entities such as companies are protected by rights and freedoms that are regarded as fundamental to individual human beings and the societies in which they live. Customary international law and treaty law afford, for instance, considerable protection of corporate foreign investment, typically through guarantees such as non-discrimination, property protection and due process standards.[1] The rights-catalogues of national constitutions, originally designed with the concerns of individuals in mind,[2] often apply by extension to non-individual actors; as has been notoriously shown in constitutional practice in the United States, companies are prone to making use of this opening in their strategizing vis-à-vis public authorities' exercise of regulatory power.[3] The fundamental rights regime of the European Union is a potent example of the allure, at the level of supranational law, of fundamental rights and freedoms to corporate actors: corporate claims make up a large part

[1] P Malanczuk *Akehurst's Modern Introduction to International Law* (7th edn, Routledge London, 1997) 100–4. See further, eg, I Seidl-Hohenveldern *Corporations in and under International Law* (Grotius Cambridge, 1987) 1–54; L Caflisch *La protection des sociétés commerciales et des intérêts indirects en droit international public* (Martinus Nijhoff Hague, 1969); FP Feliciano 'Legal Problems of Private International Business Enterprises: An Introduction to the International Law of Private Business Associations and Economic Development' (1966-II) 118 Receuil de Cours de l'Académie de Droit International 209; and KA Al-Shawi *The Role of the Corporate Entity in International Law* (Overbeck Ann Arbor MI, 1957).

[2] W Friedmann *The Changing Structures of International Law* (University of Columbia Press New York, 1964) 232.

[3] It is a permanently contentious issue in US constitutional legal discourse, as exemplified by CJ Mayer 'Personalizing the Impersonal: Corporations and the Bill of Rights' (1990) 41 Hastings LJ 577. Overviews of the law are provided also by others, eg, P Blumberg 'The Corporate Entity in an Era of Multinational Corporations' (1990) 14 Delaware J Corp L 283, 299–326; and SG Wood and BG Scharffs 'Applicability of Human Rights Standards to Private Corporations: An American Perspective' (2002) 50 Am J Comp L 531, 547–32.

of the fundamental rights litigation brought before the European Court of Justice.[4]

International human rights discourse has only recently engaged with the coupling of business practices and fundamental rights standards,[5] though it tends to concern itself more with whether companies are or should be bound by international human rights norms than with companies as beneficiaries of human rights law.[6] This is understandable. The impression of human rights as 'the language of victims and the dispossessed' is not uncommon.[7] Experience shows, besides, that uninhibited free enterprise often is at odds with respect for individual integrity, a central tenet of international human rights. In the received tradition, moreover, corporations are often associated with power, and checks against abuse of power are central to the idea of human rights law (these themes are dealt with later). At the same time it is clear that the corpus of international human rights law, although derived from several philosophical traditions,[8] is indebted to liberalism in the vein of, say, Mill, where economic freedom in terms of private ownership is a premise for liberty.[9] This has given reason for some to argue that the ideas of free enterprise and human rights share a common ground.[10]

2 The European Convention and Corporate Rights

Philosophical commonalities or normatively laden disputes aside, it cannot be denied that civil and political rights as found in international treaties can be capable of protecting different forms of economic activity.[11] This is an aspect which is rarely comprehensively discussed in human rights theory or practice

[4] W Mattli and A-M Slaughter 'Revisiting the European Court of Justice' (1998) 52 IO 177, 188–90. Some observers criticize the business community's utilization of these norms, eg, C Harlow 'Access to Justice as a Human Right: The European Convention and the European Union' in *The EU and Human Rights* (P Alston ed) (Oxford University Press Oxford, 1999) 187, 195–197; J Coppel and A O'Neill 'The European Court of Justice: Taking Rights Seriously?' (1992) 29 CMLR 669, 689–91.

[5] An overview can be found in MK Addo (ed) *Human Rights Standards and the Responsibility of Transnational Corporations* (Kluwer Hague, 1999). See also J Dine *Companies, International Trade and Human Rights* (Cambridge University Press Cambridge, 2005)

[6] Relatively new and comprehensive discussions are found in, eg, S Joseph *Corporations and Transnational Human Rights Litigation* (Hart Oxford, 2004); N Jägers *Corporate Human Rights Obligations: In Search of Accountability* (Intersentia Antwerp, 2002); and MT Kamminga and S Zia-Zarifi (eds) *Liability of Multinational Corporations under International Law* (Kluwer Hague, 2000).

[7] J Donnelly *International Human Rights* (2nd edn Westview Boulder Col, 1998) 20.

[8] JJ Shestack 'The Philosophic Foundations of Human Rights' (1998) 20 HRQ 201.

[9] eg, JW Harris *Property and Justice* (Clarendon Press Oxford, 1996) 301.

[10] eg, EU Petersmann 'Human Rights and International Economic Law in the 21st Century. The Need to Clarify their Interrelationships' (2001) 4 JIEL 3. Contrast P Alston 'Resisting the Merger and Acquisition of Human Rights by Trade Law: A Reply to Petersmann' (2002) 13 EJIL 815.

[11] K Vasak 'Analytical Examination of Civil and Political Rights' in K Vasak and P Alston (eds) *The International Dimensions of Human Rights* (UNESCO Paris, 1982) vol 1, 142, 158–59.

and perhaps understandably so since human rights first and foremost are meant for individuals and not for corporations.

This book nonetheless investigates the ways in which human rights articulate with business law and practice, adopting as a facilitatory starting point approaches to the issue common in international and constitutional law. More closely, it examines the level of protection offered company interests by what is often described as the most effective international human rights regime in the realm of civil and political rights,[12] namely the European Convention on Human Rights.[13] The book thus offers a study of the doctrinal response developed in Strasbourg by the European Court of Human Rights to claims for ECHR protection submitted by or on behalf of companies.

The ECHR differs from other regional and global arrangements such as the closely related International Covenant on Civil and Political Rights and the American Convention on Human Rights,[14] part of what is commonly known as the international law of human rights,[15] in that it offers wide-ranging protection for business entities such as companies in addition to not-for-profit organizations and natural persons. This fact can be derived directly from the Convention's text. Thus, the Convention right to the protection of private property, an important right for companies, applies expressly to 'every natural and legal person',[16] a term naturally inclusive of corporate entities.[17] As will

12 M Janis R Kay and A Bradley *European Human Rights Law. Text and Materials* (2nd edn Oxford University Press Oxford, 2000) 6; and DJ Harris M O'Boyle and C Warbrick *Law of the European Convention on Human Rights* (Butterworths London, 1995) 28–32.

13 Convention for the Protection of Human Rights and Fundamental Freedoms (the European Human Rights Convention) (Rane, 4 November 1950; TS 71 (1953); Cmd 8969) (ECHR, or the Convention). The Convention and its supervisory system underwent a significant restructuring with the coming into force of Protocol No 11 to the Convention for the Protection of Human Rights and Fundamental Freedoms, restructuring the control machinery thereby (adopted 11 May 1994 entered into force 1 November 1998) ETS 157 (Protocol 11).

14 The International Covenant on Civil and Political Rights (adopted 16 December 1966 entered into force 23 March 1976) 999 UNTS 171 (ICCPR) is the main United Nations treaty for the protection of civil and political human rights. The American Convention on Human Rights (adopted 22 November 1969, entered into force 18 July 1978) 1144 UNTS 123, OASTS 36 (ACHR) is the main human rights convention for the American hemisphere, set up under the Organization of American States. For certain aspects of the ICCPR and ACHR approach to companies' rights, see M Emberland 'The Corporate Veil in the Jurisprudence of the Human Rights Committee and the Inter-American Court and Commission of Human Rights' (2004) 4 HRLR 257.

15 The term international human rights law, comprising the treaty norms that build on the tradition of the Universal Declaration of Human Rights (adopted 10 December 1948) UN Doc A/180 (1948) (UDHR), is believed to have been inaugurated in K Vasak 'Le droit international des droits de l'homme' (1974) 140 Receuil des Cours 343, see AA Cançado Trindade 'The Procedural Capacity of the Individual as Subject of International Human Rights Law: Recent Developments' in *Human Rights at the Dawn of the Twenty-First Century. Karel Vasak Amicorum Liber* (Bruylant Brussels, 1999) 521, 522.

16 Art 1(1) first sentence of Protocol to the Convention for the Protection of Human Rights and Fundamental Freedoms (adopted 20 March 1952, entered into force 18 May 1954) ETS 9 (Protocol 1).

17 The absence of a similar inventory of corporate rights-holders in other substantive ECHR provisions does not automatically imply that they apply exclusively to natural persons. The Convention's

be considered again later, the term 'everyone', which appears frequently in Convention provisions, can crucially also be applied to corporate entities, the most important of several cogent reasons being that set out in its Art 34 first sentence which states that the European Court of Human Rights (the Court), the authoritative international arbiter of disputes arising from the Convention,[18] 'may receive applications from any person, non-governmental organisation or group of individuals claiming to be the victim of a violation by one of the High Contracting Parties of the rights set forth in the Convention or the protocols thereto'.[19] The Court has never doubted that a company is a 'nongovernmental organisation' within the meaning of Art 34,[20] and that the Convention's system of private litigation therefore is open for corporate persons.[21]

It is important to appreciate that under the Convention the notion of companies enjoying rights protection is not disputed in principle: the Court does not per se regard corporate litigation with suspicion. This does not mean, however, that the protection of corporate interests is plain sailing in terms of ECHR law. The particular features of the corporate person and the interests pursued by such, combined with the particular structure of the ECHR and its international supervision, sometimes pose interpretative and practical challenges in terms of Convention guarantees.

3 Exposing the Structure of ECHR Protection

This book will revert to the debate on the suitability of coupling human rights norms and legal strategies of the business community. Yet, the present study

contracting States—the 45 member States of the Council of Europe—are required, according to Art 1, to 'secure to everyone within their jurisdiction' ECHR rights and freedoms.

[18] Articles 19, 32, and 47 set out the mandate of the European Court of Human Rights, which is seated in Strasbourg, France. More information on the Court's activities is found at http://www.echr.coe.int.

[19] Prior to Protocol 11, the right to application was found in Art 25, which had an identical wording in this respect.

[20] The French authentic text of the Convention in Art 34 speaks of 'toute personne physique, toute organisation non gouvernementale ou tout groupe de particuliers', thus excluding the possibility that it is the word 'person' that mandates a right of application for corporate entities. The term 'nongovernmental organisation' appears to connote a meaning akin to its understanding in the UN context, primarily referring to not-for-profit organizations such as human rights NGOs, from which is was also borrowed, see H Golsong W Karl and H Miehsler 'Artikel 25' in H Golsong and Others (eds) *Internationaler Kommentar zue Europäischen Menschenrechtskonvention* (Heymann Cologne, 1986) vol 2, 40. The Convention drafting history shows, however, that the Convention always intended to include all corporate persons. The preliminary draft prepared by the European Movement's legal committee in May 1948 spoke in Art 7 a) of a right of petition for 'any natural or corporate person', see AH Robertson (ed) *Collected Editions of the 'Travaux Préparatoires' of the European Convention on Human Rights* (Martinus Nijhoff Dordrecht, 1975) vol 1, 298. The wording was later emended, but the preparatory works contain nothing to suggest that subsequent changes were intended to delimit the scope of the right of application.

[21] *Sunday Times v UK* Series A No 30, (1980) 2 EHRR 245 was the Court's first encounter with a corporate applicant.

does not directly engage in what seems to be a recurrent and highly contentious discussion on the appropriateness of opening up human rights law to corporate persons and the business community. Nor should the book be read as a case for the unreserved inclusion of representatives of private business enterprises as beneficiaries of human rights norms, for that is not its intention. In fact, these issues, although undeniably important and thus worthy of discussion, are not that central for the purpose of the present study.

The book is rather inspired by the pragmatism adhered to by the European Court of Human Rights—it takes given facts for granted. Companies tend to rely on the Convention—what does the Court make out of that situation? More significantly, however, is the book's overall ambition to study and expose important aspects of the structure of ECHR protection, where the focus on corporate human rights litigation mainly serves as a means to discover fundamental and general aspects of the law of the ECHR.

The book firstly sets out and analyses the Court's reasoning in corporate cases, particularly those involving human rights litigation that has tended to present particular problems of treaty interpretation. The Court's views are not always readily discernible from the wording of Strasbourg case law. It is frequently the case, in fact, that we are left to speculate on the reasons that sway the opinions of the judges this way or that, though it would be highly unlikely that the factual circumstances of the dispute in question and the Convention framework within which the Court operates did not weigh heavily on the Court's deliberations. It will be argued therefore, regardless of the difficulties involved in discovering every doctrinal and other motive, that a structured consideration of those principles, mechanisms and values that inform ECHR law and adjudication can enable a wider and doctrinally more coherent understanding of the Court's approach to these types of claims than is often explicitly revealed in the decisions themselves.

The implications of these factors extend beyond the corporate context, although such situations do bring them to the fore. Their study from the perspective of the Court's response to company applications, a potentially marginal form of ECHR litigation, would, it follows, enlighten us regarding certain general features of ECHR law that sometimes are neglected in ECHR analyses. Second, therefore, and following from the above, the Court's response to corporate ECHR litigation is used as a vehicle for highlighting crucial aspects of the workings of the Court and the nature and purpose of the Convention. The academic literature on the ECHR and its supervisory mechanisms is considerable. Yet, certain fundamental features of the Convention system remain, it is suggested here, underappreciated in the existing literature. These features are aptly revealed in the Court's response to complaints submitted by or on behalf of companies and so this part of the case law is a suitable means for generating insight and awareness of fundamental aspects of this particular international human rights regime.

The aspects in question, which are introduced as the book unfolds, essentially revolve around three themes, which undeniably are related. First, the book seeks to convey the nature of the Convention as a European liberal project, a characteristic that makes the ECHR stand out from the bulk of international human rights law treaties. Second, the Convention's object and purpose are fleshed out in order to convey that the Court's teleology, its principal interpretative approach, reflects a complexity that gets lost when we merely refer to the Convention system as an instrument 'for the protection of human rights and fundamental freedoms'. Third, the book aims at highlighting the collective and economic aspects of the civil and political rights contained in the Convention. By shedding fresh light on ECHR discourse in these areas, it is hoped that the book may pave the way for further analyses in the field.

B. Overview

The book is divided into three parts. The first (chapters 1 and 2) provides an introduction to the topic and describes the structural basis of subsequent analyses. The second part (chapters 3, 4, and 5) analyses the Court's responses to corporate litigation in three different situations, each of which roughly corresponds to one of the Court's procedural stages. The third and final part (chapter 6) concludes the discussion and ventures certain observations of general import.

The remainder of the present chapter covers several essentials. First it describes the material relied upon. Then follows a description of the basic principles of Convention interpretation, as they are instrumental to the subsequent analyses, and a word on the obligatory nature of the ECHR system. The chapter goes on to indicate the methodological challenges posed by the Court's method of reasoning, and how these challenges inform the way in which the analyses are carried out.

Chapter 2 introduces the general framework within which, it will be suggested, the Court decides its responses to corporate litigation. The methodological and structural framework is then presented in the form of a detailed rebuttal, on the basis of the ECHR protection *de lege lata*, of certain observers' intermittently published views, ie, that the protection of corporate and other for-profit actors under the Convention is controversial in principle. Chapter 2 attempts to explain why it is that corporate claims are not by presumption dismissed by the Court and why, due to their special nature, they are occasionally considered to be marginal ECHR issues and therefore pose a challenge to Convention interpretation.

Chapters 3, 4, and 5 examines the Court's adjudicatory response to three types of problems of treaty interpretation that are typical of corporate applications either due to the structure of the corporate person or the nature of the activities typically pursued by them. The three issues together paint a representative picture of the Court's construal in marginal cases of the corporate person, the status of for-profit activities under the Convention and the nature and purpose of ECHR protection in this area. Chapter 3 surveys the Court's handling of applications submitted by shareholders arguing for the admission of their claims for consideration although the alleged violation at the root of their complaint in formal terms befell the company in which they owned shares. Roughly speaking, the chapter is an analysis of the construction of a 'corporate veil' in the Court's jurisprudence. This is an important indication of how the Court looks upon an essential constituent of the corporate person, and thus, indirectly, how it views this engine of business enterprise in light of the Convention.

Chapter 4 proceeds to examine the Court's handling of applications where companies, as protagonists of for-profit business activity, have sought refuge under Convention guarantees normally conceived in relation to the needs of the natural person, and as such far removed from a business context. An examination of the Court's accommodating response to corporate claims reveals major doctrinal mechanisms at play at Strasbourg. To a large part they explain the success of corporate claimants in entering onto Convention territory which in the past was the exclusive province of not-for-profit and natural persons.

Chapter 5 considers the standards of judicial review as applied by the Court in the corporate context. The Court for various reasons tends to adopt a lenient standard of review when it is alleged that public authorities' regulation of private economic activity is in violation of Convention standards. This analysis of judicial scrutiny reveals the prevailing double standards of ECHR protection in this area, and might be suggestive of the manner in which the Court sees the Convention system in light of the conflicting ideas of free enterprise and the regulatory state.

Chapter 6 marshals the findings of the foregoing chapters where a pattern emerges concerning the place accorded by the Court to for-profit enterprises within the framework of the Convention system. Adopting a pragmatic outlook on ECHR law as a reflection of the Court's own approach—the meaning of 'pragmatism' in our context is explained in due course—the book largely refrains from recommending that the Court change or improve its handling of corporate applications. Instead, it is argued that the complex nature of the Convention, which has been revealed by this book, needs further theoretical consideration. The status of corporate ECHR protection is finally seen in light of the most recent effort to restructure the Strasbourg Court.

C. Materials

This being a study of the Strasbourg system's doctrinal response to a particular form of ECHR litigation, the Court's case law naturally constitutes its primary source of material.[22] The Court delivers two main forms of decisions,[23] both of which are important for this study: admissibility decisions, in which the Court, normally sitting in committees of three judges,[24] decides on whether a complaint satisfies the admissibility criteria set forth in the Convention; and judgments, in which the substance of the private applicant's complaint is examined by the Court either sitting as a Chamber of seven judges or, exceptionally, as a Grand Chamber consisting of a panel of 17 judges.[25] Judgments on the merits decide whether the applicant is correct in maintaining that his or her Convention rights or freedoms have been violated. A judgment may also determine whether the applicant whose rights have been breached is entitled to remedies ('just satisfaction') in accordance with Art 41 of the Convention. Both types of judgments inform the analyses carried out below.[26]

Two other ECHR organs were formerly, that is, prior to the implementation of Protocol 11 in 1998, also entrusted with supervisory powers in disputes arising from private applications.[27] The European Commission of Human Rights,

[22] The inter-state application procedure provided for in Art 33 is not considered, as no issues of relevance for the corporate context have thus far been handled. Since the book focuses on select issues of Convention interpretation, the case law referred to and analysed does not constitute the whole body of relevant judgments and decisions that concern corporate applicants. In fact, the judicial decisions drawn upon comprise merely a fraction of the total body of corporate case law.

[23] Judgments concerning requests of interpretation of earlier judgments, see Rule 79 of the Rules of Court of the European Court of Human Rights (adopted November 2003, immediately in force) available at: <http://www.echr.coe.int/Eng/EDocs/RULES%20OF%20COURTNOV2003.htm> (5 June 2005) claims for revision of a delivered judgments (Rules of Court Rule 80), and the confirmation of friendly settlements reached by the parties (Rules of Court Rules 44 and 54A) are of little relevance for the present study.

[24] Art 28. In exceptional cases admissibility decisions are taken either by a Chamber (seven judges) (Art 29) or a Grand Chamber (Art 31 a).

[25] Art 43 and Rules of Court Rules 71–73 provide the criteria for the referral of a case to a Grand Chamber. Prior to the enactment of Protocol 11, the Court could decide cases sitting as a Plenary Court.

[26] The Court's determination of just satisfaction is normally included in the main judgment but may be delivered in a subsequent and separate judgment if the question is not ready for decision at the time of the original judgment, see Rules of Court Rule 75. Since separate judgments on just satisfaction concern the interpretation of Art 41 (formerly Art 50), they are identified in the following with the suffix Art 41 or Art 50 so as to distinguish them from the judgments on the merits bearing the same name.

[27] AZ Drzemczewski 'A Major Overhaul of the European Human Rights Convention Control Mechanism: Protocol No 11' (1997-II) 6 AEL 121 introduces the changes to the supervisory machinery pursuant to Protocol 11.

which formerly screened incoming cases (former Art 28), was made defunct, its tasks taken over by the new permanent Court.[28] According to Art 46(2), the powers of the Committee of Ministers are now restricted to the overseeing of the execution of Court judgments.[29] Neither the Commission nor the Committee had jurisdiction to settle individual disputes as a court proper,[30] as has the Court, but they frequently considered private applications, including applications submitted by companies or their agents.[31] A large part of their decisions has been consulted for the purpose of the present study. The Commission's interpretation of the Convention in the corporate context is occasionally included when it illuminates the approach of the Court (none of the decisions delivered by the Committee of Ministers are directly relevant for the discussion).

The domestic courts of many ECHR Member States have been required to handle companies' reliance on Convention rights and freedoms. In the United Kingdom, for instance, corporate human rights litigation seems to be on the rise.[32] But such cases are not considered here. Comparisons are however drawn between the case law of the European Court of Human Rights and that of certain constitutional courts and international courts and tribunals. Beneficial in this respect are the practices of the Inter-American Commission and Court of Human Rights (the tribunals entrusted with the supervision of the ACHR), the United Nations' Human Rights Committee (which is the dispute-settling organ of the ICCPR), the International Court of Justice, the European Court of Justice (the supreme arbiter of fundamental rights dispute in the European

[28] The Commission delivered decisions on admissibility and issued reports on the merits of admitted complaints. On the Commission's former functions, see, eg, E Friedbergh and ME Villiger 'The European Commission of Human Rights' in R St John Macdonald F Matscher and H Petzold (eds) *The European System for the Protection of Human Rights* (Martinus Nijhoff Dordrecht, 1993) 605.

[29] The Committee is the decision-making body of the Council of Europe. It consists of the foreign ministers of the Council's member states, see arts 10 and 15–21 of the Statute of the Council of Europe (adopted 5 May 1949, entered into force 3 August 1949) ETS 1 with subsequent amendments (Council of Europe Statute). Prior to Protocol 11, the Committee could settle private complaints not submitted to the Court within the specified period of time, see former Art 32; details are provided in AZ Drzemczewski 'Decisions on the Merits: By the Committee of Ministers' in R St John Macdonald F Matscher and H Petzold (eds) *The European System for the Protection of Human Rights* (Martinus Nijhoff Dordrecht, 1993) 733.

[30] There is no uniform agreement of what constitutes an international 'court', eg, C Tomuschat 'International Courts and Tribunals with Regionally Restricted and/or Specialized Jurisdiction' in *Judicial Settlement of International Disputes: International Court of Justice, other Courts and Tribunals, Arbitration and Conciliation: An International Symposium* (Max-Planck-Institut für ausländisches öffentliches Recht und Völkerrecht Heidelberg, 1987) 285.

[31] Eg, app 7987/77 *Andorfer Tonwerke, Walter Hannak and Co. iL v Austria*, Committee of Ministers resolution adopted 23 June 1983, DH (83) 9; and app 20471/92 *Kustannus Oy Vapaa Ajattelija AB and Others v Finland* (1996) 85 DR 29 (1996) 22 EHRR 69.

[32] Eg, the intra-business nature of the case of *Cream Holdings Ltd v Banerjee* [2004] 3 WLR 918, [2004] 4 All ER 617, HL (freedom of speech complaint; interim injunctions restraining publication of financial information).

Union), the Supreme Court of the United States of America and the federal German *Bundesverfassungsgericht*. The two latter courts in particular have over time developed a sophisticated jurisprudence and comparisons between their approaches and that of the Court are generally instructive.

The Convention text, in its English and French authentic versions,[33] is naturally a source of great pertinence. The preparatory works of the Convention (the original *travaux préparatoires* and the Explanatory Reports prepared for the Convention's additional protocols) have also been consulted.[34] Finally, the discussions rely on English and German-language literature, although some French sources have also been consulted.

D. Companies and the ECHR: an Overview

1 The Company: Protagonist of Private Business Enterprise

The analyses of this book focus on one particular form of business entity, notably the limited liability company (hereinafter called 'the company', sometimes also referred to as 'the corporation').[35] The ECHR does not authoritatively define the term 'company'.[36] It must be assumed that the Convention drafters did not envisage a situation in which companies would require much consideration; at least they paid scant attention to them. The Court is not inclined to provide

[33] The Convention's final sentence, immediately following Art 59, states: 'Done at Rome this 4th day of November 1950, in English and French, both texts being equally authentic.'

[34] AH Robertson (ed) *Collected Editions of the 'Travaux Préparatoires' of the European Convention on Human Rights* (Martinus Nijhoff Dordrecht, 1975–1985) vols 1–9. Explanatory Reports are available at <http://www.coe.int> (see also the appended bibliography).

[35] Terminologically speaking, a 'company' may comprise entities with unlimited liability as well as not-for-profit entities, eg, SK Miller 'Piercing the Corporate Veil among Affiliated Companies in the European Community and in the US: A Comparative Analysis of US, German, and UK Veilpiercing Approaches' (1998) 36 Am Bus L J 73, 109. A 'corporation' may likewise denote more than limited liability companies. The limited liability company is referred to as 'company' and 'corporation' interchangeably in the following.

[36] 'Company' as used in the European Convention on Establishment of Companies (adopted 20 January 1966) ETS 57 corresponds with the usage in the present dissertation. But Council of Europe treaties vary in their terminology, eg, the European Convention on Compulsory Insurance against Civil Liability in respect of Motor Vehicles (adopted 20 April 1959, entered into force 22 September 1959) ETS 29, Annex II para 7 (the limited liability company is referred to as the 'corporate person', while a 'company' comprises partnerships with unlimited liability); and the Civil Law Convention on Corruption (adopted 4 November 1999, entered into force 1 November 2003) ETS 174 (which speaks generally of 'companies' regardless of the form of a business entity). Article 10 of the Convention on Laundering, Search, Seizure and Confiscation of the Proceeds from Crime and on the Financing of Terrorism (adopted 15 May 2005, not yet in force) ETS 198 refers to 'corporate' persons and 'legal persons' without distinction in meaning. The Convention on Mutual Assistance in Tax Matters (adopted 25 January 1988, entered into force 1 April 1995) ETS 127 uses 'enterprise' for all forms of business entities.

conceptual clarification other than as a necessary step in its decision-making process; a definition of 'company' is rarely required in Strasbourg adjudication. The international character of the Convention system defies, too, a precise ECHR definition, since the corporate entity traditionally is regarded as a product of national law.[37] The details of what is regarded as necessary elements of a limited liability company obviously vary from one municipal jurisdiction to another.

We are generally aware, nonetheless, of the core characteristics of the company regardless of jurisdictional affiliation.[38] The company is an organization of persons and material resources which is licensed by a State for the purpose of conducting some form of business activity. A company's limited liability means that its capital suppliers are not subject to losses greater than the amount of their original investment. This investment is the company's capital, divided among shares whose transferability does not as such affect the company's constitution. Having separate juristic personhood, the company's lifetime is also of indefinite duration; its existence extends beyond the participation of its incorporators. There is considerable dispute as to what the essential purpose of the company may be. It is incompatible with current corporate theory to suggest that the company's only *raison d'être* is pursuit of profit for the ultimate benefit of the company ownership, eg, the shareholders. In fact, it is generally assumed today that the company is a complex social institution with various participants and, consequently, various objectives and interests. The activities of a company may therefore be seen as a fulfilment of the interests not only of its shareholders but also those of its various stakeholders, that is, the company's employees, creditors, suppliers, and customers and others 'having a relation of sufficient intimacy with the corporation or subject to its power in a sufficiently specialized way'.[39] Consideration of the pecuniary interests of corporate shareholders remains nonetheless a central objective of the company and is likely to be considered thus from the viewpoint of practical life and corporate litigation.[40]

[37] The European Company, set up in accordance with European Union legislation, is a notable exception. For details, see, eg, C Tavares Da Costa and A de Meester Bilreiro *The European Company Statute* (Kluwer Hague, 2003).

[38] 'Corporation' *Encyclopaedia Britannica* from Encyclopaedia Online <http://search.eb.com> (5 June 2005). M Lutter 'Limited Liability Companies and Private Companies' in D Vagts (ed) *International Encyclopedia of Comparative Law: Business and Private Organizations* (Mohr Siebeck Tübingen, 1998) vol 13 is a very useful comparative identification of the company's core characteristics.

[39] A Chayes 'The Modern Corporation and the Rule of Law' in ES Mason (ed) *The Corporation in Modern Society* (Harvard University Press Cambridge, Mass 1959) 41. E Wymeersch 'A Status Report on Corporate Governance Rules and Practices in Some Continental European States' in KJ Hopt and others (eds) *Comparative Corporate Governance: The State of the Art and Emerging Research* (Clarendon Press Oxford, 1998) 1045 notes a European convergence towards common principles on corporate governance and, by implication, what a company represents

[40] LA Cunningham 'Commonalities and Prescriptions in the Vertical Dimensions of Global Corporate Governance' (1999) 84 Cornell L Rev 1133 is a representative of this view.

Organizations that match the description set out above are counted as companies and meet therefore the criteria for inclusion as objects of study for the purposes of this thesis. Whether they are privately or publicly held makes no difference at this point. In the European legal order they are known under various linguistic guises. Examples are the *Aktiengesellschaft (AG), Gesellschaft mit begrensder Haftung (GmbH), société anonyme (SA), société d'une personne à responsibilité limitée (Sprl)*, and so forth. All companies have a management that in formal terms is separate from their ownership; here, however, a company's management may or may not consist of its ownership. Companies are eligible for inclusion in the study regardless of the number of shareholders (companies with only one shareholder, known in certain jurisdictions, are therefore eligible). The company may have few or many stakeholders.The size of the enterprise or the nature of its business is principally irrelevant as an eligibility criterion. A company may or may not be established by the laws of the State allegedly violating the company's ECHR rights, and it may or may not carry out activities or have its head (or any other) office within the territory of the Council of Europe member states. The nature of state responsibility under the Convention as laid down in Art 1 informs us that the decisive criterion for enjoying ECHR protection is not the territorial or national affiliation of the applicant but whether any action or inaction by the authorities of an ECHR member State has affected the applicant's interests.

Limited liability companies are, in short, eligible regardless of type and form: the Court does not appear to treat them differently. It should be noted, however, that so-called multinational or transnational corporations, which are the traditional focus of international human rights discourse when it engages with business, are rare visitors to Strasbourg.[41] The typical Strasbourg litigant seems from the case law's description of the facts of each case to be smaller or medium-size business enterprise that are set up pursuant to the laws of the State it claims has violated its Convention rights.

The limited liability company is the protagonist of private business enterprise in the Council of Europe area as it is in most developed countries. It is a highly attractive vehicle for undertakings of a profit-seeking purpose and its study offers a valuable insight into the stance taken by the ECHR system concerning private business enterprise. The distinct make-up of the corporate entity—its nature as a collective unity of interests, its separate legal nature, its public aspects and formal affiliation with the state, and the importance of profit-making—makes it a worthwhile object of study from the viewpoint

[41] See, however, *British-American Tobacco Company Ltd v Netherlands* Series No A 331, (1996) 21 EHRR 404 as an example proving that there are always exceptions to a rule. On multinational companies as beneficiaries of international law, see, PT Muchlinski *Multinational Enterprises and the Law* (2nd edn Blackwell Oxford, 1999).

of ECHR law, since all these features set it apart from the archetypical Strasbourg litigant.

Other forms of business entities may however well share some or even many of the characteristics of the limited liability company, and there exist various hybrid corporate forms that resemble companies as described above. That said, there is little likelihood that the Court would treat them altogether differently from the traditional limited liability company, and to the extent they are treated in a similar manner, and there is good reason to do so when significant features are identical, judgments and decisions concerning other business entities are referred to where appropriate. The 'company' is a fluid concept, also in terms of ECHR law.

2 Companies and the ECHR: Basic Facts

The fact that for-profit entities are entitled to have recourse to the Court is certainly not something the literature devotes much attention, although notable exceptions can be found.[42] The lack of scholarly interest has doubtless several reasons, though it is not hard to imagine that it reflects the relatively speaking diminutive presence of corporate claims in Strasbourg.

Some statistical measures are suggestive of the frequency of corporate litigation that comes before the Court. In the five-year period from 1998 to 2003, the

[42] The following list of (mostly brief and introductory) works on the subject is by no means exhaustive (listed in alphabetical order): MK Addo 'The Corporation as a Victim of Human Rights Violations' in MK Addo (ed) *Human Rights Standards and the Responsibility of Transnational Corporations* (Kluwer Hague, 1999) 187; R Bernhardt 'Einwirkungen der Europäischen Menschenrechts-Konvention auf das Staatliche Wirtschaftsrecht' in R Briner and others (eds) *Law of International Business and Dispute Settlement. Liber Amicorum Karl-Heinz Böckstiegel* (Heymann Cologne, 2001) 67; S Bottomley 'Corporations and Human Rights' in S Bottomley and D Kinley (eds) *Commercial Law and Human Rights* (Dartmouth Ashgate Aldershot, 2002) 61; N Bratza 'The Implications of the Human Rights Act 1998 for Commercial Practice' [2000] EHRLR 1; AJ Dignam and D Allen *Company Law and the Human Rights Act 1998* (Butterworths London, 2000); T Douraki: 'Les associations devant la Commission et la Cour européenne des Droits de l'Homme' (1989) 2 Hague Ybk Intl L 139; PJ Duffy 'The Protection of Commercial Interests Under the European Convention on Human Rights' in R Cranston (ed) *Making Commercial Law. Essays in Honour of Roy Goode* (Clarendon Press Oxford, 1997) 525; F Ermacora 'L'accès aux mécanismes jurisdictionnels de protection des personnes privée dans la Convention européenne des droits de l'homme' (1973) 6 HRJ 645; S Marcus Helmons 'L'applicabilité de la Convention européenne des droits de l'homme aux personnes morales (1996) 4 JdT 150; J de Meyer 'Human Rights in a Commercial Context' (1984) 5 HRLJ 139; M Smyth *Business and the Human Rights Act 1998* (Bristol: Jordans, 2000); O de Schutter 'L'accès des personnes morales à la Cour européenne des droits de l'homme' in *Mélanges offerts à Silvio Marcus Helmons, Avancées et confines actuels des droits de l'homme aux niveaux international, européen et national* (Bruylant Bruxelles, 2003) 83; C Schwaighofer 'Legal Persons, Organisations, Shareholders as Applicants (Article 25 of the Convention)' in M de Salvia and ME Villiger (eds) *The Birth of European Human Rights Law: Liber Amicorum Carl Aage Nørgaard* (Nomos Baden-Baden, 1998) 321; and J Strachan 'The Human Rights Act 1998 and Commercial Law in the United Kingdom' in S Bottomley and D Kinley (eds) *Commercial Law and Human Rights* (Dartmouth Ashgate Aldershot, 2002) 161.

Court delivered no less than 3307 judgments (including judgments concerning just satisfaction pursuant to Art 41 and judgments confirming settlements between the parties). Of these judgments only 126 originated in applications filed by companies or by other persons clearly pursuing corporate interests. Approximately 3.8 per cent of the Strasbourg case law was directly concerned with corporate litigation in this five-year period. This rate seems fairly consistent, nor does it deviate significantly from the numbers of corporate applications handled at the admissibility stage. Whatever the representativeness of this figure, it can nonetheless be inferred that it is unlikely that companies dominate the Strasbourg supervisory machinery.

Companies concentrate their litigious efforts within a small band of ECHR provisions. A perusal of judgments concerning company applicants shows a recurrence of claims of violations of Art 6(1) (various due process guarantees) with regard to civil proceedings to which the applicants have been parties; alleged breaches of Protocol 1 Art 1 (property protection) concerning various forms of regulation of economic activity; and claims of illegitimate interference with their freedom of expression guaranteed by Art 10, the latter group of claims naturally dominated by the media industry. Although companies do occasionally seek refuge in other rights and freedoms, even provisions that conventional wisdom would see as wholly irrelevant in a corporate context, corporate litigation tends to revolve around a small area of ECHR law. Quantitatively and qualitatively speaking, then, an analysis of the applicability of the Convention to the business world is bound to rest on a relatively small piece of Strasbourg case law. Such factors obviously contribute to the limited interest paid to this particular aspect of the Convention.

3 The System of Private Application: Overview

Much has been written about the system of dispute resolution at Strasbourg and it is not a concern of this thesis to replicate the work done elsewhere in this area.[43] This section sets out in summary form the workings of the current private application system at Strasbourg especially as they relate to claims submitted by or on behalf of companies.

(a) The Admissibility Stage

Rule 36(1) of Rules of Court adopted by the European Court of Human Rights states that a company is free, via the individuals or organs properly authorised to act on its behalf, to submit an application to the Court in which

[43] C Ovey and RCA White *Jacobs and White The European Convention on Human Rights* (3rd edn Oxford University Press Oxford, 2002) 396–419 is a recent introduction.

it alleges that its rights or freedoms under the Convention have been violated by the authorities of one or more of the ECHR member States.[44] All applications received by the Court's Registry are subjected to a preliminary screening by the legal secretariat with a view to establishing whether the application meets the minimum requirement for further consideration by the judge appointed as rapporteur. In such an event, this judge will proceed to examine the application and decide whether it is worthy to be considered by the Court in a Committee or a Chamber (Rule 49 of the Rules of Court), which makes the final decision on admissibility (Rules 54 of the Rules of Court).

The admissibility criteria, governed by Arts 34 and 35, are generally applicable to all types of applicants. Some conditions of admissibility are more frequently addressed than others with regard to corporate applicants and other applicants purporting to act on the company's behalf.[45] The so-called 'victim' requirement in Art 34—stipulating that it is the applicant personally who needs to be 'claiming to be the victim of a violation by one of the High Contracting Parties of the rights set forth in this Convention'—stimulates discussion at the Court typically when a company shareholder claims to be the 'victim' of a violation in respect of government action or inaction formally with the corporate entity, and not the shareholder, as an addressee. This question is considered in depth in chapter 3.

It is also required, for an application to be found admissible, that the subject-matter of the complaint has been unsuccessfully pursued before national dispute-settling organs prior to its submission in Strasbourg. This question, too, raises certain problems depending on which of various persons having stakes in the company has litigated the question before the domestic courts.[46] Whether all domestic remedies have been exhausted, pursuant to Art 35(1), is a further procedural hurdle. This, too, is considered thoroughly in chapter 3 below.

The admissibility requirements also include the Court's assessment of the extent to which the matter complained of falls within the Convention's material scope. The Court is barred from dealing with complaints concerning rights or freedoms that are not listed in the Convention or its Protocols. This question entails essentially an interpretation of the extent to which the provisions relied upon are applicable to corporate interests. As we shall see, this is not always the case. Complaints that fall outside the scope of the Convention in this respect are normally rejected under Art 35(3) as incompatible *ratione materiae* with the

44 See also de Schutter (n 42) 89.

45 Ovey and White (n 43) 405–13 give an overview of the admissibility requirements.

46 AM Aronovitz 'Notes on the Current Status of the Rule of Exhaustion of Local Remedies in the European Convention on Human Rights' (1995) 25 Israel Ybk HR 73 gives an overview of this requirement. For a more comprehensive treatment, see AA Cançado Trindade *The Application of the Rule of Exhaustion of Local Remedies in International Law. Its Rationale in the International Protection of Human Rights* (Cambridge University Press Cambridge, 1983).

provisions of the Convention. This particular examination may raise difficult problems of interpretation and may also be dealt with by the Court when it considers the merits of the case.[47] In any event, this is an issue to be discussed in detail in chapter 4.

(b) *Examination on the Merits*

An admissible complaint will be considered by the Court, normally constituted as a Chamber, in the manner appropriate to a court with contentious jurisdiction. Unless the parties agree to settle their differences amicably, the Court's examination of the merits of the case will result in a judgment in which the Court declares that a violation of the Convention has or has not taken place with respect to the interests of the applicant.

The Court approaches the merits of an application in a standardized manner. First, it examines and decides upon the question of applicability of the provision(s) on which the applicant has relied in the complaint. Thereafter the Court assesses whether the applicable right has indeed been violated by the respondent state. For some provisions, the applicability and violation assessment stages are undertaken in a joint operation, though they are mostly kept separate in the Court's opinion-writing.[48]

During the first stage of the proceedings, the applicability stage, the nature of the applicant's complaint (or, occasionally, the nature of the applicant person) is considered in light of the material scope of the ECHR provisions claimed in the application and whether the respondent state's authorities in fact can be said to have acted in compliance with the obligations contained in the provisions in question. This is dealt with in some detail in chapter 4.

If the Court finds that the rights or freedoms relied upon by the petitioner are applicable and that they have been interfered with, the Court then goes on to examine whether the government has interfered legitimately or not with the applicant person's rights or freedoms. This examination may take different forms depending on the provision under scrutiny. In all events this stage of the proceedings involves a complex assessment of facts, conflicting private and public interests and vague standards and norms in which the Court's discretion is generally wide. With regard to provisions such as Art 8 (respect for private life), Art 10 (freedom of expression) and First Protocol Art 1 (protection of private property), which are central to the present study, the Court's discussion on the violation stage follows a standard procedure laid down in the provisions and having been refined through longstanding jurisprudence.[49] Chapter 5 touches upon the Court's approach to this assessment.

[47] P van Dijk and GJH van Hoof *Theory and Practice of the European Convention on Human Rights* (2nd edn Kluwer Hague, 1998) 204–6 discuss the issue further.

[48] Ovey and White (n 43) 5.

[49] Harris O'Boyle and Warbrick (n 12) 283–301 give an overview. Provisions that do not in the same manner reflect the needs of the regulatory state do not necessarily adhere to the same two-stage

If the Court concludes that a violation has occurred, the applicant may claim a monetary or other remedy for suffering sustained due to the violation. This issue is governed by Art 41 (former Art 50).[50] The applicability of one particular part of Art 41 to companies has caused problems in the Court's case law. For the sake of convenience, this question of applicability, although being different than the other issues because it concerns a remedy rather than a right, is dealt with together with other contentious applicability questions in chapter 4.

4 Providing a Structural Framework: Preliminary Issues

It was suggested above that this book is mainly a book on ECHR structures. Before chapter 2 introduces the complexities of the Convention's object and purpose, it is appropriate to introduce other issues that also have a bearing on the structural framework within which the Court operates.

(a) *The Regulatory State and the Nature of ECHR Obligations*

It will become evident in due course that the Court's handling of corporate claims normally concern situations where the applicant in question seeks Convention shelter against the exercise of regulatory authority that impinges on the company's activities or interests. Corporate applicants squarely use the Convention as a means to restrain regulatory authority in the economic sphere. Corporate utilisation of the ECHR as means of curbing regulatory authority remains therefore the issue with which the study is mainly concerned. This approach requires some comments on the nature of State responsibility under the Convention and in the material consulted for the purpose of this study.

Article 1 proclaims that ECHR member States, through all branches of government, are required to 'secure' Convention rights and freedoms of persons within their jurisdictional reach. The nature of this obligation to 'secure' protection varies. It is common to distinguish conceptually between governmental obligations to not interfere with the rights guaranteed to the private party ('negative obligations') and obligations to promote or protect the guarantees set forth ('positive obligations').[51]

procedure as described above, yet it is clear that examinations of other provisions require the same close assessment of various facts and norms. Such provisions do not, however, fall within the scope of the present discussion.

50 G Dannemann *Schadenersatz bei Verletzung der Europäischen Menschenrechtskonvention. Eine rechtsvergleichende Untersuchung zur Haftung nach Art. 50 EMRK* (Heymann Cologne, 1994) is a comprehensive and still relevant analysis of the remedies clause.

51 Literature abounds. Comprehensive analyses include A Mowbray 'The Development of Positive Obligations under the European Convention on Human Rights by the European Court of Human Rights' (Hart Oxford, 2004); B Conforti 'Reflections on State Responsibility for the Breach of Positive Obligations: the Case-law of the European Court of Human Rights' (2003) 13 Italian YB Intl L 3; C Dröge *Positive Verpflichtungen der Staaten in der Europäischen Menschenrechtskonvention* (Springer Berlin, 2003); A Clapham *Human Rights in the Private Sphere* (Clarendon Press Oxford 1993)

While the discussion of rights and freedoms in chapters 4 and 5 concentrates on the negative obligations approach, this should not be interpreted as a lack of appreciation of the importance of the positive obligations of ECHR member States to safeguard corporate persons adequately under the Convention. Typically, the due process guarantees contained, inter alia, in Art 6(1) put obligations of a positive nature on national authorities, and particularly the national courts. A well-functioning judiciary capable of settling intra-corporate, intra-private, and public-private disputes at a national level is, for instance, paramount to the efficacy of private business enterprise. The discussion in chapter 3 bears tangentially on these issues. The thrust of the study deals, nonetheless, with the State's negative obligations only.

(b) ECHR Compliance

The ECHR system boasts a high measure of State compliance.[52] This feature is an important part of structure on which the Court's response to controversial corporate claims rests. This is not the place to discuss regime and compliance theories and their compatibility with ECHR realities,[53] but a few words on the main elements that make up the special form of effectiveness pertaining to the Convention system are required since they do have a bearing on the issue under consideration here.[54]

Having accepted obligations under an international treaty, the contracting States are naturally bound to respect ECHR rights and freedoms as a matter of international law. Being a human rights treaty, the Convention builds on the premise that its substantive content be implemented domestically.[55] The

178–244; and P van Dijk ' "Positive Obligations" Implied in the European Convention on Human Rights: Are the States Still the "Masters" of the Convention?' in M Castermans-Holleman F van Hoof and J Smith (eds) *The Role of the Nation-State in the 21st Century: Human Rights, International Organisations, and Foreign Policy. Essays in Honour of Peter Baer* (Kluwer Hague, 1998) 17.

[52] On the difficulties involved in measuring effectiveness of human rights treaties in general, see, O Hathaway 'Do Human Rights Treaties Make a Difference?' (2002) 111 YLJ 1935; and the ensuing debate in R Goodman and D Jinks 'Measuring the Effects of Human Rights Treaties' (2003) 14 EJIL 171; and O Hathaway 'Testing Conventional Wisdom' (2003) 13 EJIL 185.

[53] M Burgstaller *Theories of Compliance with International Law* (Martinus Nijhoff Leiden, 2005) provides an excellent discussion on international law compliance, human rights compliance included.

[54] See chapters 3 and 5 in particular. The following rendition closely follows the overview given in Ovey and White (n 43) 431–35. Further on the issue, see, L Helfer and A-M Slaughter 'Toward a Theory of Effective Supranational Adjudication' (1992) 107 YLJ 273; P Leuprecht 'The Execution of Judgments and Decisions' in R St John Macdonald F Matscher and H Petzold (eds) *The European System for the Protection of Human Rights* (Martinus Nijhoff Dordrecht, 1993) 791; Andrew Moravcsik: 'The Origins of Human Rights Regimes: Democratic Delegation in Postward Europe' (2000) 54 IO 217; and R Ryssdal 'The Enforcement System set up under the European Convention on Human Rights' in MK Bulterman and M Kuijer (eds) *Compliance with Judgments of International Courts: Symposium in Honour of Henry G Schermers* (Martinus Nijhoff Hague, 1996) 49.

[55] This follows from various provisions, including arts 1, 19, 41, and 46. Harris O'Boyle and Warbrick (n 12) 23–26 gives an overview of domestic implementation.

Convention has a stronger obligatory nature than the majority of other international human rights law regimes. Acceptance of the jurisdiction of the Court is compulsory for all member States.[56] In this the ECHR system differs fundamentally from, say, the ACHR and ICCPR, under which the supervisory organs' competence still builds on a facultative arrangement.[57] According to ECHR Art 46(1), the contracting States 'undertake to abide by the final judgment of the Court in any case to which they are parties'. The Committee of Ministers makes sure that judgments are implemented by the violating State (Art 46(2)).

Contracting States are in principle entitled to denounce the treaty if they so wish;[58] and although the Committee of Ministers undertakes its task of securing compliance diligently it is generally admitted that the States' follow-up procedures fall short of perfection. Delay in the payment of compensation afforded pursuant to Art 41 is, for instance, not entirely uncommon.[59] Yet, such inroads into the legally binding effect of the Convention cannot outweigh the political effectiveness of the treaty, whose importance for the work of the Court should not be underestimated. As Clare Ovey and Robin White note, 'in addition to good faith, a number of pressures and interests combine to encourage States to comply with the legal obligation to take restitutory measures created by a finding of a violation by the Court'.[60] The Committee of Ministers have various means available through which to seek implementation via extra-judicial channels:[61] the Statute of the Council of Europe provides in Arts 3 and 8 for the exclusion from Council of Europe membership for States that have 'seriously violated' the human rights and freedoms set forth, inter alia, in the Convention. Convention member States have in addition an obvious interest in maintaining stability in Europe, and the Convention system is seen as one of several guarantors of this stability.[62] Perhaps most importantly, Convention membership is effectively a precondition for membership in the European Union, and a good record in Strasbourg is significant for States which are not part of the EU but that wish to join or to remain on amicable terms with it.[63]

56 Protocol 11 introduced mandatory jurisdiction for the Court, see Explanatory Report to Protocol No 11 to the Convention for the Protection of Human Rights and Fundamental Freedoms restructuring the control machinery established thereby (Protocol 11 Explanatory Report), available at <http://conventions.coe.int/Treaty/en/Reports/Html/155.htm> §§ 85–86.

57 Emberland (n 14) 271.

58 Art 58 sets, however, a six-month notice requirement for being absolved from Convention duties.

59 Rules of Court Rule 75(3) provides that the Court stipulates interest to be added to the original compensation sum if payment is not honoured within three months after the delivery of the judgment. As from 11 July 2002, the Court sets the default interest to three percentage points above the current marginal lending rate of the European Central Bank, see *Christine Goodwin v UK* judgment 11 July 2002 [GC] Reports 2002-VI §§ 123–24.

60 Ovey and White (n 43) 431.

61 ibid 432.

62 ibid.

63 M Nowak 'Human Rights "Conditionality" in Relation to Entry to, and Full Participation in, the EU' in P Alston (ed) *The EU and Human Rights* (Oxford University Press Oxford, 1999) 687.

Naturally, the Court is barred from exceeding its mandate to interpret and apply the Convention. It is not allowed to add international obligations by creating new rights and freedoms. And the work done by the Court depend on financial support from its creators, the Council of Europe member States; a factor which also encourages diligence by the Court to maintain a proper balance between the private and public interests involved in every dispute. Having said that, the Court, thanks to the legal and political climate in which the system functions, is conceivably able to adjudicate without undue political pressure. This has created an atmosphere at Strasbourg for breathing space for the Court when it decides matters that may challenge settled interpretation of the Convention.[64]

(c) The Court's Methodology and Mode of Reasoning

The Court's special form of legal reasoning is part and parcel of the structure against which its response to corporate litigation must be measured. According to Art 32(1), the Court's primary task is to interpret and apply the Convention and its Protocols in individual disputes. In so doing, the Court adheres to the general principles of treaty interpretation as developed in international law. In *Golder v UK*, the Court accepted Arts 31 to 33 of the Vienna Convention on the Law of Treaties as a guide for its interpretative action. Even if the latter treaty (see its Art 4) does not apply retrospectively, it largely expresses generally accepted principles of international law.[65] Naturally, in corporate cases as elsewhere the Court deliberates on the basis of the words of the treaty itself, in accordance with Art 31(1) of the Vienna Convention. Much has been written on the methodology applied by the Court and there is no reason to restate the various positions in their entirety here.[66] Certain aspects of the Court's methodology will, besides, receive attention as the thesis unfolds. At this stage, two critical aspects of the Court's mode of reasoning are introduced inasmuch as they bear on the study as a whole and its analytical approach in particular.

(i) The Teleological Approach

Article 31(1) of the Vienna Convention states that a treaty text shall be interpreted in light of its 'object and purpose', a principle with which the Court

[64] Chapters 3 through 5 investigate further how the Court—in the corporate context—relates to the structural aspects just introduced.

[65] *Golder v UK* Series A No 18, (1979) 1 EHRR 524 § 29. Vienna Convention on the Law of Treaties (adopted 22 May 1969, entered into force 27 January 1980) 1155 UNTS 331 (Vienna Convention).

[66] F Matscher 'Methods of Interpretation of the Convention' in R St John Macdonald F Matscher and H Petzold (eds) *The European System for the Protection of Human Rights* (Martinus Nijhoff Dordrecht, 1993) 63; and P Wachsmann 'L'interprétation de la Convention européenne des droits de l'homme' in F Sudre (ed) *L'interprétation de la Convention européenne des droits de l'homme. Actues du colloque des 13 et 14 mars 1998* (Bruylant Bruxelles, 1998) 335.

generally complies.[67] There is in fact good reason to say that the Court regards teleology as the pre-eminent principle of Convention interpretation.[68] The Court's approach differs in this regard fundamentally from, say, the approach taken by the dispute settlement body set to adjudicate disputes arising under the World Trade Organization (WTO) treaties—an arena for international litigation for the economic sector of far greater importance than the ECHR—where a textual interpretative approach is favoured.[69] It might be ventured that the difference is due to the fact that the ECHR, after all, is a human rights treaty where, so the received tradition will have it, consideration of non-state interests is vitally important.[70]

Two essential principles of interpretation are intimately linked with—or rather they are variables of—the Court's teleological approach. They are now introduced.

The Court's consistent reliance on the principle of *effective interpretation*, which implies that Convention guarantees shall be interpreted in a manner that renders them practical and effective for the applicant,[71] is a natural extension of its teleological approach.[72] The principle of *dynamic (or evolutive) interpretation*, which implies that the Court 'takes into account contemporary realities and attitudes, not the situation prevailing at the time of the drafting of the Convention',[73] is also closely connected with the teleological premise since it assumes that interpretation of Convention provisions in light of present-day conditions is required for achieving effective interpretation.[74] The principles of effective and dynamic interpretation have a special function with regard to justifying the Court's approach to corporate complaints. They deserve closer examination later when appropriate.

The teleological approach in its various forms requires, however, that the Convention's object and purpose can be identified.[75] This is not an easy task. Sporadically the Court may suggest what the object and purpose of the treaty is,

[67] Harris O'Boyle and Warbrick (n 12) 6–7.

[68] Matscher (n 66) 65–66; and, eg, *Pretto and Others v Italy* Series A No 71, (1984) 6 EHRR 182 § 26.

[69] See, eg, T Skouteris 'Customary Rules of Interpretation of Public International Law and Interpretative Practices in the WTO Dispute Settlement System' in P Mengozzi (ed) *International Trade Law on the 50th Anniversary of the Multilateral Trade System* (Giuffrè Milan, 1999) 113. The author is grateful to Peter Muchlinski for this information.

[70] See, however chapter 5 below.

[71] *Artico v Italy* Series A No 37 (1981), 3 EHRR 1 § 33.

[72] van Dijk and van Hoof (n 47) 74–76; and Matscher (n 66) 67.

[73] van Dijk and van Hoof (n 47) 77–78.

[74] JG Merrills *The Development of International Law by the European Court of Human Rights* (2nd edn Manchester University Press Manchester, 1988) 73–75. More literature on effectiveness and dynamism is referred to in chapters 3 and 4.

[75] This study follows J Klabbers 'Some Problems Regarding the Object and Purpose of Treaties' (1997) 8 Finnish Ybk Intl L 138, 144–48 in stating that, without evidence to the contrary, the terms 'object' and 'purpose' have mainly the same meaning. There is little in the Court's practice to believe that the Court distinguishes between the two.

but it prefers to reiterate variants of the standard phrase—of little help for our present purposes—that the ECHR object and purpose is the protection of human rights.[76] This begs the more fundamental question of what 'human rights' (and fundamental freedoms) within the meaning of the Convention actually comprise, and whether the Convention exhibits other objectives that also require implementation by the Court in its dispute-settling work. There is also a question whether the general understanding of the Convention's object and purpose can be 'translated' to the corporate context.

The Court has stated that guidance as to what constitutes the treaty's object and purpose is found in the treaty's Preamble,[77] and that the Convention's character as a law-making treaty makes it

> necessary to seek the interpretation that is most appropriate in order to realise the aim and achieve the object of the treaty, and not that which would restrict to the greatest possible degree the obligations undertaken by the parties.[78]

Such renditions of the teleological method, which are frequently cited in ECHR literature, have, however, mostly been adopted in cases that are remote from business-related matters that are the topic of interest in the present study. Further investigation is required for clarifying what, exactly, is the object and purpose of the treaty in the context at issue. As corporate human rights litigation before the European Court of Human Rights predominantly aims (rightly or unjustifiably) at curbing regulatory policies of the ECHR member States, it is not unlikely that the law requires a balance to be struck between legitimate regulatory practices and the enjoyment of corporate rights—a balance that may imply that in the corporate context the teleological thrust of the Court takes the law in a slightly different direction than would have been the case were the litigant in question the protagonist of 'human rights talk'[79]—the individual person *qua* human being. These matters will be dealt with comprehensively as part of the discussion in chapter 2.

(ii) The Court's Minimalist Reasoning

Article 45(1) provides that 'reasons shall be given' for judgments and decisions, and Rule 74(h) of the Rules of Court states that the judgment shall contain 'reasons in point of law'. Any student of the structural motives underlying Strasbourg jurisprudence will be challenged by the Court's singular style and mode of reasoning.[80] As visualised in judgments and decisions, the Court's rendered reasons incline more towards the minimalist than the loquacious.

[76] *Soering v UK* Series A No 161, (1989) 11 EHRR 439 § 87.

[77] *Golder* (n 65) § 34(1).

[78] *Wemhoff v Germany* Series A No 7, (1979) 1 EHRR 55 § 8.

[79] MA Glendon *Rights Talk. The Impoverishment of Political Discourse* (Free Press New York, 1991).

[80] Merrills (n 74) 21–32 gives a detailed comment on the Court's distinctive opinion writing.

The Court gives careful attention to the factual circumstances of each case. Doctrinal justification is characterized by brief and mechanical reference to a streamlined and general phraseology, prepared by the Court's staff of jurists,[81] which tends to obscure the 'true' rationale behind the outcome of the case. As John Merrills has observed, this practice

> not only makes the Court's judgments less interesting than they might be, but also ensures that they rarely display either the forcefulness or the depth of juridical analysis characteristic of the best individual opinions.[82]

It is particularly challenging when the decisions in question are or appear controversial in terms of ECHR law, because a modest presence of doctrinal individuality in cases that do not rest on a body of prior case law refined by use makes it extremely difficult to say with absolute conviction why and how the Court arrived at its conclusion.

In *Colas Est SA and Others v France* from 2002, for instance, which the study will consider subsequently in chapter 4, the Court came to the conclusion that the right to 'respect for one's . . . home' pursuant to Art 8(1) extended to the business premises of construction companies, regardless of any presence of infringement of individual privacy matters in the course of the investigations carried out on the properties. The Court arrived at this conclusion without responding directly to the litigants' arguments concerning the fundamental issues evidently at stake (notably that the Court was urged to expand the scope of private life protection to corporate persons despite the fact that there was evidence in the provision's doctrinal history to suggest that this sector was not a target for this form of human rights protection).[83] Its reasoning was predominantly based on simple reference to previous case law the essence of which, objectively speaking, diverged considerably from the matters at stake in the *Colas Est* application,[84] and on reliance on the principle of dynamic interpretation,[85] without specifying why the element of dynamism and prior decisions would support the outcome of the case. Yet it cannot be doubted that the Court had valid reasons, beyond mere technicalities, for extending 'home' protection to business premises in that particular case. From where can a comprehensive rationale for the judgment be extracted?

The argument in this study builds on the presumption that the Court does not interpret the Convention in a vacuum, devoid of doctrinal rationality. In its adjudicatory process it is informed—and this comes as no surprise—by various

[81] P Mahoney 'The Status of the Registry of the European Court of Human Rights: Past, Present and Future' in P Mahoney and others (eds) *Protecting Human Rights: The European Perspective: Studies in Memory of Rolv Ryssdal* (Heymann Cologne, 2000) 845 considers this further.

[82] Merrills (n 74) 25. [83] *Colas Est SA and Others v France* Reports 2002-III §§ 28–29.

[84] ibid § 40. [85] ibid §§ 41–42.

sources of law, including those that are external to the Convention as legal text.[86] The Court is, moreover, obviously constrained as much as it is enlightened by the structural framework within which it functions and which is laid down in the treaty itself. Factors such as the object and purpose of the Convention, the finite nature of its rights-catalogue and the supervisory system's international and subsidiary character necessarily play their part in the shaping of the Court's approach to contentious disputes.

It is assumed in the following that the Court's articulated reasons for judgments and decisions can be understood on various planes, where the apparent reasons given by the Court in its brief and technical language reflect and result from contextual and fundamental considerations. It will be maintained that the context and foundations of the Court's reasoning can be inferred from the Court's general mandate, the principles of interpretation used by the Court (and their underlying rationale) and the value system on which the Convention builds (which for a large part is reflected in the treaty's operative text and Preamble). In this attempt to explain and make sense of Court's occasionally controversial views in cases concerning corporate claims, the study draws considerably, therefore, on the insight gained from the prior study of these factors.

[86] R Bernhardt 'Comparative Law in the Interpretation and Application of the European Convention on Human Rights' in S Busuttil (ed) *Mainly Human Rights. Studies in Honour of JJ Cremona* (Fondation Internationale Malte Valletta, 1999) 33.

2

Companies and the Structure of Convention Protection

This chapter explores in depth whether corporate human rights protection accords with the basic structures of ECHR protection. The purpose of this manoeuvre is to suggest a foundation upon which the Court's approach to corporate litigation may be analysed and made sense of.

This is done firstly by addressing the criticism often seen and heard against the fact that companies and other corporate actors make use of human rights law for the protection of their own interests. Conventional wisdom will probably have it that there is something peculiar, even controversial, about companies 'having' human rights. Corporate entities are manifestly not natural persons; are not human rights meant for human beings? A sentiment of controversy is also brought forward, at times, by commentators who know that human rights law can be infinitely more complex than what the name suggests. Sentiments range from moral indignation (surely, companies, who are potential human rights abusers, deserve no protection by human rights norms) to politically or ideologically motivated opposition to this form of human rights law. Part A sets out the tenor of this criticism, using illustrations from the ECHR discourse in the United Kingdom and thereafter addresses it point by point from the standpoint of applied ECHR law.

The rest of the chapter explains further why it is that companies are principally welcomed in the Convention's legal order, but why they nonetheless tend, on occasion, to be met with a particular type of treatment by the Court. The ECHR builds on a European liberal system, which fundamentally welcomes and facilitates private enterprise. On the other hand, the European liberal order does not—and should not—give free enterprise unmitigated free rein. The social dimensions of European liberalism and the pervasiveness of the regulated market model may well mean that corporate reliance upon Convention guarantees may fail if up against certain public interests. Part B investigates the tacit acceptance of corporate protection found in the Convention text and drafting history. Part C represents an attempt to explain why the Convention's value system on the whole suggests that companies should not be excluded from its protective framework. In part D, it is argued that the nature of the rights-catalogue and the purpose of ECHR supervision are additional factors that shape the Court's response to corporate complaints. Part E assembles the various strands of the discussion.

A. An Occasional Sense of Controversy

1 Voices of Dissent: the United Kingdom's ECHR Discourse

Members of the Court, and, previously, the Commission, have sometimes held that companies' complaints in certain instances challenge long-held perceptions of ECHR law or somehow give rise to doctrinal difficulty. Although examples of these views will be offered in the following chapters, one would be hard put to say that a genuine sense of controversy in the form of a principled opposition to corporate protection is a manifest feature of the case law. The bulk of the Convention literature, which on the whole relates to the *lex lata* of ECHR protection, similarly conveys no sense of contentiousness as far as companies are concerned. While this may in part be explained by the quantitatively marginal role played by companies in Strasbourg case law—its diminutive importance failing to ignite debate—it may just as well suggest a matter-of-fact approach to ECHR realities where the notion of companies 'having' human rights is seen as principally uncontroversial.

Disagreement tends to be encountered on the normative plane. Such *de lege ferenda* views marshalled against corporate protection are not necessarily well-versed in the structural realities of ECHR law. It is, however, useful to be acquainted with the critics of corporate human rights enjoyment because although the views may not necessarily relate to or affect Court practice, it helps in the identification of some of the underlying issues to be encountered in the wider analysis of the Court's approach.

The voices of dissent presented here will doubtless be familiar to students of the United Kingdom's ECHR discourse. Indeed, the presentation draws on arguments found—mostly—in legal literature in Britain on the Convention as such and on the debate on the Convention's incorporation in domestic law in the UK.[1] (Arguments that pertain exclusively to the domestic effects of incorporation are nonetheless sought left out.) In thus delimiting the examination it is not intended to suggest that opposition to corporate ECHR utilisation

[1] Parts of the Convention were incorporated by the Human Rights Act 1998) (fully in force 2 October 2000), eg, R Blackburn 'The United Kingdom' in R Blackburn and J Polakiewicz (eds) *Fundamental Rights in Europe. The ECHR and Its Member States, 1950–2000* (Oxford University Press Oxford, 2001) 935, 960–71.

does not pertain to other Council of Europe jurisdictions; it is simply that these particular voices of dissent are transparent and therefore readily available to us. That said, the arguments against corporate ECHR enjoyment are not very much unlike those found in comparable fundamental rights regimes.[2] The following list is not exhaustive, and the arguments are sometimes interconnected and partly overlapping.

(a) A Conceptual Mismatch?

One recurrent argument is that the very idea of companies 'having' human rights is in itself a conceptual oxymoron.[3] A company, unlike a human person, has 'no soul to be damned, and no body to be kicked'.[4] Human rights are for human beings, not for non-human persons. This conceptual peculiarity can be put to good, narrative use, as when the counsel for the applicant in *Air Canada v UK*—a case concerning the observance of procedural safeguards in relation to the seizure of a commercial airliner by customs officers at Heathrow airport—observed in his opening statement before the Court that '[w]e are not human . . . the question whether we have any rights, remains for your Lordships' decision'.[5]

Comments such as these, and indeed, the conceptually inspired critique, fall short of the mark inasmuch as they fail to take into account the Convention's quality not merely as a treaty for the protection of 'human rights' but additionally of 'fundamental freedoms'. The latter term lacks, at least linguistically, the intimate bond with the qualities of natural persons that characterises 'human rights'.[6] From the viewpoint of applied ECHR law, it is at any rate inadvisable to deduce the scope of the Convention from concepts alone. The principle of effectiveness defies, as will be shown later, an application of the Convention that is based on deduction from concepts and formal categorisations.

[2] In US constitutional law, CJ Mayer 'Personalizing the Impersonal: Corporations and the Bill of Rights' (1990) 41 Hastings L J 577; and T Hartmann *Unequal Protection: the Rise of Corporate Dominance and the Theft of Human Rights* (Rodale Press Erasmus PA, 2002); in the EU context, C Harlow 'Access to Justice as a Human Right: The European Convention and the European Union' in P Alston (ed) *The EU and Human Rights* (Oxford University Press Oxford, 1999) 187, 195–97; G de Búrca 'The Language of Rights and European Integration' in J Shaw and G More (eds) *New Legal Dynamics of European Union* (Clarendon Press Oxford, 1995) 29; and J Coppel and A O'Neill 'The European Court of Justice: Taking Rights Seriously?' (1992) 29 CMLR 669, 689–91.

[3] eg, K Ewing 'The Human Rights Act and Parliamentary Democracy' (1999) 62 MLR 79, 93.

[4] E Knowles (ed) *The Oxford Dictionary of Quotations* (6th edn, Oxford University Press Oxford, 2004) 550 (quoting Edward, Baron Thurlow).

[5] *Air Canada v United Kingdom* Series A No 316, (1995) 20 EHRR 150. The quotation is found in N Bratza 'The Implications of the Human Rights Act 1998 for Commercial Practice' [2000] EHRLR 1, 1.

[6] H Guradze *Die Europäische Menschenrechtskonvention. Konvention zum Schutze der Menschenrechte und Grundfreiheiten nebst Zusatsprotokollen. Kommentar* (Vahlen Berlin, 1968) 43 and 45–46 sees the two concepts as synonymous in light of the drafting process of the UDHR, where a similar terminology was adopted.

The argument that the Convention's 'human rights' cannot apply to artificial persons such as companies seems to rest on a classical liberal understanding of human rights that individuals need protection from governmental excesses, and that, consequently, human rights are for natural persons, in particular the weak and vulnerable. This conception of human rights fails to take into account that human rights has become, in the words of Michael Addo:

> a lot more persuasive, especially in our ever more pluralistic communities in which we are able to recognise more than just governments and human beings as the generators of the legal order.[7]

The conceptually inspired critique requires in other words clarification of what, exactly, human rights (and fundamental freedoms) mean in the context of the ECHR. This will be dealt with soon.

(b) Ideological and Political Motives

Ideological views and political priorities can be potent driving forces against corporate Convention protection, especially when they operate in tandem. At least three examples are found in the UK debate.

Ideological differences with regard to companies' protection arose already in the drafting process that led to the Convention's eventual adoption in 1950. British delegates were apparently alone in airing their opposition to a business-friendly rights catalogue. As one of the delegates said in the first stages of the drafting process (with regard to the protection of private property):

> [In] the United Kingdom we are at the moment—I am not arguing the rights or wrongs of this—completing highly important legislation involving the steel industry of our country. The steel industry objects, as it is perfectly entitled to do, and they have used every legitimate means of opposition that the law permits. I ask the Rapporteur: is the steel industry of the United Kingdom, having gone through all the processes of the State, entitled to appeal to the Commission? . . . I honestly believe that to pass this as we now have it would be grossly opposed to the interests of Europe.[8]

A member of the Cabinet at the time, much preoccupied with schemes to nationalise large industries, similarly considered that the Convention's 'standpoint [was that] of a laissez-faire economy,'[9] and its adoption therefore undesirable.[10]

[7] MK Addo 'The Corporation as a Victim of Human Rights Violations' in MK Addo (ed) *Human Rights Standards and the Responsibility of Transnational Corporations* (Kluwer Hague, 1999) 187, 188. See also M Zander *A Bill of Rights?* (4th edn Sweet & Maxwell London, 1997) 153–55.

[8] AH Robertson (ed) *Collected Editions of the 'Travaux Préparatoires' of the European Convention on Human Rights* (Martinus Nijhoff Dordrecht, 1975) vol 2, 192–94 (Mr Nally).

[9] G Marston 'The United Kingdom's Part in the Preparation of the European Convention on Human Rights, 1950' (1993) 42 ICLQ 796, 813.

[10] The protection of property was postponed inter alia to placate British opposition, see AWB Simpson *Human Rights and the End of Empire. Britain and the Genesis of the European Convention* (Oxford University Press Oxford, 2001) 754–807.

Political opposition to corporate rights enjoyment under the Convention was in fact the crucial reason for the British government's deferred acceptance of a right to private petition under the Convention. Fearing massive compensation claims arising out of British military forces' scorched earth tactics in Asia in 1942, the War Damage Act of 1965 retrospectively abandoned the obligation to pay compensation for the lawful destruction of private property in times of war. The Burmah Oil Company, whose industrial plant in Burma was destroyed in 1942, would have made use of the right to apply to the Court to challenge the Act. It would almost certainly have been seized upon by some as '[a] luminous . . . example of an attempt by private capital to exploit the . . . Convention and of the concern on part of the executive to which this gave rise'.[11] The UK government delayed the acceptance of the private application until December 1965, by which time the deadline for the Burmah Oil Company to file a Strasbourg claim had come and gone.[12]

Ideological resistance also flared up in the wake of the debate to incorporate the Convention in domestic law in Britain. The Labour Party had for long resisted domestic implementation because it was seen as a guarantor of free enterprise.[13] When Labour Chairman John Smith in 1993 finally recommended incorporation, he wanted companies left unprotected.[14]

It is of course wholly legitimate to argue against corporate ECHR enjoyment on ideological or political grounds. The Convention rests firmly, however, on a platform of European liberalism. It is not 'laissez-faire' liberalism, but neither does the Convention's value system support the form of planned economy that was in vogue in some corners immediately after WWII. These aspects of the Convention, too, are dealt with soon.

(c) Disproportional Litigious Advantages

The perennial case workload problem in Strasbourg is naturally augmented by every fresh complaint submitted to the Court.[15] In this respect, the acceptance of corporate complaints must take its share of the blame for an overburdened

[11] M Smyth *Business and the Human Rights Act 1998* (Jordans Bristol, 2000) 12.

[12] eg, A Lester 'The United Kingdom Acceptance of the Statutory Jurisdiction: What Went on in Whitehall in 1965' [1998] PL 237; and Simpson (n 10) 1092–1101.

[13] AJ Dignam and D Allen *Company Law and the Human Rights Act 1998* (Butterworths London, 2000) 150.

[14] J Smith 'A Citizens' Democracy' (speech 1 March 1993) reprinted in R Blackburn (ed) *Towards a Constitutional Bill of Rights for the United Kingdom. Commentary and Documents* (Pinter London, 1999) 932, 935.

[15] Generally on the workload problem, eg, T Said and J Wadham 'What Price the Right of Individual Petition: Report of the Evaluation Group to the Committee of Ministers on the European Court of Human Rights' [2002] EHRLR 169. The results of recent initiatives in the Council of Europe to mitigate the problem are considered separately in chapter 5.

Court. Some critics oppose corporate human rights litigation on the presumption that companies are resourceful societal actors and that their economically motivated litigation would be disproportionably represented in human rights litigation to the implicit disadvantage of other litigants that are presumptively needier of protection.[16] It is likely that this concern prompted the human rights advocacy group Liberty, for instance, to disallow companies and other business entities from utilising the catalogue of rights and freedoms that were proposed in Liberty's 1991 draft UK Bill of Rights.[17]

The dreaded *Lochner* era in US constitutional legal history, during which the corporate world supported by a laissez-faire-minded Supreme Court undermined on fundamental rights grounds economic and social reform in the United States, is a powerful historical example of the drawbacks of combining business interests and human rights arguments in the courts.[18] The United Kingdom ECHR discourse is naturally familiar with the US experience with serious attempts to undermine democratically founded and even much needed regulatory policies. Some critics thus argue that by virtue of their resourcefulness, companies are able to advance their policies under a Convention mantle to the detriment of democratic processes.[19]

The stereotypical image of the corporate actor as presumptively litigious, and a powerful one at that, does not necessarily coincide with the realities of Strasbourg jurisprudence. Companies' complaints have so far not caused the Court to drown in work. The image of the individual complainant as a weak litigant should besides be reconsidered in light of the fact that many individual human rights complaints today are sponsored by human rights groups or other organizations.[20] Corporate defiance of regulatory power by Strasbourg means may at times have economic ramifications for the respondent State, and in this sense the Court is entitled, as will become clear later, to consider the complaint in a particular manner. But on the whole, the Strasbourg system does not permit adjudication on the basis of the real or presumed strength of the applicant person. The right to Convention protection applies

[16] K Ewing and C Gearty 'Rocky Foundations for Labour's New Rights' [1997] EHRLR 146, 146; and J Wadham 'Why Incorporation of the European Convention on Human Rights Is Not Enough' in R Gordon and R Wilmot-Smith (eds) *Human Rights in the United Kingdom* (Oxford University Press Oxford, 1996) 25, 34–35.

[17] F Klug (ed) *A People's Charter: Liberty's Bill of Rights: A Consultation Paper* (National Council for Civil Liberties London, 1991) 82 (draft art 21).

[18] Named after *Lochner v New York* 198 US 45 (1905). See further, eg, BH Siegan *Economic Liberties and the Constitution* (University of Chicago Press Chicago, 1980) 110–83; and RG McCloskey 'Economic Due Process and the Supreme Court' [1962] S Ct Rev 34.

[19] S Sedley 'Opinion: A Bill of Rights for Britain' [1997] EHRLR 458, 464.

[20] MA Nowicki 'Non-Governmental Organisations (NGOs) before the European Commission of Human Rights' in M de Salvia and Villiger (eds) *The Birth of European Human Rights Law. Liber Amicorum Carl Aage Nørgaard* (Nomos Baden-Baden, 1988) 267, 269.

to everyone regardless of status; the treaty's provisions are universal in all senses of the word.[21]

(d) Considerations of Symmetry and Merit

Some critics assume that ECHR protection is somehow conditional. Companies, they assert, represent private capital, which historically has threatened the human rights of other persons, typically their employees. This uneven track record, they argue, should disqualify companies from relying on human rights standards.[22]

There is arguably some truth in the claim that companies have shown and continue to show a propensity for infringing the human rights of individuals and groups. The doctrine of corporate human rights accountability, as we know it in international legal discourse today, arose from this well-documented fact.[23] In terms of ECHR law, however, the germaneness of such arguments is dubious. Human rights protection under the treaty does not depend on historical or current proclivities for human rights abuse in the generic group which the applicant represents. Neither does the past or present conduct of the actual person applying to the Court qualify the right to benefit from Convention protection.[24] This is indeed an essential aspect of ECHR protection.

A related view concerns symmetry rather than merit. Having no responsibility to respect the human rights of others, companies, so the argument goes, deserve no ECHR protection.[25] This argument can be logically defensible. Yet it should be recalled that the ECHR is not entirely symmetrical. Under the Convention public persons have duties while private persons have rights. As a rule, capability of protection is not contingent on an equivalent human rights responsibility for the same person.[26] The notion that companies should

[21] In *Sunday Times v UK* Series A No 30, (1980) 2 EHRR 245 § 66(1) the Court spoke of the industrial concern on whose activities the applicant company sought newspaper coverage as a 'powerful company' in a negative light. In *Groppera Radio and Others v Switzerland* Series A No 173, (1990) 12 EHRR 321 § 68 the Court considered that the extent to which the legality requirement in Art 10(2) was fulfilled depended inter alia on the 'status' of the applicant as a business enterprise, and considered that it could be expected of a 'business company' to familiarize itself with the law in question.

[22] S Kentridge 'The Incorporation of the European Convention on Human Rights' in J Beatson (ed) *Constitutional Reform in the United Kingdom: Practice and Principles* (Hart Oxford, 1998) 69, 70.

[23] SR Ratner 'Corporations and Human Rights: A Theory of Legal Responsibility' (2001) 111 YLJ 443 provides a detailed account on the human rights responsibility for companies.

[24] JES Fawcett *The Application of The European Convention on Human Rights* (Clarendon Press Oxford, 1987) 346.

[25] Sedley (n 19) 31: Ewing (n 3) 93; and AH Robertson (ed) *Collected Editions of the 'Travaux Préparatoires' of the European Convention on Human Rights* (Martinus Nijhoff Dordrecht, 1975) vol 1, 144–48 (Mr Nally).

[26] Some modifications do, however, exist, eg, Art 10(2): 'the exercise of these freedoms, since it carries with it duties and responsibilities'.

be unprotected because they cannot be held responsible for ECHR violations therefore takes little account of the main design of Convention protection.

2 The ECHR's Singular Human Rights Ideology

A human rights treaty, particularly if concerned with civil and political rights, aims primarily at tackling other issues than the conditions of free enterprise in the regulatory state. The majority of international human rights conventions limit their scope to the individual human being or to organizations whose relation to profit is at best indirect. The international supervisory practice under other human rights treaties shows that the typical human rights violations are largely removed from the business context, although some treaties do in fact open up for a consideration of claims arising from the business sector.[27] From the vantage point of a large part of international human rights law, therefore, it would not be entirely outlandish to suggest that the protection of companies' human rights is taken as an affront to the ideals of the international human rights movement.[28]

There is, however, reason to question the reach of terminology and discursive traditions. The Convention is a human rights treaty. But the fact that it belongs to the international law of human rights cannot by itself govern the form of protection it offers. The Convention is a human rights treaty of a different kind to, say, the majority of United Nations treaties for the protection of human rights. It might very well be that the human rights of the ECHR signifies a particular human rights ideology which differs from that reflected in other international treaties for the protection of civil and political rights. It is a European treaty with particular features tailored to the needs of the societies in which it is meant to operate. This significant point is pursued in the following section.

B. Treaty Text and Drafting History

The ECHR is a treaty negotiated and adopted by sovereign States. The parties' intentions, as they are articulated primarily in the treaty text and the

[27] M Emberland 'The Corporate Veil in the Jurisprudence of the Human Rights Committee and the Inter-American Court and Commission of Human Rights' (2004) 4 HRLR 257 introduces the protection of business actors in the ICCPR and ACHR.

[28] The human rights movement is, however, no uniform group and various actors within the movement may pursue a human rights agenda with different objectives, see critical remarks from two different angles, D Kennedy 'The International Human Rights Movement: Part of the Problem?' (2002) 15 Harv HRJ 101; and HJ Steiner *Diverse Partners: Non-Governmental Organizations in the Human Rights Movement: The Report of a Retreat of Human Rights Activists* (Harvard Law School Human Rights Program Cambridge Mass, 1991).

Convention's drafting history, should enable us to discover the object and purpose of the Convention,[29] which is the essential task for any ECHR interpretation, also with regard to the proper place of companies in its protective framework. Let us consider further what the text and drafting history can tell us about companies and Strasbourg protection.

1 The Text Read in Isolation

Some Convention guarantees are by their textual reference aimed at matters that are exclusively human, such as the right to 'life' (Art 2), the prohibition against 'torture or inhuman or degrading treatment and punishment' (Art 3) and the right to 'marry' (Art 12). But most textual references only dimly identify whose rights and freedoms are protected. Reading the text in isolation, it is not easy to decide whether companies enjoy, say, freedom of 'association' (Art 11) or a 'right to a fair hearing' (Art 6(1)).[30]

The treaty text provides limited assistance also with regard to its designation of rights-holders. Protocol 1 Art 1(1) first sentence uniquely says that property protection is for '[e]very natural or legal person', the latter term clearly encompassing for-profit entities such as companies. Two other provisions too suggest the protection of corporate actors: Art 10(1) third sentence proposes by negation that various media 'enterprises' are protected by the right to freedom of expression; this term includes companies.[31] Article 34, which provides for the right to private petition, speaks enigmatically of a right of application for 'any person, non-governmental organisation or group of individuals'.[32] The word 'person' in its English form is linguistically capable of designating legal persons such as companies,[33] but since the French authentic text of Art 34 uses '*personne physique*', the right for companies to apply to the Strasbourg institutions is subsumed under the concept of 'non-governmental organisation'.[34]

[29] Vienna Convention Art 31(1) and (2).

[30] The title of Art 6 refers to 'trial' rather than 'hearing' (which is the word used in the operative text of the clause).

[31] *Autronic AG v Switzerland* Series A No 178, (1990) 12 EHRR 485 § 47.

[32] Former Art 25(1) was identically phrased.

[33] Note, for instance, that the General Framework Agreement for Peace in Bosnia and Herzegovina (adopted 14 December 1995) (1996) 35 ILM 89130 and 133, refers in Annex VI 'On Human Rights' to the rights-catalogue of the ECHR and refers in Art I to 'persons' as its beneficiaries; the agreement's tribunal—the Human Rights Chamber—has mandate to consider claims from the same group of persons as the one listed in Art 34 of the European Convention on Human Rights, see Art VIII.

[34] W Peukert 'Artikel 25 (Individualbeschwerde)' in JA Frowein and W Peukert *Europäische Menschenrechtskonvention. EMRK-Kommentar* (2nd edn Engel Kehl am Rhein, 1996) 523, 531 and 534; and App 11921/86 *Verein 'Kontakt-Information-Therapie' (KIT) and Hagen v Austria* (1988) 57 DR 81 §§ 1(4) and 2.

The Convention's meaning of a 'non-governmental organisation' is thus broader than its specific connotation within the United Nations system.[35]

Article 1, which institutes the scope of the member States' obligations under the treaty, refers to the protection for 'everyone' within the States' jurisdiction. In this respect, the ECHR differs from its closest siblings, the ICCPR and ACHR, where states undertake to respect the rights of the individual only.[36] (The reasons for this difference in approach taken to corporate persons are largely unknown with regard to the ACHR; the ICCPR drafters were apparently anxious that human rights organizations' use of the Covenant could affect sovereign interests more than the States could accept.)[37] Even if the terms 'everyone' and its antonym 'no-one' have different meanings depending on the provision in which they are found the special wording of ECHR Art 1, when viewed in a comparative light, allow of a broad construction in which companies can be included. The concept of 'everyone' is thus sometimes taken in favour of an inclusion of non-individual persons such as with regard to Art 6(1) and its procedural guarantees.[38] In other provisions, the Strasbourg authorities have drawn the opposite conclusion.[39] One cannot, therefore, base the investigation of corporate protection under the Convention on the wording of Art 1 alone.

Only two substantive provisions—Protocol 1 Art 1 directly and Art 10 indirectly—describe rights-holders in a way which accommodates the company form in the treaty text itself. This does not mean that companies are unprotected by other provisions. But the textual basis remains ambiguous and needs be supplemented by other sources in order to establish with certainty the extent to which companies have a place within the Convention system.

35 C Schwaighofer 'Legal Persons, Organisations, Shareholders as Applicants (Art 25 of the Convention)' in M de Salvia and Villiger (eds) *The Birth of European Human Rights Law: Liber Amicorum Carl Aage Nørgaard* (Nomos Baden-Baden, 1998) 321, 323. Outside the UN context, the concept might include business entities, eg, PR Baehr 'Mobilization of the Conscience of Mankind: Conditions of Effectiveness of Human Rights NGOs' in E Denters and N Schrijver (eds) *Reflections on International law from the Low Countries in Honour of Paul de Waart* (Martinus Nijhoff Hague, 1998) 135, 137.

36 ICCPR art 2(1) ('all individuals'). ACHR art 1(1) speaks of 'all persons', but makes clear in (2) that 'person' means 'human being' for the purpose of Convention interpretation. Art 2 of the African Charter on Human and Peoples' Rights (adopted 27 June 1981, entered into force 21 October 1986) OAU Doc. CAB/LEG/67/3 rev. 5 (1982) 21 ILM 58 speaks of 'every individual'. The Arab Charter on Human Rights (adopted 15 September 1994) (1997) 18 HRLJ 151, 152 refers similarly to 'all individuals' (art 2).

37 Emberland (n 27) 261 and 274 considers the two treaties' drafting history on this matter.

38 *Firestone Tire and Rubber Co and Others v UK* Application 5460/72, (1973) 43 CD 99 is an early example.

39 App 14438/88 *Boucheras and Groupe Information Asiles v France* Application 14438/88, (1991) 69 DR 236 § 1(1) (art 5); and *Verein 'Kontakt-Information-Therapie' (KIT) and Hagen* (n 34) § 1(4) (Art 3).

2 Tacit Acceptance in the *Travaux Préparatoires*

The drafters' subjective intentions, spoors of which are found in the preparatory works, are pertinent insofar as they help clarify what objectively speaking is the treaty's object and purpose.[40] A striking aspect of the *travaux préparatoires* is that they, except from the dissents presented above, seem to take for granted that companies and other for-profit actors were to be included in the Convention. Evidence is primarily found in the discussions to clarify who should be entitled to apply to the international authority which ultimately became the Court.

The first preliminary draft of a European Convention on Human Rights, which was prepared by the Juridical Section of the International Council of the European Movement, a private organization predating the formation of the Council of Europe,[41] contained a right of petition to a Court of Human Rights for 'any natural or corporate person'.[42] The term 'corporate body', a later variant, was eventually replaced with the term 'non-governmental organisation', but there is no evidence that it was meant to have any doctrinal significance.[43] The provision was adopted without discussion in the subsequent drafting process under the auspices of the Council of Europe.[44] As observed by Pierre-Henri Teitgen, who was co-author of both the European Movement draft and the subsequent Convention, this first draft became 'the effective source of the [ECHR]' because the 'Assembly of the Council of Europe . . . tacitly accepted it without comment as a basis for its work'.[45] It cannot be doubted, then, that companies were seen, together with other corporate persons, as included as rights-holders under the proposed human rights catalogue.[46]

According to the treaty text as read in light of the preparatory works, companies are undoubtedly entitled to some degree of ECHR protection. But

[40] Vienna Convention art 31. Eg, F Matscher 'Methods of Interpretation of the Convention' in R St John Macdonald F Matscher and H Petzold (eds) *The European System for the Protection of Human Rights* (Martinus Nijhoff Dordrecht, 1993) 63, 66; and H Golsong 'Interpreting the European Convention on Human Rights Beyond the Confines of the Vienna Convention on the Law of Treaties?' in R St John Macdonald F Matscher and H Petzold (eds) *The European System for the Protection of Human Rights* (Martinus Nijhoff Dordrecht, 1993) 147, 147–48.

[41] Simpson (n 10) 629 and 649–55 considers this draft.

[42] Robertson *Travaux Préparatoires* vol 1 (n 25) 296 and 298 (draft Art 7 a).

[43] Robertson *Travaux Préparatoires* vol 2 (n 8) 3 and 68 (draft Art 17). There were no substantial changes in later drafts, ibid, 98, 132, 194, 228, 286 and 318 (draft Art 25).

[44] Robertson *Travaux Préparatoires* vol 1 (n 25) 156 and 202; AH Robertson (ed) *Collected Editions of the 'Travaux Préparatoires' of the European Convention on Human Rights* (Martinus Nijhoff Dordrecht, 1979) vol 5, 318.

[45] P-H Teitgen 'Introduction to the European Convention on Human Rights' in R St John Macdonald F Matscher and H Petzold (eds) *The European System for the Protection of Human Rights* (Martinus Nijhoff Dordrecht, 1993) 3, 9.

[46] There is no evidence in the drafting material to suggest that 'corporate bodies' comprised, say, only not-for-profit entities.

neither source informs us why companies so straightforwardly were integrated in the Convention, or, for that matter, what form of protection corporate applicants actually enjoy. Answers to these questions must be found elsewhere.

C. The Convention's Value System

The ECHR was adopted for many reasons and all of them cannot be enumerated here. An important motivation, however, was for the countries of Western Europe, the Council of Europe member States at the time, to pledge their commitment to certain values that over time had developed to become (and remain) essential to their social and legal order.[47] The need to proclaim the virtues of European liberalism was genuinely felt at the time. The ideals of the liberal state espoused by the better part of Western Europe had been threatened by totalitarianism and barbarianism and faced new dangers in the shape of a rapidly expanding communist East. This was the post-war climate in which the Convention was adopted,[48] and which provided its value system and general purpose. In this section, it is argued that significant portions of the treaty's underlying system of values,[49] as expressed in the Preamble of the Convention, does not bar in any way corporate litigants from the pursuit of Convention claims in Strasbourg. In fact, they provide avenues for companies' legitimate use of the Convention's rights and freedoms.

1 The Preamble's Significance

The Convention's fundamental values can conceivably be drawn from several sources. They find expression in the treaty provisions because they re-articulate the basic elements of a legal order to which the Council of Europe pledges allegiance. The Court's case law similarly enunciates a set of basic values. The Convention's value system is, however, systematically spelled out in the Preamble, which hence may act as a very helpful guide to the treaty's fundamental

[47] C Ovey and RCA White *Jacobs and White The European Convention on Human Rights* (3rd edn Oxford University Press Oxford, 2002) 1–4.

[48] JG Merrills and AH Robertson *Human Rights in Europe. A Study of the European Convention on Human Rights* (4th edn Manchester University Press Manchester, 2001) 3–5; and DJ Harris M O'Boyle and C Warbrick *Law of the European Convention on Human Rights* (Butterworths London, 1995) 1–2.

[49] 'Values' are understood here in the sense applied by ML Fernández Esteban *The Rule of Law in the European Constitution* (Kluwer Hague, 1999) 39–40, as 'the foundation of a group of other norms' that plays a 'structural role inside the legal order'. It is not the intention here to enter upon a philosophical debate on this question.

values. Since it has important implications for the status of companies in the treaty system, it is useful to cite the Preamble in full:

The governments signatory hereto, being members of the Council of Europe,

[1] Considering the Universal Declaration of Human Rights proclaimed by the General Assembly of the United Nations on 10th December 1948;
[2] Considering that this Declaration aims at securing the universal and effective recognition and observance of the Rights therein declared;
[3] Considering that the aim of the Council of Europe is the achievement of greater unity between its members and that one of the methods by which that aim is to be pursued is the maintenance and further realisation of human rights and fundamental freedoms;
[4] Reaffirming their profound belief in those fundamental freedoms which are the foundation of justice and peace in the world and are best maintained on the one hand by an effective political democracy and on the other by a common understanding and observance of the human rights upon which they depend;
[5] Being resolved, as the governments of European countries which are like-minded and have a common heritage of political traditions, ideals, freedom and the rule of law, to take the first steps for the collective enforcement of certain of the rights stated in the Universal Declaration,

The Preamble is not part of the Convention's operative clauses. But it is not empty of doctrinal significance. In accordance with Art 31(2) of the Vienna Convention on the Law of Treaties, the Court takes the Preamble's guidelines into account when it interprets the treaty text. In *Golder v UK*, the Preamble was regarded as 'generally very useful for the determination of the "object" and "purpose" of the instrument construed'.[50] It is asserted here that it similarly is useful for determining the place of companies within the Convention.

Four aspects of the Convention's value system are now considered. They are central components of the structural framework against which the Court's response to corporate human rights litigation can be seen—and will be seen in the subsequent chapters.

2 Individual Dignity

Human rights can be justified on various philosophical grounds.[51] It is not in the Court's nature to philosophize, and it has not expressed its loyalty to one philosophical school over another. There is similarly no evidence that the drafters, after careful consideration, committed themselves to one particular theory of human rights protection above another. It might well be that the

[50] *Golder v UK* Series A No 18, (1979) 1 EHRR 524 § 34(1).
[51] JJ Shestack 'The Philosophic Foundations of Human Rights' (1998) 20 HRQ 201.

ECHR can be explained in light of different contemporary and ancient schools of thought (if, indeed, such an endeavour is fruitful).

The Preamble nonetheless informs us that one approach to the protection of human rights has greatly influenced the Convention, notably that taken in the Universal Declaration of Human Rights.[52] Although this was not its only function,[53] the Convention was a regional implementation of the civil and political rights of the UDHR at the level of pan-European law.[54] Now although the UDHR drafters, too, rejected allegiance to a particular philosophical school,[55] the 'inherent dignity' of the human being is a prominent UDHR value. The Declaration's Preamble regards it as an absolute precondition for 'justice and freedom',[56] if not the very origin of human rights protection.[57] Individual dignity is not expressly referred to in the ECHR,[58] but its Preamble's reference to the UDHR suggests that the Convention also regards individual dignity as one of its basic values.[59]

The Court has occasionally referred to individual dignity,[60] but not elaborated on its meaning. The notion of individual dignity is besides generally contested.[61] Given the limited attention thus far paid in legal discourse to

[52] Ovey and White (n 47) 4.

[53] KJ Partsch 'Die Rechte und Freiheiten der europäischen Menschenrechtskonvention' in KA Bettermann FL Neumann and HC Nipperdey (eds) *Die Grundrechte. Handbuch der Theorie und Praxis der Grundrechte* (Duncker & Humblot Berlin, 1966) vol 1, 237, 245–46.

[54] E Decaux 'Les États parties et leurs engagements' in L-E Pettiti E Decaux and P-H Imbert (eds) *La Convention européenne des droits de l'homme. Commentaire article par article* (Economica Paris, 1995) 3, 4–5. See Preamble 1st, 2nd, and 5th recitals.

[55] Å Samnøy 'The Origins of the Universal Declaration of Human Rights' in G Alfredsson and A Eide (eds) *The Universal Declaration of Human Rights. A Common Standard of Achievement* (Martinus Nijhoff Hague, 1999) 3, 17–18.

[56] UDHR Preamble 1st recital and art 1; and M Koskenniemi 'The Preamble of the UDHR' in G Alfredsson and A Eide (eds) *The Universal Declaration of Human Rights. A Common Standard of Achievement* (Martinus Nijhoff Hague, 1999) 27, 30, and 35.

[57] ICCPR Preamble 2nd recital states that human rights 'derive from the inherent dignity of the human person'.

[58] Conversely, the Conference on Security and Co-operation in Europe, Helsinki Final Act (adopted 1 August 1975), available at <http://www.osce.org/mc/13017.html> (Helsinki Final Act) (9 May 2004) Principle VII proclaims that all human rights and fundamental freedoms 'derive from the inherent dignity of the human person'.

[59] JA Frowein 'Human Dignity in International Law' in D Kretzmer and E Klein (eds) *The Concept of Dignity in Human Rights Discourse* (Kluwer Hague, 2002) 121, 123; L-E Pettiti 'Réflexions sur les principes et les mécanismes de la Convention. De l'idéal de 1950 à l'humble réalité d'aujourd'hui' in L-E Pettiti E Decaux and P-H Imbert (ed) *La Convention européenne des droits de l'homme. Commentaire article par article* (Economica Paris 1995) 27, 32; and JA Carrillo Salcedo 'The Place of the European Convention in International Law' in R St John Macdonald F Matscher and H Petzold (eds) *The European System for the Protection of Human Rights* (Martinus Nijhoff Dordrecht, 1993) 15, 20.

[60] *Lawless v Ireland (Preliminary Objections)* Series A No 1, (1979) 1 EHRR 1, Individual Opinion of Judge Mariadakis.

[61] O Schachter 'Human Dignity as a Normative Concept' (1983) 77 AJIL 848, 849.

developing the concept in a human rights setting,[62] this is not the place to seek clarification of its actual scope. In essence, however, the concept of human dignity is intimately linked with the faculties of the natural person,[63] and is reminiscent of the natural law tradition of human rights justification.[64] It includes at least respect for 'everyone's humanity' and 'the creation and protection of individual self-fulfilment'.[65]

Given the impersonal character of the company, the inclusion of corporate entities in the Convention system will enjoy little direct support on the basis of the value of individual dignity. At best, it can only indirectly, or derivatively, support the protection of companies, in the sense that companies ought to be protected to the extent that they ultimately stem from human activity.[66] That the Convention builds in part on the notion that human rights derive from human dignity may therefore support a restrictive interpretation of the provisions which would not therefore encompass rights for non-individual persons such as companies, and especially those companies whose individual *substratum* is remote or insignificant.[67] The status of corporate human rights in Strasbourg practice must primarily be explained on the basis of other Convention values.

3 Democracy

Democracy is one such value.

Democracy is also an elusive and essentially contested concept.[68] In the context of the ECHR, however, many aspects of it are known to us. It is not the intention of this study to detail the findings of other studies,[69] but some

[62] E Klein and D Kretzmer 'Foreword' in D Kretzmer and E Klein (eds) *The Concept of Dignity in Human Rights Discourse* (Kluwer Hague, 2002) v–vii.

[63] K Dicke 'The Founding Function of Human Dignity' in D Kretzmer and E Klein (eds) *The Concept of Dignity in Human Rights Discourse* (Kluwer Hague, 2002) 111, 114–18 (which considers the UDHR concept in detail).

[64] J Morsink *The Universal Declaration of Human Rights. Origins, Drafting and Intent* (University of Pennsylvania Press Philadelphia, 1999) 281.

[65] A Clapham *Human Rights in the Private Sphere* (Clarendon Press Oxford, 1993) 148–49.

[66] C Starck 'Artikel 1' in H von Mangoldt F Klein and C Starck (eds) *Das Bonner Grundgesetz* (4th edn Vahlen Munich, 1999) vol 1 [17 ff].

[67] The term 'individual substratum' is borrowed from German constitutional discourse, where it is taken to mean the extent to which the company's composition has a clear element of natural persons' interests and influence; eg, PM Huber 'Artikel 19' in H von Mangoldt F Klein and C Starck (eds) *Das Bonner Grundgesetz. Kommentar* (4th edn Vahlen Munich, 1999) vol 1, 2174, 2239.

[68] S Marks *The Riddle of All Constitutions. International Law, Democracy, and the Critique of Ideology* (Oxford University Press Oxford, 2000) 50.

[69] Studies include S Marks 'The European Convention on Human Rights and Its "Democratic Society"' (1996) 66 BYIL 209; and JG Merrills *The Development of International Law by the European Convention of Human Rights* (Manchester University Press Manchester, 1988) 112–35.

knowledge is necessary to substantiate the present study's contention that democracy, as a fundamental treaty value, does provide an opening for the inclusion of companies in the Convention.

(a) Democracy's Importance

The Convention does not as such guarantee democracy as a 'human right',[70] but the whole treaty is immersed in the value of democratic governance. The Court has held, perhaps most eloquently in the case of *United Communist Party of Turkey and Others v Turkey* in 1998, that democracy is 'the only political model contemplated by the Convention, and, accordingly, the only one compatible with it'; it is one of its 'underlying values' and a very influential one at that since it constitutes 'without doubt a fundamental feature of the European public order'.[71]

The role of democracy as a spiritual bedrock of the Convention is intimated in several ways. The Preamble refers to it as a precondition for the enjoyment of Convention rights and freedoms.[72] Democracy is also a condition for legitimate governmental interference with several Convention rights, including those spelled out in Arts 8 to 11, in the sense that interferences must be assessed by the yardstick of what is 'necessary in a democratic society'.[73] Specific rights, most notably Art 10, Art 6(1) (procedural guarantees) and Protocol 1 Art 3 (free elections), are besides 'characteristic of democratic society',[74] but, as will soon be explained, the list of rights and freedoms that articulate aspects of democracy can be expanded.

By virtue of its importance, democracy constitutes—importantly for the present study—a general principle for Convention interpretation.[75] It may therefore be taken into account for the purpose of determining the place of companies within the Convention system.

[70] T Franck 'The Emerging Right to Democratic Governance' (1992) 86 AJIL 46 is a notable protagonist of democracy as a human right under international law.

[71] *United Communist Party of Turkey and Others v Turkey* Reports 1998-I (1998) 26 EHRR 121 § 45. The case is a landmark in the Court's articulation of democracy, as observed, eg, by L-A Sicilianos *L'ONU et la démocratisation de l'état. Systèmes régionaux et ordre juridique universel* (Pedone Paris, 2000) 61.

[72] *United Communist Party of Turkey and Others* (n 71) § 45(2); see Preamble 4th recital. The 3rd recital of the Preamble of the Statute of the Council of Europe (adopted 5 May 1949, entered into force 3 August 1949) ETS 1 states that 'genuine democracy' is fundamental for the organization.

[73] *United Communist Party of Turkey and Others* (n 71) § 45(3).

[74] ibid § 45(4). The Court also considers freedom of religion one of the foundations of a democratic society, see *Kokkinakis v Greece* Series A No 260, (1994) 17 EHRR 397 § 31.

[75] O Jacot-Guillarmod 'The Relationship Between Democracy and Human Rights' in Council of Europe (ed) *Democracy and Human Rights, Proceedings of a Colloquy organized by the Government of Greece and the Council of Europe, Thessaloniki, 24–26 September 1987* (Engel Kehl am Rhein, 1990) 43, 57.

(b) The Pre-eminence of Political Discourse

Susan Marks observed in 1995 that the Convention builds on 'a relatively thin conception' of democracy.[76] It rests on a liberal democratic model in which the formal guarantees of the traditional liberal state, where '[d]emocracy is taken to be about institutions and procedures of public decision-making',[77] overshadow communitarian perceptions that tend to emphasise substantive values such as redistribution and democratisation of the private sphere. There is little in Strasbourg case law developments over the last ten years to incite a reconsideration of her observation.

This means, typically, that the people's entitlement to choose a representative government through the political procedure of free elections figures prominently in the ECHR's perception of democracy. As the Parliamentary Assembly of the Council of Europe has affirmed, Protocol 1 Art 3 (the right to vote and stand for election) enshrines a fundamentally 'political' conception of democracy in which the focal point is institutional facilitation of free elections in order to secure a government 'of the people by the people'.[78]

More importantly for our purpose, free elections require uninhibited political discourse. Freedom of political debate is 'at the very core' of the Convention's democracy,[79] so freedom of expression, and particularly the freedom to hold political opinions, has a prominent place in the Convention's democracy model. The right to form political parties and to assemble for political purposes pursuant to Art 11 is likewise important.[80]

In the ECHR, '[t]he proper scope of democracy is taken to be the "public" realm'.[81] The company and its interests, however, involve economic activity undertaken primarily in the private sphere. Such persons are normally and nominally connected to activities far from party politics, franchise, political opposition, and heated political debate. In this sense, democracy does not immediately support protection of companies in the Convention. The importance attached to political discourse in the ECHR's democracy model may in fact mean that companies, to the extent they are protected, are of little interest for the Court since their activities are removed from the Convention's inner core. This is an issue to which this study will return in chapter 5.

[76] Marks (n 69) 237. [77] ibid 232.

[78] Resolution 800(1983) adopted by the Parliamentary Assembly of the Council of Europe 1 July 1983 defines democracy as 'the government of people by the people'. For details on Protocol 1 art 3, see, eg, J de Meyer 'Electoral Rights' in R St John Macdonald F Matscher and H Petzold (eds) *The European System for the Protection of Human Rights* (Martinus Nijhoff Dordrecht, 1993) 553.

[79] *Lingens v Austria* Series A No 103, (1986) 8 EHRR 329 § 42.

[80] *Refah Partisi and Others v Turkey (No 2)* (2003) 37 EHRR 1 §§ 87–88; and *Plattform 'Ärtze für das Leben' v Austria* Series A No 139, (1991) 13 EHRR 204 § 32(1) last sentence.

[81] Marks (n 69) 234.

The Convention's democracy concept has, however, other elements than those related to political debate in a narrow sense. The value of democracy supports a place for companies in the Convention on several grounds. They will now be considered.

(c) Private Enterprise and Liberal Democracy

It would be meaningless to disconnect the Convention's democratic model from core values of a capitalist system since it embraces the value system of the liberal state,[82] in which the company as protagonist of private enterprise has a natural place.

The interconnection between democracy and capitalism is evident in several ways in the Convention.

For one, essential components of democracy are simultaneously foundational for free enterprise and, consequently, for companies' activities. The right to freedom of association, for instance, plays a vital role in securing democracy,[83] since it '[permits] people to articulate their concerns by demonstrating or forming interest groups' to pursue democratic ends.[84] The Court has conceded that freedom of association, as guaranteed by Art 11,[85] includes the possibility of establishing 'a legal entity in order to act collectively in a field of mutual interest', and that the 'practical application of [this right] by the authorities reveal the state of democracy in the country concerned'.[86] Restrictions on the freedom of association potentially endanger the effectiveness of political democracy under the Convention.[87] It is also necessary for a capitalist system. The right therefore applies to 'all kinds of legal persons'.[88]

82 L Henkin 'Constitutionalism and Human Rights' in L Henkin and AJ Rosenthal (eds) *Constitutionalism and Rights. The Influence of the United States Constitution Abroad* (Columbia University Press New York, 1990) 383, 388: 'Repeated references . . . to "a democratic society" imply a particular Western conception of such a society'. More generally on the interconnection between democracy and capitalism, CB Macpherson *The Life and Times of Liberal Democracy* (Oxford University Press Oxford, 1977) 42–43; and D Held *Models of Democracy* (3rd edn Stanford University Press Stanford Ca 2004) 70 and 168–201.

83 *Le Compte, Van Leuven and De Meyere v Belgium* Series A No 43, (1982) 1 EHRR 1 § 65.

84 Merrills (n 69) 125.

85 The literature on this provision is sparse, see, however, G Jörundsson 'The Case-Law of the Commission as Regards the Freedom of Assembly and Association' in M de Salvia and Villiger (eds) *The Birth of European Human Rights Law. Liber Amicorum Carl Aage Nørgaard* (Nomos Baden-Baden, 1998) 101; and C Tomuschat 'Freedom of association' in R St John Macdonald F Matscher and H Petzold (eds) *The European System for the Protection of Human Rights* (Martinus Nijhoff Dordrecht, 1993) 493.

86 *Sidiropoulos and Others v Greece* Reports 1998-IV (1999) 27 EHRR 633 § 40.

87 R Bernhardt 'Einwirkungen der Europäischen Menschenrechts-Konvention auf das Staatliche Wirtschaftsrecht' in R Briner and others (eds) *Law of International Business and Dispute Settlement. Liber Amicorum Karl-Heinz Böckstiegel* (Heymann Cologne, 2001) 67, 72 states that Art 11 must include the freedom to establish business enterprises.

88 EA Alkema 'Freedom of Association and Civil Society' in Council of Europe (ed) *Freedom of Association. Proceedings. Seminar organised by the Secretariat-General of the Council of Europe in*

Likewise, private ownership is indispensable for democracy because it provides an essential basis for any opposition to form a political platform against those in position.[89] The Court has held that the protection of private property, in terms of guaranteeing privately owned media, is instrumental to secure pluralism in political discourse.[90] The protection of private property is obviously also crucial for private business enterprise.

Another important component of the Convention's democracy model is transparency, be it in the form of freedom of expression, the right of access to publicly held information, accessible and foreseeable laws, or fair and transparent judicial proceedings.[91] The Court has said that '[t]he right to a fair administration of justice holds so prominent a place in a democratic society that a restrictive interpretation' of Art 6(1) would not correspond to the provision's democratic purpose.[92] Experience shows that the right to settle disputes in independent courts is also essential for a capitalist society.

'Political democracy' is, according to the Preamble, an invaluable tool for the preservation of 'freedom'. Freedom, in the sense of absence of (arbitrary) public encroachment of the private sphere, and in fact the very public/private divide, is without a question a requisite for the Convention's conception of democracy.[93] The drafters saw democracy primarily as the corollary of totalitarian public authority.[94] As a result, the Convention's democracy concept places considerable emphasis on the ability of the private sphere to keep 'critical control of the exercise of public power'.[95] Free elections, in Protocol 1 Art 3, are one means of securing this control,[96] but transparency and accountability also serve important functions in this regard, and the latter two are also requisites for a thriving private enterprise.

The fact that democracy and the capitalist model are entwined suggests that it would be unlikely that an interpretation of the Convention inspired by the

collaboration with the Ministry of Justice of Iceland (Reykjavik, 26–28 August 1998) (Council of Europe Press Strasbourg, 1994) 55, 74; and J Velu and R Ergec *La Convention européenne des Droits de l'homme* (Bruylant Bruxelles, 1990) 650.

89 J Waldron *The Right to Private Property* (Clarendon Press Oxford, 1988) 230–317 with references.

90 *Informationsverein Lentia and Others v Austria* Series A No 276, (1994) 17 EHRR 93 § 33.

91 G Cohen-Jonathan 'Transparence, démocratie et effectivité des droits fondamenteaux dans la Convention européenne des droits de l'homme' in P Mahoney and others (eds) *Protecting Human Rights: The European Perspective:Studies in Memory of Rolv Ryssdal* (Heymann Cologne, 2000) 245, 245.

92 *Delcourt v Belgium* Series A No 11, (1979) 1 EHRR 355 § 25. See further, Jacot-Guillarmod (n 75) 62–63; *United Communist Party of Turkey and Others* (n 71) § 45(4); and *Lawless* (n 60).

93 Jacot-Guillarmod (n 75) 61; and Marks (n 69) 212 and 228.

94 Marks (n 69) 210; see, eg, Robertson *Travaux Préparatoires* vol 2 (n 8) 90 (Mr Sweetman); Robertson *Travaux Préparatoires* vol 5 (n 44) 294 (M Teitgen).

95 App 11508/85 *Barfod v Denmark* (report) (1987) § 64; and Marks (n 69) 212.

96 *Mathieu-Mohin and Clerfayt v Belgium* Series A No 113, (1988) 10 EHRR 1 § 47; see further Merrills (n 69) 113–14.

value of democracy would lead to the exclusion of companies from treaty protection if the source material in other respects was sufficiently open-ended. Democracy can, however, also support the inclusion of companies in the Convention in an instrumental sense. This is considered separately in section D below.

4 The Rule of Law

The rule of law is another underlying value of the Convention, to which the Preamble makes explicit reference (in the 5th recital).[97] Observance of the principle is integral to the treaty's object and purpose.[98] The entire Convention is inspired by it.[99] It is therefore a generally relevant source for its interpretation.[100] The rule of law also helps explain why corporate persons enjoy ECHR protection.

(a) The Convention's Rule of Law Principle

As with the Convention's concept of democracy, it is necessary to introduce the principle of the rule of law before its significance for the present study is considered.

Unlike democracy, however, little work has been done to extrapolate ECHR rule of law perceptions.[101] It is a widely contested concept also outside the Convention realm. A construction of the Convention's meaning of it must relate to the fact that the principle traditionally is understood differently in various corners of Europe, while at the same time, its incorporation in the Convention must mean that it has some form of autonomous meaning which reflects the commonalities of the basic values represented by the rule of law in various European jurisdictions and legal traditions.

The treaty text itself refers to two different traditions: the 'rule of law' of the English authentic text connotes the perception of the principle in the tradition of the common law; the French authentic text gives its equivalent, the principle of '*préeminence du droit*'. A third tradition, not authentically mentioned in the treaty text, is the German variant of the rule of law, notably the '*Rechtsstaat*'

[97] Art 3 of Statute of the Council of Europe (n 72) requires adherence to the rule of law for membership in the organization (see also the 3rd recital of the Statute's Preamble).

[98] *Golder* (n 50) § 34; and *Silver and Others v UK* Series A No 61, (1983) 5 EHRR 347 § 90 (the effectiveness principle has a central function in securing the rule of law).

[99] *Engel and Others v Netherlands* Series A No 22, (1979) 1 EHRR 647 § 69.

[100] *Golder* (n 50) § 34.

[101] See, however, O Jacot-Guillarmod 'Règles, méthods et principes d'interprétation dans la jurisprudence de la Cour européenne des droits de l'homme' in L-E Pettiti E Decauz and P-H Imbert (eds) *La Convention européenne des droits de l'homme. Commentaire article par article* (Economica Paris, 1995) 41, 56–57; and Merrills (n 69) 116–22.

tradition,[102] which has exerted considerable influence in Europe. These three concepts rest on different traditions and they are far from identical. But they capture many of the same essential characteristics of a liberal constitutional state.[103] That they are different does not mean that there is no agreement on the basic values they represent.[104]

The Court has sporadically conceptualized the principle. Based on its case law it can be inferred that the Convention's notion of the rule of law equals a 'formal' rather than a 'substantial' conception of the principle.[105] The formal conception is occupied with providing a system in which governmental action is subjected to law in order to prevent arbitrary exercise of power and to secure equality and foreseeability in law.[106] It thus focuses on legal procedures and institutions, and does not comprise a substantial approach whereby distribution of resources and opportunities, and the protection of individual human rights, are also central elements.[107]

The right for private persons to have access to an independent judiciary for the settlement of disputes on legal matters, provided for in Art 6(1), is one important aspect of the rule of law.[108] The Court says that the rule of law generally consecrates the principle of due process as found in Art 6.[109] Freedom from arbitrary detention, in Art 5, is another important aspect of the rule of law.[110] The safeguards against arbitrary interference with certain Convention rights as spelled out in Arts 8(2) through 11(2), that is, the requirements of legality, purposefulness and proportionality, are likewise part and parcel of the rule of law principle.[111] The requirement that governmental interference with the private sphere needs a basis in law, expressed in Art 7(1) as well as in many other provisions, is generally a natural expression of the rule of law.[112]

102 JA Frowein 'Präambel' in JA Frowein and W Peukert *Europäische Menschenrechtskonvention. EMRK-Kommentar* (2nd edn Engel Kehl am Rhein, 1996) 13, 15.

103 Fernández Esteban (n 49) 65–101 succinctly present the three traditions for the purpose of establishing a supranational rule of law concept in the framework of the EU.

104 NS Marsh 'The Rule of Law as a Supra-National Concept' in A Guest (ed) *Oxford Essays on Jurisprudence. First Series* (Clarendon Press Oxford, 1961) 223, 260.

105 PP Craig 'Formal and Substantive Conceptions of the Rule of Law' (1995) 1 Diritto Pubblico 35 on this distinction.

106 Fernández Esteban (n 49) 93. See, eg, *Malone v UK* judgment 2 August 1984 [PC] Series A 82 (1985) 7 EHRR 14 § 68; and *Huvig v France* judgment 24 April 1990 Series A 176-B (1990) 12 EHRR 528 § 29. *Brumarescu v Romania* Reports 1999-VII (2001) 33 EHRR 35 § 61 emphasizes foreseeability and legal certainty.

107 International Commission of Jurists (ed) *The Rule of Law and Human Rights. Principles and Definitions as Elaborated at the Congresses and Conferences held under the auspices of the International Commission of Jurists, 1955–1966* (International Commission of Jurists Geneva 1966) details a wide conception of the rule of law in which such substantial issues are included alongside the formal components. See also Fernández Esteban (n 49) 94–97.

108 *Klass and Others v Germany* Series A No 28, (1980) 2 EHRR 214 § 55; and Merrills (n 69) 116–17.

109 *Salabiaku v Austria* Series A No 141, (1991) 13 EHRR 379 § 28; and *Sunday Times* (n 21) § 55.

110 Merrills (n 69) 116. 111 *Malone* (n 106) § 67. 112 Merrills (n 69) 117–20.

(b) *The Rule of Law and Companies*

How can the rule of law, as a Convention value, tell us how the Court might respond to corporate claims? As is the case with democracy, the rule of law as an underlying Convention value is intimately linked to the liberal state, and in the liberal state it is essential to provide fertile ground for private business enterprise. An interpretation of the Convention heeding the principle of the rule of law would therefore, again as was the case with democracy, be unlikely to lead to an exclusion of companies from the Convention's protective scope.

John Merrills has defined the rule of law in the Convention context as:

> the principle that the *individual's* dealings with the State and his fellow citizens should be regulated by a framework of legal rules, whose interpretation and application are in the hands of independent courts'.[113]

If we grant his rendition cogency, it appears that the rule of law as a value pertains solely to the individual human being and, as such, could work to exclude companies from the Convention rather than serve as an argument for inclusion.

There is, however, reason to question the precision of this definition since it does not appreciate the 'objective' character of the formal rule of law principle.[114] Unlike the substantive conception of the rule of law, which observes the needs of the individual human being,[115] and is sometimes said to derive from the inherent dignity of the natural person,[116] the formal version is not dependent on the nature of the person who should benefit from the principle. As put by María Fernández Esteban in a related context, '[u]niversality and predictability are the two basic elements in the formal conception of the Rule of Law'.[117] When the Court invokes the rule of law as an interpretive argument, it emphasises its capacity to prevent governmental arbitrariness and the excessive wielding of public power and pays scant, if any, attention to what form of person or what kinds of interests that would benefit from its application.[118] Thus, Joseph Raz's view of the rule of law principle could just as well have been a description of its Convention variant:

> The Rule of Law is just one of the virtues which a legal system may possess and by which it is to be judged. *It is not to be confused with* democracy, justice, equality (before

[113] Merrills (n 69) 116 (emphasis added).

[114] The mention of 'fellow citizens' is confusing in a Convention context, as the Convention does not apply merely to citizens but to 'everyone' within the member States' jurisdiction, art 1.

[115] Marsh (n 104) 232–34. [116] Fernández Esteban (n 49) 94. [117] ibid 93.

[118] This was essential in the path-breaking judgments in *Niemietz v Germany* Series A No 251-B, (1993) 16 EHRR 97; and *Colas Est SA and Others v France* Reports 2002-III (with regard to Art 8); and in *Comingersoll SA v Portugal* Reports 2000-IV (2001) 31 EHRR 772 (with regard to Art 41), which expanded the scope of rights or entitlements that were previously thought to be aimed at the protection to human beings only. This is considered further in chapter 4.

the law or otherwise), *human rights of any kind or respect for persons or for the dignity of man.*[119]

As a matter of illustration, it might be added that under the German federal constitution companies and other juristic persons are entitled to enjoy protection under the fundamental rights catalogue spelled out in its part 1 only by virtue of the special procedure provided for in Art 19(3) of the *Grundgesetz*. This provision makes it possible to apply fundamental rights, otherwise deemed to derive normatively from the inherent dignity of the individual human being, to non-human persons to the extent that is compatible with the nature of the right in question.[120] Prominent procedural rights, however, set out in part 4 of the *Grundgesetz*,[121] are believed to derive normatively from the *Rechtstaat* principle,[122] and apply thus by default to any person.

The rule of law as a supporting argument for corporate ECHR protection is justified because the principle has an 'objectiveness' to it that makes it pertain to society as a whole.[123] It is not merely a quality of society that pertains to the individual human being. The 'objectiveness' of Convention protection is further examined in section D below.

5 European Liberalism

(a) European Liberalism as Convention Value

It has been maintained above that human dignity, democracy, and the rule of law are values that inform the Convention. They are essential aspects of the European liberal order. In the same vein it may be argued that the European liberal model, which lacks correspondence with the value order expressed in the universal instruments for human rights protection,[124] can be understood as an underlying Convention value in its own right. For the purpose of the present study, 'European liberalism' broadly connotes the constitutional values

[119] J Raz 'The Rule of Law and Its Virtue' (1977) 93 LQR 196, 198 (emphasis added).

[120] The debate over juristic persons' protection by the *Grundrechte* is too complex to be restated here. Two ideologically distant but comprehensive introductions are the collectivist view of A von Mutius 'Artikel 19 Abs. 3' in R Dolzer and others (eds) *Kommentar zum Bonner Grundgesetz* (2nd edn Müller Heidelberg 1975) vol 2 [26 ff].

[121] Arts 101 (access to court), 103(1) (due process), 103(2) (*nulla poena sine lege*) and 103(3) (*ne bis in idem*). A Tschentscher *The Basic Law (Grundgesetz). The Constitution of the Federal Republic of Germany (May 23, 1949)* (Jurisprudentia Würzburg, 2002) gives an English translation of the *Grundgesetz*.

[122] A Bleckmann *Staatsrecht. Die Grundrechte* (4th edn Heymann Cologne, 1997) 1172 with references to judgments of the *Bundesverfassungsgericht*.

[123] The German equivalent of 'objectiveness' is the term used by the *Bundesverfassungsrecht*, eg, BVerfGE 21, 362 (373).

[124] C Leben 'Is there a European Approach to Human Rights?' in P Alston (ed) *The EU and Human Rights* (Oxford University Press Oxford, 1999) 69, 93.

of the Council of Europe member States, which include democracy, protection of human rights, rule of law, social justice, and a regulated market economy.[125] This value suggests that companies, and the whole business sector, are naturally situated in the Convention landscape.

The Convention's character as a liberal document is an observation so obvious that its relevance is often overlooked. Yet, the Convention without question represents a project of pan-European liberalism. Its inception was—as observed earlier—motivated by threats to the existence of this model of governance.[126] Its entire rights-catalogue is made up of rights and freedoms that reek of liberal ideals. The Court's jurisprudence bears evidence of it down to the last detail. The nature of the treaty suggests the same: being a law-making treaty meant for domestic implementation in Europe, the Convention naturally draws on a common European heritage of constitutional issues.[127] The Preamble's 5th recital says that 'European countries . . . are like-minded and have a common heritage of political traditions, ideals, freedom and the rule of law'. As an underlying value, this European constitutional consensus—which must coincide with the central tenets of European liberalism—informs the treaty's interpretation.[128]

(b) Liberalism and Companies' Rights

To establish that European liberalism represents a Convention value is one thing. To say that it supports the inclusion of companies is another. This is an assertion which requires additional evidence as the ECHR, unlike, for instance, the EU system for fundamental rights protection, contains no open acknowledgement of the economic aspects of liberalism,[129] even if the protection of

[125] *The EU and Human Rights* provides an informative background to this topic from an EU as well as an ECHR perspective.

[126] Ovey and White (n 47) 1–4. European liberalism naturally predates the Convention, eg, H Laski *The Rise of European Liberalism* (Allen & Unwin London, 1936).

[127] *Sunday Times* (n 21) § 61: the main purpose of the Convention is 'to lay down certain international standards to be observed by the Contracting States in their relations with persons under their jurisdiction.' See further, eg, M de Salvia 'L'élaboration d'un "ius commune" des droits de l'homme et des libertés fondamentales dans la perspective de l'unité européenne: l'oeuvre accomplie par la Commission et la Cour européenne des droits de l'homme' in F Matshcer and H Petzold (eds) *Protecting Human Rights: The European Dimension. Studies in Honour of Gérard J Wiarda* (Heymann Cologne, 1988) 555.

[128] *Marckx v Belgium* Series A No 31, (1980) 2 EHRR 330 § 41. Further, eg, WJ Ganshof van der Meersch 'Reliance, in the Case-Law of the European Court of Human Rights, on the Domestic Law of the States' (1980) 1 HRLJ 13, 15–16.

[129] The normative bases of the EU fundamental rights system are documented, eg, in the Preamble of the Charter of Fundamental Rights of the European Union (adopted 18 December 2000) [2000] OJ C364/1 (EU Charter of Fundamental Rights). Its second recital refers to concepts such as 'human dignity, freedom, equality and solidarity' and 'democracy and the rule of law', whereas its third recital makes clear that the rights are cherished since they seek to 'promote balanced and sustainable development' and ensure 'free movement of goods, persons, services and capital, and the freedom of establishment'. Although not a legally binding catalogue, the CFR implicitly carries doctrinal weight, see S Alber and U Widmaier 'Die EU-Charta der Grundrechte und ihre Auswirkungen auf die Rechtsprechung' (2000) 27 EuGRZ 497.

property in Protocol 1 Art 1 surely suggests that it finds some degree of protection under the Convention.[130]

From an extra-doctrinal viewpoint, it cannot be doubted that the 'like-mindedness' and 'common heritage' to which the Preamble refers include a social and legal order of which free enterprise, and its very useful vehicle the limited liability company, is an integral component. All Council of Europe member States adhere in principle to a liberal state in which private enterprise is a central characteristic. The significance of this element re-emerged in the Council of Europe setting when Central and East European countries joined the Convention in the early 1990s.[131]

The Court, however, has never had or grasped an opportunity to say clearly that the Convention builds on a structure that includes private business enterprise. It has in fact only rarely elaborated on the substance of European constitutional commonality, although it has held that the 'common heritage [is] to be found [in] the underlying values of the Convention',[132] and they include at least (and this we already know) democratic governance,[133] and various aspects of the rule of law,[134] in addition to certain other aspects that are less important for our purpose.[135]

A direct link to free enterprise is thus absent in the Convention. The Convention's rights and freedoms, as interpreted by the Court, nonetheless intimate a system based on free enterprise.[136] As this study unfolds several instances confirming this assumption will come to light. As was mentioned above, the right to freedom of association is said to include the right to establish juristic persons, and, as will be explained in the next chapter, the Court accepts the concept of juristic personhood, genuinely important for private enterprise, in its interpretation of Art 34. Freedom of contract, another basis for economic liberalism, is not recognized as a human right as such in the treaty, but it is indirectly guaranteed, also in the business context, by Art 6(1) and its concept of 'civil rights',[137] as well as by the concept of 'possessions' in Protocol 1

[130] D Gomien DJ Harris and L Zwaak *Law and Practice of the European Convention on Human Rights and the European Social Charter* (Council of Europe Publishing Strasbourg, 1996) 311.

[131] R Dworkin and S Lukes 'The Political Culture of Liberalism and the Prospects for Eastern and Central Europe. Panel Discussion' (1993-II) 2 AEL 273.

[132] *United Communist Party of Turkey and Others* (n 71) § 45(1).

[133] *Refah Partisi and Others v Turkey (No 1)* (2001) 35 EHRR 3 § 45; *United Communist Party of Turkey and Others* (n 71) § 45(1).

[134] *Brumarescu* (n 106) § 61; *Sovtransavto Holding v Ukraine* Reports 2002-VII § 72.

[135] *Soering v UK* Series A No 161, (1989) 11 EHRR 439 § 89 (prohibition of extradition when facing death-row in receiving state); and *Wemhoff v Germany* Series A No 7, (1979) 1 EHRR 55 Dissenting Opinion of Judge Zekia (prohibition of arbitrary detention).

[136] eg, A Ogus 'Property Rights and Freedom of Economic Activity' in L Henkin and AJ Rosenthal (eds) *Constitutionalism and Rights. The Influence of the United States Constitution Abroad* (Columbia University Press New York, 1990) 125, 134–45 (which also includes the ECHR).

[137] Harris O'Boyle and Warbrick (n 48) 177. *Ringeisen v Austria* Series A No 13, (1979) 1 EHRR 455 § 94 is an early example.

Art 1.[138] The latter provision, which guarantees private property, provides a crucial platform not only for business enterprise but also for the enjoyment of the other Convention rights.[139]

(c) *Free Enterprise and European Integration*

The Preamble of the Statute of the Council of Europe states that the organization's aim is, inter alia, 'to achieve a greater unity between its Members for the purpose of . . . facilitating their economic . . . progress'.[140] It cannot be doubted that the protection of the rights and freedoms spelled out in the Convention represent powerful incentives for private business.[141] It should be added here that the Convention has an integrationist purpose; its Preamble's 3rd recital recalls that the Council of Europe's aim is:

> the achievement of greater unity between its members and that one of the methods by which that aim is to be pursued is the maintenance and further realisation of human rights and fundamental freedoms.

The Council of Europe's precursor, the European Movement, was also a forerunner to the European Economic Community,[142] whose founders clearly saw business as a method of building links between countries to bring about a closer union and to prevent new wars between European powers.[143] 'Peace' was, incidentally, also a goal for the Convention fathers, as the Preamble's 4th recital confirms. There is perhaps no direct evidence in the written material available

[138] Harris O'Boyle and Warbrick (n 48) 517; and *Mellacher and Others v Austria* Series A No 169, (1990) 12 EHRR 391 § 43.

[139] JA Frowein 'The Protection of Property' in R St John Macdonald F Matscher and H Petzold (eds) *The European System for the Protection of Human Rights* (Martinus Nijhoff Dordrecht 1993) 515, 515: 'It is certainly correct to say that freedom as enshrined in the Convention cannot subsist without a meaningful protection of private property'.

[140] Statute of the Council of Europe (n 72) art 1(1). See also 1st recital of the Preamble of European Social Charter (revised) (adopted 3 May 1996, entered into force 1 July 1999) ETS 163: 'Considering that the aim of the Council of Europe is the achievement of greater unity between its members for the purpose of safeguarding and realising the ideals and principles which are their common heritage and of facilitating their economic and social progress, in particular by the maintenance and further realisation of human rights and fundamental freedoms . . .'.

[141] G Bannock (ed) *The Promotion of Small and Medium-Sized Enterprises in Europe* (Council of Europe Press Strasbourg, 1994) 22–23.

[142] Literature on the origins of the European Union project abounds. One comprehensive study is AJ Zurcher *The Struggle to Unite Europe, 1940–1958: An Historical Account of the Development of the Contemporary European Movement from its Origin in the Pan-European Union to the Drafting of the Treaties for Euratom and the European Common Market* (New York University Press New York, 1958).

Simpson (n 1110) 596–648 is a detailed study, from the viewpoint of Britain, of the inception of the European movement and the establishment of the Council of Europe

[143] On the common origin of the Convention and the European Economic Community, see, eg, JA Frowein 'Fundamental Human Rights as a Vehicle of Legal Integration in Europe' in M Cappelletti M Seccombe and J Weiler (eds) *Integration Through Law. Vol 1 Methods, Tools and Institutions* (de Gruyter Berlin, 1986) 300, 329.

to us that economic integration and the role of private enterprise in building bridges across borders were the most important motivating factors for the adoption of the Convention. Yet, given the common heritage shared by the Convention and the treaties establishing the European Economic Community and its successors, it is unlikely that the ECHR is wholly unfamiliar with this objective.

Given these arguments relating to the European liberal project, company claims should theoretically expect a favourable response from the Court since such claims are part and parcel of the order sought realised by the Convention. Yet, European liberalism is no neo-liberal order. It fundamentally includes a social dimension and takes account of the needs of the regulatory state. This leads us naturally to the next topic.

D. Consideration of Whose Interests?

Commitment to the protection of human rights and fundamental freedoms has a central place in European liberalism,[144] and the fundamental values of European liberalism are a robust platform from which to argue the inclusion of companies under Convention protection. But the status of companies in the Convention structure can also be explained on other grounds than those described above. The Convention title articulates its concern as the 'protection of human rights and fundamental freedoms'. Two implications spring from the wording of this title. The first relates to the nature of the 'human rights and fundamental freedoms' of the Convention (section 1), and the second to the interpretation of the 'protection' of such rights and freedoms (section 2). There are, additionally, public interests to be considered by the Court, and they are fleshed out in section 3.

1 What Kinds of Rights and Freedoms?

What is meant by 'human rights and fundamental freedoms' in the ECHR context? The easy answer is that the terms comprise those substantive norms that are contained in the treaty, typically those found in the Convention's section I. But we find little help in such an answer when we seek to identify the fundamental nature of the Convention's substantive provisions and their

144 JHH Weiler 'Fundamental Rights and Fundamental Boundaries: On the Conflict of Standards and Values in the Protection of Human Rights in the European Legal Space' in JHH Weiler *The Constitution of Europe. 'Do the New Clothes Have an Emperor?' and Other Essays on European Integration* (Cambridge University Press Cambridge, 2000) 102, 103: 'Within this constitutional ethos the judicial protection of fundamental human rights has a central place.'

implications for corporate actors. If we compare ECHR rights and freedoms with those enumerated in other treaty regimes within the international human rights law tradition that seek to protect civil and political rights, we may be able shed a brighter defining light on features particular to ECHR rights and freedoms. The ECHR catalogue differs, or appears to differ, from the construction of civil and political rights in related treaty regimes in at least two ways. They are considered separately.

(a) *Collective and Individual Aspects of Convention Rights*

A striking feature of the construction of civil and political rights in the tradition derived from the Universal Declaration of Human Rights is the emphasis often placed on an individualized conception of human rights—the interests of the individual are uppermost. Not untypically, Louis Henkin describes human rights in the tradition of the UDHR as 'rights of individuals in society',[145] and he observes that, with the exception of the right for 'peoples' to self-determination, which is guaranteed in ICCPR Article 27, the interests of collective entities and groups have not been addressed by the international human rights law of civil and political rights.[146] The UDHR confines itself to rights for the individual.[147] The ICCPR and the ACHR are but with a very few exceptions structurally limited to the protection of the rights of the individual human person.[148]

Historically, civil and political rights have not contemplated collectiveness to the same extent as they have worked to ensure the interests of the individual person. Classical liberalism, it has been said, had a '*phobie des groupements*': the French Declaration of the Rights of Man contained, for instance, no affirmation of freedom of association.[149] Structurally, it seems fair to say, the civil and political rights regimes of international law embrace a type of individualism reminiscent of classical liberalism. Contemporary society, however, is massively corporatist by any measure.[150]

Economic and social rights, for their part, while often applicable to individuals, do possess collective features and often provide protection for individuals in

[145] L Henkin *The Age of Rights* (Columbia University Press New York, 1990). J Donnelly *Universal Human Rights in Theory and Practice* (2nd edn Cornell University Press Ithaca NY, 2003) 7 says that human rights are simply 'the rights that one has because one is human'.

[146] Henkin (n 145) 5. On group rights in the ICCPR, see, eg, B Kingsbury 'Claims by Non-State Groups in International Law' (1992) 25 Cornell Intl L J 481, 494–95.

[147] Donnelly (n 145) 23–27 and 204–24.

[148] See, for details, Emberland (n 27) 259–262; and (as far as the ICCPR goes) M Nowak *UN Covenant on Civil and Political Rights. CCPR Commentary* (2nd edn Engel Kehl am Rhein, 2005) 825 and 829–37.

[149] W Kaegi *Die Verfassung als rechtliche Grundordnung des Staates. Untersuchungen über die Entwicklungen im modernen Verfassungsrecht* (Polygraphischer Verlag Zürich, 1945) 47.

[150] R Cotterrell *The Sociology of Law. An Introduction* (2nd edn Butterworths London, 1992) 123–30 for a socio-legal introduction to corporatism in contemporary society.

community with others.[151] The European Social Charter, the Council of Europe variant of some of the economic and social rights that were programmatically established by the UDHR, gives expression to an underlying sense of collectivism in many ways, including the establishment of a right of application not for individual persons or entities but for organizations of such persons only.[152]

As its global and regional counterparts, the Convention is an instrument for the protection of individuals' rights. But the Convention acknowledges collective aspects of these rights more so than its siblings. Unlike the private petition systems under the ICCPR and ACHR, the ECHR variant accepts that collective entities have rights on their own.[153] Article 34, which bestows on 'non-governmental organisations [and] groups of individuals' a right to petition the Court for alleged violations of their own affairs as protected by the treaty, is an obvious example of the collectivism of the Convention. Aspects of collectivism are, however, also contained in various substantive provisions (such as Art 10(1) third sentence's reference to 'enterprises'; and Protocol 1 Art 1 first sentence's reference to 'legal person'). An element of collectivism is naturally found also in the rights to freedom of association and assembly (Art 11).[154]

The Strasbourg organs have confirmed that the Convention addresses collective and individual interests even though it concedes that it depends on the specific right or freedom in question whether collective or individual aspects are dominant. The whole of Art 3 (prohibition against torture or inhuman or degrading treatment or punishment) and the part of Art 9 that protects

[151] R Stavenhagen 'Cultural Rights: A Social Science Perspective' in A Eide C Krause and A Rosas (eds) *Economic, Social and Cultural Rights. A Textbook* (2nd edn Martinus Nijhoff Dordrecht, 2001) 85, 92–93.

[152] ESC Pt IV art D ('Collective complaints') provides for a collective complaints mechanism through which businesses as employers indirectly may be protected, see generally DJ Harris 'The Collective Complaints Procedure' in Council of Europe (ed) *The Social Charter of the 21st Century* (Council of Europe Publishing Strasbourg, 1998) 100; and R Brillat 'A New Protocol to the European Social Charter Providing for Collective Complaints' [1996] EHRLR 52. On the case law, see L Samuel *Fundamental Social Rights: Case Law of the European Social Charter* (Council of Europe Publishing Strasbourg, 2002). The ILO system allow for business enterprises to pursue claims collectively, see, generally, eg, F Maupain 'The Settlement of Disputes within the International Labour Organization' (1999) 2 JIEL 273.

[153] The ICCPR system accepts only individuals' complaints, see, eg, Communication No 360/1989, A *Newspaper Publishing Company v Trinidad and Tobago*, admissibility decision 14 July 1989, UN Doc Supp No 40 (A/44/40) 1989 307; and Communication No 361/1989, *A Publication and a Printing Company v Trinidad and Tobago*, admissibility decision 14 July 1989, UN Doc Supp No 40 (A/44/40) (1989) 309. Under the ACHR, collective entities have a right to petition but only insofar as their application concerns alleged violations of individual human beings; see, eg, *Tabacalera Boquerón SA v Paraguay*, admissibility decision 6 October 1997, Report No 47/97 (1997) Annual Report of the Inter-American Commission of Human Rights 229 (§§ 24–27). The cases, and other in the same vein from the two systems, are considered in Emberland (n 27).

[154] The right to education in Protocol 1 Art 2 has been said to be sufficiently collective to include associations' claims, see App 23419/94 *Verein Gemeinsam Lernen v Austria* (1995) §§ 3–4.

freedom of 'conscience' are applicable only to individuals and not to collective entities.[155] Article 5 (freedom from arbitrary detention) is likewise said to be reserved for the protection of natural persons.[156] The right to freedom of 'religion' in Art 9 has, however, collective elements and may therefore protect entities in addition to individual claimants.[157]

In *Church of Scientology of Paris v France*, the European Commission of Human Rights considered that 'unlike Article 9, Article 8 of the Convention has more an individual than a collective character'.[158] But even individualistic provisions such as Art 8 have certain collective aspects, since, for instance and as stated by the Court, the right to protection of one's 'private life must also comprise to a certain degree the right to establish and develop relationships with other human beings'.[159] As chapter 4 will show, the Court has even taken the collectivism of Art 8 one step further, including within it in at least some protection of corporate entities regardless of their individual *substratum*.[160]

The conclusion to be drawn from this discussion is that the Convention's catalogue of rights and freedoms, since it inhibits collective elements, is also an apt instrument for the protection of collective entities such as companies. The special nature of the Convention's civil and political rights can therefore justify corporate ECHR protection in specific circumstances.

(b) Economic Aspects of Civil and Political Rights

The international legal protection of civil and political rights is often seen as an equivalent of the protection of non-economic interests so that an inclusion of the interests of business entities, being predominantly profit-oriented, requires reconsideration of otherwise well-known concepts.[161] The UDHR arguably contains the right to property protection, 'alone' and 'in association with others', and its concept of property protection largely reflects its conception in Western liberalist thought.[162] Yet in the general language of international human rights law, the possibility that human rights could also protect economic activity remains largely unexplored and is generally considered controversial

[155] *Verein 'Kontakt-Information-Therapie' (KIT) and Hagen* (n 34) § 1(4).

[156] *Boucheras and Groupe Information Asiles* (n 39) § 1(1); and *Wouterse Marpa Zeeland BV and Metal Welding Service BV v Netherlands* decision 1 October 2002 § B.2.

[157] *Verein 'Kontakt-Information-Therapie' (KIT) and Hagen* (n 34) § 1(4) draws an explicit distinction in this sense between the right to freedom of conscience and the right to freedom of religion, citing App 7805/77 *X and Church of Scientology v Sweden* (1979) 16 DR 68.

[158] App 19509/92 *Church of Scientology of Paris v France* (1995) § 1(5).

[159] *Niemietz* (n 118) § 29(1).

[160] *Colas Est SA and Others* (n 118).

[161] Bratza (n 5) 2 asks rhetorically: 'Does a Convention which is designed to protect the fundamental rights of individuals to life, liberty, fair trial, privacy, freedom of thought, expression and association have any relevance in what may loosely be described as a commercial context?'

[162] C Krause and G Alfredsson 'Article 17' in G Alfredsson and A Eide (eds) *The Universal Declaration of Human Rights. A Common Standard of Achievement* (Kluwer Hague, 1999) 359, 359.

from a human rights proponent perspective.[163] In the ACHR and ICCPR, claims for the protection of for-profit activity have only recently been brought to the attention of their respective supervisory tribunal. While they do not seem to deny the possibility of certain provisions to cater for for-profit interests, this form of litigation clearly represents a novel type of claim at the tribunals, to which they are still struggling to find a suitable response.[164]

The well-known distinction between civil and political rights on one hand and economic, social, and cultural rights on the other supports the sentiment that economic activities do not entirely belong in the realm of civil and political rights, even if for-profit activity is not the kind of activity with which conventions on economic and social rights are primarily concerned either.[165] Today, it is accepted that the two groups of rights cannot meaningfully be separated in all respects,[166] but in the Council of Europe context the distinction is reflected in that the ECHR is primarily intended for the protection of civil and political rights while economic (and social) rights are mainly protected by the European Social Charter.[167]

Nevertheless, the Convention does stray into the field of economic rights,[168] and civil and political rights by their nature will entail protection of certain aspects of economic life.[169] The Court has therefore predictably held that

> Whilst the Convention sets forth what are essentially civil and political rights, many of them have implications of a social or economic nature. The Court therefore considers... that the mere fact that an interpretation of the Convention may extend into the sphere of social and economic rights should not be a decisive factor against such an interpretation; there is no water-tight division separating that sphere from the field covered by the Convention.[170]

In principle, therefore, various Convention rights have the capacity of protecting economic activity in one way or another.[171] Whether or not a provision can

163 ibid 378. 164 Emberland (n 27).

165 'Economic' human rights may more precisely be referred to as rights of a 'socio-economic' nature, see, eg, C Krause 'The Right to Property' in A Eide C Krause and A Rosas (eds) *Economic, Social and Cultural Rights. A Textbook* (2nd edn Martinus Nijhoff Dordrecht, 2001) 191, 191.

166 GJH van Hoof 'The Legal Nature of Economic, Social and Cultural Rights: A Rebuttal of Some Traditional Views' in P Alston and K Tomasevski (eds) *The Right to Food* (Martinus Nijhoff Hague 1984) 97.

167 Gomien Harris and Zwaak (n 130) 14; and DJ Harris and J Darcy *The European Social Charter* (2nd edn Transnational Ardsley NY, 2001) 2–3. 168 Harris O'Boyle and Warbrick (n 48) 3.

169 C Flinterman 'The Protection of Economic, Social and Cultural Rights and the European Convention on Human Rights' in R Lawson and M de Blois (eds) *The Dynamics of the Protection of Human Rights in Europe. Essays in Honour of Henry G Schermers* (Martinus Nijhoff Dordrecht, 1994) vol 3, 165; and K Vasak 'Analytical Examination of Civil and Political Rights' in K Vasak and P Alston (eds) *The International Dimensions of Human Rights* (UNESCO Paris, 1982) vol 1, 142, 158–59.

170 *Airey v Ireland* Series A No 32, (1980) 2 EHRR 305 § 26; repeated in *Annoni di Gussola Debordes and Omer v France* Reports 2000-XI § 56. 171 Bernhardt (n 87) 67, 67.

protect economic activity depends on an interpretation of it in light of the nature of the claim brought before the Court.

Protocol 1 Art 1 obviously protects economic activity in the sense that the provision affords protection to interests that correspond to a 'sufficiently pecuniary right'.[172] The broad construction of 'possessions' in the provision includes property regardless of origin (labour as well as speculation) or its intended use,[173] so it clearly can cater for the activities of business actors. Strasbourg case law has unearthed economic implications of other rights and freedoms in the sense that they enable the protection of for-profit activity. Significant examples include Art 6(1) (right to a fair trial) (which afford fundamental procedural guarantees to civil disputes over economic matters),[174] Art 7(1) (prohibiting retroactive criminal laws that impinge upon economic activity),[175] and Art 11 (freedom of association also applies to for-profit employees).[176] This list is not exhaustive, as will be demonstrated later.

Other provisions, or aspects of provisions, remain, however, not-for-profit territory. Thus, the Court has suggested that the protection against self-incrimination in Art 6(2) cannot be used as means to refuse to disclose information of a mere financial nature when no criminal liability is involved.[177] Article 9 seems to be confined in scope to not-for-profit activity, but some claimants whose interests are both economic and non-economic may be protected to the extent that the economic aspects are overshadowed by non-economic matters. The Commission has thus held that an applicant that is a 'profit-making corporate body can neither enjoy nor rely on the rights referred to in Article 9', but to the extent a company 'was created principally in order to publish and sell books promoting the aims of the freethinkers and not in order to produce profit', it nonetheless enjoy protection.[178]

To be sure, the Convention does not as such protect a freedom of economic activity, in the sense of offering a guarantee regulating 'the extent to which individuals and firms may engage in enterprise untrammelled by state

[172] *Willis v UK* Reports 2002-IV (2002) 35 EHRR 21 § 36.

[173] HG Schermers 'The International Protection of the Right to Property' in F Matscher and H Petzold (eds) *Protecting Human Rights: The European Dimension. Studies in Honour of Gérard J Wiarda* (Heymann Cologne, 1988) 565, 574–75 (who opposes this from a normative viewpoint).

[174] *Balmer-Schafroth and Others v Switzerland* Reports 1997-IV (1998), 25 EHRR 598 §§ 30–33.

[175] *Cantoni v France* Reports 1996-V; and *Radio France v France* judgment 30 March 2004.

[176] *Gustafsson v Sweden* Reports 1996-II (1996) 22 EHRR 409 § 44.

[177] *Allen v UK* decision 10 September 2002 § 1(3).

[178] *Kustannus Oy Vapaa Ajattelija AB and Others v Finland* Application 20471/92, (1996) 85 DR 29, (1996) 22 EHRR CD 69 § 1(b)(iii)(2) and (3). In *Cha'are Shalom Ve Tsedek v France* Reports 2000-VII § 67, the respondent government had held that Art 9 was inapplicable because the religious association was really seeking protection of commercial activity. The Court saw the issue as raising questions concerning the association's religious activity, see §§ 72–73. The elements of property interests protected by the right to freedom of conscience were left undecided in *Chassagnou and Others v France* Reports 1999-III (2000) 20 EHRR 615 §§ 122–25.

intervention'.[179] But the Convention is largely an instrument for the protection of economic aspects of civil and political rights, and when it does offer this form of protection, the place of companies in the treaty system is justifiable.

2 Objective and Instrumental Functions of Convention Protection

Further support for the protection of corporate interests is found in the Convention's occasional indifference regarding the status of the corporate applicant or the nature of its interests. This particular feature relates, one might say, to the sense in which the Convention is an international legal instrument 'for the protection' of its rights and freedoms. Two functional aspects, which are to some extent interrelated, are important inasmuch as they provide structural support for corporate Convention protection also where the treaty text and the value system do not as such provide clear arguments for inclusion. They are referred to here as objective and instrumental aspects of the system for Convention protection.

(a) The Subjective Approach

First, however, some words on how the Convention primarily has been perceived. It is usual to see the ECHR system in what may be referred to as a 'subjective' mode, that is, as an instrument whose reach is dependent on the legal interests of the individual applicant bringing his or her complaint before the Court and that the Court—following a 'private law' model of dispute resolution[180]—is set up for the settling of the dispute that has arisen between the parties to the Strasbourg application.

There are certain features of the system that suggests a subjective approach like this. The Convention does not accept the institution of *actio popularis* under Art 34,[181] and by requiring that the applicant person personally must be directly affected by the contested measures set our in the complaint, the 'victim' requirement in Art 34 (discussed further in chapter 3) surely supports a commonly held view of Strasbourg litigation as primarily a means for the protection of the rights or freedoms of the particular person who asserts protection before the Court. The Court is certainly an organ authorised to settle concrete disputes between parties; this is for instance intimated in Arts 34 and 32(1),[182] and it also follows from the entitlement

179 Ogus (n 136) 134.

180 M Dan-Cohen *Rights, Persons, and Organizations* (University of California Press Berkeley, Ca 1986) 123–29 on the two main models of dispute settlement; the public law and private law models.

181 *Klass and Others* (n 108) § 33; and *Norris v Ireland* Series A No 142, (1991) 13 EHRR 186 § 30.

182 Article 32(1): 'The jurisdiction of the Court shall extend to all matters concerning the interpretation and application of the Convention and the protocols thereto'.

for a person whose rights have been violated to seek compensation pursuant to Art 41.

In many instances, this subjective understanding of the purpose of Convention protection, where the focus remains on the applicant person's legal interests, will suffice to explain why companies enjoy Convention protection. As was just discussed, corporate enjoyment of rights or freedoms is often intrinsically justified as their economic or collective or other nature also encompasses the activity of corporate applicants.

(b) The Objective Approach

But apart from this subjective approach, there is an additional approach which justifies Convention protection because the protection of one applicant has ramifications for others or for society in general. This approach to understanding the nature and purpose of Convention protection, which has been called 'objective',[183] and will be so here, can augment the rationale for accepting corporate protection where it simultaneously is supported on intrinsic or subjective grounds. But it provides an independent justification for corporate enjoyment of rights in instances in which the rights or freedoms in question cannot readily be said to 'fit' the nature of the applicant person who pursues the claim or the interests pursued by that person.

According to the objective approach, the inclusion of corporate applicants' claims is defensible because protection of such claims can generate a radiance of human rights observance that is beneficial to other private persons or society in general. The actual circumstances of the application brought before the Court are thus less important than what a protection of it may entail in more general terms. This objective approach is a generally accepted purpose of human rights adjudication.[184] It is an acknowledged form of constitutional adjudication in the context of fundamental rights in various legal systems.[185] But its place in the Convention is rarely discussed at length in the literature.

[183] P van Dijk and GJH van Hoof *Theory and Practice of the European Convention on Human Rights* (2nd edn Kluwer Hague, 1998) 40–41. J Miles 'Standing under the Human Rights Act 1998. Theories of Rights Enforcement and the Nature of Public Law Adjudication' (2000) 59 CLJ 133 convincingly argues for a public law litigation model in the ECHR context. See also T Zwart 'Standing to Sue in Human Rights Litigation: Abstract and Hypothetical Cases' in R Lawson and M de Blois (eds) *The Dynamics of the Protection of Human Rights in Europe. Essays in Honour of Henry G Schermers* (Martinus Nijhoff Dordrecht, 1994) vol 3, 361.

[184] A Byrnes 'An Effective Complaints Procedure in the Context of International Human Rights Law' in AF Bayefsky (ed) *The UN Human Rights Treaty System in the 21st Century* (Kluwer Hague, 2000) 139, 142.

[185] Dan-Cohen (n 180) 123–29. On the US constitutional perspective, see, eg, A Chayes 'The Role of the Judge in Public Law Litigation' (1976) 89 Harv L Rev 1281; on German constitutional adjudication, see, K Schlaich *Das Bundesverfassungsgericht: Stellung, Verfahren, Entscheidungen: ein Studienbuch* (4th edn Beck Munich, 1997) 180; T Gawron and R Rogowski 'Implementation von

Clearly, this objective approach has a significant instrumental element, since it presupposes that human rights protection for one may be beneficial to others or to society as a whole.[186] Instrumentality is not a stranger to the Convention, which is evident already in the Preamble's 3rd and 4th recitals: the protection of the Convention's rights and freedoms is, for instance, meant to achieve 'greater unity between the members of the Council of Europe' and 'justice and peace in the world'. European integration in human rights matters is another aim that may be fulfilled by the protection of the treaty's rights and freedoms.[187]

Other aspects of the supervisory system also build on the premise that adjudication has a wider purpose than to settle the dispute between the parties in the case. The right of third parties to intervene as *amici curiae* before the Court, guaranteed by Art 36(2) and Rule 44 of the Rules of Court is an expression of this rationale,[188] since it allows interest groups to assist the applicant's litigious efforts.[189] The inter-state application procedure, provided for in Art 33, is a special form of *actio popularis*, the purpose of which being to bring before the Court 'an alleged violation of the public order of Europe'.[190] Pursuant to Art 37(1) (former Art 30), the Court, moreover, can decide to pursue a case in the public interest even if the applicant withdraws the application.[191]

As observed by van Dijk and van Hoof, Strasbourg adjudication is thus

> concerned not only with . . . the personal interest of the applicant, but also with the public interest, and thus the procedure that originates from an individual complaint may in some respects also assume an objective character.[192]

Bundesverfassungsgerichtsentscheidungen' in E Blankenburg and others (eds) *Implementation von Gerichtentscheidungen* (Westdeutsches Verlag Opladen, 1987) 352, 365; and P Häberle 'Grundprobleme der Verfassungsgerichtbarkeit' in P Häberle (ed) *Verfassungsgerichtbarkeit* (Wissenschaftlichers Buchgesellschaft Darmstadt, 1976) 15.

[186] The instrumental function of human rights is known particularly in the context of development, eg, AK Sen *Development as Freedom* (Oxford University Press Oxford, 1999) 10–11; and United Nations Development Program (ed) *Human Development Report 2000* (Oxford University Press New York, 2000) 14. Contrasting intrinsic and instrumental justifications of rights is a method borrowed here from C McCrudden 'The Future of the EU Charter for Fundamental Rights' (Jean Monnet Working Paper 2001:10) 24–25.

[187] JA Frowein S Schulhofer and M Shapiro 'Fundamental Human Rights as a Vehicle of Legal Integration in Europe' in M Cappelletti M Seccombe and J Weiler (eds) *Integration Through Law. Vol 1 Methods, Tools and Institutions* (de Gruyter Berlin, 1986) 230, 244.

[188] A Lester 'Amici curiae: third-party interventions before the European Court of Human Rights' in F Matscher and H Petzold (eds) *Protecting Human Rights: The European Dimension. Studies in Honour of Gérard J Wiarda* (Heymann Cologne, 1988) 341, 342.

[189] Nowicki (n 20) 268–73.

[190] *Austria v Italy* Application 788/60 (1961) 6 Yearbook 116, 140; and van Dijk and van Hoof (n 183) 40–41.

[191] The provision states that 'the Court shall continue the examination of the application if respect for human rights as defined in the Convention and the protocols thereto so requires'.

[192] van Dijk and van Hoof (n 183) 47.

This was early affirmed in the Commission's practice,[193] and has later been re-stated by the Court itself, typically with regard to the protection of procedural guarantees in Art 6(1).[194]

Meir Dan-Cohen argues that corporate rights adjudication is well suited for an objective approach, because the nature of a corporate entity, being the aggregate of a variety of individual interests, 'will have relatively far-reaching consequences for many individuals (possibly for society as a whole)', and also because

> the organization represents the diverse interests of different groups of individuals. These interests will often (though not always) be significantly affected in various ways by the judicial decision aimed at the organization. Even a judge who habitually purports to focus only on the parties before her must realize that when those parties are organizations her decision will affect many individuals who populate the area behind the 'corporate veil' but do not participate in the proceedings, and that the soundness of the decision must ultimately be measured by those effects.[195]

While it cannot be ascertained whether this view also applies to our context, it nonetheless remains a fact that corporate complaints brought before the Court can be understood in a broader sense than as just representing the interests of the applicant corporate person.

3 Public Interests

Thus far this study has concentrated on arguing in favour of a place for companies in the ECHR legal order. Many of the arguments that suggest exclusion of corporate entities from the Convention, or at least a careful application of its rights and freedoms to for-profit business entities, make sense from a normative viewpoint. The majority of the concerns enumerated in part A above lacks however structural support in the present ECHR system and they are therefore not pursued further here. Be that as it may, there are still certain features of the Convention framework that do not unequivocally support the protection of companies' interests.

(a) Community Interests

Human rights enjoy a prima facie, presumptive inviolability, and will often 'trump' public interests that conflict with them in a given case.[196] But human

[193] The Commission early stated that 'the interests served by the protection of human rights and fundamental freedoms guaranteed by the Convention extend beyond the individual interests of the persons concerned', see App 2294/64 *H G and W G v Germany* (1965) 8 Yearbook 314, 320 (1964) 15 CD 50.

[194] *Kostovski v Netherlands* Series A No 166, (1990) 12 EHRR 434 § 44(3); and *De Becker v Belgium* Series A No 4, (1979) 1 EHRR 43 § 25.

[195] Dan-Cohen (n 180) 131.

[196] R Dworkin 'Rights as Trumps' (1981) 1 OJLS 177.

rights are not absolute in the sense that they always will take priority over conflicting community interests. In the very concept of human rights there is consideration of community interests as well as those of the particular individual person.[197] The Convention, as any other fundamental rights regime, is built on a careful equilibrium of public and private concerns.

This can be explained by way of many approaches. For instance, the principle of the *raison d'état*, as a view not to respect the law of human rights in the name of a more important interest of the national community or of the State, plays in fact an important role under the ECHR.[198] One might also contemplate the extent to which the ECHR in practice embraces the idea of the State's legitimate 'right to regulate' in face of the private sector's default inclination to resist regulatory measures by relying on fundamental rights and freedoms.[199] But more matter-of-factly, consideration of public interests is structurally ingrained in the Convention; it finds textual support in various provisions (including Art 8(2)—11(2); Art 15 and Arts 17 and 18).[200] The Convention, in short,

> implies a balance between the protection of the general interest of the community and the respect due to fundamental human rights, while attaching particular importance to the latter.[201]

Significantly for us, the principle of proportionality, an interpretative mode which will be considered later, is an instrument used by the Court to handle the conflict between the individual and the society.[202]

[197] Henkin (n 145) 4–5.

[198] M Delmas-Marty 'General Introduction' in M Delmas-Marty (ed) *The European Convention for the Protection of Human Rights: International Protection Versus National Restrictions* (Martinus Nijhoff Dordrecht, 1992) 1, 1; and JC Soyer 'Retour discret de la raison d'état dans ces états soumis à la raison du droit (La function publique nationale)' in J-L Aujol (ed) *Mélanges en hommage à Louis-Edmond Pettiti* (Bruylant Bruxelles, 1998) 661, 661.

[199] The 'right to regulate', a concept which has regained prominence in international investment law, is 'a "shield" against an expansive use of expropriation claims by investors that have threatened to encroach on a sovereign government's right to regulate in the public interest', see, eg, UNCTAD *World Investment Report 2003. FDI Policies for Development: National and International Perspectives* (United Nations Conference on Trade and Development New York/Geneva, 2003), esp chapter V 'The Importance of National Policy Space' 145, 146–47; and C Yannaca-Small '"Indirect Expropriation" and the "Right to Regulate" in *International Investment Law*' (OECD Directorate for Financial and Enterprise Affairs Working Paper on International Investment 4:2004) (which also considers ECHR law).

[200] M Delmas-Marty and G Soulier 'Restraining or Legitimating the Reason of State?' in M Delmas-Marty (ed) *The European Convention for the Protection of Human Rights: International Protection Versus National Restrictions* (Martinus Nijhoff Dordrecht, 1992) 7.

[201] *Case relating to certain aspects of the laws on the use of languages in education in Belgium (Belgian Linguistics Case) (Merits)* Series A No 6, (1979) 1 EHRR 252 § 5.

[202] Y Arai-Takahashi *The Margin of Appreciation Doctrine and the Principle of Proportionality in the Jurisprudence of the ECHR* (Intersentia Antwerp, 2002) 245.

(b) Sovereignty Concerns

Human rights treaties entail by their very nature a significant curtailment of sovereign power. Like any other human rights convention, the ECHR will not be interpreted as a reciprocal agreement between States in which sovereignty concerns take priority over contrasting interests.[203] It is the Strasbourg organs' consistent view that:

> The over-riding function of this Convention is to protect the rights of the individual and not to lay down as between States mutual obligations which are to be restrictively interpreted having regard to the sovereignty of these States. On the contrary, the role of the Convention and the function of its interpretation is to make the protection of the individual effective.[204]

Yet, being a treaty entered into by the Council of Europe member States by their own volition, the Convention inevitably needs to relate also to the sovereign interests of the potential human rights violator. The Court's task is to apply the finite rights-catalogue of the Convention;[205] the power of amendment rests with the member States.[206] To the extent that the Court interprets the treaty extensively in a way which smacks of illegitimate judicial activism close to court-made legislation, the respondent States' sovereign interests may be engaged in ways that are counterproductive for the effectiveness of Convention protection.[207] Sovereign interests of the treaty's signatory States are thus also fixed in the structure of Convention protection,[208] and they have required the invention of the principle of a margin of appreciation.[209] The study will return to the significance of this interpretative approach in due course.

[203] *Austria* (n 190) 138 and 140. See further M Craven 'Legal Differentiation and the Concept of the Human Rights Treaty in International Law' (2000) 11 EJIL 489, 510–13.

[204] Ovey and White (n 47) 39–41.

[205] Art 19. The finite nature of the Convention emerges, inter alia, in the Preamble's 5th recital '*certain* of the rights stated in the [UDHR]' (emphasis added).

[206] Further, eg, E Møse 'New Rights for a New Court?' in P Mahoney and others (eds) *Protecting Human Rights: The European Perspective: Studies in Memory of Rolv Ryssdal* (Heymann Cologne, 2000) 943.

[207] For details, eg, P Mahoney 'Judicial Activism and Judicial Self-Restraint in the European Court of Human Rights: Two Sides of the Same Coin' (1990) 11 HRLJ 57. See also chapter 1 (pp 26–29).

[208] M Oreja 'Souverainité des Etats et respect des droits de l'homme' in F Matscher and H Petzold (eds) *Protecting Human Rights: The European Dimension. Studies in Honour of Gérard J Wiarda* (Heymann Cologne, 1988) 7; H Petzold 'The Convention and the Principle of Subsidiarity' in R St John Macdonald F Matscher and H Petzold (eds) *The European System for the Protection of Human Rights* (Martinus Nijhoff Dordrecht, 1993) 41, 55.

[209] E Brems 'The Margin of Appreciation Doctrine in the Case-Law of the European Court of Human Rights' (1996) 56 ZaöRV 240, 298.

E. A Many-Sided Convention

The company was described in chapter 1 as a private impersonal organization of individual and economic activity set up to undertake a business enterprise predominantly for the purpose of obtaining pecuniary gain for its shareholders. Critics of corporate utilisation of the ECHR apparatus may, of course, be normatively justified in presuming that the company is unfit to rely on human rights because its characteristics remove it too far from the individual human being whose Strasbourg application is wholly unrelated to the pursuit of profit.

The validity of that critique is not tested here since it cannot be implemented on the Convention as it stands today. From a descriptive viewpoint, that is, based on the way in which the Court actually operates in response to corporate litigation, this chapter has shown that the treaty and its structure makes it impossible for the Court to exclude companies altogether from the Convention system. There is, in fact, a range of factors that suggest that companies have a natural place in the ECHR even if they are not always protected on par with the individual applicant.

The Convention framework informs us of a treaty system whose compatibility with interests sought protected by companies depends on a detailed assessment of both the claim pursued and the Convention right or freedom on which the corporate applicant relies. The Convention exhibits a heterogeneous catalogue of rights and freedoms. This has obvious ramifications for corporate applicants.

In the context of corporate complaints, the Convention rights and freedoms can roughly be divided in three groups. Some provisions, or aspects of provisions, are wholly inapplicable to corporate entities' complaints because their orientation is primarily individualistic and dignity-based. According to Strasbourg case law, this group comprises rights such as freedom of conscience in Art 9, the prohibition against torture or inhuman or degrading treatment or punishment in Art 3 and the prohibition against arbitrary detention in Art 5. Another group consists of provisions, or aspects of provisions, that apply *ipso facto* to corporate entities pursuing economic goals because they by their nature have collective aspects, economic facets, and/or are more or less objectively construed. Article 6(1), Art 9 (freedom of religion) and Protocol 1 Art 1 are examples of this group according to the Court's practice. In between these two groups are certain rights and freedoms whose compatibility with corporate complaints is less sure. They are considered in more detail in chapter 4.

The Convention's many-faceted structure can also inform the Court's handling of other issues of interpretation, such as the 'victim' requirement in

Art 34 (which is considered in chapter 3) and the appropriate standard of judicial review applied by the Court with respect to rights or freedoms that have been found to apply to corporate applicants (discussed in chapter 5). In all matters of interpretation the Court is required to look to what is the most reasonable outcome provided it keeps its adjudicatory discretion within the boundaries set by the Convention's object and purpose, which, as has been shown above, is an assortment of different, sometimes even conflicting, considerations, values and interests. The three next chapters present and seek to make structural sense of the Court's response to issues of treaty interpretation where corporate complaints have a tinge of doctrinal controversy. It will become clear that the Court's approach in such instances can be rationalized on the basis of the structure outlined in the chapters 1 and 2.

3

The Court's Approach to Corporate Personality

This chapter attempts to derive from relevant case law Strasbourg's conception of corporate personality.[1] Corporate legal personality entails the conferment of rights (and duties) under municipal law on companies as were they human beings.[2] It also signifies a distinction between the rights (and duties) of the company and those of other persons,[3] including shareholders, the pre-eminent group of corporate constituents. It was observed in chapter 1 that separate juristic personhood is a salient feature of the limited liability company. Without it, the company's function as an attractive instrument for business investment would be undermined. A study of the Court's stance on corporate legal personality, as found in Strasbourg case law, is an indispensable part of this study's exploration of private business enterprise within the Convention system and demonstrates, as we shall see, doctrinal peculiarities of the Court's handling of difficult questions of treaty interpretation in the field of corporate litigation.

The nature of Strasbourg adjudication means that the Court rarely expounds on matters of theory, whether of pertinence to corporate issues or not.[4] It is conceivable, besides, that questions of corporate theory—understood here as

[1] This topic has also been considered in part in M Emberland 'The Corporate Veil in the Case Law of the European Court of Human Rights' (2003) 63 ZaöRV 945.

[2] A 'right-and-duty-bearing unit' in the words of FW Maitland 'Moral Personality and Legal Personality' in HAL Fischer (ed) *Collected Papers* (London University Press London, 1911) vol 3, 307.

[3] On corporate legal personality in municipal law, see, eg, PL Davies *Gower's Principles of Modern Company Law* (6th edn Sweet & Maxwell London, 1997) 77–83 (with regard to English company law).

[4] In *Comingersoll SA v Portugal* Reports 2000-IV (2001) 31 EHRR 772 §§ 35–36, the Court majority afforded compensation (art 41) for immaterial loss sustained by a company partly because the loss had affected its individual members. Four judges wished to award compensation purely on grounds of the inconvenience caused by the corporate entity as such, see Concurring Opinion of Judges Rozakis, Bratza, Caflisch, and Vajić. The opinions may derive from different theories of corporate personhood, see further M Emberland 'Compensating Companies for Non-Pecuniary Damage: *Comingersoll v Portugal* before the European Court of Human Rights and the Ambivalent Expansion of the ECHR Scope' (2003) 74 BYIL 409. A study of the Court's approach to various theories of corporate personhood falls outside the dissertation's scope. F Hallis *Corporate Personality. A Study in Jurisprudence* (Oxford University Press Oxford, 1930) is a classical exposition of such theories.

conceptions of the nature, composition and purpose of the limited liability company—lack the social and legal urgency in Europe today that would require specific handling by a court of human rights. The Court has therefore not developed a corporate theory for the ECHR and we will not attempt to contrive one here. Having said that, however, corporate legal personality is undeniably a 'classical' subject of corporate theory, and the Court's construction of it gives some credence to the view that Strasbourg's company case law generally reflects the relatively uniform approach to such matters by jurisdictions across the Council of Europe area.

The present effort to determine the perception of the corporate legal personality at Strasbourg is subject to certain constraints. Firstly, this chapter attempts solely to identify the corporate person with its shareholders in situations in which shareholders seek Convention protection in matters that formally concern the company in which they own shares. Secondly, this chapter considers only claims of identification in relation to the 'victim' requirement in Art 34 (former Art 25(1)), either when the Court interprets Art 34 directly or (as occasionally happens) when the Court incorporates the 'victim' test in its interpretation of the substantive provision under which protection is sought. It is here that Strasbourg litigation has generated a body of case law sufficiently comprehensive to enable reliable conclusions to be drawn with regard to separate corporate personality. Although this has attracted some attention in ECHR literature,[5] a wider-ranging discussion is still justified.[6] The Court, now and again, touches upon issues relevant to a discussion of separate corporate personality when other company constituents than shareholders and other questions than 'victimhood' are involved, but this case law is too sporadic to yield valid insights and is therefore excluded from this analysis.[7] Empirically, then, this chapter proceeds on the basis of a shareholder model

[5] MK Addo 'The Corporation as a Victim of Human Rights Violations' in MK Addo (ed) *Human Rights Standards and the Responsibility of Transnational Corporations* (Kluwer Hague 1999) 187 191–92; P van Dijk and GJH van Hoof *Theory and Practice of the European Convention on Human Rights* (2nd edn Kluwer Hague, 1998) 58; and W Peukert 'Artikel 25 (Individualbeschwerde)' in JA Frowein and W Peukert *Europäische Menschenrechtskonvention. EMRK-Kommentar* (2nd edn Engel Kehl am Rhein, 1996) 523, 538–39 are representative examples.

[6] AJ Dignam and D Allen *Company Law and the Human Rights Act 1998* (Butterworths London, 2000) 172–92 is a fairly detailed study, which deserves mention.

[7] In *Groppera Radio and Others v Switzerland* Series A No 173, (1990) 12 EHRR 321 § 49, for instance, the Court identified an employee with his corporate employer under art 10. In *CDI Holding AG and Others v Slovakia* decision 18 October 2001 § 4, the Court dismissed a claim submitted by a board of directors as lying outside its jurisdiction *ratione personae* because the measure complained of had concerned the 'company as such and not . . . its . . . official representatives' in their personal capacity. Shareholders' claims for compensation pursuant to Art 41 for loss formally sustained by their company are not uniformly handled by the Court, contrast, eg, *Veeber v Estonia (No 1)* judgment 7 November 2002 §§ 79–81 (no identification) with *Ruiz-Mateos v Spain* Series A No 262, (1993) 16 EHRR 505 §§ 69–70 (identification).

of the company,[8] and confines itself to a limited sector of the Convention. Despite these constraints, however, the significance of the chapter's findings arguably remains of value.

Section A introduces the 'victim' requirement of Art 34 and the crucial distinction between shareholder rights and interests. Section B examines the Court's justification for dismissing shareholder claims for identification with the corporate entity with reference to the corporate veil. Section C examines the exceptions to this main rule. Section D concludes.

A. The 'Victim' Requirement and Shareholders' Claims

1 The 'Victim' Requirement

The 'victim' requirement in Article 34 is one of several admissibility conditions,[9] but it has evoked particular discussion in Strasbourg as far as separate corporate personality is concerned. The provision states that:

> The Court may receive applications from any person, non-governmental organisation or group of individuals claiming to be the victim of a violation by one of the High Contracting Parties of the rights set forth in the Convention or the protocols therein.

There is an extensive interpretative practice of the requirement by the Court and, obviously, the Commission as its former screening organ, whose case law remains relevant since former Art 25(1) was emended to Art 34 without substantive changes.[10] This is not the place to restate all aspects of the Strasbourg organs' rendition of 'victimhood',[11] but three points deserve attention since they bear significantly on the discussion below.

[8] M Dan-Cohen *Rights, Persons, and Organizations* (University of California Press Berkeley Ca, 1986) 17–25 introduces the shareholder and stakeholder models.

[9] C Ovey and RCA White *Jacobs and White The European Convention on Human Rights* (3rd edn Oxford University Press Oxford, 2002) 405–13.

[10] Explanatory Report to Protocol No 11 to the Convention for the Protection of Human Rights and Fundamental Freedoms restructuring the control machinery established thereby (Protocol No 11 Explanatory Report), available at <http://conventions.coe.int/Treaty/en/Reports/Html/155.htm> (Protocol 11 Explanatory Report) §§ 85–86.

[11] Comprehensive studies of the 'victim' requirements include JA Frowein 'La notion de victime dans la Convention Européenne des Droits de l'Homme' in *Studi in onore di Giuseppe Sperduti: fonti internazionali e rapporti fra ordinamenti, l'individuo nel diritto internazionale, altri contribute* (Giuffrè Milano, 1984) 585; HC Krüger and CA Nørgaard 'The Right of Application' in R St John Macdonald F Matscher and H Petzold (eds) *The European System for the Protection of Human Rights* (Martinus Nijhoff Dordrecht, 1993) 657, 663–64; K Rogge 'The "Victim" Requirement in Article 25 of the European Convention on Human Rights' in F Matscher and H Petzold (eds) *Protecting Human Rights: The European Dimension. Studies in Honour of Gérard J Wiarda* (Heymann Cologne, 1988) 539; and van Dijk and van Hoof (n 5) 46–60.

First, the 'victim' requirement denotes an autonomous concept.[12] The Court is thereby not bound to interpret it in consideration of how it, or related concepts, is understood in municipal law.[13] Solutions adopted in municipal law concerning shareholders' ability to protest against measures that directly concern their company rather than themselves, or, for that matter, the very construct of separate legal personality, which is inherently municipal, do not necessarily control the Court's perception of 'victimhood'.

Second, the Court consistently holds that 'the word "victim"... denotes the person directly affected by the act or omission which is in issue'.[14] The requirement of 'direct affectedness' presupposes a special relationship between the applicant and the interference of which he or she complains. An applicant cannot therefore, as a rule, complain of matters that have befallen other persons. The 'direct affectedness' criterion does intuitively seem to indicate that the concept of a separate corporate personality puts a formidable barrier in the way of all persons except the company itself (via its legally appointed organs) to start Strasbourg proceedings for matters that concern the company. Shareholders would, it can be surmised, fail to meet a necessary condition for admissibility when the complaint refers to such matters.

Third, the Court also takes cognizance of the principle of effectiveness when it interprets the requirement,[15] which is unsurprising as the provision's last sentence adjures ECHR member States to 'undertake not to hinder in any way the effective exercise of this right'. Effective interpretation, which was briefly introduced in chapter 1, suggests a repudiation of formal or theoretical categorizations as determining principles for Convention interpretation (this is dealt with in detail in chapter 4). It admits of considerable flexibility and pragmatism in the application of ambiguous treaty expressions, the 'victim' requirement included.

Applied in the corporate context, the effectiveness principle may suggest that the Court does not feel constrained by the construct of separate corporate personality if it hinders effective Convention protection for the shareholder applicant. This conjecture is not wholly unsubstantiated. The effectiveness principle has, significantly, led the Court to establish an 'indirect victim' doctrine, which confers 'victim' status to individuals who strictly speaking have not

[12] *Middelburg van der Zee and Het Parool BV v Netherlands* Application 28202/95, (1998) § 1(3).

[13] F Sudre 'Le recours aux "notions autonomes" ' in F Sudre (ed) *L'interprétation de la Convention européenne des droits de l'homme. Actes du colloque des 13 et 14 mars 1998* (Bruylant Bruxelles, 1998) 93; and D Evrigenis 'L'interaction entre la dimension internationale et la dimension nationale de la Convention européenne des Droits de l'homme: notions autonomes et effet direct' in R Bernhardt and others (eds) *Völkerrecht als Rechtordnung, Internationale Gerichtbarkeit, Menschenrechte: Festschrift für Hermann Mosler* (Springer Berlin, 1983) 193.

[14] *Eckle v Germany* Series A No 51, (1983) 5 EHRR 1 § 66(1).

[15] *Ilhan v Turkey* Reports 2000-VII §§ 51–55.

themselves been the subject of an interference but who have close affinity with the person against whom the contested measure was directed.[16] The doctrine represents a means for remedying wrongs that, in the Court's opinion, require international denunciation regardless of formal barriers otherwise inherent in Art 34. While it is not, however, habitually linked with the topic under discussion here,[17] the doctrine illustrates the inclination of the Court to approach the 'victim' requirement pragmatically when it deems that it is appropriate to do so.

2 Shareholding and ECHR Protection

Before we explore the Court's position on shareholder claims for identification, we need to know whether the difficulties met by shareholders are theoretical or practical or both. This requires a rehearsal of basic shareholder axioms and the protective status of shareholding under the Convention.

A shareholder may appear before the Court in various capacities. As a member of, say, a company's management and in the function as the company's representative, the shareholder may claim that the company's rights have been breached. As a member of the company board, a shareholder may petition the Court about the manner in which domestic courts have handled a dispute concerning the lawfulness of his of her forced ousting from the board of directors.[18] A shareholder who is directly involved in the company's business activities may assert before the Court that the personal sphere has been infringed because competition authorities have carried out investigatory measures in his or her private home in search of evidence for unlawful corporate activity.[19]

In none of these instances will a shareholder's claim for Convention protection concern the position *qua* shareholder. Shareholders appear before the Court in two fundamentally different situations: either they claim protection for matters that concern their rights as shareholders directly or they claim protection for matters that merely concern their interests in the company in which they own shares. The Court responds differently to these two types of claims. Why this is so deserves explanation (see sections (a) and (b)) since basic aspects of shareholding lie outside the purview of general ECHR discourse. Readers acquainted with corporate law will notice that ECHR law and municipal law are not dissimilar in their treatment of such issues.

(a) Protection of Shareholders' Rights

Sovtransavto Holding v Ukraine concerned allegations from a Russian holding company that Ukrainian courts had been nationally biased when settling a

[16] van Dijk and van Hoof (n 5) 56–57. [17] ibid 58.
[18] *Tsatsos and Others v Greece* decision 9 March 2000.
[19] *Tee v UK* Application 26663/95, (1996) 21 EHRR 108.

dispute on the lawfulness of the Ukrainian company management's decision to increase the company's share capital so that the applicant lost control of it. In that case, the Court remarked that:

> a company share is a complex thing. It certifies that the holder possesses a share in the company together with corresponding rights. This is not only an indirect claim on company assets but other rights, especially voting rights and the right to influence the company, may follow the share.[20]

The Court here reflects two essential aspects of shareholding, both of which enjoy direct Convention protection for an applicant shareholder. Let us consider them in turn.

(i) Shares as Property

A share is only 'an indirect claim on company assets'; it entails no ownership of them. But the share itself is the shareholder's property and is considered as such by international law.[21] The Convention protects shares as the property of shareholders mainly under two guarantees.

Shares constitute 'possessions' within the meaning of Protocol 1 Art 1. This is unsurprising since a share, being a share in a company's capital stock, is susceptible of economic assessment, the basic requirement for Protocol 1 Art 1 protection.[22] Shares are consequently protected against deprivation and certain forms of governmental control and interference. In *Olczak v Poland*, for instance, the applicant claimed to have suffered a Protocol 1 Art 1 violation following a decision of the Board of Receivers of a limited liability bank to increase the share capital of the bank with the effect of reducing the applicant's shareholding percentage from 45 percent to 0.4 percent. The measure entailed a severe reduction in the value of the applicant's shares. This, considered the Court, amounted to a deprivation of property within the meaning of the provision.[23]

Property rights in shares also constitute 'civil rights' within the meaning of Art 6(1). Domestic legal disputes concerning property rights in shares must satisfy the provision's due process guarantees and this provides a certain amount of protection, inter alia, of minority shareholder rights. In *Sovtransavto Holding v Ukraine*, for instance, referred to above, the Court found the judicial process in Ukraine to be in contravention of the requirements of independence and impartiality contained in Art 6(1).[24]

[20] *Sovtransavto Holding v Ukraine* Reports 2002-VII § 92(2).

[21] WK Geck 'Diplomatic Protection' in R Bernhardt (ed) *Encyclopedia of Public International Law* (North-Holland Amsterdam, 1992) vol 1, 1045, 1054. One central example from judicial practice is the matter underlying the ICJ's *Interhandel* Case *(Switzerland v United States of America) (Preliminary Objections)* [1959] ICJ Rep 6, 16.

[22] *Gasus Dosier- und Fördertechnik GmbH v Netherlands* Series A No 306-B, (1995) 20 EHRR 403 § 53.

[23] *Olczak v Poland* decision 7 November 2002 Reports 2002-X § 61.

[24] *Sovtransavto Holding* (n 20) § 82.

(ii) Shareholder Rights

As the Court indicated in *Sovtransavto Holding*, municipal law recognizes a host of other legal positions that emanate from the share in addition to the property right. These so-called shareholder rights are necessarily linked with the corporate entity: they would not exist without it. But they belong to the shareholder and not to the company. A shareholder could therefore without difficulty lay claim to 'victimhood' in pursuance of shareholder rights before the Court.

Although they may vary across national jurisdictions,[25] there is a consensus as to which rights normally count as shareholder rights. A cluster of them is also recognized in international law, where they have long enjoyed considerable protection.[26] Some of these rights are pecuniary, others relate more directly to the governance of the company.[27] But which rights are, exactly, regarded as shareholder rights for Convention purposes?

The catalogue provided in *Olczak v Poland* is slightly longer than that provided in *Sovtransavto Holding*; in the former case the Court referred to shareholder rights as 'the right to a share in the company's assets in the event of its being wound up,' and other 'unconditioned rights, especially voting rights and the right to influence the company's conduct'.[28] But neither list is exhaustive.

It would be instructive here to consider the International Court of Justice's 1970 *Barcelona Traction* judgment, a milestone in international law with regard to shareholder protection and separate corporate personality. There is no need to rehearse every particular of the *Barcelona Traction* case, for it has generated a wealth of literature.[29] The judgment essentially concerned the question of effective shareholder protection in customary international law; the specific issue addressed by the ICJ was the proper allocation of national affiliation for corporate constituents in the law of diplomatic protection. Although evidently not immediately relevant for ECHR purposes, it bears on

[25] L Caflisch *La protection des sociétés commerciales et des interêts indirects en droit international public* (Martinus Nijhoff Hague, 1969) 154.

[26] A Kiss 'La protection diplomatique des actionnaires dans la jurisprudence et la pratique internationales' in S Bastid and others (eds) *La personnalité morale et ses limites* (Pichon et Durand-Auzias Paris, 1960) 179; and J-P de Hochepied *La protection diplomatique des sociétés et des actionnaires* (Pedone Paris, 1965) 145.

[27] S Beyer *Der diplomatische Schutz der Aktionäre im Völkerrecht* (Nomos Baden-Baden 1977) 131–32.

[28] *Olczak* (n 23) § 60.

[29] Early comments include L Caflisch 'The Protection of Corporate Investments Abroad in the Light of the Barcelona Traction Case' (1971) 31 ZaöRV 162, 171–72 and 183; and R Higgins 'Aspects Concerning the Barcelona Traction Light and Power Company, Ltd' (1970–71) 11 VJIL 327. V Lowe 'Shareholders' Rights to Control and Manage: From Barcelona Traction to ELSI' in N Ando E McWhinney and R Wolfrum (eds) *Liber Amicorum Judge Shigeru Oda* (Kluwer Hague, 2002) vol 1, 269 introduces the present legal situation.

the present chapter for various reasons (see below) and also helps us expand the list of shareholder rights protected by the Convention. The ICJ referred to shareholder rights as:

> rights which municipal law confers upon the [shareholder] distinct from those of the company, including the right to any declared dividend, the right to attend and vote at general meetings, the right to share in the residual assets of the company on liquidation.[30]

The *Barcelona Traction* list reflects generally accepted shareholder rights and is frequently cited in international decisions.[31] Most probably, therefore, it articulates also those rights regarded as shareholder rights in the Convention.

The Convention may, in fact, offer valuable protection for minority shareholders who may see their influence and positions in the company threatened by restructuring measures or internal turmoil.[32] Typically, shareholder rights are affected when domestic courts adjudicate in derivative suits, litigation initiated by minority shareholders against the company's controlling majority. In *Pafitis and Others v Greece*, for instance, the Court found a violation of Art 6(1) in a lengthy dispute over the applicant shareholders' right to vote at the general meeting of a limited liability bank which had decided to increase the bank's capital stock. There was no doubt at the Court that the right to vote, and other direct shareholder rights, counted as 'civil rights'. They were therefore susceptible Art 6(1) protection.[33]

Shareholder rights also constitute property within the meaning of the Convention. In *Olczak v Poland*, the Court agreed with the applicant that the sharp reduction in his percentage of the shareholding after a capital increase had severely curtailed his procedural ability to 'influence the company and to vote' at the general meeting, and that it therefore raised an issue under Protocol 1 Art 1.[34] The Court regarded his shareholder rights as 'possessions' pursuant to the provision because they were bound to the share, whose character is essentially pecuniary. In the Court's view, they constituted an indirect claim on company assets.[35]

[30] *Case concerning the Barcelona Traction, Light & Power Co Ltd (Belgium v Spain) (Merits)* [1970] ICJ Rep 3, 36 (§ 47).

[31] eg *Cantos Case (Preliminary Objections)* Inter-American Court of Human Rights Series C No 85 (7 September 2001) § 29. On the *Cantos* judgment, see also M Emberland 'The Corporate Veil in the Jurisprudence of the Human Rights Committee and the Inter-American Court and Commission of Human Rights' (2004) 4 HRLR 257, 269.

[32] See M Krohn 'Minority Squeeze-outs and the European Convention on Human Rights' (2004) 10 Tidsskrift for forretningsjus 394 for details.

[33] *Pafitis and Others v Greece* Reports 1998-I (1999) 27 EHRR 566 § 87.

[34] *Olczak* (n 23) § 61. The Commission raised but did not decide the issue in *Company S-S I AB and B T v Sweden* Application 11189/84, (1986) 50 DR 121, 138–39.

[35] *Olczak* (n 23) § 60. See also *Company S-S I AB and B T* (n 34) 138; and *Bramelid and Malmström v Sweden* Application 8588–89/79, (1982) 29 DR 64, 81; (1983) 5 EHRR 249.

(b) *Protection of Shareholder Interests: Identification Claims*

(i) The Rights/Interests Distinction

But let us come to what is the main focus of the present chapter, notably shareholders' identification claims. Intrinsic to investment in a company is the potential for financial prejudice as well as economic gain. Any matter influencing the company's legal position or activities may, ultimately, also influence the value of the shareholder's investment and is therefore of consequence for the shareholder. These stakes may be called the shareholder's 'indirect interests' in the company.[36]

Shareholder interests are linked with the legal position of the company—they concern the company's rights (and obligations)—and the concept of separate corporate personality commands that shareholder interests are distinguished from the shareholder's own rights in municipal law.[37] The shareholder is barred from coming to the company's rescue with regard to such interests in other ways than to make use of the procedures set up in the corporate constitution. Only when infringements of the legal positions of the company affect directly the shareholder's property or shareholder rights will the shareholder be able to take independent action.

The rights/interests distinction is an accepted means for allocating the legal spheres of companies and shareholders in international law:[38] it has long since been adopted for determining state responsibility.[39] In the *Barcelona Traction* case, the International Court of Justice observed that 'a distinction must be drawn between a direct infringement of the shareholder's rights and difficulties or financial losses to which he may be exposed as the result of the situation in the company'.[40] The ICJ majority continued:

> Notwithstanding the separate corporate personality, a wrong done to the company frequently causes prejudice to its shareholders. However, the mere fact that both company and shareholder sustain damage does not imply that both are entitled to claim compensation. Thus, no legal conclusion can be drawn from the fact that the same event caused damage simultaneously affecting several natural or juristic persons.... In such cases, no doubt, the interests of the aggrieved are affected, but not their rights. Thus whenever a shareholder's interests are harmed by an act done to the company, it is to the latter that he must look to institute appropriate action: for although two separate entities may have suffered from the same wrong, it is only one entity whose rights have been infringed.[41]

[36] Caflisch (n 25) 155.

[37] On the distinction in municipal law from the perspective of international law, see, eg, M Diéz de Velasco 'La protection diplomatique des sociétés et des actionnaires' (1974-I) 141 Receuil de Cours de l'Académie de Droit International 87, 155; and *Barcelona Traction* (n 30) 33 (§ 37 last sentence) and 35 (§ 44).

[38] Beyer (n 27) 45.

[39] E Jiménez de Aréchaga 'Diplomatic Protection of Shareholders in International Law' (1965) 4 Phil Intl L J 71, 74, gives references to early arbitral practice.

[40] *Barcelona Traction* (n 30) 33 (§37 last sentence).

[41] *Barcelona Traction* (n 30) 35 (§ 44).

In *Olczak v Poland*, the Court similarly attested to the significance of the distinction for Art 34 purposes:

> Whenever a shareholder's interests are harmed by a measure directed at the company, it is up to the latter to take appropriate action. An act infringing only the company's rights does not involve responsibility towards the shareholders, even if their interests are affected. Such responsibility arises only if the act complained of is aimed at the rights of the shareholders as such.[42]

The rights/interests distinction, as an aspect of separate corporate personality, is however not necessarily watertight, and modifications to it may, besides, apply when it is transported from its municipal legal origin to the level of international law. The ICJ's reliance on separate corporate personality was vigorously contested by judges at the court, and the *Barcelona Traction* doctrine remains contentious in international legal discourse.[43] The extent to which the rights/interests distinction is to be upheld for Convention purposes is the essential question under discussion in the present chapter.

(ii) 'Veil-piercing' *à la* Strasbourg

The partition separating the legal positions of the company and those of its shareholders is often referred to as the corporate veil; it signifies that the legal rights and responsibilities of a company and its shareholders shall remain separate. Experience has shown that there is a practical need sometimes to identify the corporate person with the shareholder, a process of identification often referred to as the 'piercing' or 'lifting' of the corporate veil. The terminology assumes that shareholders are prone to hiding behind the company construct for the sake of exploiting the corporate form for purposes that do not correspond with the company's essential function.[44] 'Veil-piercing' is therefore chiefly undertaken by courts or legislators for the purpose of holding shareholders accountable for matters that formally pertain to the company person.[45]

The Convention exclusively concerns the bestowment of rights, not duties, on private persons. 'Veil-piercing' *à la* Strasbourg must therefore necessarily take a reverse form, in which a disregard of separate corporate personality is carried out for the benefit of shareholders who otherwise would be barred from Convention protection.

[42] *Olczak* (n 23) § 59.

[43] RB Lillich 'Two Perspectives on the Barcelona Traction Case: The Rigidity of Barcelona' (1971) 65 AJIL 522 is an early critic of the majority's holding.

[44] Davies (n 3) 148–77 gives an English perspective on this matter.

[45] Presumably, the concept is known to most ECHR jurisdictions, see, eg, the early overview provided in EJ Cohn and C Simitis ' "Lifting the Veil" in the Company Laws of the European Continent' (1963) 12 ICLQ 189.

To some extent, the Court has itself had recourse to 'veil-piercing' terminology. In *Agrotexim Hellas SA and Others v Greece* from 1995, an essential judgment in relation to the concerns of this chapter (see below), it observed

> at the outset that the applicant companies did not complain of a violation of the rights vested in them as shareholders of Fix Brewery, such as the right to attend the general meeting and to vote. Their complaint was based exclusively on the proposition that the alleged violation of the Brewery's right to the peaceful enjoyment of its possessions had adversely affected their own financial interests. They considered that the financial losses sustained by the company and the latter's rights were to be regarded as their own, and that they were therefore victims, albeit indirectly, of the alleged violation. In sum, they sought to have the company's corporate veil pierced in their favour.[46]

But the Court does not consistently use this terminology and in some instances in which shareholders seek to traverse the rights/interests distinction for Art 34 purposes the terminology does not fit entirely. To speak of the process in terms of the 'identification' of shareholders with their company captures all instances under discussion.

If municipal law distinguishes between the corporate person and the shareholder, the latter has little or no opportunity to pursue claims that concern his or her interests in the company before national courts. It is up to the company to assert its own rights. So what motivates shareholders to initiate Strasbourg proceedings when they are barred from similar procedures on the domestic front?

Current case law reveals a diverse group of claims. Some reflect misunderstandings of the conditions for admissibility and who is entitled to represent the company before the Court. Occasionally, various corporate constituents file a joint complaint in the belief that it will increase their chance of success that the essence of the claim be admitted at least for some of them.[47] Some applicants, typically majority shareholders, believe that they and their business are, in practice, the same and should therefore be regarded as a 'victim'.[48] A shareholder may also file identification claims because the company interests for which they claim protection are not safeguarded by the corporate organs set up to protect them, typically because the company is in the process of liquidation. In this situation, a shareholder might see himself (or herself) as the only person genuinely representing the company's concerns.[49] It may also happen that the company, as controlled by a shareholding majority, has no desire to pursue a Strasbourg complaint because the dispute essentially is over

46 *Agrotexim Hellas and Others v Greece* Series A No 330, (1996) 21 EHRR 250 § 62. See also, eg, *T.W. Computeranimation GmbH v Austria* decision 1 February 2005; and *Lebedev v Russia* decision 25 November 2004.

47 eg, *Matrot SA and Others v France* decision 3 February 2000.

48 eg, *Ankarcrona v Sweden* Reports 2000-VI § 1(4).

49 eg, *GJ v Luxembourg* (2003) 36 EHRR 40.

corporate policy, about which the applicant shareholder may hold divergent views.[50] There are, in sum, rational and less convincing reasons why shareholders sometimes pursue identification claims before the Court. Let us now turn to a review the of Court's response to such claims.

B. The Starting Point: Preservation of Corporate Personality

After this fairly detailed setting of the background, it is time to analyse the Court's view on separate corporate personality with regard to the 'victim' requirement. Today, the Court adopts a consistent approach to shareholders' identification claims for the purpose of the 'victim' requirement in Article 34. It has, however, been a lengthy journey since the Commission's first encounter with the problem in 1966.[51] This section introduces the Court's starting point and general rule, notably that shareholders cannot claim 'victim' status for matters that do not concern their shareholder property or shareholder rights (section 1). The Court's motivation for upholding the construct of the corporate veil is sought explained in section 2.

1 Starting Point: No Identification

(a) The Agrotexim *Case*

The Court's point of departure is that shareholders cannot achieve 'victim' status under Art 34 for matters that concern the corporate person and not directly their own rights. The Court bases its reasoning on the 1995 judgment in the case of *Agrotexim Hellas SA and Others v Greece*. Its substance is presented in some detail here since the dispute amply fleshes out the issue under consideration.

The applicants were six limited liability companies who jointly held slightly more then 51 per cent of the shares of Karolos Fix Brewery ('Fix'). Heavily in debt to the National Bank of Greece, the Greek government in November 1982 ordered the liquidation of Fix under a special procedure which allowed for the appointment of one liquidator representing the National Bank of Greece, and one representing the company's management. Fix allegedly suffered financial ruin because its plans to sell its two factory plants in central Athens to a development venture were thwarted by the municipal council of the city of Athens. The city of Athens had publicly stated its intention to utilize the areas for public purposes and their involvement scared off potential investors in the project. Athens' sustained, yet informal, interest in the property amounted, in

[50] eg, *Santos Lda and Fachadas v Portugal* Reports 2000-X.

[51] App 1706/62 *X v Austria* (1966) 21 CD 26.

the applicants' view, to a de facto expropriation of Fix's property in contravention of their right to protection of their possessions in Protocol 1 Art 1. They also complained of violations of Arts 6(1) and 13 concerning the manner in which the domestic proceedings in the dispute had been carried out.[52]

The Court majority, eight out of nine judges, dismissed the application as failing to meet the 'victim' requirement (the dissenting opinion will be discussed later). It observed that the applicants did not complain of infringements of their shareholding rights, but that the alleged violation of the brewery's right to the peaceful enjoyment of its possessions 'had adversely affected their own financial interests because of the resulting fall in the value of their shares'. Seeing the claim as one in which the shareholders 'sought to have the company's corporate veil pierced in their favour',[53] the Court considered that:

> the piercing of the 'corporate veil' or the disregarding of a company's legal personality will be justified only in exceptional circumstances, in particular where it is clearly established that it is impossible for the company to apply to the Convention institutions through the organs set up under its articles of incorporation or—in the event of liquidation—through its liquidators. The Supreme Courts of certain member States of the Council of Europe have taken the same line. This principle has also been confirmed with regard to the diplomatic protection of companies by the International Court of Justice [in the Barcelona Traction judgment] pp. 39 and 41, paras. 56–58 and 66.[54]

Since no 'exceptional circumstances' were found, the claim was consequently dismissed.

The cited statement, found in § 66 of the judgment, is noteworthy since the Court explicitly diverged from the Commission's views in the same case, where the corporate veil had in fact been lifted. In its admissibility decision, the Commission held that the shareholders were 'victims' of the measures taken against Fix because they had had 'an interest in the subject matter of the application' and that Fix, because of its situation as debtor and its special liquidation scheme, had been 'under effective State control' since its liquidation.[55] Other Commission cases had foreshadowed some form of flexibility with regard to 'victimhood' for shareholders claiming identification,[56] but in the *Agrotexim* case the Commission, in its report in the case before sending the case to the Court, took its mode of interpretation one step further. The relevant passage in the Commission's report, to which the *Agrotexim* majority objected,[57] signals a far greater willingness to accommodate the shareholders' demands:

> The Commission notes that the applicant's rights at issue are their rights as majority shareholders in the company Karolos Fix Brewery SA. The measures complained of

[52] On the facts, see *Agrotexim* (n 46) §§ 6–38. [53] ibid § 62. [54] ibid § 66.

[55] App 14807/89 *Agrotexim Hellas SA and Others v Greece* (1992) 72 DR 148 'The Law' (ii) (6) and (8). [56] App 7598/76 *Kaplan v UK* (report) (1980) 21 DR 5, (1982) 4 EHRR 64 § 130.

[57] *Agrotexim* (n 46) §§ 63–64.

were directed against the company but also indirectly affected the applicant's rights. Consequently, insofar as there has been an interference with the company's property rights, this interference *must* be considered to extend to the applicants' property rights as well.[58]

The Court majority thought this an inadvisable interpretation of the 'victim' requirement. In noting that the Commission

> seems to accept that where a violation of a company's rights protected by Article 1 of Protocol 1 . . . results in a fall in the value of its shares, there is *automatically* an infringement of the shareholders' right under that Article

the majority considered that the Commission's view amounted to something equivalent to a default rule of identification between shareholders and their company.[59] Clearly, the Court was unhappy with what it perceived as the Commission's readiness to let considerations of equity take precedence over the formal barrier represented by the corporate veil; it expressly dismissed the Commission's stress on the 'specific circumstances of each case' and the fact that the applicants had a 'personal interest in the subject-matter of the complaint'.[60]

(b) The Reach of Agrotexim

The Court remains faithful to what may be referred to as the *Agrotexim* approach. Not only is it applied in the context under scrutiny here,[61] it has also been adopted with regard to other corporate constituents' applications for 'victim' status for matters that directly concern their company.[62] But how far does the doctrine actually reach? This is worth exploring since there has been little discussion on this issue in the literature.

Alan Dignam and David Allen have suggested that the substantive reach of the principle is uncertain outside Protocol 1 Art 1.[63] In their view, it is conceivable that the inherent exposure of financial risk in shareholding explains the Court's negative approach to claims of property protection for matters that concern the company directly. The principle, it is true, was established under Protocol 1 Art 1, and there is some evidence in the case law to support their

[58] App 14807/89 *Agrotexim Hellas SA and Others v Greece* (report) (1994) § 59 (emphasis added) (two of 16 Commission members dissented).

[59] *Agrotexim* (n 46) § 64 (emphasis added).

[60] ibid § 63.

[61] Court cases are on the increase, and include *TW Computeranimation GmbH and Others v Austria* (n 46); *Paparatti and Others v Italy* decision 1 June 1999; *Matrot SA and Others* (n 47); and *CDI Holding AG and Others* (n 7). The Commission relied on *Agrotexim* in, eg, App 30381/96 *Mironov v Bulgaria* (1997); and App 24463/94 *Penton v Turkey* (1998).

[62] *Société Géneral de Investissement (SGI) and Others v France* decision 4 May 1999 (claim for identification between companies within the same corporate group); and *Farbers and Harlanova v Lithuania* decision 6 September 2001 (manager seeking identification with company).

[63] Dignam and Allen (n 6) 183.

contention that identification with regard to 'victimhood' under other Convention rights may rest on different considerations than those immediately concerned with the exposure of financial risk. The Court in the *Agrotexim* case, when discussing, in a separate assessment, the applicant shareholders' claim for Arts 6(1) and 13 protection for the way in which their company had been treated, dismissed the complaint by reference to the judgment's § 65 rather than its § 66. The Court thereby relied on the rationale for non-identification rather than the principle itself, and observed that

> [n]either Article 6 nor Article 13 ... impl[ies] that under the national law of the Contracting State shareholders in a limited company should have the right to bring an action seeking an injunction or damages in respect of an act or omission that is prejudicial to 'their' company.[64]

CDI Holding AG and Others v Slovakia, where the Court considered the admissibility of complaints filed by various shareholders of violations of Protocol 1 Art 1 and Art 10 (freedom of expression), reveals what appears to be a detailed assessment of the impact of the *Agrotexim* case outside Protocol 1 Art 1. While the Court under this provision dismissed the complaint by reference to the *Agrotexim* case,[65] the Art 10 complaint was rejected merely by stating that the contested termination of the company's broadcasts 'were linked to the applicant company and not to its shareholders'.[66] In other cases claims under Arts 8 and 9 have been resolved (with a similar negative outcome for the applicants) without any mentioning of separate corporate personality or the *Agrotexim* statement.[67]

In *GJ v Luxembourg*, however, the Court did rely on *Agrotexim* when it decided on the admissibility of a shareholder claim for identification with regard to Art 6(1) (the case is examined in detail later).[68] Since that judgment is the most recent of these decisions, it can be argued that the Court has confirmed the possibility of the principle to apply outside Protocol 1 Art 1.

The case law's incoherent signals have at any rate little practical significance. In cases in which the principle is not reiterated the Court upholds the 'victim' requirement's essential condition that the applicant must be 'directly affected' by the measure.[69] As far as Arts 6 and 13 complaints go, this is generally taken to mean that the applicant, save for the existence of other special circumstances warranting 'victimhood', must personally have been party to the contested

[64] *Agrotexim* (n 46) § 73(2).

[65] *CDI Holding AG and Others* (n 7) § 4(1) and (2).

[66] ibid § 4(3).

[67] *Keslassy v France* decision 8 January 2002 (Art 8); and *Kustannus Oy Vapaa Ajattelija AB and Others v Finland* Application 20471/92, (1996) 85 DR 29 (1996) 22 EHRR 69 (Art 9).

[68] *GJ* (n 49) §§ 23–24. See also, eg, *Credit and Industrial Bank and Moravec v Czech Republic* Application 29010/95, (1998) 93 DR 137, (1998) 26 EHRR 88; and *Société Générale d'Investissement (SGI) and Others* (n 62).

[69] eg, *Eckle v Germany* Series A 51 § 66.

judicial proceedings. For Arts 8, 9, and 10 complaints, elements of personal affectedness may play a part in the Court's deliberation, considering the individualistic core of these provisions (see chapter 4 for this), and this may entail modifications of the principle of non-identification. As will be explained below, it is instructive to see the Court's response, regardless of any formal application of *Agrotexim*, as being shaped by a set of recurrent considerations and the facts of every case. The differences that do obtain between approaches that rely on *Agrotexim* and those in which general considerations of the 'victim' requirement is applied are therefore extremely slight and hinge more on matters of form than substance.

2 Exploring the Court's Approach: the Given Justifications

The Court, then, in principle, prefers the adoption of a municipal legal maxim to the Convention plane over the needs of individual applicants whose financial interests have been prejudiced by an ECHR member State. Is the Court here at odds with its otherwise generally maintained disposition to secure effective Convention protection? Judge Walsh appears to have been of that opinion in his dissenting opinion in *Agrotexim*, where he objected to the Court's negation of 'victimhood' as it in his opinion was 'anomalous that the defence of human rights in the field of property, or otherwise, should yield to the commercially sacred impenetrability of the "corporate veil"'.[70]

To assess the valence of Judge Walsh's concern one might study the Court's rationale for adhering in principle to separate corporate personality. As the *Agrotexim* judgment contains important pointers to this rationale, it merits closer study.[71] Sections (a), (b), and (c) introduce the three groups of justifications for preserving the corporate veil as given in the judgment. None of them, it will be argued, is sufficiently convincing to justify the Court's non-identification line. Section 3 places the Court's approach in a broader context whereby is can be fully appreciated as a judicious solution.

(a) Difficulties in Determining Who Can Represent the Company in Strasbourg

(i) The Reasoning

The *Agrotexim* Court's majority first of all justified the preservation of separate corporate personality under Art 34 in consideration of the following:

It is a perfectly normal occurrence in the life of a limited liability company for there to be differences of opinion among its shareholders or between its shareholders and its

[70] *Agrotexim* (n 46) Dissenting Opinion of Judge Walsh § 3.1.

[71] An anonymous commentator found the Court majority's view unconvincing without, however, specifying why, see case comment in 'Company Law: Victim—Shareholders in Company—Lifting the Corporate Veil' [1996] EHRLR 191, 193. Besides this, little has been written on the Court's rationale for upholding corporate personality on the level of ECHR law, or, in exceptional cases, to disregard it.

board of directors as to the reality of an infringement of the right to the peaceful enjoyment of the company's possessions or concerning the most appropriate way of reacting to such an infringement. Such differences of opinion may, however, be more serious where the company is in the process of liquidation because the realisation of its assets and the discharging of its liabilities are intended primarily to meet the claims of the creditors of the company whose survival is rendered impossible by its financial situation, and only a secondary aim to satisfy the claims of the shareholders, among whom any remaining assets are divided up.

To adopt the Commission's position would be to run the risk of creating—in view of these competing interests—difficulties in determining who is entitled to apply to the Strasbourg institutions.[72]

The Court's statement can conceivably be understood on different levels. Ostensibly, the Court gives a procedural rationale for its rejection of 'victim' status. To allow shareholders to apply to the Court for corporate matters, the Court proposes, would complicate the application of the right of individual petition: it would lead to 'difficulties in determining who is entitled to apply' to the Court. Thereby, the Court—quite sensibly—presupposes that the Convention system designates who, among corporate constituents, is uniquely entrusted with the right to apply to Strasbourg for matters that affect the company.

Indeed, as was established in chapter 1, Rule 36(1) of the Rules of Court appears to allocate this mandate to those organs that are endowed with the right to represent the company pursuant to municipal law (typically, the Board of Directors and the Managing Director). The Court also, again sensibly, assumes that it is advantageous for its '[determination of] who is entitled to apply' that a line of clarity is retained with regard to corporate representation. The adoption of an arrangement that diverges from municipal regulation would create 'difficulties' for the Court's screening of incoming applications because it would not suffice merely to establish whether the application has been submitted by persons or organs duly and ordinarily authorised to act on the company's behalf.

(ii) Sufficiently Coherent?

The Court's justification is not, however, entirely in line with its general application of the requirement. Since the 'victim' requirement denotes an autonomous concept, the assessment of who is entitled to apply to the Court is in principle undertaken independently of domestic legal arrangements, such as the designation of company representatives. The Court's sole task is to consider whether the applicant has been directly affected by the measure in question pursuant to the Convention. To the extent that the corporate entity and one of its constituents have, in fact, been directly affected by those same measures, even if they were formally directed at the corporate entity alone, the Court has

[72] *Agrotexim* (n 46) § 65(1) and (2).

the capacity to admit both persons' complaints. This view has long been favoured in Strasbourg. In *A Association and H v Austria*, where an association as well as its chair (as a private person) were complaining of an Art 11 violation following a demonstration ban that had been issued on the first applicant only, the Commission was asked to examine whether both persons could achieve 'victim' status. The Commission stated that:

> As the right invoked by the applicants . . . can be exercised both by the organiser of a meeting even it should be a legal person in the present case, and by the individual participants, the Commission accepts that both applicants are entitled to claim to be victims . . . of a violation of their rights under Article 11.[73]

The Court also admits, on occasion, applications concerning matters that formally were directed towards the corporate person even when the applicant person is not duly authorised to act on the company's behalf, and it does not in such instances express concern about the need to retain a clear *locus standi* rule. In *Matos e Silva Lda and Others v Portugal*, for instance, the company applicant and its individual and institutional shareholders jointly, and successfully, complained, inter alia, of a violation of Art 6(1) on account of the length of administrative proceedings to which only the applicant company had been a party.[74] The Court did not raise the issue of corporate representation and the underlying need for clarity.[75]

Although concern for clarity has a certain merit, then, it does not get in the way of the Court's reasoning when it considers it outweighed by other concerns. It should be added that since the *Barcelona Traction* judgment international practice now allows for the submission of competing claims, at least to some extent.[76] While this is not a decisive argument in any direction, the Court's first justification, prima facie, is not necessarily in tune with the international legal trend.

It is reasonable to assume that the Court's case for preserving the corporate veil rests on more fundamental considerations than merely a simple need for practical clarity as to who should exercise the right to apply on the company's behalf. One key to their understanding can be found in the *Agrotexim* judgment's accentuated concern for practical clarity when 'competing interests' involve various corporate constituents, typically when two groups of shareholders disagree on matters of corporate policy and, more frequently, when a company

[73] App 9905/82 *A Association and H v Austria* (1984) 36 DR 187, 191–92.

[74] *Matos e Silva Lda and Others v Portugal* 1996 Reports 1996-IV (1997) 24 EHRR 573 §§ 9, 68–70.

[75] The Commission examined the shareholders' 'victim' status, see App 15777/89 *Matos e Silva Lda and Others v Portugal* (1993) § 1(8) and (9). The question of difficulties in determining who is entitled to submit the application was, however, not discussed.

[76] F Orrego Vicuña 'Changing Approaches to the Nationality of Claims in the Context of Diplomatic Protection and International Dispute Settlement' (2000) 15 ICSID Rev 340, 355–58.

is in financial ruin and the interests of shareholders and creditors differ fundamentally. This aspect of the Court's approach is examined more closely in section 3.

(b) Unreasonable Application of the Local Remedies Rule

(i) The Reasoning

The Court's second justification for non-identification also signals the import of procedural matters. The Court chose to preserve the integrity of corporate personality because a different solution

> would also engender considerable problems concerning the requirement of exhaustion of remedies. It may be assumed that in the majority of national legal systems shareholders do not normally have the right to bring an action for damages in respect of an act or an omission that is prejudicial to 'their' company. It would accordingly be unreasonable to require them to do so before complaining of such an act or omission before the Convention institutions. Nor could, conversely, a company be required to exhaust domestic institutions itself, because the shareholders are of course not empowered to take such proceedings on behalf of 'their' company.[77]

To fully appreciate this argument we need to revisit the local remedies requirement, which was briefly introduced in chapter 1. Article 35(1) (former Art 26) requires for admissibility that the applicant has exhausted all domestic remedies:

> The Court may only deal with the matter after all domestic remedies have been exhausted, according to the generally recognised rule of international law.

Only the absence of an occasion for domestic redress entitles the applicant to initiate international proceedings.[78] The criterion is meant to encourage the respondent State to redress the alleged wrong on the domestic plane.[79]

According to the *Agrotexim* judgment, recognition of 'veil-piercing' to enable 'victimhood' requires that the shareholder applicant has availed himself (or herself) of all national legal remedies with regard to the essence of the dispute. As the municipal legal adherence to separate legal personality effectively bars the shareholder from litigating matters on the company's behalf (as it is for the company itself to undertake this form of action), he or she will be unable to fulfil a basic criterion for admissibility. An acceptance of identification under

[77] *Agrotexim* (n 46) § 65(3), reiterated in *Olczak* (n 23) § 57 and *JW v Poland* Application 27917/95 (1997) 90 DR 69 § (19).

[78] HG Schermers 'Exhaustion of Domestic Remedies' in N Ando E McWhinney and R Wolfrum (eds) *Liber Amicorum Judge Shigeru Oda* (Kluwer Hague, 2002) vol 2, 947, 954.

[79] *Van Oosterwijck v Belgium* Series A No 40, (1981) 3 EHRR 557 § 34; and T Zwart *The Admissibility of Human Rights Petitions. The Case Law of the European Commission of Human Rights and the Human Rights* Committee (Martinus Nijhoff Dordrecht, 1994) 187.

the 'victim' requirement would therefore be futile, since the shareholder will at any rate be unable to satisfy the local remedies requirement. The 'unreasonableness' of requiring the fulfilment of the Art 35(1) condition justifies, as the Court sees it, a rejection of identification for Art 34 purposes.

It would also, in the Court's opinion, be 'unreasonable' to demand of the company that it satisfy the local remedies requirement in lieu of the shareholder because this would clearly be an anomaly: a shareholder would seek identification in Strasbourg mainly if the company is unwilling or unable to initiate proceedings. A doctrine of identification under Art 34 would consequently endorse an arrangement that effectively empowers shareholders to demand their companies to take domestic procedural steps for matters in which they cannot act or with which they disagree. The Court is not inclined to welcome this scenario.

(ii) Sufficiently Coherent?

The Court's second justification for preserving the corporate veil fails to correspond entirely to what appears to be the Court's general application of the local remedies requirement. Admittedly, how the local remedies requirement in Art 35(1) should be understood in the context of shareholder identification claims remains partially a matter of guesswork. These claims are, as we know, generally dismissed (or, exceptionally, admitted) following an assessment of the 'victim' requirement, and not (also) the local remedies rule (exceptions are soon introduced), so the Court has not yet rendered authoritatively the meaning of the requirement in the present context. The immediate sense of doctrinal uncertainty notwithstanding, one could, with some confidence, predict how the Court would interpret Art 35(1) with regard to shareholders' 'veil-piercing' claims.

The Court has said that the local remedies requirement is to be applied with 'some degree of flexibility and without excessive formalism'.[80] In reviewing whether the rule has been observed it is essential, says the Court, to have regard to the particular circumstances of each individual case.[81] The local remedies rule demands of the 'victim' that he utilize only those remedies that are likely to be adequate and effective.[82] An applicant's obligation to have utilised national

[80] *Cardot v France* Series A No 200, (1991) 13 EHRR 853 § 34.

[81] *Van Oosterwijck* (n 79) § 35.

[82] These exact terms are rarely applied explicitly by the Court and the Commission. In the words of the Commission in one of its first encounters with the condition: '. . . the rules governing the exhaustion of the local remedies, as they are generally recognized today, in principle require that recourse should be had to all legal remedies available under the local law which are in principle capable of providing an effective and sufficient means of redressing the wrongs for which, on the international plane, the Respondent State is alleged to be responsible'; see *Schouw Nielsen v Denmark* Application 343/57, (1958–9) 2 Yearbook 412, 440. In *Deweer v Belgium* Series A No 35, (1980) 2

means of redress can be waived if in the circumstances of the case they will be ineffective or inadequate.[83] Shareholder claims for identification with a company often arise from disputes in which no adequate or effective remedy can exist. In this respect, it would make sense if the local remedies requirement is dispensed with in the corporate context.[84]

Significantly, the Commission in two instances has expressed its views on the matter, and they have not been subsequently contested at the Court. The Commission has affirmed that a matter is not adequate and effective and, hence, not in need of being exhausted, when it is only available to the company and not to the applicant shareholder. When it decided on the admissibility of the *Agrotexim* complaint, the Commission thus remarked, in assessing whether the local remedies requirement had been fulfilled, that:

> according to the generally recognised rules of international law, it should not take into consideration measures which were not open to the applicants themselves... Only those remedies which are capable of remedying the criticised state of affairs directly, and not merely indirectly, are to be considered as effective.[85]

As there was little prospect that the applicant shareholders would have been able to initiate proceedings on behalf of the company under Greek law and pursue the remedies on behalf of the 'person directly affected by the litigious measures', the applicants had satisfied the local remedies requirement.[86]

In *GJ v Luxembourg*, the applicant shareholder had not taken any legal action for the matter complained of. He had only written a letter to the Commercial Court (as liquidator) in which he complained of the 'conduct of the insolvency proceedings and particularly the time it had taken to conclude the proceedings'. The respondent government maintained that the applicant had failed to exhaust domestic remedies, as there was a possibility under local law to take litigious action to seek to replace the Commercial Court as liquidator. Not subsequently contested by the Court, the Commission observed the following:

> As regards the applicant's alleged prolonged silence the Commission agrees that this is not a matter which in the present case falls to be examined under Article 26... As regards the exhaustion of domestic remedies the Commission recalls that only

EHRR 439 § 29 the Court spoke of 'available and sufficient' remedies. But it is undoubtedly the essence of the rule in Art 35(1), eg, van Dijk and van Hoof (n 5) 136. On adequacy and effectiveness, see in particular AA Cançado Trindade *The Application of the Rule of Exhaustion of Local Remedies in International Law. Its Rationale in the International Protection of Human Rights* (Cambridge University Press Cambridge, 1983) 69–80.

[83] van Dijk and van Hoof (n 5) 136.

[84] Schermers (n 78) 955 points at the 'unfairness' of an opposite solution; he appears to believe that it does not run counter to present interpretative practice.

[85] *Agrotexim* (admissibility decision) (n 55) 158. The Commission cited as authority *Baraona v Portugal* Application 10092/82, (1984) 40 DR 118, 136, which again quotes *Deweer* (n 82) § 29(5) (neither case considers our form of identification directly).

[86] *Agrotexim* (n 55) 158.

remedies which are likely to provide redress for an applicant's complaints need to be taken into account. In particular the existence of such remedies must be sufficiently certain not only in theory but also in practice, failing which they will lack the requisite accessibility and effectiveness.[87]

The Commission's approach is consistent with the Court's handling of the local remedies requirement in cases of 'indirect victimhood', which, as was observed by way of introduction in this chapter, clearly resembles the shareholder identification claims. In such cases, the Court does not adhere to the assumption it advances in the *Agrotexim* case, that the applicant always need satisfy the local remedies rule. Instead, it requires the 'indirect victim' to fulfil the requirement only when the direct victim has failed to do so. If the direct victim has, conversely, fulfilled the criterion, the Court will identify the 'indirect victim' with the direct victim so that the former pass the local remedies criterion accessorily.[88] If the Court heeds consistency in its interpretation of Art 35(1), a shareholder's claim for identification with the company will satisfy the local remedies rule either if the shareholder personally, or the company, has indeed unsuccessfully used all adequate and effective remedies in the national legal system.

The Commission's approach fits, moreover, the rationale of the local remedies rule. A general rule of international law and an expression of the subsidiary nature of the ECHR, the Convention's local remedies requirement derives from two fundamental axioms: the sovereignty of the respondent State and the effective protection of the applicant's human rights.[89] Sovereignty is important, so it is highly relevant to ask whether the essence of the dispute has, objectively speaking, been sufficiently examined by domestic authorities rather than who, among various constituents having stakes in the dispute, has is fact sought legal redress.[90] The Court's person-focused (or subjective) conception on the local remedies rule implied in the *Agrotexim* case does not seem to take this into account.

The approach of the Commission in the *Agrotexim* and *GJ* cases is finally in line with prevailing understanding of the local remedies rule in international law.[91]

[87] App 21156/93 *GJ v Luxembourg* (1996) § 2(8). See also similar views implicitly adhered to, undisputed, by the Commission in *Matos e Silva, Lda and Others* (admissibility decision) (n 75) § 2(5); and *Pine Valley Developments Ltd and Others v Ireland* Application 12742/87, (1989) 61 DR 206 'The Law' § 12.

[88] This was at least the Commission's approach, see *X v Germany* Application 4185/69, (1970) 35 CD 140 (identification between husband and wife); and L Mikaelsen *European Protection of Human Rights: the Practice and Procedure of the European Commission of Human Rights on the Admissibility of Applications from Individuals and States* (Sijthoff & Nordhoff Alphen aan den Rijn, 1980) 134.

[89] Cançado Trindade (n 82) 14–18 and 46–56; and AM Aronovitz 'Notes on the Current Status of the Rule of Exhaustion of Local Remedies in the European Convention on Human Rights' (1995) 25 Israel Ybk HR 73, 76–77.

[90] This aspect can only be inferred from the case law, eg, *Airey v Ireland* Series A No 32, (1980) 2 EHRR 305 § 19(b) (2).

[91] CF Amerasinghe *Local Remedies in International Law* (Grotius Cambridge, 1990) 179–81 with further references. CF Amerasinghe *Local Remedies in International Law* (2nd edn Cambridge University Press Cambridge, 2004) 196–97 is less detailed with regard to this matter.

Based on the above considerations, it is to be assumed that the Court would interpret the local remedies requirement much in the way of the Commission. This would suggest that the 'unreasonableness' referred to as a justificatory factor in the *Agrotexim* case need not pertain. The Court's justification for non-identification fits only those instances in which the company has not taken domestic legal action against the contested measure. The strength of the second argument for preserving the corporate veil with regard to the 'victim' requirement loses some of its force and there is consequently room for supporting the Court's reasoning with additional arguments that renders its non-identification approach sensible in spite of some shortcomings (see section 3).

(c) The Comparative Legal Context

The Court in the *Agrotexim* case finally reached its conclusion by consulting comparable legal sources.[92] An approach to identification claims such as that laid down in the judgment's § 66 was, said the Court, 'in . . . line' with the practice of 'Supreme Courts of certain member States of the Council of Europe'. It added that the 'principle has also been confirmed with regard to the diplomatic protection of companies', and referred specifically to the solution adopted by the ICJ in the *Barcelona Traction* case.[93] The two arguments are now considered separately.

(i) **Constitutional Solutions**

The Court does not reveal which of Europe's constitutional courts have adopted, as a principle, a doctrine of upholding the corporate veil in instances of 'reverse piercing'. Neither does it explain whether this constitutional practice has been developed in the context of domestic interpretation of the Convention, or in light of comparable constitutional rights. Yet it must be assumed that the Court has specific jurisdictional solutions in mind and it can be safely assumed that its observation is correct in the sense that respect for separate corporate personality is a feature of municipal law which also enjoys constitutional reverence in certain jurisdictions. The *Bundesverfassungsgericht*, for instance, applies it when it interprets the 'victim' requirement set out in Art 93 of the German *Grundgesetz*.[94]

A Court whose task it is to observe an international treaty for the protection of human rights might have been inclined to hesitate twice before making

[92] On the Court's use of comparative law arguments, see, eg, R Bernhardt 'Comparative Law in the Interpretation and Application of the European Convention on Human Rights' in S Busuttil (ed) *Mainly Human Rights. Studies in Honour of JJ Cremona* (Fondation Internationale Malte Valletta, 1999) 33.

[93] *Agrotexim* (n 46) § 66.

[94] A Vosskuhle 'Artikel 93' in H Dreier (ed) *Grundgesetz. Kommentar* (Mohr Siebeck Tübingen, 2000) 1077, 1087 with references to case law.

renvoi-like manoeuvres in respect of domestic legal solutions.[95] But the Court does rely on domestic solutions when appropriate, including when it interprets autonomous concepts. The force of the Court's reference to municipal law is especially strong if the domestic arrangement reflects a European consensus on the issue under consideration.[96] The Court's *Agrotexim* reference does not help us ascertain the extent to which the solutions adopted in 'certain' jurisdictions do convey a European consensus on the level of constitutional law, although the prevalence of separate corporate personality in municipal law is a very strong indication that consensus in this field actually does exist.

(ii) The *Barcelona Traction* Citation

The *Agrotexim* approach, so the Court admits, corresponds with the principle of non-identification developed in the international legal context and confirmed by the ICJ in the *Barcelona Traction* judgment. The *Barcelona Traction* majority found that only in exceptional circumstances would it consent to look beyond the corporate person and regard the nationality of its shareholders.[97] The Strasbourg Court evidently sees the judgment as a comparative legal factor with some relevance for ECHR purposes.

The Court is not unknown to take international legal solutions into account.[98] In *Al-Adsani v UK*, the Court sitting as a Grand Chamber unanimously confirmed, in an unrelated situation, what has long been its practice, notably that:

> the Convention has to be interpreted in the light of the rules set out in the Vienna Convention on the Law of Treaties . . . and that Article 31 § 3 (c) of that treaty indicates that account is to be taken of 'any relevant rules of international law applicable to relations between the parties'. The Convention . . . cannot be interpreted in a vacuum. The Court must be mindful of the Convention's special character as a human rights

[95] PG Carozza 'Uses and Misuses of Comparative Law in International Human Rights: Some Reflections on the Jurisprudence of the European Court of Human Rights' (1998) 73 Notre Dame L Rev 1217, 1218. The ICJ majority's approach was referred to as a form of 'renvoi' in the Separate Opinion of Judge Gros, see *Barcelona Traction* (n 30) 272 (§§ 9–10); the terminology was criticized in the Dissenting Opinion of Judge Riphagen, ibid 338 (§ 7).

[96] WJ Ganshof van der Meersch 'Reliance, in the Case Law of the European Court of Human Rights, on the Domestic Law of States' (1980) 1 HRLJ 13; L Helfer 'Consensus, Coherence and the European Convention on Human Rights' (1993) 26 Cornell Intl L J 133, 134; and JG Merrills *The Development of International Law by the European Court of Human Rights* (Manchester University Press Manchester, 1993) 78–81.

[97] *Barcelona Traction* (n 30) §§ 56–58 and § 66. The two exceptions acknowledged as permissible by the court were demise of the corporate structure or, alternatively, the company's home State's inability to assert protection. Finally, protection of interests may be asserted by way of diplomatic protection regardless of nationality if the case involves grave human rights violations amounting to *jus cogens*, thus enabling an obligation *erga omnes* under international law, see § 91.

[98] F Matscher 'Methods of Interpretation of the Convention' in R St John Macdonald F Matscher and H Petzold (eds) *The European System for the Protection of Human Rights* (Martinus Nijhoff Dordrecht 1993) 63, 74–75.

treaty, and it must also take the relevant rules of international law into account . . . The Court should so far as possible be interpreted in harmony with other rules of international law of which it forms part.[99]

The Court is clearly not bound by rules or principles confirmed by another international court in a different, albeit partly related, part of international law. The *Barcelona Traction* judgment was, besides, cited only; the Court did not go into details with regard to the degree of influence it exerted on its reasoning. The *Barcelona Traction* judgment is an old decision and there are obvious dissimilarities between an ECHR Art 34 investigation and the determination of national affiliation in the context of diplomatic protection. The *Barcelona Traction* decision was highly contested at the time, both at the ICJ and by international scholars. The bone of contention in that judgment, also raised in the *Agrotexim* case, was precisely whether equity considerations or formal legal concepts should be favoured with regard to shareholders' protection under international law.[100] International legal developments subsequent to the holding have gone far to soften the 'rigidity' of the ICJ majority's view in favour of a more holistic approach in which the underlying need for shareholder protection is given increased attention.[101] The importance of the Court's citation of *Barcelona Traction*'s preservation of the corporate veil should not, therefore, be overestimated.

3 The *Agrotexim* Approach in Context

The critique that has now been given of the three groups of justifications presented in the *Agrotexim* case does not mean that the Court's preservation of the distinctiveness of corporate personality is flawed. But the Court's generally minimalist reasoning suggests that the rendered explanations must be viewed in their proper context in order to make perfect doctrinal sense. The purpose of this section is to suggest a structural support for the Court's approach in the *Agrotexim* case.

As a point of departure for our examination, it must be assumed that the Court has decided to transport the construct of separate corporate personality

[99] *Al-Adsani v UK* Reports 2001-XI (2002) 34 EHRR 11 § 55 (further on the judgment, see M Emberland 'Case Comment: McElhinney v Ireland, Fogarty v United Kingdom, Al-Adsani v United Kingdom' (2002) 96 AJIL 699). This method is naturally not controversial; see further F Matscher 'Vertragsauslegung durch Vertragsrechtsvergleichung in der Judikatur internationaler Gerichte, vornemlich vor den Organen der EMRK' in R Bernhardt and others (eds) *Völkerrecht als Rechtsordnung, Internationale Gerichtbarkeit, Menschenrechte Festschrift für Hermann Mosler* (Springer Berlin, 1983) 545.

[100] The majority in *Barcelona Traction* (n 30) 48 (§§92–93), dismissed an approach to the company veil influenced by equity considerations, a viewpoint vehemently favoured by some dissenting judges.

[101] Lillich (n 43) referred to the judgment's 'rigidity'. The currency of *Barcelona Traction* in contemporary international law is considered, eg, in R Jennings and A Watts *Oppenheim's International Law* (9th edn Longman London, 1992) vol 1, 517–22 and vol 2, 859–64.

to the Convention plane because it believes that it is the most sensible solution. The Court does not, it is true, have to abide by domestic legal solutions when interpreting Art 34. But it is entitled to use common sense. It is submitted here that at least two sets of considerations augment the rationality of the Court's principled adherence to the corporate veil. One set of arguments refers to a concern for the nature and purpose of the company form—see (a); the other to the structure of the system for Convention protection—see (b).

(a) Concern for the Company's Fundamental Attractiveness

In instances of 'reverse piercing' of the corporate veil—the instances under consideration here—the impenetrability of the veil is in the main justified by a symmetry argument. It basically says that since the shareholder's liability for the company's debts and obligations is limited to the shareholder investment, the opportunity of the shareholder to influence the company's affairs must be equally limited. In the *Barcelona Traction* case, the ICJ majority reiterated the municipal legal axiom that 'the shareholders' rights in relation to the company . . . remain limited, this being . . . a corollary to the limited nature of their liability',[102] and that this limited influence follows inevitably from this form of investment.[103]

As regards the underlying rationale of symmetry, the ICJ explained that:

> in forming a company, its promoters are guided by all various factors involved, the advantages and disadvantages of which they take into account. So equally does a shareholder, whether he is an original subscriber to the capital or a subsequent purchaser of the company's shares from another shareholder. He may be seeking safety of investment, high dividends or capital appreciation—or a combination of two or more of these. Whichever it is, it does not alter the legal status of the corporate entity or affect the rights of the shareholder. In any event, he is bound to take account of the risk of reduced dividends, capital depreciation or even loss, resulting form ordinary commercial hazard or from prejudice caused to the company by illegal treatment of some kind.[104]

Limited influence in a company is, in other words, integral to the very nature of shareholder investment. The preservation of the corporate veil in face of shareholders' claims for identification is founded essentially on the conception of the limited liability company: its great appeal as a vehicle for business undertakings derives precisely from its separateness from its owners. Absent this quality, the company's attractiveness would be seriously impaired.

To sustain the popularity of shareholding, regardless of its limited influence over the company's affairs, requires, however, that the corporate organs assume the role as agents for the shareholder's interests, or, in the event of disagreement

[102] *Barcelona Traction* (n 30) 35 (§ 42). [103] ibid 50 (§ 99). [104] ibid 35 (§ 43).

between those organs and the shareholders, that internal disagreement can be sought resolved internally. The corporate veil builds on the premise that the company normally caters for the shareholder's interests and, if it does not do so, the shareholder may, to a certain extent, make use of the decision-making and dispute-settlement procedures set up by the company's constitution. As stated by Sir Gerald Fitzmaurice—who later became the British judge at the European Court of Human Rights—in his separate opinion in *Barcelona Traction*:

> The true rationale . . . of denying to the shareholder the possibility of action in respect of infringements of company rights is that, normally, he does not need this.[105]

The ICJ majority in the *Barcelona Traction* judgment more elaborately stated:

> It is a basic characteristic of the corporate structure that the company alone, through its directors or management acting in its name, can take action in respect of matters that are of a corporate character. The underlying justification for this is that, in seeking to serve its own best interests, the company will serve the shareholders too. Ordinarily, no individual shareholder can take legal steps, either in the name of the company or in his own name. If the shareholders disagree with the decisions taken on behalf of the company they may, in accordance with its articles or the relevant provisions of law, change them or replace its officers, or take such actions as is provided by law. Thus to protect the company against abuse by its management or the majority of shareholders, several municipal legal systems have vested in shareholders (sometimes a particular number is specified) the right to bring an action for the defence of the company, and conferred upon the minority of shareholders certain rights to guard against decisions affecting the rights of the company vis-à-vis its management or controlling shareholders. Nonetheless the shareholders' rights in relation to the company and its assets remain limited, this being, moreover, a corollary of the limited nature of their liability.[106]

The Court in Strasbourg has not invoked the same arguments to justify its upholding of the corporate veil. But it has shown awareness of the company's constitutional arrangement with regard to representation of its affairs. In *Olczak v Poland*, the Court expressly observed that '[w]henever a shareholder's interests are harmed by a measure directed at the company, *it is up to the latter to take appropriate action*'.[107] In recognizing the corporate allocation of representation, the Court indirectly acknowledges the underlying assumption of limited shareholder influence, and thereby accepts the significance of those factors that make the company an attractive instrument for business investment. The Court is concerned with securing fertile ground for business enterprise by upholding the characteristic features of the limited liability company. This is revealed in

[105] *Barcelona Traction* (n 30) Separate Opinion of Judge Fitzmaurice, 64 (§§ 10–11).

[106] *Barcelona Traction* (n 30) 35 (§ 42).

[107] *Olczak* (n 23) § 59 (emphasis added); and (implicitly) *Agrotexim* (n 46) § 65(1) and (2).

the statement in the *Agrotexim* case that an identification approach 'would create a source of uncertainty in commercial transactions and relations'.[108]

This is in accordance with the Convention mandate. Private enterprise represents a component of the Convention's value system and corporate entities are recognized by implication in the Convention text. The drafters intended companies to enjoy some degree of ECHR protection. It would be a curious paradox if the Court did not heed, at least in principle, something as intrinsic to the company as its separate legal personality. It is natural to see the *Agrotexim* principle therefore in extension of this circumstance.

(b) *Structural Aspects of Convention Protection*

The principle established in the *Agrotexim* case is also compatible with other structural features of the Convention system that are not as intimately connected with the Court's concern for the corporate form. They add to the coherence of adopting non-identification as a rule and starting point in face of shareholders' claims for 'victim' status.

(i) Subsidiarity

The Convention system is of a subsidiary nature; the principle of subsidiarity generally informs the Court. An essential tenet of the principle of subsidiarity is that the Convention should assume responsibility for functions, and thereby superimpose legal solutions domestically, only insofar as the national legal system is unable to do so.[109] As the Court has observed with regard to its subsidiary function in another context, it will not, when it interprets the Convention, 'disregard those legal and factual features which characterise the life of the society in the [respondent] State',[110] provided, it should be added, that they do not contravene the Convention.

The Court has not invoked the principle of subsidiarity in support of its decision to uphold the corporate veil. But as we have seen, it does refer to the municipal legal arrangement of separate corporate personality as a given fact of consequence for Convention interpretation. It must assume that the corporate veil is an artefact which works well and is, in principle, in no need of reform. In the *Agrotexim* case, for instance, the Court:

> assumed that in the majority of national legal systems shareholders do not normally have the right to bring an action for damages in respect of an act or omission that is prejudicial to 'their' company.[111]

[108] *Agrotexim* (n 46) § 59(3).

[109] H Petzold 'The Convention and the Principle of Subsidiarity' in R St John Macdonald F Matscher and H Petzold (eds) *The European System for the Protection of Human Rights* (Martinus Nijhoff Dordrecht, 1993) 41, 41.

[110] *Case relating to certain aspects of the laws on the use of languages in education in Belgium (Belgian Linguistics Case) (Merits)* Series A No 6, (1979) 1 EHRR 252 § 10.

[111] *Agrotexim* (n 46) § 65(3) (emphasis added).

It based its conclusion on the fact that the liquidators, as those organs appointed to represent the company, were still able to pursue claims on the company's behalf,[112] thus intimating that there was no need to interfere with a system that worked. The Court, it can be conjectured, accepted the underlying motivation for subsidiarity. An ECHR disregard of the concept of separate corporate personality would not rhyme well with the subsidiary character of the Court's supervision.

(ii) Domestic Implementation

The Court's reverence of municipal legal functions can also be seen in light of the Convention's domestic implementation function.[113] The Court's refusal to interfere with the construct of separate corporate personality makes sense in that its views on the matter are prone to affect that arrangement on the domestic plane. As we know, the respondent State is expected to execute diligently the Court's judgments, and the views of the Court also serve as guidelines for Council of Europe member States on a general basis, regardless of participation in the relevant dispute. An adoption by the Court of an identification approach as that developed by the Commission in its report *Agrotexim* on would not directly require the Greek, or any other ECHR State, to alter its legal system with regard to corporate personality and representation. But it would signal that a domestic softening up of the corporate veil was appropriate in light of the Convention.

That the domestic implementation function may influence the Court's construction of the corporate veil for ECHR purposes is revealed in the *Agrotexim* judgment's handling of the shareholders' allegation that they had been the victims of a violation of Arts 6(1) and 13 (a 'victimhood' discussion undertaken separately from the claim under Protocol 1 Art 1). The Court remarked that neither provision could be interpreted in an identification mode because that would

> imply that *under the national law of the Contracting States* shareholders in a limited company should have the right to bring an action seeking an injunction or damages in respect of an act or omission that is prejudicial to 'their' company.[114]

The Court thus accepted, in its rationale for non-identification, the domestic legal bearing of its own actions. Obviously, the Court is required to take into account the effects its renditions will have in the Council of Europe jurisdictions, including its handling of 'veil-piercing' complaints.

(iii) Concern for National Interests

An interpretation that would run the risk of affecting generally well-functioning domestic legal arrangements is also problematic inasmuch as protection and

[112] ibid § 70.

[113] AZ Drzemczewski *European Human Rights Convention in Domestic Law: A Comparative Study* (Clarendon Press Oxford, 1983) remains the authoritative study of this field.

[114] *Agrotexim* (n 46) § 73(2) (emphasis added).

promotion of democratic values are inherent to the Convention's overall purpose (see chapter 2 for this). It would not be unreasonable to assume that a democracy argument supports the preservation of a municipal legal arrangement which has been introduced by the legislatures of the Convention's member States. Disregarding it would similarly be potentially at odds with the corporate veil's democratic basis.

The interests of the nation-state and sovereign authority permeate the Convention just as much as the interests of the individual person that has suffered an ECHR violation. The economic interests of the respondent State are a legitimate concern which is ingrained in the Convention text and structure and the Court's mode of reasoning. The significance of public and national concerns for Convention interpretation will be dealt with in depth in chapter 5. Suffice it here to observe that the *Agrotexim* approach fits in with the Convention's built-in awareness of the respondent party's interest in sustaining a thriving national economy. To undercut, on the Convention plane, the attractiveness of an important economic instrument could also, ultimately, affect negatively the State's economy. A preparedness to favour interests of a general nature—in this case the safeguarding of fertile ground for corporate business enterprise which is important for the general public—over the economic exigencies of individual shareholders is a natural consequence of the Court's responsibility to contemplate, in a balanced assessment, not only the interests of the applicant party, but also those of the respondent government and society as a whole. As we saw in chapter 2, the Court is entitled to take such considerations into account.

By upholding, at least in principle, the corporate veil in the context of Art 34, the Court safeguards and facilitates structural support for a significant vehicle for economic progress in the ECHR member States. The principle laid down in the *Agrotexim* case favours general exigencies over individual needs; the interests of the respondent State prevail over the applicants' claim to protect them against financial prejudice. In part, the Court's approach is the result of an assessment of the competing interests presented before it in that particular dispute. The structural aspects considered in this section, however, also demonstrate the Court's ability take into account issues that do not exclusively concern the matters at stake in the dispute. The Court's dismissal of shareholders' identification claims favours objective criteria such as the need to uphold a well-functioning, and indeed, profitable and democratically legitimate municipal legal arrangement of national economic significance. The adoption of the corporate veil at the level of Art 34 is therefore also a good illustration of the objective function of the Convention system for human rights protection, introduced in chapter 2.

C. Disregard for the Corporate Veil in Exceptional Circumstances

The Court in the *Agrotexim* case dismissed the comprehensive 'veil-piercing' approach taken in the Commission's report, yet did not wholly rule out that shareholders are entitled to be protected against measures formally taken against their company. It conceded that identification was permitted in 'exceptional circumstances'.[115] The Court thereby effectively endorsed significant portions of an extant jurisprudence in which shareholders had been found sufficiently affected by interferences with the company's rights to warrant their identification with the corporate entity. Viewed in this context, the *Agrotexim* case suggests that identification be permitted in two types of instances, each with a distinct doctrinal history. They are introduced and an explanation sought in sections 1 and 2 respectively.

1 The 'Impossibility' Exception

(a) 'Impossibility' as Ground for Admissibility

In the *Agrotexim* case, the Court acknowledged that the

> piercing of the 'corporate veil'... will be justified... where it is clearly established that it is impossible for the company to apply to the Convention institutions through the organs set up under its articles of incorporation or—in the event of liquidation—through its liquidators.[116]

In doing so, the Court confirmed one form of legitimate identification which had been applied for a long time in Commission practice.[117]

The criteria for identification are exacting and strictly applied. In the *Agrotexim* case the Court asserts that it must be impossible for the company as such to initiate Strasbourg proceedings and that this 'impossibility' must be 'clearly established'. The Court also maintains, presumably as a guiding norm, that 'impossibility' most easily will occur when the applicant company has ceased to be a legal personality altogether.[118]

This form of identification is not easily attainable for an applicant shareholder. In the *Agrotexim* case, the applicants complained of measures affecting a company under liquidation where one of the two liquidators, who were required to act in concert, represented authorities of the respondent party of

[115] *Agrotexim* (n 46) § 66.

[116] ibid.

[117] *Yarrow PLC and Others v UK* Application 9266/81, (1983) 30 DR 155, 184; and *Company S-S IAB and B T* (n 35) 138.

[118] *Agrotexim* (n 46) § 68 'had not ceased to exist as a legal person'.

the Strasbourg case. From a public/private distinction viewpoint, it is not entirely unlikely—or so the Commission at least surmised in its admissibility decision—that the State-appointed liquidator would be disinclined to take action against the municipal authorities of Athens, another (albeit local) entity of the Greek state.[119] The Court, however, emphasized that it had been at least theoretically 'possible' for Fix, via its liquidators, to act against the city of Athens had it so wanted. Absent such procedural steps taken, the 'impossibility' requirement was not fulfilled and the shareholders' Strasbourg intervention was deemed inadmissible.[120]

'Impossibility' does not always equal corporate demise. The company may be barred from filing a Strasbourg complaint because the nature of the complaint makes corporate action 'impossible'. Typically, if the shareholder's complaint relates to infringements perpetrated by the corporate organs themselves, it is fair to say that those same organs cannot sensibly initiate Strasbourg proceedings regarding the matter. In *GJ v Luxembourg*, for instance, the applicant shareholder submitted an application of an Art 6(1) violation with regard to the manner in which the company's liquidation proceedings had been carried out. The Court agreed with the respondent government that the contested proceedings 'concerned . . . the limited liability company' and not the shareholder personally,[121] But it accepted 'victim' status for Mr GJ nonetheless because:

> the complaint brought before the Court relates to the activities of the liquidators, ie the official receiver and the Commercial Court. In these circumstances the Court considers that it was not possible for the company, as a legal personality, at the time, to bring the case before the former Commission.[122]

This approach—focusing on circumstances in a given case that suggest that the corporate person itself be effectively unable to pursue the claim—has been taken by the Court also after the *GJ v Luxembourg* case. *Camberrow MM5 AD v Bulgaria* from 2004, for instance, concerned a claim filed by a corporate applicant, in which it was maintained that the Bulgarian National Bank's decision to revoke the licence of a bank in which the applicant held 90 per cent of the shares violated Art 6 of the Convention. The Court reiterated its *Agrotexim* approach, yet noted that

> in the present case [the bank] was first managed and represented by special administrators appointed by [the Bulgarian National Bank] and then, when it was declared bankrupt, by trustees in bankruptcy appointed by the court, while the application before the Court relates precisely to the complex of events leading to the appointment of the special administrators and the trustees and the action of the trustees. In these circumstances, the Court considers that because of the conflict of interests between

[119] *Agrotexim* (admissibility decision) (n 55) § ii)(10).
[120] *Agrotexim* (n 46) §§ 68–72.
[121] *GJ* (n 49) § 23.
[122] ibid § 24 first sentence.

[the bank] and its special administrators and trustees it was not possible for the bank itself to bring the case before the Court.[123]

(b) The 'Impossibility' Exception's Rationale

(i) No Risk of Competing Claims

What is the rationale of the 'impossibility' exception? In the *Agrotexim* judgment the Court provides, inversely, one important justification for it. The risk of creating, in view of the competing interests of various corporate constituents, 'difficulties in determining who is entitled to apply to the Strasbourg institutions', that was instrumental for establishing a principle of non-identification,[124] is reduced when the corporate entity cannot in fact initiate Strasbourg proceedings in the case at hand. It was assumed above that the Court's concern for competing claims reflects fundamental aspects of the nature and purpose of the company as an investment instrument. When the company entity and its internal processes for handling disputes and decision-making fail to function as intended, some of the underlying purpose of paying respect to the separateness of corporate personality is eroded. This argument is repeatedly advanced in municipal corporate theory,[125] and it has also found its way into international legal discourse, as the *Barcelona Traction* judgment demonstrates,[126] so it is not unthinkable that it might help explain the Court's approach too.

But can the inverse application of one reason for non-identification wholly explain the Court's willingness to admit shareholder claims when the company is no longer able to pursue its own interests? The fear of an unreasonable application of the local remedies requirement, which also justified the Court's rejection of 'victim' status for shareholders, remains, for what it is worth, valid in a situation of corporate demise and perhaps even more so since it would be even more 'unreasonable' to expect a shareholder to have a malfunctioning company to exhaust local remedies on his or her behalf.

The logic of corporate legal personality retains, besides, validity when the company has no possibility to go to the Court with its claims. Even if the corporate entity no longer works as envisaged, the shareholder may still claim to be protected under the Convention for matters that concern the rights or obligations of the corporate entity, not his or her own legal positions under municipal law. Does not the construct of the limited liability company as a general fact, esteemed by the Court as we have seen, demand respect even in the event of a company failing to work properly? Must not the shareholder accept the risk of corporate involvement also in situations of corporate demise?

[123] *Camberrow MM5 AD v Bulgaria* decision 1 April 2004.

[124] *Agrotexim* (n 46) § 65(2).

[125] Dignam and Allen (n 6) 177.

[126] *Barcelona Traction* (n 30) 41 (§ 66) the 'legal demise' exception; see also Separate Opinion of Judge Fitzmaurice, ibid 70 (§ 11(4)).

(ii) The Court Ascertains Effective Protection of Central Convention Values

As is the case with the rationale for preserving the corporate veil, the Court's motivation for accepting an 'impossibility' exception is not known to us in its entirety, though one might surmise that wider considerations may, on occasion, outweigh reasons for upholding separate corporate personality. The existence of such considerations clarifies the consistency of the Court's 'impossibility' exception.

The Court is especially inclined to invoke the 'impossibility' requirement if by so doing it secures effective protection of values that are central to the Convention. In *GJ v Luxembourg*, where the Court did conclude that 'impossibility' existed, the 'activities of the liquidators' caused the Court to admit the complaint. The nature of the complaint made adherence to the corporate veil artificial. The Court overlooked a formality because its application would be unreasonable. A similar factor was present in the *Camberrow* case.

This is reminiscent of the thrust of the principle of effectiveness (stated several times already in this book), in which formal constructs shall not impede effective Convention protection. In the *GJ* case, the Convention interest effectively being protected by admitting the claim was the right to have legal proceedings concluded within a 'reasonable time',[127] a central aspect of the rule of law principle. Had the shareholder's claim been rejected, the matter would not have been subject to Convention scrutiny since the shareholder was the only person in a position to defend the principle of the rule of law. Undoubtedly, the Court is interested in ensuring effective observance of this principle, as an underlying Convention value, and it makes sense that it can sometimes outweigh the otherwise legitimate need to uphold the formality of the corporate veil on the ECHR level.

Further grounds for this inference can be found in another recent case in which the Court discussed the reach of the *Agrotexim* case. In *Credit and Industrial Bank v the Czech Republic*, the Court was called to assess an Art 6(1) complaint submitted by the applicant bank (via its ordinarily authorized representatives, who acted on behalf of the bank's majority shareholder). The applicant alleged that its rights had been violated in that it had had no remedy against the administrative decision concerning the imposition of compulsory administration on the bank, and the subsequent decisions by various administrative and judicial organs.[128] The Czech government submitted before the Court that the case failed to satisfy the 'victim' requirement in Art 34 since the bank, which was in the process of liquidation, could only be

[127] *GJ* (n 49) § 36.

[128] *Credit and Industrial Bank v Czech Republic* 2003 Reports 2003-XI § 3.

represented in Strasbourg proceedings by its liquidators and not, as was the case in the complaint, its formerly authorized representatives.[129]

While the judgment does not directly concern a shareholder claim for identification with a company, the Court saw sufficient similarities in the case to the facts of the *Agrotexim* case to pause at length at the *Agrotexim* principle, and to assess its impact on the dispute under consideration. Assessing the 'victim' requirement, the Court endorsed the effectiveness principle as a relevant means for interpreting Art 34.[130] It conceded that it was the compulsory administrator who had had the capacity to represent the company at the time of the lodging of the Strasbourg application, but it raised the question 'whether in the circumstances [he] alone was authorised to lodge an application ... on behalf of the bank' and distinguished the present case from *Agrotexim*, where, it observed, the corporate veil had been upheld because the *Agrotexim* liquidators 'had taken all the measures which they considered to be in the interests of the insolvent company's assets'.[131]

In contrast, the present application was admitted because it

> relates not to an alleged interference with the property rights of the bank which the compulsory administrator had been appointed to protect and manage and in respect of which the administrator could apply on the bank's behalf to the Convention institutions. On the contrary, the complaint made relates to the very fact that a compulsory administrator was appointed ... without a proper opportunity being granted to the bank which was the subject of the administration order to oppose it. Where, as in the present case, the essence of the complaint is the denial of effective access to court to oppose or appeal against the appointment of a compulsory administrator, to hold that the administrator alone was authorised to represent the bank ... would be to render the right of individual petition conferred by Article 34 theoretical and illusory.[132]

The *GJ, Camberrow and Credit and Financial Bank* cases illustrate how the 'impossibility' exception tunes in with the Court's task of effectively securing underlying Convention values. In the cases, the rule of law was the value at risk. Other values may presumably also be invoked when needed.

2 The 'Vehicle' Approach

(a) The Approach of Pine Valley v Ireland

Although other exceptions to the Court's negation of 'victim' status for shareholders were not mentioned in the *Agrotexim* judgment, the Court did not dismiss the prospect that other 'exceptional circumstances' could justify a disregard of separate corporate personality; it merely referred to impossibility

[129] ibid §§ 43 and 47. [130] ibid § 48. [131] ibid §§ 49–50. [132] ibid §§ 51–52.

'in particular'.[133] In fact, in its rebuttal of the Commission's identification approach there is nothing to suggest that the Court intended to discount one special tradition of identification that had evolved in Commission jurisprudence.[134]

This tradition was confirmed by the Court in 1991 in the case of *Pine Valley Developments Ltd and Others v Ireland*. In a situation far removed from corporate demise the Court identified the legal positions of a limited liability company (Pine Valley Developments Ltd), its sole shareholder (Healy Holding Ltd) and the latter holding company's sole shareholder (Mr Healy), although it was Pine Valley, the corporate person, that was the subject of the alleged violation.[135] The complaint concerned allegations of unjustified government control over Pine Valley's property in violation of Protocol 1 Art 1. Public authorities had failed to validate retrospectively a planning permission or, alternatively, to compensate for the reduction in value of the property which had been subject to regulation.[136] Healy Holding and Mr Healy were not directly affected since the permission was given to their company, but they owned 90 per cent of Pine Valley's capital stock and Mr Healy, through Healy Holding, personally controlled the company in question. The Court accepted all three persons as 'victims' because:

> Pine Valley and Healy Holdings were no more than vehicles through which Mr Healy proposed to implement the development for which outline planning permission had been granted. On this ground alone it would be artificial to draw distinctions between the three applicants as regards their entitlement to claim to be 'victims' of a violation.[137]

This approach is evidently different from the 'impossibility' ground for identification. The Court accepts a disregard of corporate personality for 'victim' purposes when the company whose rights have been interfered with is the vehicle for the applicant shareholders' business ventures. The 'vehicle' approach uses the applicant shareholders' effective control of the corporate entity as reason for establishing 'victim' status for the shareholder.

The *Pine Valley* approach has been applied in subsequent decisions by the Strasbourg organs' relying directly on that judgment or by their invoking arguments of a similar kind.[138] That the subsequent *Agrotexim* judgment did not affect its vitality was demonstrated in *Ankarcrona v Sweden*. Mr Ankarcrona was the sole owner of Skyddsvakt Herbert Ankarcrona AB, a limited liability company licensed to trade in military equipment. The company's application

[133] *Agrotexim* (n 46) § 66.

[134] ibid §§ 62–64. In *Pine Valley* (n 87) § 5, the Commission accepted identification by relying on *Kaplan v UK* (n 56) which again builds on *X v Austria* (n 51).

[135] *Pine Valley Developments Ltd and Others v Ireland* Series A No 222, (1992) 16 EHRR 379.

[136] ibid §§ 35–37.

[137] ibid § 42.

[138] *Eugenia Michaelidou Developments Ltd and Michael Tymvios v Turkey* judgment 31 July 2003 § 21.

for an extension of its licence to include trade in armoured vehicles was rejected by the relevant public authority. There existed no possibility to appeal against this decision. Mr Ankarcrona applied to the Court, claiming that the company was denied access to court, in breach of Art 6(1), and that his right to peaceful enjoyment of its possessions pursuant to Protocol 1 Art 1 had also been violated. The Court accepted that Mr Ankarcrona because of his status as the company's sole shareholder:

> reasonably [could] claim to be a victim within the meaning of Article 34 . . . in so far as the impugned measures taken with regard to his company are concerned.[139]

Similarly, in *GJ v Luxembourg*, the Court found that the 'vehicle' approach justified identification alongside the 'impossibility' exception.[140] The Court observed that:

> the applicant held a substantial shareholding of 90% in the company. He was in effect carrying out his business through his company and has, therefore, a direct personal interest in the subject-matter of the complaint. Therefore, the Court finds that the applicant may claim to be a victim of the alleged violation of the Convention affecting rights of the limited liability company.[141]

The Court provides a similar rationale in the *Camberrow v Bulgaria* decision, where it, in addition to observing the impossibility of the affected bank to maintain ECHR protection itself, noted that 'the applicant [ie Camberrow MM5 AD] held a substantial shareholding of 98% of the bank' and thus 'was in effect carrying out parts of its business through the bank' so that it had 'a direct personal interest in the subject-matter of the application'.[142]

(b) Explaining the 'Vehicle' Approach

Why does the fact that a shareholder 'in effect [carries] out his business through his company' justify a disregard for the corporate veil? Several reasons can be marshalled in support of this identification approach. They help to rationalize the *Pine Valley* judgment's minimalist reasoning.

(i) No Risk of Competing Claims

When shareholder and company in reality represent the same interests, there is no risk of competing claims being filed in Strasbourg. The absence of this risk

139 *Ankarcrona* (n 48) § 1(5) and (6).

140 Dignam and Allen (n 6) 185 suggests that the combination of two grounds for identification in this judgment may signal a softening of the *Agrotexim* principle, presumably because the 'vehicle' approach was added to the 'impossibility' justification. It is rather reasonable to see the judgment as one in which two different grounds happened to be present at the same time.

141 *GJ* (n 49) § 24 last sentence.

142 *Camberrow* (n 123) § 1(4) third sentence.

undermines one part of the rationale for upholding the corporate veil that was given in the *Agrotexim* judgment. In *Ankarcrona v Sweden*, the Court noted that:

[c]ontrary to what was the situation in... Agrotexim..., where the applicant companies... owned only half of the shares in the company in question, there is no risk of differences of opinion among shareholders or between shareholders and a board of directors as to the reality of infringements of the rights protected under the Convention... or concerning the most appropriate way of reacting to such infringements.[143]

Having 'regard to the absence of competing interests which could create difficulties, for example, in determining who is entitled to apply to the Court',[144] the Court decided to admit the shareholder's claim for Convention protection although indubitably the proceedings in question had concerned his company only.

(ii) Effective Protection of Shareholder Investment

The absence of competing claims is not, however, the only possible consideration on which the Court can build its 'vehicle' approach. As with the 'impossibility' exception, the Court's concern for effective protection of Convention values seems to be an additional motor for adopting an identification approach. This assertion requires a closer study of the relevant case law.

In the *Pine Valley* case, the Court allowed 'victim' status to Healy Holding and Mr Healy because ultimately, the two companies 'were no more than vehicles through which Mr Healy proposed the development for which outline planning permission had been granted'. It '*would be artificial* to draw distinctions between the three applicants' as far as the 'victim' requirement was concerned, the Court significantly noted.[145] Responding directly to the government's objections to the applicants' 'victim' status, the Court in the *Pine Valley* case observed that the

pleas all turn, directly or indirectly, on the *financial status* of Healy Holdings and Mr Healy. Whilst that status may, of course, be of importance or have effects on the domestic level, it is, in the Court's opinion, of no relevance as far as the entitlement to claim to be a victim of a violation is concerned.[146]

The Court does not explain why, exactly, the use of a company as a vehicle for shareholder business enterprise suffices to justify a disregard of separate legal personality. On the level of municipal law, dominant ownership or control of a company does not suggest or entail identification to the benefit of

[143] *Ankarcrona* (n 48) § 1(5). [144] ibid § 1(6).
[145] *Pine Valley* (n 135) § 42(1) (emphasis added). [146] ibid § 42(3).

the shareholder. Quite the opposite; the corporate veil is generally upheld by reference to the inevitable risk that follows from this form of investment. The Court's statement that the corporate veil, although important on the level of municipal law, has 'no relevance' for Art 34 purposes does not seem entirely convincing, either, especially in light of the *Agrotexim* judgment's subsequent reference to this very arrangement.

However, the Court's mentioning of 'artificiality' in upholding a distinction between shareholder and company is reminiscent of the central tenet of the effectiveness principle: as was noted in chapter 2, the Court looks behind pretence and formal categorizations and concentrates pragmatically on the 'reality' of the claim insofar as that may assist in Convention protection for the applicant person in question. As we now know, the effectiveness principle obviously has a potential for modifying the impregnability of the corporate veil if the latter represents an undesirable barrier against Convention protection.

In instances of 'impossibility' we saw that consideration for an effective protection of the rule of law supported identification. In 'vehicle' instances, it is asserted here, the Court can be seen as being mindful of the importance, in certain instances, of effective investment protection since it represents an element of private property, which is an acknowledged Convention value.

Thus, in *GJ v Luxembourg*, the Court permitted identification because Mr GJ

> held a substantial shareholding of 90 per cent in the company. He was in effect carrying out his business through the company and has, *therefore, a direct personal interest in the subject-matter of the complaint.*[147]

In the *Camberrow* case, the 'direct personal interest' was one held by an applicant company, and not, as in the *GJ* case, an individual businessman. Undoubtedly, the 'direct personal interest' referred to is of a pecuniary nature, ie, the shareholder's investment in the company. The Court in the *Pine Valley* case stressed the 'financial status' of the shareholders, and decided to ignore the formal distinction between shareholder rights and shareholder interests.[148] A share is, after all, 'an indirect claim on company assets'.[149] When the shareholder owns all shares, the indirect nature of the claim is little more than a formality.

The Court in short is willing, sometimes, to look at the underlying economic realities for the applicant shareholder and to respond doctrinally in a way which secures effective protection of the shareholder's financial situation. The concepts of private property and economic enterprise are accepted values on which the Convention builds. The rationale of the 'vehicle' approach is consistent with these values. It is also consistent with the effectiveness principle's concern for underlying realities, in this respect, the reality that shareholders

[147] *GJ* (n 49) § 24 last sentence (emphasis added).
[148] *Pine Valley* (n 135) § 42(3).
[149] *Sovtransavto Holding* (n 20) § 92(2).

sometimes suffer financial or other form of prejudice as a result of their involvement in a limited liability company and that there is sometimes a perceived need in Strasbourg to come to their assistance.

It may also be said to be in line with international legal developments with regard to investment protection. The critique of the *Barcelona Traction* judgment's approach to the corporate veil reflected widespread concern for the climate for (foreign) investment protection. Some bi- and multilateral investment treaties secure the interests of shareholders in ways that may, fundamentally, resemble the 'vehicle' approach taken by the Court at Strasbourg.[150]

The 'vehicle' approach signals that the Court does recognize the Convention value of individual economic investment and that it sometimes is considered more important than heeding the municipal legal construct of the corporate veil. But the 'vehicle' judgments rarely accept identification merely on the ground of substantial financial involvement. In the *Pine Valley* case, for instance, the Court emphasized that Mr Healy and Healy Holding also had been party to the proceedings complained of, and the *Ankarcrona* judgment accepted identification 'in light of the circumstances of the case as a whole',[151] and not only on the basis of the shareholder's financial situation. This leads to the next section.

3 A Pragmatic Overall Assessment

It is easy to over-emphasize apparent adherence to legal maxims and play down the adjudicator's careful tailoring of principled approaches to the specific circumstances of each case. It is not in the Court's nature to see itself as unconditionally bound by any particular 'principle', or exceptions to them, although it does subscribe to such devices as guiding principles.[152] The *Agrotexim* principle and its two exceptions provide good and objectively identifiable starting points for establishing the Court's response. But obviously, the Court applies them with flexibility in an overall assessment in which a variety of elements come into play. The factors that were presented in the two preceding sections, whether they are found expressly in the case law or not, are

[150] Orrego Vicuña (n 76) 357–58; C Schreuer *The ICSID Convention: A Commentary on the Convention on the Settlement of Investment Disputes between States and Nationals of Other States* (Cambridge University Press Cambridge, 2001) 285 and 322; and CN Brower and JD Brueschke *The Iran-United States Claims Tribunal* (Martinus Nijhoff Hague, 1998) 55–56. But there is no uniform approach here, as the solutions will vary in accordance with the treaty in question. See, eg, examples of treaties that extend coverage only to the 'enterprise' and not individual shareholders referred to in UNCTAD *Scope and Definition. UNCTAD Series on issues of international investment agreements* (United Nations Conference on Trade and Development New York/Geneva, 1999).

[151] *Ankarcrona* (n 48) § 1(6).

[152] This emerges, for instance, implicitly, from the discussion in *Agrotexim* (n 46) §§ 67–71; see also Zwart (n 79) 48.

important because they have immediate bearing on the underlying rationale. But the Court (formerly also the Commission) also consider other factors, some of them subjective and very concrete, which they openly acknowledge to have relevance in determining whether or not a shareholder applicant will attain 'victim' status for measures that formally have impinged on the company. By examining some of the recurring factors we gain valuable insight into the pragmatic nature of the Court's mode of reasoning in face of shareholders' identification claims.

The Court considers, as one among many factors, the amount of ownership exerted by the applicant even in situations in which the percentage of ownership fails to meet the 'vehicle' requirement of almost 100 per cent.[153] As remarked by the Commission in its admissibility decision in *Agrotexim*, the 'victim' test

> cannot be determined on the sole criterion of whether the shareholder retains the majority of the company shares. This element is an objective and important indication but other elements may be relevant in view of the circumstances of each particular case.[154]

The relatively few shares held by the *Agrotexim* shareholders undoubtedly contributed to the Court's dismissal of the applicants' claim.[155] Majority shareholding below the 'vehicle' threshold may be taken into account, but it does not result in 'victim' status by default.[156] If the applicants jointly represent dominant ownership, this may indicate admission of the claim because they represent 'la totalité du capital de la société',[157] but this too does not guarantee admissibility.[158]

The Court also bears in mind various forms of stakeholder involvement in the company. In *Kaplan v UK*, the applicant was managing director and majority shareholder (with more than 90 per cent ownership).[159] Due to misrepresentations by him in his capacity of managing director, the company

153 It might be that the Court does not feel constrained by a view of shareholder influence in the company in terms of the number of shares held. Yet without available case law in this area, whether the Court will apply a 'control test' as that increasingly encountered in international law remains an open question (literature in n 150), in which shareholder influence is quantified in terms of voting rights, etc also are considered.

154 *Agrotexim* (admissibility decision) (n 55) 156.

155 Shareholder identification claims are frequently dismissed when the applicant is but one of several shareholders in the company, eg, *Mironov* (n 61); and *Santos Lda and Fachadas* (n 50).

156 *Credit and Industrial Bank and Moravec* (n 68) (complaint from majority shareholder dismissed).

157 *Matos e Silva Lda and Others* (admissibility decision) (n 75). The Court did not consider this issue in its subsequent judgment.

158 *Matrot SA and Others* (n 47). See also App 18737/91 *Dias da Fonseca da Costa and Dias e Costa Lda v Portugal* (1994); and App 19157/91 *Pires da Silva and Pereira v Portugal* (1993) (majority shareholder's complaint dismissed although the application was joined by another shareholder).

159 *Kaplan v UK* (n 56) 14.

was served a notice imposing restrictions on its ability to enter into various insurance contracts.[160] The Commission observed that the applicant, with regard to the Art 6(1) complaint:

> had a clear interest in the outcome insofar as it affected the company. This arose from his investment interest in the company *and his position as an officer*.[161]

In *MB v France*, the Commission found that the applicant was a 'victim' of an Art 6(1) violation that concerned proceedings to which only his company had been a party. It took into account the applicant's shareholding, but also his position as manager and status as the company's joint debtor.[162]

It seems that the more directly involved an organ of the State has been in the alleged contravention, the more likely it is that the shareholder may be identified with the company. In its admissibility decision, the Commission in the *Agrotexim* case placed considerable emphasis on the special liquidation procedure in which one of the liquidators was appointed by the State. The company, Fix, had 'essentially been under state control', and it was therefore effectively incapable of complaining of a violation on its own.[163] The Court did not as such contest the validity of this argument (although it disagreed that the company had been effectively paralysed),[164] and indicated its relevance in noting that there were no indications that they had:

> failed to perform their duties satisfactorily. On the contrary, there is sufficient evidence to show that they took all the measures that they considered to be in the interests of the insolvent company's assets.[165]

In *GJ v Luxembourg*, the Court justified identification in part on grounds that the claim concerned the behaviour and activities of the company liquidators, both having been publicly appointed.[166]

Little financial or other prejudice suffered by the company is presumably less pressing for the shareholder also, and there is therefore less reason to allow the claim to be considered on its merits. In *Kustannus Oy Vapaa Ajattelija AB and Others v Finland*, the Commission observed that it 'also [had] regard to the minor amounts at stake', when it found the claim inadmissible.[167] Conversely, in *EuroArt Centre BV v Netherlands*, the Commission accepted the claim from a shareholder applicant who received his 'sole income' from the company in which he was majority shareholder.[168]

[160] *Kaplan v UK* (n 56) 7.

[161] ibid 23 (emphasis added).

[162] App 12547/86 *MB v France* (1990) § 2(19) and (20). The case was later considered by the Court in *Bendenoun v France* Series A No 284, (1994) 18 EHRR 54 (where identification was not discussed). On joint liability as factor, see also *Sprl ANCA and Others v Belgium* Application 10259/83, (1984) 40 DR 170, 176–77.

[163] *Agrotexim* (admissibility decision) (n 55).

[164] *Agrotexim* (n 46) § 68.

[165] ibid § 70(1).

[166] *GJ* (n 49) § 24 first sentence.

[167] *Kustannus* (n 67) § 1(b)(i)(2); see also *JW* (n 77) § 1(22).

[168] App 11834/85 *EuroArt Centre BV and Others v Netherlands* (1987).

GJ v Luxembourg suggests that personal affectedness beyond that which flows from business involvement such as shareholding also may come into play. The applicant shareholder's son in this case had died during the period in which the process of liquidating the company was delayed. In these circumstances the applicant had asked for a swift settling of the proceedings, but to no avail.[169] The Court and Commission found that his direct personal interests were involved in the complaint, and linked their view to his shareholding.[170] Yet, it is possible that all factors available in the case, the element of personal suffering included, helped the Court on its way to the conclusion of admissibility: the 'activities of the liquidators' were taken into account,[171] and they did not ensure an end to the proceedings despite of their knowledge of the applicant's personal trauma.

Shareholder intervention on the company's behalf is less deserving of Strasbourg attention when the company joins the application. In *Dias da Fonseca, da Costa and Dias e Costa, Lda v Portugal*, the Commission observed that the company itself, and not only its two shareholders, in fact submitted the application. There was therefore no reason to permit identification.[172] Presumably, the Strasbourg authorities regard the admittance of the company's claim as a sufficient (albeit indirect) mode of redress for the applicant shareholder and that the shareholder is therefore in no need of 'victim' status. But part of the case law diverges here; companies and shareholders may well be admitted even if they all complain about the same measure since other factors are considered relevant also.[173]

There is also evidence that a perception of 'victim' status in the sense that the shareholder applicant has participated in the domestic proceedings, also seems to have the potential to influence the assessment, and not only when the dispute concerns those proceedings' fulfilment of the standards laid down in Art 6(1).[174] In *JW v Poland*, the Commission dismissed the claim for identification under Art 6(1) and Protocol 1 Art 1. The shareholder applicant had not been party to the domestic proceedings and this was taken as evidence that he had not considered himself directly affected by the violation, and, consequently, that he did not have to be regarded as immediately affected on the supranational plane either.[175]

The extent to which the shareholder through actions or omissions has contributed to the situation that has arisen, and which forms the basis for the

169 *GJ* (n 49) §§ 14–15. 170 ibid § 24. 171 *GJ* (n 49) § 24 first sentence.

172 *Dias da Fonseca, da Costa and Dias e Costa Lda* (n 157) § 5; see also *SGI and Others* (n 62); and *Credit and Industrial Bank and Moravec* (n 68). 173 *Matos e Silva Lda and Others* (n 75).

174 *Neves e Silva v Portugal* Series A No 153-A, (1991) 13 EHRR 535 § 39.

175 *JW* (n 77) § 1(21). A similar factor is applied, and with greater impact it seems, in the case law under the ICCPR and ACHR systems, see Emberland (n 31) 270.

Strasbourg claim, also seems to be a relevant factor. In the *Agrotexim* case, the Court took into account, in its decision to uphold the 'veil', the applicant shareholders' failure to propose the removal of the liquidators for alleged malperformance.[176]

D. Concluding Observations

This chapter has shown that the Court has developed a nuanced view of separate corporate legal personality when dealing with shareholders' requests for 'victim' status regarding matters that formally pertain to their company. As a rule, the Court adheres to the distinction between shareholder rights and shareholder interests that follows from the construct of separate corporate personality under municipal law. The Court is, then, sympathetic to the member States' contention that a domestic legal arrangement which is a sensible and essential for private business enterprise should be acknowledged by the Convention. In this sense, the Court's non-identification approach, as pronounced in *Agrotexim v Greece*, illustrates the favourable business climate provided on the general level by the Convention. It also suggests the lengths to which the Court is willing to go to acknowledge the signatory States' need to preserve their autonomy in matters concerning national economy and the democratic basis of municipal law.

The *Agrotexim* principle's rejection of identification claims is not good news for the individual shareholders suffering financial or other prejudice from their corporate involvement. From the individual applicant's viewpoint, structural support for corporate investment may well be regarded 'anomalous' because, as put by Judge Walsh in the *Agrotexim* judgment, 'the defence of human rights in the field of property' in the actual dispute 'yield[s] to the commercially sacred impenetrability of the "corporate veil"'.[177] Although rejecting a comprehensive identification doctrine, the Court is, however, prepared to come to the individual shareholder's rescue when, in the Court's opinion, it is required and appropriate to do so. The 'impossibility' exception provides an opportunity for redress for shareholders who would otherwise suffer from their company's failure to operate as intended. The 'vehicle' approach provides, in fact, extended protection for corporate investment in exceptional circumstances. The Court's application of both exceptions shows that its occasional preference for shareholder interests rests on concrete considerations, of which its concern for effective Convention protection is central. In applying the principle of effectiveness

[176] *Agrotexim* (n 46) § 70(2).

[177] *Agrotexim* (n 46) Dissenting Opinion of Judge Walsh para 3.1.

the Court is enabled to consider not only the concrete and individual exigencies of each case but also the underlying Convention values, such as the rule of law principle, respect for individual dignity and consideration for economic enterprise.

One might legitimately ask whether the Court has, in fact, adopted a particular—an autonomous—ECHR conception of what a 'company' is and where the distinction between upholding and disregarding corporate personhood should be drawn. Such an autonomous construction is dependent, in that case, on the Court's tendency to see the law of the Convention pragmatically. The Court's approach to the corporate veil and modifications of the construct of separate legal personality signifies a type of pragmatism in which micro and macro considerations go hand in hand but are carefully balanced. In the face of the corporate veil, individual human rights protection remains a valid consideration for the Court, also as far as shareholders' interests are concerned. Effective ECHR protection will not, however, take precedence by default over macro-economic and political realities. This insight reflects a profound aspect of Strasbourg jurisprudence.

4

The Court's Response to Hard Cases of Applicability

A. Hard Cases of Applicability

The Court's admissibility of a private complaint does not merely depend on whether it holds that it has competence *ratione personae* to deal with it (as was essentially the matter discussed in the previous chapter). A complaint is also assessed to determine whether there is compatibility between the interests pursued and the interests protected by the provision. This question concerns the Court's jurisdiction *ratione materiae* to examine the merits of an application; this is the topic of the present chapter.[1]

The Court's consideration of the existence of 'fit' between interests pursued and interests protected may raise difficult questions of interpretation when corporate complaints are at stake. The Convention's differentiated rights-catalogue, introduced in chapter 2, suggests that such applicability assessments result in different answers depending on the right or entitlement invoked. Some rights have always and without discussion been regarded as applicable to companies, including the right to enjoyment of the procedural guarantees in Arts 6(1) and 13, and property protection pursuant to Protocol 1 Art 1. Others have equally indisputably been found wholly inapplicable to them, typically Art 3 (prohibition of torture) and Art 5 (freedom from arbitrary deprivation of physical liberty).

Between these extremes lie certain rights and entitlements—a 'middle group' of provisions—whose relevance to company litigants was at least once open to debate. Companies' claims for protection under them have previously been regarded as controversial due to the provisions' open-textured nature and their ambiguous doctrinal backdrop. The Court, in exercising its discretion, has had to balance a variety of competing considerations in establishing the appropriate doctrinal solution. Paraphrasing Ronald Dworkin's well-known

[1] Art 35(3). DJ Harris M O'Boyle and C Warbrick *Law of the European Convention on Human Rights* (Butterworths London, 1995) 629–40 presents in detail this ground for inadmissibility.

epithet, these groups of complaints have represented 'hard cases' for the Court to solve.[2] In principle, it could have decided to include companies wholly or in part or exclude corporate claims from the protective ambit of the rights and entitlements altogether. Today, most of these issues are hard cases no longer. Despite initial reluctance, internal dissent and—in exceptional cases—some remaining doubt, the Court eventually settled on a surprisingly favourable view of the applicability of the rights and entitlement to corporate claimants. Three judgments were landmark decisions in the development of the respective provisions; and they are introduced shortly.

This chapter scrutinizes the Court's solutions with regard to the applicability of this 'middle group' of provisions, and explores some important reasons why the Court, against a background of considerable doctrinal ambiguity, arrived at its conclusions. More precisely, it considers the Court's handling of 1) the right for companies to enjoy protection by Art 8(1), which, among other things, guarantees 'respect for one's . . . home' against searches and seizures on their business premises; 2) companies' ability to assert protection under Art 10(1) for what will be referred to as 'corporate commercial expression'; and 3) companies' entitlement to be awarded monetary compensation for non-pecuniary loss pursuant to Art 41.[3] The discussion is guided by the empirical material at hand; case law on the applicability of other 'middle group' rights to corporate claimants is sparse and undeveloped.[4]

While part B considers the likely causes of divergence at the Court, part C discusses the Court's ultimately favourable response. The Court is in some cases fairly generous in setting out its arguments, but it would be counterproductive to subject every detail to exhaustive analysis. Part D does attempt to interpret the Court's arguments from a teleological perspective and thus tie them to the structural landscape provided in chapters 1 and 2. It will be asserted that the Court's teleology was developed or modified in the landmark judgments, leaning towards an objective teleological approach that made the inclusion of corporate claims within the provisions' ambit a viable proposition. The Court's bold approach loses some of its edge in its progressive reasoning, however. Part E ties the conclusions of this chapter to the concerns of the next

[2] R Dworkin *Taking Rights Seriously* (Harvard University Press Cambridge Mass, 1977) 81–130.

[3] Art 41 guarantees an entitlement and not a right proper, as any award of 'just satisfaction' awarded under Art 41 rests on the Court's discretion, see *Sunday Times v UK (Art 50)* Series A No 38 (1981) 3 EHRR 317 § 15.

[4] The applicability of Art 9 and Protocol No 4 Art 2 to the Convention for the Protection of Human Rights and Fundamental Freedoms, securing certain rights and freedoms other than those already included in the Convention and in the first Protocol thereto (adopted 16 September 1963, entered into force 2 May 1968) ETS 46 (Protocol 4) (freedom of movement) has been raised, see eg *Cha'are Shalom Ve Tsedek v France* Reports 2000-VII §§ 69 and 73 (Art 9); and *Eugenia Michaelidou Developments Ltd and Michael Tymvios v Turkey* decision 8 June 1999 § 4 (Protocol 4 Art 2 (question not discussed in the subsequent judgment).

B. Object and Purpose as Arguments against Applicability

Apart from the wording of and circumstances surrounding the judgments (see part C), there is ample evidence in prior case law that corporate complaints involved tortuous interpretation—that they represented 'hard cases'. This lack of poise is frequently reflected in the Court's disinclination to confront the matter head on, though it has on occasion confessed to the difficulties involved, without achieving a final stance.[5] The Court has also occasionally conceded that the question was difficult, but without determining it at that juncture.[6] Indeed, the members of the Court have expressed divergent views—also in the landmark judgments—as to the appropriateness of protecting company applicants under the provisions (such dissents are considered later).[7]

The following discussion examines the considerations mainly invoked in support of a restrictive reading of Arts 8, 10, and 41 whereby they are taken as not applying to corporate applicants engaged in for-profit pursuits. Some of the arguments apply to other entities than companies and/or to all persons that pursue commercial objectives. The limited liability company, especially when publicly held, is, however, in a special position because of its organizational form, its unmitigated legal personality and the absence of an immediate individual *substratum*.[8] The arguments against inclusion affect them the strongest. Each provision is considered separately according to their order in the Convention. It will become evident that the main thrust of the argument against applicability derives from a particular conception of what the object and purpose of the provisions are. An alternative teleology is considered in part D.

Before this chapter ventures to discuss the Court's case law, some general information on the provisions discussed is warranted.

[5] *Immobiliare Saffi v Italy* Reports 1999-V (2000) 30 EHRR 756 §§ 77 and 79 (with regard to Art 41); *Banco de Finanzas e Inversiones (Fibanc) SA v Spain* decision 27 April 1999 § 5 (with regard to Art 8(1)); and *Barthold v Germany* Series A No 90, (1985) 7 EHRR 383 §§ 42 and 38(1) (with regard to Art 10(1)).

[6] *Manifattura FL v Italy* Series A 230-B §§ 21–22; and *News Verlags GmbH & Co KG v Austria* 2000 Reports 2000-I (2001) 31 EHRR 246 §§ 64 and 66 (Art 41).

[7] *Comingersoll SA v Portugal* Reports 2000-IV (2001) 31 EHRR 772, Concurring Opinion of Judges Rozakis, Bratza, Caflisch and Vajić paras 2–3 (with regard to Art 41). With regard to Art 10, see *Groppera Radio and Others v Switzerland* Series A No 173, (1990) 12 EHRR 321, Concurring Opinion of Judges Matscher and Bindschedler-Robert para 2; and Concurring Opinion of Judge Valticos para 3, especially when contrasted with the Dissenting Opinion of Judge Pettit and the Dissenting Opinion of Judge De Meyer; and *Autronic AG v Switzerland* Series A No 178, (1990) 12 EHRR 485, Dissenting Opinion of Judges Bindschedler-Robert and Matscher para 1. Similar disagreement has not been seen in Art 8, but the landmark judgment is clearly confined to the 'circumstances of the case', see *Colas Est SA and Others v France* Reports 2002-III § 41.

[8] *Comingersoll* (n 7) Concurring Opinion of Judges Rozakis, Bratza, Caflisch and Vajič para 3.

1 Article 8(1): Business Premises as a Company's 'Home'

(a) A Distinction between the Private Sphere and General Private Activity

Article 8(1) states that '[e]veryone has the right to respect for his private and family life, his home and his correspondence'.[9] The provision embodies four different, yet interrelated and sometimes overlapping rights. They can be referred to jointly as rights protecting the 'privacy' or 'private sphere' of the persons benefiting from them.[10] The present discussion is only concerned with one function of one of the 'private sphere' rights, whether the right to respect for one's 'home' puts restraints on public authorities' ability to raid the business premises of company applicants. This issue has engendered a comprehensive discussion at Strasbourg with regard to the scope of Art 8(1) in the corporate context.[11]

A person's 'home' (French: 'domicile') presupposes as a minimum the existence of occupational premises in which the applicant has 'sufficient continuing' links.[12] This requirement also applies to a corporate 'home'. Beyond this starting point, however, the concept is vague.[13] Here, as elsewhere in Art 8, a distinction is drawn between matters concerning a person's 'private sphere' and matters more broadly connected with private activity. When a company asserts 'home' protection it seeks safeguard for its for-profit activity, but for-profit activity as such is not an issue with which 'privacy' and 'home' protection are concerned.[14] Art 8 reflects, one might say, the conceptual distinction between privacy and liberty to which privacy theorists tend to adhere.[15] Allegiance to liberty may explain some interpretative aspects of the

[9] The French authentic text has some relevance for the discussion: 'Toute personne a droit au respect de sa vie privée et familiale, de son domicile et de sa correspondence.'

[10] 'Private sphere' is the term preferred in AM Connelly 'Problems of Interpretation of Article 8 of the European Convention on Human Rights' (1986) 35 ICLQ 567, 568. Commentators disagree on the meaning of 'privacy' in the Convention context, contrast, eg, the narrow understanding in Harris O'Boyle and Warbrick (n 1) 305–6, with the wide one in P van Dijk and GJH van Hoof *Theory and Practice of the European Convention on Human Rights* (Kluwer Hague, 1998) 489.

[11] Aspects of the discussion are considered in M Emberland 'Protection against Unwarranted Searches and Seizures of Corporate Premises under Art 8 of the European Convention on Human Rights: the *Colas Est SA v France* Approach' (2003) 25 Mich J Intl L 77. Some doubt as to the applicability of 'private life' and 'correspondence' to companies has been expressed, see, eg, App 20062/92 *B Company and Others v Netherlands* (1993) (as regards 'private life'); App 14369/88 *Noviflora AB v Sweden* (1992) ('private life' as well as 'correspondence'). 'Family life' applies, it can safely be assumed, by default to individuals only.

[12] *Gillow v UK* judgment 24 November 1986 Series A 109 (1989) 11 EHRR 335 § 46.

[13] The concept of 'privacy' is also inherently elusive, eg, E Barendt 'Introduction' in E Barendt (ed) *Privacy* (Ashgate Dartmouth Aldershot, 2001) i, xi.

[14] *SCP Huglo Lepage & Associés and Others v France* decision 11 February 2003 § 3. Some for-profit activities are protected by Protocol 1 Art 1.

[15] E Barendt 'Privacy as a Constitutional Right and Value' in P Birks (ed) *Privacy and Loyalty* (Clarendon Press Oxford, 1997) 1, 2.

notion of 'private life' in the EU context,[16] and why the concept of 'home' in the German *Grundgesetz* is generously interpreted so as to include corporate premises.[17] But Art 8 is not a clause broadly providing for the protection of liberty.[18] A line must consequently be drawn between an economic actor's private sphere and his or her private economic activity but this is problematic since the distinction will depend on the circumstances of each case

The present section presupposes that the Court has identified the 'privacy' aspects of a company's complaint so that the question of Art 8's applicability is actuated in the corporate context. Two main arguments, both of which concern the object and purpose of the provision, have been levelled against an interpretation of 'home' that encompasses corporate premises. They are now considered.

(b) Article 8 Primarily Protects the Natural Person

A central argument against an inclusion of corporate premises in the term 'home' in Art 8 is that the Convention was fashioned primarily with the individual human being and its particular interests in mind.[19] A number of doctrinal sources support this contention (the philosophical justifications are considered next).

The English authentic text, at least, connotes the permanent residence of a human being rather than the offices or other locales of a corporate entity.[20] A 'domicile', the French text's equivalent, it is true, does have a greater semantic capacity for encompassing the residence of non-individuals.[21] That said, however, a contextual reading of the provision suggests relatively strongly that 'home' protection was included so as to afford protection to individuals. Two

[16] Cases 46/87 and 227/88 *Hoechst AG v Commission* [1989] ECR 1575 § 19; Case 85/87 *Dow Benelux NV v Commission* [1989] ECR 3137 § 30; and Cases 97–99/87 *Dow Iberica SA v Commission* [1989] ECR 3165 § 16: 'any intervention by public authorities in the sphere of private activities of any person, whether natural or legal, must have a legal basis and be justified on the grounds laid down by law, and . . . provide . . . protection against arbitrary and disproportionate intervention'.

[17] C Starck 'Artikel 2' in H von Mangoldt F Klein and C Starck (eds) *Das Bonner Grundgesetz. Kommentar* (4th edn Vahlen Munich, 1999) vol 1, 186, 211; and T Maunz and H-J Papier 'Artikel 13' in T Maunz and G Dürig (eds) *Grundgesetz. Kommentar* (Beck Munich, 1999) [10–18].

[18] The Convention's liberty protection is confined to selected areas, including aspects of physical liberty (art 5), expressive liberty (art 10); and organizational freedom (art 11).

[19] N Bratza 'The Implications of the Human Rights Act 1998 for Commercial Practice' [2000] EHRLR 1, 2. See, eg, the respondent government in *Niemietz v Germany* Series A No 251-B, (1993) 16 EHRR 97 § 27 second sentence.

[20] Among various definitions available, a 'home' is '[a] dwelling-place, house, abode; the fixed residence of a family or household; the seat of domestic life and interests; one's own house; the dwelling in which one habitually lives, or which one regards as one's proper abode,' *Oxford English Dictionary Online* (Oxford University Press Oxford, 2003), available at<http://dictionary.oed.com> (24 June 2005).

[21] *Niemietz* (n 19) § 30. The text does not, for instance, speak of 'logis' or 'maison', both of which having connotations more similar to those of a 'home'.

of the other rights guaranteed by Art 8 speak of (private and family) 'life' and refer thus to qualities that are directly attributable to human beings.[22] Moreover, the Commission in 1974 on a general basis held that 'home' connoted what its literal meaning in English implied and that it was not to be extensively interpreted.[23] Heinz Gurazde, a well-informed early commentator on the ECHR, likewise wrote in 1968 that he considered that 'private life' was equivalent with 'Achtung der Intimsphäre', and that the concepts of 'home'/'domicile' when read in light of 'private' and 'family life' suggested that business premises were left unprotected by Art 8(1).[24]

Although the *travaux préparatoires* are generally not very helpful in clarifying the intended object and purpose of Art 8(1),[25] the drafting process nonetheless supports an individualized reading of the provision. Article 12 of the Universal Declaration of Human Rights, which served as a model for ECHR Art 8, was primarily concerned with the protection of individuals.[26] Louise Doswald-Beck in her 'overall assessment of the [drafting material]' has suggested that, given the time of the Convention's adoption in the aftermath of WWII, the drafters primarily had in mind a safeguard against totalitarian regimes' disrespect for individual integrity.[27]

The Court has always held that the object and purpose of Art 8 is 'essentially that of protecting the *individual* against arbitrary interference by . . . public authorities'.[28] This doctrine was reiterated in judgments that, prior to the Court's clarification, came close to examining the possibility of extending 'home' protection to corporate premises. In *Niemietz v Germany*, for instance, the Court relied on it when it concluded that a lawyer's home office was to be protected against searches and seizures carried out by the police in their investigation of a case involving one of his clients.[29] The Court evidently thought the lawyer's personal interests were a significant argument for extending 'home' protection to encompass his office.[30] The Commission explicitly favoured a

22 Vienna Convention art 31(1): A treaty shall be interpreted 'in good faith in accordance with the ordinary meaning to be given to the terms of the treaty in their context'.

23 *X v Belgium* Application 5488/72, (1974) 45 CD 20.

24 H Guradze *Die Europäische Menschenrechtskonvention. Konvention zum Schutze der Menschenrechte und Grundfreiheiten nebst Zusatsprotokollen. Kommentar* (Vahlen Berlin, 1968) 118.

25 Connelly (n 10) 568–70; and L Loucaides 'Personality and Privacy under the European Convention on Human Rights' (1991) 61 BYIL 175, 176.

26 On the provision, see, eg, LA Rehof 'Article 12' in G Alfredsson and A Eide (eds) *The Universal Declaration of Human Rights. A Common Standard of Achievement* (Martinus Nijhoff Hague, 1999) 251.

27 L Doswald-Beck 'The Meaning of the "Right to Respect for Private Life" under the European Convention on Human Rights' (1983) 4 HRLJ 283, 286–87.

28 *Case relating to certain aspects of the laws on the use of languages in education in Belgium (Belgian Linguistics Case) (Merits)* Series A No 6, (1979) 1 EHRR 252 § 7 (emphasis added).

29 *Niemietz* (n 19) § 31.

30 See also *Chappell v UK* Series A No 152-A, (1990) 12 EHRR 1 §§ 26b and 63.

restrictive scope of the provision at the time when it had a mandate to interpret the treaty. In *Church of Scientology of Paris v France* it remarked, in a case which concerned the protection of non-disclosure of private information of a religious association, that 'unlike Article 9, Article 8 was of an individual rather than a collective character'.[31] Such opinions on the provision's object and purpose do not actually spell a favourable approach towards the inclusion of company premises in the concept of 'home' in Art 8.

(c) Absence of 'Fit' with Philosophical Justifications

The philosophical justifications for privacy protection, which are relevant for determining the meaning of Art 8,[32] reinforce the doctrinally founded sentiment that corporate claims are located at best on the margins of the provision's compass. Privacy is believed to require protection for two main reasons,[33] both of which refer to qualities intrinsic to the natural person.

Privacy is, above all, cherished out of consideration for the individual's inner personal sphere: the individual *qua* human being has a right to be let alone.[34] Without an area free from outside intrusion, the individual cannot make free moral and rational choices, establish an identity and develop his or her personhood.[35] This theory would be clearly difficult to apply to non-individual entities. Obviously, a corporate entity is ultimately made up of individuals and their activity. But at face value, this normative basis has the individual's personal aspects in mind, not the interests of non-individual entities.

Privacy protection is also justified on social grounds (and consequently extended to include certain relationships).[36] Privacy, it is held, is valuable because it is conducive for the development of social relationships with other human beings, which again is considered important for individual and society alike.[37] Again, although a company may comprise an aggregate of individual interests, there is little doubt that this rationale, as originally developed, had in mind the social needs and abilities of the individual person in a different form than a perceived urge of individuals to enter into business associations.

Theorists mainly agree that the case for privacy protection is weakened when the individual leaves the inner sanctum of her home and enters the public

[31] App 19509/92 *Church of Scientology of Paris v France* (1995) § 1(5). See also *Scientology Kirche eV v Germany* Application 34614/97, (1997) 89 DR 163.

[32] Doswald-Beck (n 27) 287–89; *X v Iceland* Application 6825/74, (1976) 5 DR 86, 87.

[33] Barendt (n 13) xi.

[34] *X v Iceland* (n 32) 87. Generally, SD Warren and LD Brandeis 'The Right to Privacy' (1890) 4 Harv L Rev 193.

[35] G Negley 'Philosophical Views on the Value of Privacy' (1966) 31 L & Contemp Probs 319.

[36] *X v Iceland* (n 32) 87.

[37] D Feldman 'Privacy-related Rights: Their Social Value' in P Birks (ed) *Privacy and Loyalty* (Clarendon Press Oxford, 1997) 15, 21.

sphere.[38] This is a view which also is adhered to in Strasbourg practice.[39] The argument gains force for companies since they tend to have public sides to their person and activities. Being a creature of the law of the state, a company pursues its activities by public licence. A company's enterprise involves extrovert activity in that its business relies on contractual and other relationships with others.[40] For many businesses public access to their premises is essential.[41] The company's expectation of privacy protection cannot be compared to that of individual human beings. Privacy protection might therefore apply, at the least, in a tempered version when company interests are involved.[42]

Against this sketch of the philosophical backdrop, an extension of 'home' protection to corporate business premises does arguably seem like an uphill struggle.

2 Article 10(1): (Corporate) Commercial Expression

(a) Defining 'Commercial Expression'

A comparable set of arguments is found with regard to Art 10(1), which provides:

> Everyone has the right to freedom of expression. This right shall include freedom to hold opinions and to receive and impart information and ideas without interference by public authority and regardless of frontiers. This Article shall not prevent States from requiring the licensing of broadcasting, television or cinema enterprise.

Corporate invocation of the free speech clause has engendered discussion at the Court when the complaints concern interests defined by the Court as 'commercial speech'. Before proceeding with the examination of the causes of divergence, we need to identify what 'commercial speech' is taken to comprise. There are at least two issues here.

As with Art 8, Art 10 does not protect any and all private activity. The provision protects (freedom of) 'expression'. What 'expression' is taken to mean in the context of the ECHR remains somewhat uncertain, although it includes at least activity which embodies an expressive statement represented

[38] H Nissenbaum 'Protecting Privacy in an Information Age: The Problem of Privacy in Public' (1998) 17 L & Phil 559 presents and critiques this position.

[39] *Brüggeman and Scheuten v Germany* (report) App 6959/75, (1977) 10 DR 100, § 56. Further, eg, PJ Duffy 'The Protection of Privacy, Family Life and Other Rights under Article 8 of the European Convention on Human Rights' (1982) 2 YEL 191, 198.

[40] IN Walden and RN Savage 'Data Protection and Privacy Laws: Should Organisations Be Protected?' (1988) 37 ICLQ 337, 346 (in the context of data protection); and J Wright 'The Protection of Corporate Privacy' (1983) 11 Intl Bus Lawyer 119, 119.

[41] *Dow Chemical Co v United States* 476 US 227, 236 and 239 (1986).

[42] The US Supreme Court interprets the Fourth Amendment in light of this view; the 'houses' of 'people' are extended to include corporate premises, see *United States v Morton Salt Co* 338 US 632, 641and 652 (1950); and Emberland (n 11) 96–97.

in written and spoken words, pictures, images and expressive conduct,[43] and which therefore has an element of public outreach. For-profit activity not embodied in an expressive statement is subsequently not an 'expression': the provision therefore does not protect, say, the 'freedom to conduct business'.[44] Nor is it likely to cover various communicative actions within, from and to a company that are part of normal business undertakings and unrelated to the process of reaching a broader audience.[45] Obviously it is difficult to identify clearly when a communicative action is regarded as an 'expression' within the meaning of the provision; and the case law is not a very helpful assistant in this regard.[46] It is nonetheless plausible that a line must be drawn and that the justifications for freedom of expression may be instrumental in determining how that operation is conducted.

The Court also distinguishes between 'expression' that is relevant to political discourse and speech which is purely 'commercial'. The Court defines 'commercial expression' as dissemination of information for the purpose of 'inciting the public to purchase a particular product'.[47] This form of expression may, in principle, come from any person, whether commercial in nature or not. It is, however, most likely to be the speech of individuals and entities that pursue for-profit objectives. 'Political expression', on the other hand, comprises statements that, although they may be commercially motivated or otherwise commercial in their origin, concern the speaker's 'participation in a debate affecting the general interest',[48] or reflect 'controversial opinions pertaining to modern society in general'.[49]

Only the former type of 'expression'—pure 'commercial speech' as understood by the Court—has caused dissension on the question of applicability.[50]

[43] Harris O'Boyle and Warbrick (n 1) 378.

[44] *markt intern Verlag GmbH and Klaus Beermann v Germany* Series A No 165, (1990) 12 EHRR 161 § 25 last sentence (submitted by the respondent government). It is difficult to draw a clear line in this regard. Contrast, for instance, *Tokarczyk v Poland* decision 31 January 2002 § 3(4) and (5) with App 16555/90 *R GmbH v Germany* (1990) § 5.

[45] E Barendt *Freedom of Speech* (Clarendon Press Oxford 1985) 60.

[46] Contrast, eg, *Fressoz and Roire v France* Reports 1999-I (2001) 31 EHRR 28 § 50; with App 11617/85 *SB v UK* (1986) § 4 (ii)

[47] *VGT Verein gegen Tierfabriken v Switzerland* judgment 28 June 2001 Reports 2001-VI (2002) 34 EHRR 4 § 57 first sentence. See also comparable definitions given in PM Twomey 'Freedom of Expression for Commercial Actors' in NA Neuwahl and A Rosas (eds) *The European Union and Human Rights* (Martinus Nijhoff Hague, 1995) 265, 265–66; and AM Collins 'Commercial Speech and the Free Movement of Goods and Services at Community Law' in J O'Reilly (ed) *Human Rights and Constitutional Law. Essays in Honour of Brian Walsh* (Round Hall Press Dublin, 1992) 319, 320.

[48] *Hertel v Switzerland* Reports 1998-VI (1999) 28 EHRR 534 § 47.

[49] *VGT Verein gegen Tierfabriken* (n 47) § 70.

[50] But there is disagreement about where to draw the line, see, eg, Judge Jörundsson's Dissenting opinion in *Demuth v Switzerland* Reports 2002-IX (2004) 38 EHRR 20. In US constitutional law one also sees interpretative challenges posed by speech in the form of advertisements with an alleged

'Political' elements in the speech tend, however, to consume whatever commercial motivation may have prompted the statement at the outset. This explains why not all corporate complaints raise difficult questions of interpretation under Art 10(1): corporate entities may pursue objectives and convey expressions that are not entirely for-profit oriented but are relevant for societal and political discourse—the media business is the quintessential example here. The third sentence of the provision is in fact, by implication, sympathetic to this particular category of corporate claimants. '[B]roadcasting, television [and] cinema enterprises', and the media sector generally, enjoy considerable protection under the provision, logically enough given the Court's description of the press as a 'public watchdog'.[51] The Court's first encounter with an applicant company, the first *Sunday Times v UK* judgment, concerned a newspaper corporation's freedom of expression. In that judgment, the applicant was afforded protection without any discussion as to the relevance of its corporate nature or the underlying for-profit motivations it may have had for its newspaper activities.[52]

When the 'political' element of corporate 'expression' is missing, however, problems arise with regard to 'commercial speech' because general for-profit activity as such enjoys no Art 10 protection. Even individuals that apply for protection of their commercial statements are regarded with apprehension by the Court.[53] In this respect, corporate commercial speech, it could be argued, should raise no particularly difficult interpretative challenges.[54] Yet the Court appears to have been particularly vigilant in its approach when commercial speech is pursued by corporate claimants. On what grounds may the Court have developed this opinion? The answer has to do with the philosophical justifications for freedom of expression.

(b) The Rationale for Free Expression Does Not Fit

A potent argument for the dismissal of (corporate) commercial expression from free speech protection is that the philosophical foundation for freedom of expression does not readily apply to this form of speech. Indeed, the media

political content coming from for-profit corporations, see in particular the recent decision in *Nike, Inc v Kasky* 539 US 654 (2003), as commented in S Joseph *Corporations and Transnational Human Rights Litigation* (Hart Oxford, 2004) chapter 5.

[51] *Observer and Guardian v UK* Series A No 216, (1992) 14 EHRR 153 § 59(b).

[52] *Sunday Times v UK* Series A No 30, (1980) 2 EHRR 245 § 45, as observed in *Autronic* (n 7) § 47(1).

[53] *Barthold* (n 5); *Casado Coca v Spain* Series A No 285, (1994) 18 EHRR 1; and *Jacubowski v Germany* Series A No 291, (1995) 19 EHRR 64. Commercial speech of not-for-profit entities, eg, App 18424/91 *Röda Korset Ungdomsförbund and Others v Sweden* (1993).

[54] Observed in SR Copp 'A Dignam and D Allen *Company Law and the Human Rights Act 1998* and M Smyth *Business and the Human Rights Act 1998*' (book review) (2001) 12 ICCLR 287, 287.

industry's exploitation of free speech for the pursuit of economic goals is rightly seen as a contentious issue in contemporary society's democracy debate (yet this greater theme is not considered in detail here).[55] Freedom of expression is justified chiefly for three reasons, all of which enjoy universal acceptance and are acknowledged for Art 10 purposes.[56] On each count, however, corporate commercial speech faces subsumption problems through absence of 'fit'. Let us consider them in turn.

(i) The Democracy Argument

Commentators have submitted that corporate commercial speech lacks sufficient support in the theory that free speech is necessary for promoting an informed body politic for the purpose of safeguarding and encouraging a democratic discourse.[57] Corporate commercial expression may arguably be difficult to reconcile with the democracy argument's emphasis on an informed and active citizenry because it presupposes direct and personal participation of natural persons.

The thrust of the argument concerning lack of 'fit', however, builds on the presupposition that some forms of speech are more worthy of protection than others because they concern the heart of democracy. Information on the benefits of a particular product or service, for instance, is distinguished in this respect from statements of a political, social, scientific, or cultural value. The motive for disseminating commercial information is primarily related to profit; it is not conveyed for the purpose of enlightening and inspiring the public to engage in societal discourse.[58]

This may have serious implications for Art 10 protection, because the Court, ever since its *Handyside v UK* judgment, has made it crystal clear that democracy is the pre-eminent rationale for freedom of speech in the Convention.[59] The respondent government in *markt intern Verlag GmbH and Klaus Beermann v Germany*, for instance, in which one of the first battles for the inclusion of corporate commercial field was won, invoked lack of 'fit' with the democracy argument. It contended that Art 10(1) was inapplicable to the speech in question—information to retailers concerning the business practices of competitors—because it 'was not intended to influence or mobilise public

[55] H Thorgeirsdóttir *Journalism Worthy of the Name. Freedom Within the Press and the Affirmative Side of Article 10 of the European Convention on Human Rights* (Martinus Nijhoff Leiden, 2005) provides a comprehensive analysis of these issues.

[56] M Janis R Kay and A Bradley *European Human Rights Law. Text and Materials* (2nd edn Oxford University Press Oxford, 2000) 139–40.

[57] Barendt (n 45) 20–23; generally on the democracy argument, see A Meiklejohn *Free Speech and Its Relation to Self-Government* (Harper New York, 1948).

[58] Barendt (n 45) 55 and 60 for these arguments.

[59] *Handyside v UK* Series A No 24, (1979) 1 EHRR 737 § 49(2); and Barendt (n 45) 22.

opinion, but to promote the economic interests of a given group of undertakings'.[60] In *Autronic AG v Switzerland*, the dissenting judges agreed with the respondent government that the complaint enjoyed no Art 10(1) protection since the 'expression'—the television signals sought transmitted—was not intended to reach the public, disqualifying therefore the democracy rationale.[61]

(ii) Individual Self-Fulfilment

With regard to the two other theories of free speech, there is no direct evidence in the case law that lack of 'fit' has been invoked to justify inapplicability. But commentators on free speech in the ECHR context and in comparable legal regimes generally agree that commercial expression also lacks support in them.

The individual self-fulfilment argument for free speech protection states that freedom of expression is worthy of protection because it is conducive of developing the autonomy and personality of the human being.[62] 'Freedom of expression constitutes . . . one of the basic conditions for . . . the development of every man,' the Court said in *Handyside v UK*.[63]

Corporate commercial expression lacks a perfect 'fit' with this justification for free speech, because, as Eric Barendt notes:

> the profit motive [of this kind of speech] breaks the crucial link between the real beliefs of the producer . . . and his speech, so that the latter cannot be considered a serious manifestation of his attitudes.[64]

It is argued that a company that markets a product or a service does not communicate an idea, it conveys facts for the purpose of pecuniary gain. This exchange of communicative action does not rely on intellectual reflection by the conveyor of the statement or its intended recipients, while the individual self-fulfilment argument is inherently connected with intellectual activity.[65]

The self-fulfilment argument has, moreover, obvious affinity with the capacities of the natural person. In fact, it is thought to derive from the intrinsic worth of human dignity.[66] At best, corporate commercial speech will only indirectly provide fertile ground for individual self-fulfilment. Eric Barendt thus believes that '[t]he extension of free speech rights to legal persons, such as corporations, makes little sense in terms of self-fulfilment theories', thus advocating a widely held view that corporate commercial expression enjoys no legitimacy on this particular theory.[67]

60 *markt intern* (n 44) § 25(1).

61 *Autronic* (n 7) Dissenting Opinion of Judges Bindschedler-Robert and Matscher para 1; and the government's submission in the same case, ibid § 44(2).

62 Barendt (n 45) 14–20.

63 *Handyside* (n 59) § 49(2) second sentence.

64 Barendt (n 45) 56–57.

65 ibid 56.

66 F Schauer *Free Speech: A Philosophical Inquiry* (Cambridge University Press Cambridge, 1982) chapters 4 and 5.

67 Barendt (n 45) 17.

(iii) Pursuit of Truth

Finally, commercial expression is considered to be at odds with the theory that free expression is worth protecting as a fundamental freedom because only through free and open discussion, in 'the market-place of ideas',[68] can truth be discovered.[69]

It has been suggested that advertisements—the quintessential form of commercial speech—typically concern statements that are factually verifiable, which means that they are of no or little use in the dialectic exchange aiming at truth. The content of commercial speech, it is argued, already represents one form of truth because it only has one right answer, notably the qualities of the product or services it is there to sell.[70] Commercial expression is, in other words, durable and therefore lacks the amorphous quality that opinions are believed to have.[71] Therefore, it enjoys weak theoretical support for protection.

It is maintained, on a general basis, that commercial speech has an aptitude for being deceptive in terms of 'promising results in terms that are at best vague and at worst clearly false', and therefore does not play by the rules according to which the discursive search for truth apparently adheres.[72] On this ground, too, the rationale for protection of 'commercial speech' is weakened.

The argument from truth was not part of the rationale for freedom of expression in *Handyside* v *UK*, but it is generally assumed that it at least plays some part in the justification for free speech in the Convention.[73] Applicable or not, it cannot be doubted that commercial speech (corporate and individual) gains little or nothing from it.

3 Article 41: Companies' Compensation for Non-pecuniary Loss

(a) *Cogent Reasons for Concern?*

The discussion of the applicability of monetary compensation for non-pecuniary loss for companies pursuant to Art 41 proceeds from a different set of assumptions than the discussions under Arts 8 and 10.[74] Article 41 states:

> If the Court finds that there has been a violation of the Convention or the protocols thereto, and if the internal law of the High Contracting Party concerned allows only

[68] *Abrams v United States* 250 US 616, 630–31 (1919) (Holmes, J dissenting).

[69] Barendt (n 45) 8–14.

[70] ibid 56.

[71] A Kozinski and S Banner 'Who's Afraid of Commercial Speech?' (1990) 76 Va L Rev 627, 634. This argument has been contested by those who have misgivings about seeing advertisement as mere fact based information because it, too, may be based on value judgments, eg, J Pietzcker 'The US Commercial Speech Doctrine' (1990) 59 ZaöRV 1, 23 with further references.

[72] Barendt (n 45) 56.

[73] Janis Kay and Bradley (n 56) 139.

[74] M Emberland 'Compensating Companies for Non-Pecuniary Damage: *Comingersoll SA v. Portugal* and the Ambivalent Expansion of the ECHR Scope' (2004) 74 BYIL 409 treats aspects of the same theme.

partial reparation to be made, the Court shall, if necessary, afford just satisfaction to the injured party.[75]

To begin with, Art 41 contains no rights or freedoms. It bestows an entitlement for remedies on the applicant whose rights under the Convention have been breached, as even when the applicant has satisfied all requirements it is for the Court to decide whether, to what extent and in which form remedy shall be awarded.[76] The text refers to 'just satisfaction' to denote available remedies and 'the injured party' to designate the private applicants potentially entitled to an award. The Court interprets the provision to contain four groups of remedies,[77] but the applicability of three of them to corporate applicants has never been questioned. Thus, the Court regularly orders the reimbursement of company applicants' procedural costs and expenses arising from the dispute,[78] the payment of monetary compensation for pecuniary damage sustained by companies,[79] and the issuing of declarations of violations for pecuniary—and significantly—non-pecuniary harm suffered by company applicants.[80]

With regard to the fourth remedy, however, monetary compensation for non-pecuniary loss, the Court for a long time held that corporate enjoyment of it represented a controversial issue of Convention interpretation. In *Comingersoll SA v Portugal*, where the issue was finally decided to the benefit of the corporate applicant, the respondent government merely echoed received tradition when it contended that the purpose for awarding compensation for non-pecuniary damage 'was to provide reparation for anxiety, the mental stress of having to wait for the outcome of the case and uncertainty'. In the government's view, 'such feelings were peculiar to natural persons and could under no circumstances entitle a juristic person to compensation'.[81]

Article 41 in the present context also differs from Arts 8 and 10 because it is difficult to assemble cogent reasons why companies' claims for monetary

75 Prior to Protocol 11, the provision was known as Art 50.

76 *Sunday Times (Art 50)* (n 3) § 15. W Peukert 'Artikel 50' in JA Frowein and W Peukert *Europäische MenschenrechtsKonvention. EMRK-Kommentar* (2nd edn Engel Kehl am Rhein, 1996) 667, 671–719 introduces the general requirements.

77 Other international law remedies, such as restitution in kind, cannot be awarded directly by the Court, but it tends increasingly to suggest to the violating State what remedies be most appropriate, see, eg *Belvedere Alberghieria Srl v Italy* judgment 30 May 2000 Reports 2000-VI § 69 and *Belvedere Alberghieria Srl v Italy (Art 41)* judgment 30 October 2003 § 29.

78 *Tre Traktörer AB v Sweden* Series A No 159, (1991) 13 EHRR 309 §§ 67–69. See further on this remedy, eg, N Sansonetis 'Costs and Expenses' in R St J Macdonald F Matscher and H Petzold (eds) *The European System for the Protection of Human Rights* (Martinus Nijhoff Dordrecht, 1993) 755.

79 *Unión Alimentaria Sanders SA v Spain* judgment 7 July 1989 Series A 157 (1990) 12 EHRR 24 § 44.

80 *News Verlags* (n 8) § 66; and Emberland (n 74) 3–4. G Dannemann *Schadenersatz bei Verletzung der Europäischen Menschenrechtskonvention. Eine rechtsvergleichende Untersuchung zur Haftung nach Art. 50 EMRK* (Heymann Cologne, 1994) 365–68 gives an overview of the remedy.

81 *Comingersoll* (n 7) § 28(2).

compensation for non-pecuniary loss are doctrinally controversial. The philosophical justifications generally marshalled for remedies under international law—considerations of corrective justice, apology and deterrence—do not bar companies from receiving such compensation. Thus, the theory of corrective justice emphasizes the resumption of imbalance between two persons' legal positions, not qualities of their person. The theory of deterrence focuses either on the situation of the wrongdoer (rather than that on the victim) or emphasizes the societal impact of the remedy. The person who claims the remedy is likewise of little importance in the theory of penalizing the wrongdoer through compensation; here the wrongdoer himself naturally is in focus.[82] If we rely on philosophical justification alone, then, the obstacles facing companies should not be insurmountable.

(b) Contested Opinions and Probable Causes

There must, notwithstanding, be some reason why the Court evidently regarded the question as problematic. Three interconnected factors would, it is suggested here, help us clear a way through the thicket.

(i) Difficulties in Determining the Meaning of Non-pecuniary Loss

There is reason to believe that confusion, in the corporate context, about the actual meaning of non-pecuniary loss (or identical terms, such as immaterial loss, moral damage, *préjudice moral*, etc) could be one cause of the difficulties. The topic has rarely been analysed by scholars, whether within or outside the ECHR context.[83] Obviously, Art 41 can not provide definitional support since it does not even address the injuries for which an applicant may claim 'satisfaction'. Nor has the Court defined the concept; it prefers to refer to concrete forms of non-pecuniary damage without theoretical amplification.

The concept of non-pecuniary damage is, in short, a form of injury whose components remain obscure. This obscurity is helped by the fact that it is sometimes difficult to determine whether an injury is pecuniary or non-pecuniary.[84] In fact, the type of claim being analysed in this chapter has on occasion been construed in international practice as pecuniary rather than non-pecuniary loss. A well-known example is the Permanent Court of International Justice's

[82] D Shelton *Remedies in International Human Rights Law* (2nd edn Oxford University Press Oxford, 2005) 10–16.

[83] Dannemann (n 80) 386–89; and G Ress 'Schmerzengeld für juristische Personen?' in G Lüke T Mikami and H Prütting (eds) *Festschrift für Akira Ishikawa zum 70. Geburtstag am 27. November 2001* (de Gruyter Berlin 2001) 429 are notable exceptions in ECHR law. WV Horton (ed) *Damages for Non-Pecuniary Loss in a Comparative Perspective* (Springer Vienna, 2001) is a helpful introduction to various domestic legal systems' views. For international law, see in particular Dannemann (n 80) 386–89; and J Personnaz *La Réparation du prejudice en droit international public* (Sirey Paris, 1939) 203.

[84] Ress (n 83) 434–35.

rendition of a claim in the *Chórzow Factory* case for compensation for lost business reputation as a loss in market shares and therefore typically pecuniary in its nature.[85] Such difficulties of conceptual distinction play a part also in the approach taken at the European Court of Human Rights, as will be shown below.

It is nonetheless clear that a defining feature of non-pecuniary loss is its intangibility. Intangibility is something which is 'incapable of being touched; not cognizable by the sense of touch'.[86] In the context of compensation, this entails that its financial assessment builds on unverifiable data: its monetary value must be presumed.[87]

The controversial question is whether non-pecuniary damage requires an additional quality, notably an individual nexus requirement, in the sense that it only refers to loss which individuals alone are capable of sustaining. The government in the *Comingersoll* judgment argued, as was shown above, in favour of this view.[88] Some factors do suggest an individual nexus requirement. The International Law Commission's Articles on State Responsibility, which, in lieu of authoritative definitions under the ECHR might offer valuable insight to how the loss is conceived in international law, refers to 'moral damage' as including 'such items as individual pain and suffering, loss of loved ones or personal affront associated with an intrusion of one's home and private life'.[89]

Support for an individual nexus requirement is also found by implication in relevant literature. Dinah Shelton in the leading treatise on remedies in international human rights law seems to take for granted that non-pecuniary damage is associated with qualities that are intrinsic to human beings when she writes that:

> Intangible injuries such as physical pain and suffering have long been recognized as legitimate elements of damages. Mental anguish independent of physical injury is also now recognized as an element of recovery, including humiliation, loss of enjoyment of life and other non-pecuniary losses . . . In civil law systems, 'préjudice moral' includes pain and suffering, sadness and humiliation caused by disfigurement, loss of amenities,

[85] *Case concerning the Factory at Chórzow (Germany v Poland) (Merits)* PCIJ Series A No 17, 56.

[86] 'Intangible', *Oxford English Dictionary Online* (Oxford University Press Oxford, 2003), available at <http://dictionary.oed.com> (24 June 2005).

[87] Shelton (n 82) 71. [88] *Comingersoll* (n 7) § 28(2).

[89] Art 31(2) of the International Law Commission's Articles on the Responsibility of States for internationally wrongful acts, UN GAOR 56th Session Supp No 10 Un Doc A/56/10, chapter IV.E.1 as acknowledged by the UN General Assembly, see UNGA Res 56/83 (28 January 2002) UN Doc A/RES/56/83 (ILC Articles on State Responsibility), as given in the Report of the International Law Commission on the work of its Fifty-third session, UN GAOR 56th Session Supp No 10 UN Doc A/56/10, ch IV.E.2—the Commentaries to the draft articles on Responsibility of States for internationally wrongful acts (ILC Draft Articles Commentary) 225. See also J Crawford *The International Law Commission's Articles on State Responsibility. Introduction, Text and Commentaries* (Cambridge University Press Cambridge, 2002) 201–6.

loss of recreational ability, loss of any of the five senses, enjoyment of sexual relations, harm to marriage possibilities, and generally damage to the enjoyment of life.[90]

Jean Personnaz intimated a comparable nexus when he suggested that privately held companies were entitled to compensation because of their immediate individual *substratum* whereas publicly held companies ought not to be compensated for non-pecuniary harm due to their impersonal character.[91]

Strasbourg appears to support an individual nexus requirement, since the Court twice has implied that associations were entitled to this form of remedy by reference to the suffering sustained by the individuals making up the organizations.[92] These judgments did not, however, settle the question under discussion here, since associations are 'looser' forms of organization than limited liability companies; their individual component is more palpable than in the corporate entity.[93] The willingness to award compensation for individual suffering in these cases may just have been a natural consequence of the facts of the cases under consideration.

In fact, an individual nexus remains unsettled in Strasbourg in terms of significance and merit, despite the clarification as to the applicability now given. The importance of the element of individual suffering in a corporate complaint was the centre of the dispute between the majority and the concurring judges in *Comingersoll SA v Portugal.* The Court majority saw it as important that an expansive reading of Art 41 entailed, albeit implicitly, the protection of individuals' concerns. Four judges, in a joint concurring opinion, saw this existence of an individual *substratum* as wholly irrelevant, and thus dismissed an individual nexus requirement.[94]

(ii) Rhetorical Incompatibility

Mere disagreement over the meaning of non-pecuniary loss cannot, however, fully explain the divergence of opinion nor why compensation for intangible harm is problematic while, as noted above, companies are conceived of as being capable of suffering non-pecuniary harm when the remedy in question is a declaratory judgment rather than economic compensation.

The absence of debate when in comes to remedying non-pecuniary loss with declarations could, however, be an artefact of tradition. For the Court declaratory judgments have a particular function that is, or (as we will see later) at least used

[90] Shelton (n 82) 306–7 (footnotes omitted). See in a similar vein in the context of the ECHR, van Dijk and van Hoof (n 13) 255; Harris O'Boyle and Warbrick (n 1) 687; and Peukert (n 77) 675–76.

[91] Personnaz (n 82) 203, as observed by Dannemann (n 81) 387.

[92] *Vereinigung demokratischer Soldaten Österreichs (VDSÖ) and Gubi v Austria* judgment 19 December 1994 Series A 302 (1995) 20 EHRR 56 §§ 60–62; and *Freedom and Democracy Party (ÖZDEP) v Turkey* judgment 8 December 1999 [GC] Reports 1999-VIII (2001) 31 EHRR 27 § 57. See also Ress (n 83) 435.

[93] As observed in *Comingersoll* (n 7) Concurring Opinion of Judges Rozakis, Bratza, Caflisch and Vajič, para 3.

[94] ibid paras 2–3.

to be, absent in monetary compensation. It is used as conciliatory means to meet the applicant's inability to procure proof that the general requirements for compensation have been met,[95] or because the Court wants to make some form of recompense because it is unsure of the doctrinal validity of offering another form of satisfaction.[96]

Tradition helps us also to analyse the contentiousness affiliated with compensation for intangible injury. For one, companies only infrequently claim economic compensation for non-pecuniary loss, be it before domestic or international tribunals. The law of torts in various nations of the Council of Europe regards this type of claim as rare, contentious, and far from doctrinally settled.[97] Action for damages in EU law is only exceptionally claimed by companies for non-pecuniary loss, and, where invoked, it has been received with the same measure of apprehension as previously in the Court.[98] Modern arbitral practice does in fact provide examples where the tribunal awards compensation for non-pecuniary loss without discussion,[99] though this form of remedial claim seems to be rare, not least because treaty regimes that would otherwise have been suitable outlets for companies' claims bar the opportunity.[100]

In short, it is suggested here that the rhetorical climate in legal discourse renders companies' claims incompatible with the very institution of compensation for non-pecuniary loss because it is plainly not encountered often enough. The remedy appears misplaced firstly when the claims are dressed in the language of the human being, as a form of strained exercise of anthropomorphism.[101] Companies have, for instance, claimed compensation because of their 'stress and anguish',[102] and their 'feelings of frustration, powerlessness, suffering and revolt'.[103] Given the context in which non-pecuniary damage is normally awarded, such claims appear out of place.

[95] *Academy Trading Ltd and Others v Greece* (2001) 33 EHRR 44 §§ 55–56.

[96] Examples include *News Verlags* (n 6) § 66; and *Manifattura* (n 6) § 22. Shelton (n 82) 203 and 205 treats both forms of conciliatory use of declarations.

[97] Ress (n 83) 436 and 438–41; and Dannemann (n 80) 388–89.

[98] Case T–52/96, *Sogecable SA v Commission* [1996] ECR 1996-II 797 § 29. Case law is dominated by individuals' claims, see A Toth 'The Concept of Damage and Causality as Elements of Non-Contractual Liability' in T Heukels and A McDonnel (eds) *The Action for Damages in Community Law* (Kluwer Hague, 1997) 179, 190–91.

[99] eg, ICSID Case No ARB/77/2 *Ltd Benvenuti et Bonfati srl v People's Republic of Congo* award 8 August 1980 (1982) 21 ILM 740, 761–62; and ICSID Case No ARB/82/1 *Société Ouest-Africaine des Bétons Industriels (SOAB) v Republic of Senegal* award 25 February 1988 (1992) 17 ICCA Ybk 42, 61.

[100] M Pellonpää 'Compensable Claims before the Tribunal: Expropriation Claims' in RB Lillich and DB Magraw (eds) *The Iran-United States Claims Tribunal: Its Contribution to the Law of State Responsibility* (Transnational Irvington NY, 1998) 185, 257–63; and *Futura Trading Inc v The National Oil Company* 13 Iran–US CTR 99, 117.

[101] Anthropomorphism: 'The attribution of human motivation, characteristics, or behaviour to inanimate objects, animals, or natural phenomena.' W Morris (ed) *American Heritage Dictionary of the English Language* (3rd edn Houghton Mifflin Boston 1992) 78.

[102] *Alithia Publishing Company v Cyprus* judgment 11 July 2002 §§ 43–45.

[103] *Matos e Silva Lda and Others v Portugal* Reports 1996-IV (1997) 24 EHRR 573 § 98.

A conceptual mismatch is also evident when companies choose the opposite tactic and refer to their alleged non-pecuniary loss in purely neutral—it is tempting to say business-like—terms, such as legal uncertainty,[104] 'deterioration of... commercial reputation and loss of customers',[105] or loss in the 'credibility and effectiveness' of their business undertakings.[106] Although referring to intangible matters, they are presented in settings which connote pecuniary more readily than non-pecuniary injuries (which, as the PCIJ showed, may well be construed of as pecuniary loss). Here, too, claims relating to non-pecuniary damage seem at odds with the traditional conception of non-pecuniary loss.

C. The Court's Favourable Response

This chapter has until now sought to explain how one approach to the object and purpose of the three provisions suggests the inapplicability of corporate claims under them. Now, it proceeds to explain the Court's response.

The Court only decides issues that concern the dispute brought before it (its mandate to issue advisory opinions pursuant to Art 47 not yet been fully availed of).[107] Nevertheless, over time its case law gradually forms patterns that reveal a general or prevailing understanding of aspects of Convention protection. Clarification of broader ECHR issues comes therefore gradually rather than in leaps and bounds; this mechanism is referred to in terms of progressiveness below.[108] That said, it cannot be denied that some judgments of the Court carry weight beyond the concrete dispute that occasioned them. The absence of a stare decisis doctrine in Strasbourg notwithstanding, the Court accepts that while it 'is not formally bound to follow its previous judgments, it is in the interests of legal certainty, foreseeability, and equality before the law that it should not depart, without good reason, from precedents laid down in previous cases',[109] so that it is 'in the interests of legal certainty and the orderly development of the Convention case law' to follow past decisions when it is cogent.[110]

[104] *Idrocalce Srl v Italy* Series A No 229-F, §§ 21–22.

[105] *Ruiz-Mateos v Spain* Series A No 262, (1993) 16 EHRR 505 §§ 69–70.

[106] *Alithia Publishing Company* (n 102) §§ 43–45.

[107] In the Court's Decision on the Competence of the Court to Give An Advisory Opinion, 2 June 2004 [GC], available at <http://www.echr.coe.int/Eng/EDocs/DecisionAdvisoryOpinionrequest.htm>, the Court unanimously held that it had no competence to consider a request for an advisory opinion submitted by the Committee of Ministers. It concerned the question whether the Commonwealth of Independent States' Human Rights Commission should be regarded as 'another procedure of international investigation or settlement' within the meaning of art 35 § 2(b).

[108] Part D section 4 below.

[109] *Christine Goodwin v UK* Reports 2002-VI § 74.

[110] *Cossey v UK* Series A No 184, (1991) 13 EHRR 622 § 35; generally, L Wildhaber 'Precedent in the European Court of Human Rights' in P Mahoney and others (eds) *Protecting Human Rights: The European Perspective: Studies in Memory of Rolv Ryssdal* (Heymann Cologne, 2000) 1529.

As mentioned above, three judgments represent the settlement of previous doctrinal uncertainty under the provisions. They have been relied upon in later disputes and remain landmarks in the development of ECHR law in the field. They are introduced below in chronological order and their reasoning cited in some detail as certain statements are crucial for the subsequent discussion. The rationale, which, it is maintained here, is conveyed in them, is analysed in part D.

1 Article 10 and Corporate Commercial Expression: *Autronic AG v Switzerland*

It is probably a matter of definition at which stage the Court decided to include corporate commercial speech within the boundaries of Art 10(1). In its judgments in the cases of *markt intern Verlag GmbH and Klaus Beermann v Germany*, from 1989, and *Groppera Radio AG and Others v Switzerland*, from 1990, the Court held that the commercial speech conveyed by corporate applicants fell within the scope of Art 10.[111] Although the corporate element was not explicitly debated at the Court in either case, the judgments form crucial steps in the development of the law in this area. Their reasoning is highly relevant and will be considered later. The status of corporate commercial speech was, however, discussed in particular first in *Autronic AG v Switzerland*, which was decided late in 1990. The *Autronic* dispute appropriately deserves to be called a watershed decision particularly because the presence of 'political' speech was less explicit than in prior case law.

The Court in *Autronic* was called upon to decide whether the reception and demonstration of satellite television signals via the applicant company's aerial dish at an electronics fair was protected by Art 10(1). The applicant company had applied for permission from Swiss authorities to receive signals from a Soviet telecommunications satellite, the purpose of which was solely to demonstrate the technical capabilities of the dish and encourage sales of it at the fair. The application for permission was rejected since Swiss authorities were unable to obtain permission from relevant Soviet authorities.[112] The applicant company asserted that this rejection constituted a violation of its right to freedom of expression under Art 10.[113] The Swiss government argued before the Court that because the content of the programmes was irrelevant to the company's objective—to promote the sale of its product—the applicant was essentially seeking Art 10 protection of its business activity. In the government's view, freedom of expression that was exercised 'exclusively for pecuniary gain came under the head of economic freedom' and fell therefore outside Art 10(1).[114]

[111] *markt intern* (n 44) § 26; and *Groppera Radio* (n 7) § 55.

[112] *Autronic* (n 7) §§ 10–27 gives the facts.

[113] ibid § 45.

[114] ibid § 44(2).

Deciding to convene as a forum for the settlement of complaints that raise 'serious questions affecting the interpretation of the Convention',[115] a Plenary Court determined by sixteen votes to two that Art 10(1) embodied the applicant company's claim and the provision consequently applied to the dispute. The Court majority provided the following reasons for its decision:

> In the Court's view, neither Autronic AG's legal status as a limited company nor the fact that its activities were commercial nor the intrinsic nature of freedom of expression can deprive Autronic AG of the protection of Article 10.... The Article...applies to 'everyone', whether natural or legal persons. The Court has, moreover, already held on three occasions that it is applicable to profit-making corporate bodies (see the Sunday Times judgment of 26 April 1979, Series A no. 30, the Markt Intern Verlag GmbH and Klaus Beermann judgment of 20 November 1989, Series A no. 165, and the Groppera Radio AG and Others judgment of 28 March 1990, Series A no. 173). Furthermore, Article 10...applies not only to the content of information but also to the means of transmission or reception since any restriction imposed on the means necessarily interferes with the right to receive and impart information. Indeed the Article...expressly mentions in the last sentence of its first paragraph...certain enterprises essentially concerned with the means of transmission.
>
> ...the Court is of the view that the reception of television programmes by means of a dish or other aerial comes within the right laid down in the first two sentences of Article 10 § 1..., without it being necessary to ascertain the reason and purpose for which the right is to be exercised. As the administrative and judicial decisions complained of...prevented Autronic AG from lawfully receiving [the] transmissions, they therefore amounted to 'interference by public authority' with the exercise of freedom of expression.[116]

This interpretation has come to enjoy unanimous support in the case law.[117]

2 Article 41 and Monetary Compensation for Non-pecuniary Loss: *Comingersoll SA v Portugal*

The next provision whose applicability was established was Art 41. In *Comingersoll SA v Portugal*, the Court in 2000 eventually confirmed that companies may be entitled to receive monetary compensation for non-pecuniary loss.[118] The applicant company successfully complained about Portuguese authorities' protracted handling of a civil dispute to which the *Comingersoll* company was party; the Court agreed that the company's right to have its 'civil rights' determined 'within a reasonable time', as provided for in Art 6(1), had not been observed.[119]

[115] Art 30 and Rules of Court Rule 72(1). A similar arrangement was in force when the judgment was adopted.

[116] *Autronic* (n 7) § 47(1) and (2).

[117] *Casado Coca* (n 53) § 35.

[118] *Comingersoll* (n 7). On the judgment, see Ress (n 83) and Emberland (n 74).

[119] *Comingersoll* (n 7) §§ 16–25.

Following this conclusion, the applicant company claimed monetary compensation for the non-pecuniary loss it had sustained, that is, the inconvenience of having to await a final result of the dispute pending in national courts.[120] The Court, sitting as a Grand Chamber due to the interpretative difficulty of the case, agreed in principle that this form of remedy could apply to a corporate applicant. The Court split, however, on the rationale for this view. The discussion of the dissenting judges' views is postponed to part D of the present chapter, as it is here their relevance will be most in evidence. At this juncture the Court majority's reasoning is considered. For a Strasbourg opinion, it is relatively elaborate:

First, the Court referred to its case law. It pointed out that 'in the *Immobiliare Saffi* case it did not consider it necessary in the light of the circumstances of the case to examine whether a commercial company could allege that it had sustained non-pecuniary damage as a result of anxiety'.[121] But it observed that the statement made in the *Immobiliare Saffi* judgment 'does not . . . imply that there is a general exclusion on compensation being awarded for non-pecuniary damage alleged by juristic persons'. It conceded that it would 'depend on the circumstances of each case' whether an award should be made, and noted that it in *Vereinigung demokratischer Soldaten Österreichs and Gubi v Austria* 'accepted that the first applicant, an association, may have suffered non-pecuniary damage'.[122] Furthermore, the Court noted that it had, in the *Freedom and Democracy Party (ÖZDEP)* case, awarded an applicant political party compensation for non-pecuniary damage 'on account of the frustration its members and founders had suffered as a result of a violation of Article 11'.[123]

The Court also referred to the practice of the Committee of Ministers, by noting that the Committee pursuant to its functions under the former Convention supervisory system

> in a number of cases awarded compensation for the non-pecuniary damage sustained by commercial companies as a result of the excessive length of proceedings. It is worth noting that the Government themselves have at no stage challenged the Committee of Ministers' power to make such awards in other Portuguese cases in which it has taken such decisions (see Resolution DH(96)604 of 15 November 1996 in the case of Dias & Costa, Lda., and Resolution DH(99)708 of 3 December 1999 in the case of Biscoiteria, Lda.).[124]

The Court also took into account the practice of the Council of Europe member States 'in such cases', and noted that

> Although it is difficult to identify a precise rule common to all the . . . States, judicial practice in several of the States shows that the possibility that a juristic

[120] ibid § 27(2). The Court mentions 'inconvenience and prolonged uncertainty' as the non-pecuniary headings under which the company had sought compensation, ibid § 36 first sentence.

[121] ibid § 32(1) citing *Immobiliare Saffi v Italy* (n 5).

[122] ibid § 32(2) citing *Vereinigung demokratischer Soldaten Österreichs and Gubi v Austria* (n 92) § 62.

[123] ibid § 32(3) citing *Freedom and Democracy Party (ÖZDEP) v Turkey* (n 92) § 57.

[124] ibid § 33.

person may be awarded compensation for non-pecuniary damage cannot be ruled out.[125]

Based on the foregoing arguments ('in light of its own case-law and that practice'), the Court could not 'exclude the possibility that a commercial company may be awarded pecuniary compensation for non-pecuniary damage'.[126] Finally, the Court made the following remarks, which deserve to be quoted in full:

> The Court reiterates that the Convention must be interpreted and applied in such a way as to guarantee rights that are practical and effective. Accordingly, since the principal form of redress which the Court may order is pecuniary compensation, it must necessarily be empowered, if the right guaranteed by Article 6 of the Convention is to be effective, to award pecuniary compensation for non-pecuniary damage to commercial companies, too. Non-pecuniary damage suffered by such companies may include heads of claim that are to a greater or lesser extent 'objective' or 'subjective'. Among these, account should be taken of the company's reputation, uncertainty in decision-planning, disruption in the management of the company (for which there is no precise method of calculating the consequences) and lastly, albeit to a lesser degree, the anxiety and inconvenience caused to the members of the management team.
>
> In the instant case, the fact that the proceedings in issue continued beyond a reasonable time must have caused Comingersoll S.A., its directors and shareholders considerable inconvenience and prolonged uncertainty, if only in the conduct of the company's everyday affairs. The applicant company was in particular deprived of the possibility of recovering its claim earlier—the claim, it will be recalled, was a liquidated one as it was based on bills of exchange—and it remains outstanding today. In this connection, it is therefore legitimate to consider that the applicant company was left in a state of uncertainty that justified making an award of compensation.[127]

Compensation was consequently provided for.[128] The *Comingersoll* doctrine has subsequently been reiterated in a considerable body of case law.[129]

3 Article 8 and Corporate 'Home' Protection: *Colas Est SA and Others v France*

The Court did not consider the applicability of the 'right to respect for one's . . . home' alternative in the provision until the 2002 case of *Colas Est SA and Others v France*.[130]

[125] *Comingersoll* (n 7) § 34. [126] ibid § 35(1).

[127] ibid §§ 35(2) and 36. [128] ibid § 37.

[129] eg, *Fertiladour SA v Portugal* judgment 18 May 2000 §§ 27–30; *F Spa v Italy* judgment 9 November 2000 §§ 17–19; and *Colas Est* (n 7) § 55.

[130] Emberland (n 11) considers the judgment. See also the case comment in J Temple Lang and C Rizza 'The Ste Colas Est and Others v France Case: European Court of Human Rights Judgment of April 16, 2002' (2002) 23 Eur Comp L Rev 413.

The applicants, three privately owned, but publicly held, limited liability companies in the construction business complained to the Court over French courts' acquiescence over a legal regime pending at the time which allowed raids of their corporate premises without a court warrant. French competition authorities had undertaken coordinated searches and seizures on the premises of the applicant companies, the purpose of which was to discover and secure documents related to suspected anticompetitive practices.[131] The applicant companies maintained that the raids infringed their right to respect for their home as provided for in Art 8(1).[132] The French government in this case conceded that the raids had indeed amounted to an interference with the applicant companies' rights under the 'home' protection alternative,[133] so there was no need for the Court to convene as a Grand Chamber to determine the applicability of the provision.

The respondent State's concession in the circumstances of the case did not, however, remove from deliberation at the Court the essential question of the claim. Discussing the question of applicability, a unanimous Chamber observed that:

> as it has previously held, the word 'domicile' (in the French version of Article 8) has a broader connotation than the word 'home' and may extend, for example, to a professional person's office (see Niemietz, cited above . . . § 30).
>
> In Chappell v the United Kingdom (judgment of 30 March 1989, Series A no. 152-A . . . § 26, and . . . § 63), the Court considered that a search conducted at a private individual's home which was also the registered office of a company run by him had amounted to interference with his right to respect for his home within the meaning of Article 8 . . .
>
> The Court reiterates that the Convention is a living instrument which must be interpreted in the light of present-day conditions (see, mutatis mutandis, Cossey v the United Kingdom, judgment of 27 September 1990, Series A no. 184 . . . § 35 in fine). As regards the rights secured to companies by the Convention, it should be pointed out that the Court has already recognised a company's right under Article 41 to compensation for non-pecuniary damage sustained as a result of a violation of Article 6 § 1 of the Convention (see Comingersoll v Portugal [GC] . . . §§ 33–35, ECHR 2000-IV). Building on its dynamic interpretation of the Convention, the Court considers that the time has come to hold that in certain circumstances the rights guaranteed by Article 8 of the Convention may be construed as including the right to respect for a company's registered office, branches or other business premises (see, mutatis mutandis, Niemietz, cited above . . . § 30).[134]

The caveat of 'certain circumstances' notwithstanding, the Court has, with this judgment, largely clarified the extent to which companies may invoke the

[131] *Colas Est* (n 7) §§ 8–21 reiterates the facts. [132] ibid §§ 28 and 35–39.
[133] ibid § 32(1). [134] ibid §§ 40–41 (the judgments referred to are considered later).

'home' protection alternative in Art 8(1) to defy administrative investigations carried out on corporate premises. There has been only a limited opportunity for the Court to extrapolate from it in subsequent case law, but what exists in case law after the judgment shows that the holding is relied upon.[135]

D. A Revamped Teleology

1 Rationalizing the Court's Approach

(a) Avant-Garde *Jurisprudence*

Representing important steps in the development of ECHR law, the judgments now introduced merit closer scrutiny. They indicate that the Convention is at the forefront of fundamental rights regimes in promoting the interests of for-profit entities. The *Comingersoll* judgment's view on compensation for companies' intangible injury represents, as was observed above, the *avant-garde* of the law of remedies.[136] The *Colas Est* judgment was a turning point for the European Court of Justice, which has revised its restrictive interpretation of 'home' protection for corporate premises by relying on the Court's holding.[137] The Court's interpretation of Art 10(1) serves as a model for the development of a budding commercial free speech doctrine in EU fundamental rights law.[138] Its business-friendly freedom of expression doctrine surpasses the German *Bundesverfassungsgericht*'s approach, in which the protection of commercial expression is reserved for statements with a minimum of political content.[139] Significantly, the ECHR approach outshines the US Supreme Court in offering protection to commercial speech,[140] which is all the more

[135] eg, *Buck v Germany* judgment 28 April 2004 § 31; *RL and M-J D v France* decision 18 September 2003 § b)(2); and *Tamosius v UK* decision 19 September 2002 § 1(6).

[136] Text accompanying fns 97–100.

[137] Case C–94/00, *Roquette Frères SA v Directeur general de la concurrence, de la consummation et de la repression des frauds* [2002] ECR I-9011 § 52; see further Emberland (n 11) 80 and 94–6.

[138] Cases C–74/99 and C–376/98 *Germany v European Parliament and Council* and *R v Secretary of State for Health, ex parte Imperial Tobacco Ltd and Others* [2000] ECR I-8419 § 153 (opinion of Advocate General Fennelly; the freedom of expression issues were not discussed by the ECJ).

[139] This doctrine was established in the *Benetton* case of 2000, BVerfGE 102, 347. See further T Sevecke ' "Schockwerbung" der Firma Benetton verstösst nicht gegen 1 UWG. Zugleich eine Anmerkung zum Urteil des Bundesverfassungsgerichts vom 12.12.2000' (2001) 32 AfP 179; and (as an English introduction) C Smith 'More Disagreement over Human Dignity: Federal Constitutional Court's Most Recent Benetton Advertising Decision' (2003) 4 German L J 533.

[140] The Strasbourg approach does not require that the commercial speech in question is legal and truthful, which are the minimum criteria for First Amendment protection, see *Virginia State Board of Pharmacy v Virginia Citizens Consumer Council* 425 US 748, 772 (1975); and *Central Hudson Gas & Electric Co v Public Service Commission* 447 US 557, 566 (1980).

noteworthy since the latter court is widely regarded to be a leading protagonist for a commercial speech doctrine.[141]

How did the European Court of Human Rights, of all courts with a mandate to adjudicate fundamental rights claims, come to assume this pioneering role? The reasoning of the landmark decisions affords several indications, as was shown by the discussion in part C. Building their holdings on a variety of arguments, the three judgments largely reflect well-known traits in the Court's methodology, such as various textual renderings, references to common European standards and elements of consent,[142] some of which sound more convincing than others in the circumstances.[143]

The variety of arguments relied upon underscores, perhaps, the need felt at the Court to provide as much justification as possible for what it perceived as controversial solutions. Be that as it may, it is not proposed here to examine in detail all the arguments invoked in support of an expansive reading of the provisions; many of them have been well covered by others on a general basis.[144] Some doctrinal moves, however, beg further inquiry. They are worthy of closer study because they recur, if to a varying degree, in the landmark judgments and supporting case law and because they suggest a particular approach to the principle of teleological interpretation in the context of the provisions under consideration, which in turn can be seen in light of the structural framework that was erected in chapters 1 and 2. Since the teleological approach also largely explained a narrow reading of the provisions, as was shown in part B above, it would be pertinent to offer more comments on the principle of teleological interpretation and the role played by it in the Court's response to hard cases of applicability.

(b) A Revamped Teleology

In accordance with the Vienna Convention on the Law of Treaties Article 31(1) the Court places 'considerable emphasis . . . in the interpretation of the Convention upon a teleological approach', that is, the method by which the object and purpose of the treaty is sought realized.[145] In chapters 1 and 2 it was suggested that the object and purpose of the ECHR had not been exhaustively identified but that it encompasses subjective as well as objective elements. The Convention is thus not only 'an instrument for the protection of individual human rights',[146] it is also 'an instrument designed to maintain and promote

141 Barendt (n 45) 54.

142 *Comingersoll* (n 7) §§ 33–34; *Niemietz* (n 19) § 30(1); and *Autronic* (n 7) § 47.

143 Emberland (n 74) 11–12 (Art 41); and Emberland (n 11) 86–93 (Art 8(1)).

144 General introductions to the interpretation of the Convention were cited in chapter 1.

145 Harris O'Boyle and Warbrick (n 1) 6.

146 *Soering v UK* Series A No 161, (1989) 11 EHRR 439 § 87.

the ideals and values of a democratic society',[147] 'the rule of law',[148] and other values underlying the Convention.

Chapter 2 introduced a distinction between subjective and objective approaches to human rights protection. This distinction is worth recalling here. Subjective elements of the Convention's teleology focus on the applicant person in general and the individual human being, as the prototype applicant, in particular. A subjective approach, which dominated the discussion in C above, only indirectly supports an inclusion of corporate entities' concerns within the provisions' ambit. Conversely, an objective approach places less emphasis on the interests of the applicant person and his or her concerns. It discusses instead the extent to which the applicability of the applicant person's claim is conducive to promoting and maintaining general Convention values. This approach more easily acknowledges the inclusion of company interests provided, of course, that their inclusion helps to safeguard the objective values embodied by the treaty.

The Court's response to hard cases of applicability in the corporate context suggests, it is asserted here, the application of a teleology in which objective elements of the Convention's object and purpose are placed in the foreground. While not the subject of wide scholarly attention, the application of an objective teleology represents no unusual strand of ECHR methodology. But in the context under discussion here the case law conveys a revamped teleology in use at the Court which has helped to bring about new areas of ECHR law. Following its invocation, the scope of Arts 8, 10, and 41 has been widened to include private activity that was formerly believed to lack the characteristics required for protection under the relevant rights and entitlements: their ambit now covers corporate and for-profit activities to an extent that at least was not discussed at the time of the Convention's adoption.

In what follows three doctrinal moves that form part of this teleology, as they are found explicitly or by implication in the landmark judgments and supporting case law, are discussed. They are all indicative of the Court's constant concern to ensure effective Convention protection. The principle of effectiveness plays a natural role in securing that aim. The principle has no exhaustive definition as applied by the Court,[149] but it cannot be doubted that it has a teleological thrust since it commands the Court to look to the purpose of the Convention to clarify vague treaty terms.[150] The effectiveness principle

[147] *Kjeldsen, Busk Madsen and Pedersen v Denmark* Series A No 23, (1979) 1 EHRR 711 § 53(3).

[148] *Golder v UK* Series A No 18, (1979) 1 EHRR 524 § 34(5); and *Silver and Others v UK* Series A No 61, (1984) 5 EHRR 347 § 90.

[149] *Botta v Italy* Reports 1998-I (1998) 26 EHRR 241 § 33.

[150] JG Merrills *The Development of International Law by the European Court of Human Rights* (Manchester University Press Manchester, 1988) 70–72.

provides a convenient framework for the presentation of the three forms of reasoning. For the sake of convenience, they are referred to below as pragmatism (section 2), objectiveness (section 3), and progressiveness (section 4) (their meaning to be soon explained). It cannot be ascertained with regard to all of them that they in fact did determine the outcome of the judgments. In any event, establishing that chain of causality is less important than demonstrating that such forms of reasoning are in accordance with generally acceptable modes of ECHR interpretation. To that end, the following analysis provides a structural justification for the Court's response to hard cases of applicability.

2 Pragmatism

The teleology of the principle of effectiveness is unmistakably pragmatic,[151] as it contains the element that the 'Convention is intended to guarantee not rights that are theoretical or illusory but rights that are practical and effective'.[152] A central element of pragmatic effectiveness as applied by the Court is the negation of an adjudication which is based on deductions from theoretical constructs and categorisation,[153] provided, it must be presumed, that this approach is not workable and would, besides, impede the realization of the treaty's object and purpose.

This form of pragmatism is evident in the Court's tendency to repudiate a respondent government's assertions of inadmissibility based on formal distinctions of various kinds. Thus in the *Comingersoll* case the Court refuted the assertion that an intrinsic conceptual link between damages for non-pecuniary harm and the faculties of the individual informed the interpretation of Art 4.[154] Observing that 'the Convention must be interpreted and applied in such a way as to guarantee rights that are practical and effective',[155] the Court rejected an understanding of non-pecuniary loss based on an individual/corporate dichotomy. Instead, it matter-of-factly observed that '[n]on-pecuniary damage suffered by . . . companies may include heads of claims that are to a greater or lesser extent "objective" or "subjective"'.[156] The Court also thought a distinction between pecuniary and non-pecuniary loss to be impracticable, observing that 'if one or more heads of damage cannot be calculated precisely' or if the

[151] It is not intended here to suggest that the Court subscribes to the pragmatic strand of philosophical inquiry (although possible similarities between the Court's methodology and the pragmatic school of legal philosophy seem a worthwhile subject of further research). Rather, 'pragmatism' is referred to in accordance with popular usage, something akin to the 'everyday pragmatism' of RA Posner *Law, Pragmatism, and Democracy* (Harvard University Press Cambridge Mass, 2003) 50–56.

[152] *Airey v Ireland* Series A No 32, (1980) 2 EHRR 305 § 24(2) (emphasis added). *Multiplex v Croatia* judgment 10 July 2003 § 44 provides a recent example of its use in the corporate context.

[153] van Dijk and van Hoof (n 10) 74.

[154] *Comingersoll* (n 7) §§ 32(2) and 28(2).

[155] ibid § 35.

[156] ibid § 35(2).

'distinction between pecuniary and non-pecuniary damage proves difficult, the Court may decide to make a global assessment' of the loss.[157]

With regard to the interpretation of Art 10(1), the respondent government in *Autronic AG v Switzerland* contended that a line should be drawn between corporate persons and commercial speech on the one hand and natural persons and non-political speech on the other out of the belief that a perfect 'fit' with the underlying rationale for free expression was unattainable for the first categories.[158] The government also suggested that Art 10 only include information that was 'intended for or made accessible to the public' and was relevant for the applicant, while information that failed to meet these requirements because it was subordinate to other motives than to reach the general public, that is pure for-profit motives, fell outside the provision's scope.[159] The Court refused to be guided by these categorizations. It confirmed that corporate commercial expression as such did not fall outside the provision's scope.[160] It rebuffed the appropriateness of a distinction between 'substance' and 'process' of free expression,[161] in stating that the provision 'applies not only to the content of information but also to the means' of its transmission and reception and that 'any restriction imposed on the means necessarily interferes with the right to receive and impart information'.[162]

With regard to the applicability of 'home' protection to corporate premises, the *Colas Est* judgment provides little direct evidence of a similar display of pragmatism since, as we know, the respondent government in the circumstances accepted that the provision did apply. The judgment relied heavily, however, on the case of *Niemietz v Germany*, where the government had resisted an inclusion in Art 8(1) of a lawyer's home office under the 'private life' as well as 'home' alternatives. The government had maintained that Art 8 did not afford protection since 'the Convention drew a clear distinction between private life and home, on the one hand, and professional and business life and premises, on the other'.[163] The Court's response to this assertion was reiterated in the *Colas Est* case, where it was held that:

> it may not always be possible to draw precise distinctions [between business activities and private activities], since activities which are related to a profession or business may well be conducted from a person's private residence and activities which are not so related may well be carried on in an office or commercial premises.[164]

[157] *Comingersoll* (n 7) § 29(4).

[158] *Autronic* (n 7) § 44(2) as read in conjunction with § 47.

[159] ibid § 44(2) and (3) first sentence.

[160] ibid § 47 first sentence: 'Neither the [applicant company's] status as a limited liability company nor the fact that its activities were commercial nor the intrinsic nature of freedom of expression' could deprive the applicant form art 10 protection.

[161] The terms are those of the applicant party, see *Autronic* (n 7) § 45 second sentence.

[162] ibid § 47 fourth sentence.

[163] *Niemietz* (n 19) § 27.

[164] *Colas Est* (n 7) 40(1), citing *Niemietz* (n 19) § 30(2).

The Court thus rejected an approach whereby an assumed distinction between business activities and personal activities informed the understanding of 'home'.

In sum, the Court, in adopting a favourable approach to three hard cases of applicability, has not wanted to be guided in its search of the provisions' object and purpose by concepts alone. This is a crucial element of the Court's revised teleology in the landmark cases.

3 Securing Objectiveness

A refutation of being constrained by conceptual categories is viable if it assists the Court in securing the observance of Convention protection. It is not an end in itself. The case law provides examples of several objectives of ECHR protection that emphasize objective rather than subjective aspects of the treaty's human rights and fundamental freedoms. These objective aspects of Convention protection are significant since they each in their own way make the inclusion of corporate claims appropriate in the provisions, even from a teleological viewpoint.

(a) Equal Treatment of Indistinguishable Cases

Concern with equality—to ensure some form of equal treatment in adjudication—is implied in some of the judgments, as seen above. Now, the Court is not bound to adhere unreservedly to a notion of equal treatment of individual and corporate applicants in the enjoyment of Convention protection. The treaty has no provision for equal treatment of all private interests, persons, and activities. The prohibition against discriminatory treatment, provided for in Art 14 and the new Protocol 12 Art 1,[165] is, besides, directed against the signatory States and not the Court.[166] The ambiguous doctrinal backdrop of the provisions under consideration here suggests at any rate that a differentiation between individual and corporate persons would not amount to discriminatory treatment since rational reasons could be marshalled in favour of differentiation.

The Court nonetheless endeavours to avoid interpretations that are at variance with the value of equal treatment, which is considered to be a Convention objective.[167] With regard to Art 10(1), the *Autronic* Court emphasized that parity between individuals and corporations was ingrained in the text: the

[165] Protocol No 12 to the Convention for the Protection of Human Rights and Fundamental Freedoms (adopted 4 November 2000, in force 1 April 2005) ETS 177 (Protocol 12).

[166] Protocol 12 Art 1(2); and ECHR Art 14 read in conjunction with Art 1.

[167] The Convention builds on and is generally informed by an 'equality maxim', see further OM Arnardóttir *Equality and Non-Discrimination under the European Convention on Human Rights* (Martinus Nijhoff Hague, 2003) 8–17.

provision applied 'to "everyone", whether natural or legal persons'.[168] It had previously held that the wording of Article 10(1) did not distinguish 'according to the content' of broadcasting programmes,[169] and thus implied equal treatment also in this respect pursuant to the text. The concurring judges in *Comingersoll SA v Portugal* were enthusiastic adherents of a universal application of the remedy of compensation for non-pecuniary loss to any private person, publicly held companies included,[170] since it is sometimes plainly difficult to distinguish between various forms of loss, and thus supported an equality maxim with regard to Art 41 in this respect.

As far as Art 8(1) is concerned, a similar expression of equal treatment is less evident in the *Colas Est* case. In the *Niemietz* judgment, however, the Court invoked pragmatism because:

> it is not always possible to distinguish clearly which of an individual's activities form part of his professional or business life and which do not. Thus, especially in the case of a person exercising a liberal profession, his work in that context may form part and parcel of his life to such a degree that it becomes impossible to know in what capacity he is acting at a given moment of time.
>
> To deny the protection of Article 8 . . . on the ground that the measure complained of related only to professional activities—as the Government suggested should be done in the present case—*could moreover lead to an inequality of treatment*, in that such protection would remain available to a person whose professional and non-professional activities were so intermingled that there was no means of distinguishing between them. In fact, the Court has not heretofore drawn such distinctions.[171]

The Court in the *Colas Est* case endorsed this equality argument by implication,[172] and this is natural enough since it may be inherently difficult to distinguish clearly between private and for-profit activity. The Court thereby pushed the argument in the *Niemietz* case one step further, since the equality approach in the *Niemietz* case did not logically reach the for-profit sector. The *Niemietz* Court was concerned with the risk of arbitrary under-inclusion of interests that pertain to the individual person. This approach is not necessarily transportable to the corporate context where an individual nexus is at best remotely present, and where the wording of the provision suggests that priority is given to individual applicants and their interests. The framing of the *Colas Est* judgment—its proviso for inclusion in 'certain circumstances'—similarly suggests adherence to a modified notion of equality.

[168] *Autronic* (n 7) 47(1) second sentence.

[169] *Groppera Radio* (n 7) § 55; and *markt intern* (n 44) § 26.

[170] *Comingersoll* (n 7) Concurring Opinion of Judge Rozakis, Bratza, Caflisch and Vajič, para 3.

[171] *Niemietz* (n 19) § 29(2) and (3) (emphasis added).

[172] *Colas Est* (n 7) § 40(1) citing *Niemietz* (n 19) § 30 last sentence, which again refers to the latter judgment's § 29.

Be this as it may, the Court is ready to rely on equal treatment for the purpose of including corporate interests in the provision, surely out of the belief that equality is a value which Strasbourg adjudication should seek to protect. Equality—as an objective Convention value—can therefore help support the Court's *avant-garde* jurisprudence to some extent.

(b) Rule of Law

Another Convention purpose for which protection is sought in the case law, and which in chapter 2 was defined as having an objective character, is the rule of law principle. The rule of law is an underlying Convention value in its own right. The 'entire Convention' is inspired by it.[173] It is also an essential pillar in the treaty's concept of democracy, which was introduced in chapter 2. An integral part of the Court's teleology is to secure adherence to the rule of law in the Convention's signatory States. The Court has held, we recall, that one of the functions of the principle of effectiveness is to ensure rule of law observance.[174]

There are elements of a rule of law inspired teleology in the case law under scrutiny here, although it cannot be established with certainty that rule of law aspects decided the Court's conclusion. Reliance upon them in support of an expansive interpretation of Arts 8, 10, and 41 would, however, be entirely in accordance with the general mode of teleological interpretation, as understood in a reconsidered manner.

In *Colas Est SA and Others v France* the Court reserved the application of 'home' protection to 'certain circumstances'.[175] Since the provision was found to apply in that case (it was indeed held to be violated), the Court must have meant that those 'circumstances' were present in the case. The context informs us that the Court saw 'circumstances' in that particular dispute to equate the fact that the applicant companies had been subjected to excessive searches and seizures without having been served a court warrant beforehand. The Court found Art 8(1) to encompass business premises because insufficient procedural safeguards existed to prevent arbitrariness. Now, freedom from arbitrariness is a cornerstone of the rule of law principle. It is also an important objective of Art 8 protection: as we know, the purpose of the provision is to 'protect the individual against *arbitrary interference* by public authorities'.[176] Even if the individual component was missing in the *Colas Est* case, arbitrary interference was indeed present. It is tempting to see the Court's expansive reading in the *Colas Est* judgment as a rule of law inspired purposeful interpretation.

[173] *Engel and Others v Netherlands* Series A No 22, (1979) 1 EHRR 647 § 69.

[174] *Golder* (n 148) § 34; and *Silver* (n 148) § 90.

[175] *Colas Est* (n 7) § 41 last sentence.

[176] *Niemietz* (n 19) § 31 (emphasis added).

With regard to Art 41, it is useful to know that protection of the rule of law constitutes part of the rationale for the international law of remedies.[177] The *Comingersoll* Court held that delays in Portuguese courts' handling of the dispute to which the applicant company was party contravened Art 6(1), which spells out that such disputes are to be settled 'within a reasonable time'. Arguing for an expansive reading of Art 41 to encompass compensation for non-pecuniary loss sustained by the applicant company, the Court invoked the effectiveness principle. It considered that 'if the right guaranteed by Article 6 . . . is to be effective' it must be entitled to afford compensation for non-pecuniary loss also when that loss is sustained by corporate entities.[178]

Why was it important to afford compensation in this case? The Court stressed that:

> the applicant company is unable to claim the value of its debt as compensation for pecuniary damage, especially bearing in mind that the proceedings are still pending and that it is impossible to speculate at this stage on their outcome.[179]

The Court applied thus the remedy of compensation for non-pecuniary loss as a substitute for compensation for pecuniary loss, which was unattainable for the applicant. It did so because the protracted proceedings, in the Court's view, had caused the company 'considerable inconvenience and prolonged uncertainty'.[180] Absence of certainty is, as we know, a significant aspect of the rule of law principle, and it cannot be doubted from reading the Court's reasoning that it emphasized the need for an effective protection of the rule of law principle inherent in Art 6. The company was plainly 'left in a state of uncertainty that justified making an award of compensation'.[181]

This substitute use of the remedy for repairing rule of law violations when compensation for material loss is doctrinally unattainable is in line with what was described above, that the Court has applied, without debate, the remedy of declaratory judgments to compensate companies' non-pecuniary loss.[182] The judgment can safely be seen as an example of the Court's particular concern to secure effective observance of the rule of law in the Convention.[183] As the principle is not primarily concerned with the faculties of private persons it

[177] eg, Shelton (n 82) 10.

[178] *Comingersoll* (n 7) § 35(2) second sentence.

[179] ibid § 30. To afford satisfaction for non-pecuniary loss as a substitute for compensation for material loss is a recurrent approach in the Court's art 41 practice, see Emberland (n 74) 3.

[180] *Comingersoll* (n 7) § 36 first sentence.

[181] ibid § 36.

[182] Emberland (n 74) 3.

[183] Case law subsequent to *Comingersoll* similarly shows that compensation for non-pecuniary loss is invoked as substitute for compensation for material loss in contexts in which the rule of law principle has not been observed, see, eg, *Entreprises Meton et Etep v Greece* judgment 21 March 2002 §§ 25–29; *Koncept-Conselho em Communicação e Sensibilizia de Públicos Lda v Portugal* judgment 31 October 2002 §§ 30–33; and *SA Sitram v Belgium* judgment 15 November 2002 §§ 22–24 (all cases concern length of civil proceedings in violation of art 6(1), legal uncertainty being the harm occasioned). *Colas Est* (n 7) § 55 (art 8; rule of law aspects at issue).

provided ample doctrinal space for an expansion of Article 41 to companies also with regard to compensation for non-pecuniary loss.

To sum up, a reliance on the effective adherence to the rule of law, which has an objective character, in support of an expansive reading of the provisions can also be seen as a reconsideration of the subjective teleology introduced in part B.

(c) Collective Aspects of Individual Rights Protection

Chapter 2 observed that the ECHR guarantees civil and political rights that to a varying degree have collective as well as individual import. The present chapter has thus far suggested that corporate reliance upon certain rights and entitlements raises controversial questions of interpretation because the rights and entitlements primarily have been regarded to protect the individual human being rather than interests pertaining to collective entities.

The judgments represent here a watershed in Strasbourg jurisprudence. They imply that the relevant parts of Arts 8(1), 10(1), and 41 do in fact hold collective elements: had they not done so the provisions would have been found inadmissible to the corporate claimants. To emphasize collective aspects of civil and political rights may also be seen as a reconsidered teleology, in which aspects other than those pertaining to the individual natural person are highlighted. The collectivism in question is not, however, identically construed in the three contexts.

(i) Collectivism in Article 41

In the *Comingersoll* judgment, it was noted above, the judges did not reach an agreement as to just how collectivist the remedy under discussion should be construed as they split with regard to the significance of an individual component in the non-pecuniary suffering on which basis compensation was given.

The majority believed that the presence of individual suffering was, at least, a supporting argument in favour of affording compensation. In deciding whether compensation for non-pecuniary damage should be afforded, it believed that 'account should be taken' of the damage sustained by the company as such, ie collective factors ('the company's reputation, uncertainty in decision-planning, disruption in the management of the company'), as well as 'albeit, to a lesser degree, the anxiety and inconvenience caused to the *members of the management team*'.[184]

[184] *Comingersoll* (n 7) § 35(2) (emphasis added).

The concurring judges, who failed to enjoin the whole Court in their view, favoured an unconditional collectivism in the remedy in question so that individual suffering should have no relevance in the Court's interpretation. In the concurring judges' opinion, the company 'is an independent living organism', which deserved compensation:

not because of the anxiety or uncertainty felt by its human components, but because, as a legal person . . . it has attributes, such as its own reputation, that may be impaired by acts or omissions of the State.[185]

Subsequent case law shows that the Court continues to be ambivalent in this regard.[186]

But regardless of the dispute over this detail, the whole Court conceded that the remedy did have collective elements. The majority did not contest this, it merely thought that individual component was a supporting argument for including a corporate entity among those entitled to the remedy. In this regard, the judgment has clarified that collective elements are inhered in all aspects of the provision. This surely represents an approach to teleology in which corporate interests are relevant and which is justified if we see Art 41 as having a redefined object, ie a collective nature to the same extent as it has an individual nature.

(ii) Article 8: Collective Aspects of Privacy

With regard to Art 8, the *Colas Est* Court, by finding the applicant companies' complaint admissible, must have recognized the existence of some collective aspects to Art 8's 'home' protection alternative, since it held the guarantee applicable without linking this view to the possibility of there being information of the companies' employees in the documents that had been seized.[187] The Court thus effectively modified the Commission's former statement, in the *Church of Scientology of Paris* case cited above, that 'unlike Article 9, Article 8 [was] of an individual rather than a collective character'.[188]

The acknowledgement of collectivist aspects of privacy protection enjoys also philosophical support,[189] as in privacy theory the social dimensions of privacy are increasingly invoked in support of corporate privacy either in the form of an analogy from individual privacy justification (companies, regardless of their individual *substrata*, need an inner sphere free from public intrusion; companies must be enabled to enter into relations with business partners and

[185] Ibid, Concurring Opinion of Judges Rozakis, Bratza, Caflisch and Vajić para 3.

[186] Contrast, eg, *Koncept-Conselho em Communicação e Sensibilizia de Públicos, Lda* (n 183) §§ 30–33, with *Colas Est* (n 7) § 55. Further, Emberland (n 74) 20.

[187] The applicant companies invoked this argument, *Colas Est* (n 7) § 38. The Court did not comment on it.

[188] *Church of Scientology of Paris* (n 31) § 1(5); and *Scientology Kirche eV v Germany* (n 34).

[189] Feldman (n 37) 21; and J Rachels 'Why Privacy Is Important' (1975) 4 Phil & Pub Aff 323.

other actors),[190] or in a derivative form which suggests privacy for corporate entities because companies ultimately consist of individuals.[191] Both theories provide support for a reading of Article 8 which accepts corporate inclusion among the provision's beneficiaries out of collective considerations. An emphasis on object and purpose in the light of this insight, where the nature of Art 8 is reconsidered, will therefore facilitate the inclusion of corporate interests, at least to a certain extent.

(iii) The Public Aspect of Free Speech Protection

The Court acknowledges that the text of Art 10 has collective features in that companies and other entities are entitled to rely on it on a par with individuals.[192] But additionally, the Court's jurisprudence signals another form of collectivism in which the objective outreach of the provision becomes particularly forceful. The Court adheres to a special teleological approach whereby it accepts that protection of a company applicant's commercial interests is worthy of protection since that protection is instrumental for the protection of the freedom of expression of the public at large or society in general. This has obvious links with the pervasiveness of democracy in the Convention.

The Preamble, we recall, refers to the importance of an 'effective' political democracy, not merely democracy as such. To the extent the activity of companies, and companies' Strasbourg complaints, can play a facilitative role in securing this effectiveness to the benefit of other persons or society as a whole, there is support in the Convention's value of democracy to protect companies, too.

This instrumentality is evident in the Court's broad interpretation of Art 10. It is paramount in Art 10 interpretation to provide for a 'free public discussion',[193] a means for securing open debate.[194] Freedom of expression constitutes a right not only for the speaker but also the audience and the general public.[195] Free speech is in 'the public interest',[196] not primarily in the interest of the applicant person.

[190] Walden and Savage (n 40) 342; Wright (n 40) 119; and RA Posner 'The Right to Privacy' (1978) 12 Ga L Rev 393, 404–6.

[191] The argument has been seen in the context of data protection, see Walden and Savage (n 43) 342; and F Hondius *Emerging Data Protection in Europe* (North-Holland Amsterdam, 1975) 100. In the context of US constitutional law, eg, *Hale v Henkel* 201 US 43, 76; and *Marshall v Barlow's Inc* 436 US 307, 311 (1978).

[192] *Autronic* (n 7) § 47(1).

[193] A Clapham *Human Rights in the Private Sphere* (Clarendon Press Oxford, 1993) 147.

[194] JES Fawcett *The Application of The European Convention on Human Rights* (2nd edn Clarendon Press Oxford, 1987) 261.

[195] *Thorgeirson v Iceland* Series A No 239, (1992) 14 EHRR 843 § 63(2); and G Cohen-Jonathan 'Transparence, démocratie et effectivité des droits fondamenteaux dans la Convention européenne des droits de l'homme' in P Mahoney and others (eds) *Protecting Human Rights: The European Perspective: Studies in Memory of Rolv Ryssdal* (Heymann Cologne, 2000) 245, 248.

[196] *Sunday Times* (n 52) § 42.

This means that companies, regardless of the nature of the activities they seek to have protected, may merit Convention protection when they in one way or another facilitate public discourse.[197] The Court, on the basis of securing an effective democracy, tends to 're-state, or generalize, the individual rights in issue as, in themselves, a community interest'.[198]

More concretely, the *Autronic* judgment emphasized, as we have seen, the importance of protecting the means of communication just as much as the content of speech 'since any restriction imposed on the means necessarily interferes with the right to receive and impart information'.[199] The provision protects 'not only the substance of the ideas and information expressed but also *the form in which they are conveyed*'.[200] Following this rationale, the protection of commercial expression, and corporate commercial speech, is justified primarily inasmuch as a different solution would be tantamount to the placing of a restriction on the free flow of information, which in turn could obstruct the exchange of ideas and opinions that is of such importance in a democratic society.

By shifting focus in this endeavour to separate the object and purpose of Convention protection from the interests of the applicant person and her interests from those who might benefit from the protection of her rights, the Court clearly facilitates a reading of the provision in which the content of the speech or the status of the expresser is of subordinate interest. The Court's approach corresponds closely with the development in US constitutional jurisprudence, where a similar shift in emphasis has taken place, from, in the words of John Hart Ely, 'ontology to teleology'.[201] We may continue to refer to the shift in our context as a move towards objectiveness in the Court's teleology—an approach that was less present in prior case law.

[197] Likewise, the protection of corporate rights under art 6 can help keep open the channels for accountability and transparency to the benefit of society in general, see generally, *Kostovski v Netherlands* Series A No 166, (1990) 12 EHRR 434 § 44.

[198] S Marks 'The European Convention on Human Rights and Its "Democratic Society" ' (1996) 66 BYIL 209, 216; Barendt (n 45) 7.

[199] *Autronic* (n 7) § 47. In his Concurring Opinion, Judge De Meyer applauded the result of the judgment 'especially as what was in issue here was measures preventing public demonstration of equipment for receiving television broadcasts'. See also *markt intern* (n 44) Joint Dissenting Opinion of Judges Gölüklü, Pettiti, Russo, Spielmann, De Meyer, Carillo Salcedo and Valticos para I(7): 'freedom of expression serves . . . the general interest'.

[200] *Dichand and Others v Austria* judgment 26 February 2002 § 37 (emphasis added). See further L Boisson de Chazournes 'Publicité commerciale et liberté d'expression dans la cadre du Conseil de l'Europe' (1988) 92 RGDIP 929, 951.

[201] JH Ely 'Flag Desecration: A Case Study' (1975) 88 Harv L Rev 1482, 1496. Cases include *Virginia Board of Pharmacy v Virginia Consumer Council, Inc* (n 140) and *First National Bank v Bellotti* 435 US 765, 775–86 (1978). See also, eg, MH Redish 'The First Amendment in the Marketplace: Commercial Speech and the Values of Free Expression' (1971) 39 Geo Wash L Rev 429, 441–44. In *Tobacco Directive* (n 138) § 154 the two dimensions of free speech protection were explicitly acknowledged.

4 Progressiveness

The Court cannot establish new Convention rights. That is for the signatory States to do at their own volition.[202] The Court's teleological approach to the hard cases of applicability results in a reading of the three provisions that borders on an expansion of the Convention's scope. It would be surprising if the Court did not feel the need to ground its interpretation to avoid any suspicion of illegitimate judicial activism. Several of the arguments invoked in favour of the result of including companies' interests in the provisions are instrumental to secure legitimacy for the Court's revamped teleology with regard to the question of applicability of Arts 8, 10, and 41.

(a) Reliance upon Prior Case Law

One mode of reasoning, which is found with regard to all three provisions, deserves special attention here. This is the Court's invocation of prior case law to substantiate its decisions. With regard to the interpretation of Art 8(1) in *Colas Est SA* and *Others v France*, the Court made a point of referring to its former *Niemietz v Germany* judgment, where it had held that 'the word "domicile" (in the French version of Art 8) has a broader connotation than the word "home" and may extend, for example, to a professional person's office'.[203] It also reiterated that in *Chappell v UK*, it had held that 'a search conducted at a private individual's home which was also the registered office of a company run by him had amounted to an interference' with 'home' protection.[204]

In *Autronic AG v Switzerland*, the Court, in a similar move, relied upon three prior judgments—the *Sunday Times, markt intern* and *Groppera Radio* cases—in support of the view that Art 10 'is applicable to profit-making bodies'.[205] With regard to the interpretation of Art 41 in the context of non-pecuniary loss sustained by corporate bodies, the *Comingersoll* Court similarly held that:

> [i]n light of its own case-law . . . the Court cannot . . . exclude the possibility that a commercial company may be awarded pecuniary compensation for non-pecuniary damage.[206]

Read in the context of § 32 of the judgment it can be inferred that the 'case-law' in question consisted of three prior judgements: *Immobiliare Saffi v Italy* from 1999;[207] *Freedom and Democracy Party (ÖZDEP) v Turkey*, also from 1999;[208]

202 *Johnston and Others v Ireland* Series A No 112, (1987) 9 EHRR 203 § 53.

203 *Colas Est* (n 7) § 40(1) referring to *Niemietz* (n 19) § 30.

204 ibid § 40(2) referring to *Chappell* (n 30) §§ 26 and 63.

205 *Autronic* (n 7) § 47 third sentences, referring to *Sunday Times* (n 52); *markt intern* (n 44); and *Groppera Radio* (n 7).

206 *Comingersoll* (n 6) § 35(1).

207 *Immobiliare Saffi* (n 5) § 79(4).

208 *ÖZDEP* (n 92).

and *Vereinigung demokratischer Soldaten Österreichs (VDSÖ) and Gubi v Austria* from 1994.[209]

(b) Analogous Matters Only

The case law to which the Court refers in the three judgments lacks the quality to satisfy the requirements of precedent—if the Court had indeed adopted a stare decisis doctrine—since the decisions reiterated and referred to in support of the conclusions do not concern and decide sufficiently comparable issues. This is now explained further with regard to all three provisions.

(i) **Article 8**

As correctly observed by the Court in *Colas Est*, the *Niemietz* judgment found that the French term 'domicile' has the capability of covering a wider range of premises than 'home' in the English authentic text,[210] and to place emphasis on the French rather than the English term is in accordance with Art 33(4) of the Vienna Convention, which directs the Court to interpret the differences in meaning between equally authentic texts 'in a way that will reconcile them as far as possible' and 'is most appropriate in order to realise the aim and achieve the object of the treaty'.[211]

But there is a substantial difference in kind and in degree of individual nexus with regard to the office of a professional lawyer who, as in the case of Mr Niemietz, has his office in his private home, and the business offices of the impersonal construction companies acting as applicants in the *Colas Est* case. The *Niemietz* Court stressed, significantly, the need for equal treatment of individuals' privacy in the workplace and at home.[212] The individual nexus was also evident in *Chappell v UK*, the other judgment referred to in the *Colas Est* case.[213] The *Chappell* case involved searches and seizures on company premises, which simultaneously were the home of its only shareholder. The indistinguishable relationship between the applicant's private residence and personal sphere and the premises of his business activities was decisive for finding Art 8 applicable.[214] The Court in the *Colas Est* case revealed no similar concern for the privacy of natural persons.[215]

[209] *Comingersoll* (n 7) § 32(2) citing *VDSÖ* (n 92) § 62.

[210] *Niemietz* (n 19) § 30(1).

[211] *Wemhoff v Germany*, judgment 27 June 1968, Series A 7 § 8.

[212] *Niemietz* (n 19) §§ 30(2) and 29.

[213] *Chappell* (n 30). The passage in this judgment cited by the Court in 2000 must be wrong; it is conceivably § 26b rather than § 25b (which does not exist).

[214] App 10461/83 *Chappell v UK* (report) (1987) §§ 96–99. The relationship also becomes evident in § 26b in the judgment in the case (to which *Colas Est* referred directly). The respondent government did not contest the applicability of Art 8(1) before the Court, see *Chappell* (n 30) § 51.

[215] The Court omitted to comment on the applicants' contention that the office premises should enjoy protection because of the possibility that the seized documents may contain private information on the companies' employees, see *Colas Est* (n 7) § 38.

(ii) Article 10

With regard to Art 10, the *Autronic* Court is correct in stating that the prior case law conveyed the view that 'profit-making corporate bodies' were included in the provision's scope. But the applicant's status as a profit-making body was not the controversial element in the *Autronic* case. The controversy lay in the exceptionally for-profit-oriented nature of the interests sought protected and the fact that the content of the programmes was unimportant for the applicant. In this respect, the *Autronic* complaint presents a fundamentally different form of 'expression' than those asserted by the corporate bodies of the three prior judgments, where the speech sought protected was at least important for an audience. The prior case law concerned, moreover, the protection of companies in the media sector, which, as we know, enjoys a special status under Art 10 as an instrument of public debate, which is also expressly recognized in the provision's text.

Thus, in the *Groppera Radio* case, the complaint concerned the inability to broadcast radio programmes whose content—mainly light music and commercials—could raise doubt as to whether they were 'information' and 'ideas' and consequently 'expression' within the meaning of Art 10(1). The Court admitted the claim because of the broadcasting nature of the claim.[216] The radio station also transmitted news bulletins and the expression of personal opinions of personal matters in addition to its non-essential speech.[217] In the *markt intern* case, to which the *Autronic* judgment also referred, the speech in question reached an audience and concerned substantive matters of interest for the recipients in question; it was in form of political information for the retail trade market.[218] The claim also related to restraints put on a publication. The Commission had observed that '[a] democratic society must leave it to the publishers to determine what matters are of sufficient interest to merit publication'.[219] Finally, the *Sunday Times* case concerned injunctions on a newspaper company's publication of articles that were acknowledged by the Court to have public interest;[220] the Court also stressed the special function attributed to the press in a democratic society.[221]

Autronic AG was not a media company nor a company intent on securing the interests of a specific part of the public; it was the producer and supplier of

[216] *Groppera Radio* (n 7) §§ 54–55. The broadcasting context was also crucial for the three dissenting judges to find the provision applicable in the present case, see Concurring Opinion of Judge Matscher, approved by Judge Bindschedler-Robert; and Concurring Opinion of Judge Valticos.

[217] This was stated by the legal representative of the applicants at the public hearing of the Court 21 November 1989, as observed in the Concurring Opinion of Judge Valticos.

[218] *markt intern* (n 44) § 26, citing *Müller and Others v Switzerland* Series A No 133, (1991) 13 EHRR 212 § 27.

[219] App 10572/83 *markt intern Verlag GmbH and Klaus Beermann v Germany* (report) (1987) § 202.

[220] *Sunday Times* (n 52) §§ 8–17.

[221] ibid § 65(4), see also §§ 66–67.

a means for receiving television broadcasts from foreign media.[222] The 'speech' in question was sought protected not in order to disseminate information or opinions or ideas to a general public, but only, and so the Court accepted, to promote the product for the purpose of its own pecuniary gain.[223] The Court nonetheless accepted a favourable approach to Autronic's claim for Article 10 protection, but referred to prior case law in support of this view that was at best analogous to the claim.

(iii) Article 41

One gains a similar impression, ie, that the case law invoked in support of expansive reading only partially substantiates the conclusion reached, from the *Comingersoll* judgment with regard to Art 41. In the *Immobiliare Saffi* case, to which the *Comingersoll* Court referred, the question for compensation for corporate non-pecuniary loss was in fact left undecided since the Court found no reason to award satisfaction.[224] It has later been confirmed that the *Immobiliare Saffi* Court had felt unsure whether companies were entitled to claim this remedy.[225]

In *Freedom and Democracy Party (ÖZDEP) v Turkey*, the other case invoked, the Court awarded monetary compensation for non-pecuniary harm to a political party.[226] In *Vereinigung demokratischer Soldaten Österreichs (VDSÖ) and Gubi v Austria*, the third case relied upon, the Court found that an association for soldiers had the capability of suffering non-pecuniary damage as a result of a violation of Arts 10 and 13.[227] Political parties and associations are 'looser organisations' than a company of Comingersoll SA's stature, since the individual *substratum* is more evident in organizations made up by individuals rather than their capital investment.[228] The award in *ÖZDEP* was besides based on the suffering sustained by the individual members and founders of the party, and not the party itself.[229] In the *VDSÖ* case, the Court opted for a declaratory judgment rather than compensation,[230] which, as has been observed previously, has never been regarded as problematic in the corporate context.[231] All these differences from the *Comingersoll* claim notwithstanding, the Court chose to recall these judgments in favour of inclusion.

[222] *Autronic* (n 7) Dissenting Opinion of Judges Bindschedler-Robert and Matscher para 1.

[223] *Autronic* (n 7) §§ 47(2) second sentence and (3).

[224] *Immobiliare Saffi* (n 5) § 79(4).

[225] In *News Verlags* (n 6) § 66(2), *Immobiliare Saffi* (n 5) was cited as example of the uncertainty of the law in the field.

[226] *ÖZDEP* (n 92).

[227] *Comingersoll* (n 7) § 32(2) citing *VDSÖ* (n 92) § 62.

[228] ibid, Concurring Opinion of Judges Rozakis, Bratza, Caflisch and Vajic para 3.

[229] *ÖZDEP* (n 92) § 57.

[230] *VDSÖ* (n 92) § 62.

[231] *Pressos Compania Naviera SA and Others v Belgium (Art 50)* judgment 3 July 1997 Reports 1997-IV §§ 7 and 21; and *Academy Trading* (n 95) § 56.

(c) *Progressive Reasoning as Legitimating Factor*

What could be the purpose of reviving prior case law of this kind in the landmark judgments?

It is natural to see the Court's invocation of prior case law as progressive reasoning, that is, an interpretative approach whereby the Court makes 'incremental additions to jurisprudence' over time,[232] in the sense that it gradually extends the protection afforded to Convention rights and guarantees.[233] Although well elaborated in the context under discussion here, it is not an approach which is restricted to companies' claims for protection under Arts 8(1), 10(1), and 41.[234] Progressiveness in the present context means the Court's ability to justify transformations or even expansions of the conceived protective scope of the provisions gradually and on a case-by-case basis in response to novel kinds of private litigation by invoking the holdings of prior decisions in analogous cases as arguments for a new reading of open-textured provisions.[235]

There is no reason to question the Court's reference to past decisions in this light. International courts inevitably develop the law they are called upon to adjudicate,[236] and a mode of reasoning which situates transformations of the law in an existing legal framework is a time-honoured form of constitutional adjudication.[237] As Ronald Dworkin explained in connection with his 'chain-novel' metaphor, good adjudication is characterized by a progressive, case-by-case process in which every court decision that paves new ground looks ahead while being embedded in the legitimacy of past judgments.[238]

The gradual transformation of the scope of certain provisions to engage collective and for-profit interests in addition to individual concerns may nonetheless come close to a form of adjudication which cannot immediately be considered as an uncontroversial result of the nature of the judicial process. Paul Mahoney has seen progressiveness at the Court as a mode 'generally taken to be a manifestation of judicial restraint'.[239] In relation to hard cases of

232 P Mahoney 'Judicial Activism and Judicial Self-Restraint in the European Court of Human Rights: Two Sides of the Same Coin' (1990) 11 HRLJ 57, 76–77.

233 *Hatton and Others v UK (No 2)* (2003) 37 EHRR 28, Joint Dissenting Opinion of judges Costa, Ress, Türmen, Zupancic and Steiner para II(2).

234 J Andriantsimbazovina ' "Chronique droits de l'homme": 1988–1995: L'élaboration progressive d'un ordre public européen des droits de l'homme' (1997) 33 CDE 655.

235 Progressiveness as understood in ECHR law should not be confused with a particular political platform. Nor does it correspond with progressiveness as normally conceived in international law, which refers to the gradual evolution and codification of custom, see, eg, R Jennings 'International Law Reform and Progressive Development' in G Hafner and K-H Böckstiegel (eds) *Liber Amicorum Professor Ignaz Seidl-Hohenveldern in Honour of His 80 th* Birthday (Kluwer Hague, 1998) 325, 325.

236 C Grewe 'Vergleich zwischen den Interpretationsmethoden europäischer Verfassungsgerichte und des Europäische Gerichtshof für Menschenrechte' (2001) 61 ZaöRV 459, 466.

237 ibid 466.

238 R Dworkin *Law's Empire* (Belknap Press Cambridge Mass, 1986) 225–38.

239 Mahoney (n 232) 77.

applicability in the company context, however, it may well be seen as the opposite of restraint. This dilemma in the Court's response to hard cases of applicability will not, however, be pursued further here.

(d) A Comment on the Dynamic Interpretation in Colas Est

Before this chapter is summed up, the case law under Art 8(1) permits a minor digression. Bearing in mind the climate of contention at the time of the Court's holdings, it is noteworthy that the Court in the *Colas Est* case relied on the principle of dynamic interpretation as an additional argument with regard to Art 8(1). The Court reiterated that:

> the Convention *is a living instrument which must be interpreted in the light of present-day* conditions . . . As regards the rights secured to companies by the Convention, it should be pointed out that the Court has already recognised a company's right under Article 41 to compensation for non-pecuniary damage sustained as a result of a violation of Article 6 § 1 of the Convention (see *Comingersoll v Portugal* [GC] . . . §§ 33–35, ECHR 2000-IV). *Building on its dynamic interpretation of the Convention*, the Court considers that the time has come to hold that in certain circumstances the rights guaranteed by Article 8 of the Convention may be construed as including the right to respect for a company's registered office, branches or other business premises (see, *mutatis mutandis, Niemietz*, . . . § 30).[240]

The principle of dynamic (or evolutive) interpretation must not be confused with progressiveness. A significant adjudicatory aid for the Court,[241] the dynamic principle assumes that the ECHR is 'a living instrument, which must be interpreted in light of present-day conditions'.[242] The principle conforms to the teleological approach taken by the Court in that the protection of human rights cannot be sufficiently effective without the infusion of an element of evolution in accordance with societal development.[243] It enjoys considerable support since it has a textual basis in the Preamble (the wording of which does give the impression of a forward-looking instrument);[244] since it injects a democratic element of adjudication in that it reflects acknowledged social and legal changes;[245] and because a Convention which is up-to-date with respect to

240 *Colas Est* (n 7) § 41 (emphasis added).

241 O de Schutter 'L'interpretation de la Convention européenne des droits de l'homme: un essai en démolition' (1992) 70 RDISPPS 83, 85–87.

242 *Tyrer v UK* Series A 26 (1980) 2 EHRR 1 § 31. See also R Bernhardt 'Thoughts on the Interpretation of Human-Rights Treaties' in F Matscher and H Petzold (eds) *Protecting Human Rights: The European Dimension. Studies in Honour of Gérard J Wiarda* (Heymann Cologne, 1988) 65, 69.

243 Grewe (n 236) 466–67.

244 Preamble 3rd and 5th recitals; and WJ Ganshof van der Meersch 'Le caractère "autonome" des termes et la "marge d'appréciation" des gouvernements dans l'interprétation de la Convention européenne des Droits de l'Homme' in F Matscher and H Petzold (eds) *Protecting Human Rights: The European Dimension. Studies in Honour of Gérard J Wiarda* (Heymann Cologne, 1988) 201, 202.

245 Grewe (n 236) 466–67.

social and legal currents in Europe cultivates public confidence and consequently State compliance.[246]

The *Colas Est* Court's reference to dynamism, however, appears to deviate from the manner in which the principle is normally rendered. As it appears, the Court says that the 'condition' that activates teleology through dynamism in the present case is the Court's own judgment in the *Comingersoll* case. Normally, the 'conditions' to which the Court refers as activating factors for change correspond to a conceived climate of opinion in the ECHR member States, as measured in their laws and societies, of a higher standard of fundamental rights awareness (and conversely a lower standard of tolerance for violating such rights).[247] They are, in other words, extrinsic to the Court's own activities. The Court's progressive adjudication, on the other hand, refers to the internal dynamics of the Court's own judicial business. The Court in the *Colas Est* case seems in other words to have referred to progressiveness in terms of dynamic interpretation.[248] The crucial reference point seems to have been factors internal to the Court's own adjudicatory business, notably the very tendency of progressiveness as such. It would have been clarifying, also for an understanding of progressive reasoning, if the Court had elaborated on its reading of dynamic interpretation.[249]

E. Summary Observations

This chapter has argued that the Court in its response to hard cases of applicability in the corporate context has applied a redefined teleological approach that justifies its novel reading of three provisions. This approach is different from an outlook on the provisions' object and purpose that focuses on the status of the applicant person and its interests. Within the framework of a subjective teleology, so part B showed, the aspects of Arts 8, 10, and 41 considered here suggested that corporate interests lie either at the provisions' margins or wholly beyond their ambit. A view on the provisions' object and purpose that focuses on other matters than those intimately connected with the applicant person tends to be more inclusive of corporate interests, perhaps primarily because the status of the corporate applicant is subordinate to the protection of underlying Convention values, such as equality, rule of law and democracy. As we have

246 Mahoney (n 232) 64.

247 M de Blois 'The Fundamental Freedom of the European Court of Human Rights' in R Lawson and M de Blois (eds) *The Dynamics of the Protection of Human Rights in Europe. Essays in Honour of Henry G Schermers* (Martinus Nijhoff Dordrecht, 1994) vol 3, 35, 57 refers to it as a 'sociological' method of Convention interpretation.

248 *Colas Est* (n 7) § 41.

249 On this point, see also Emberland (n 74) 14–17.

seen, the Court also appreciates collective facets of the provisions' civil and political rights. The teleology here used by the Court, and which draws on the complex nature and purpose of the Convention that was indicated in chapter 2, is a revamped teleological approach to this context since it deviates from how the provisions previously have been rendered.

The shift of focus in the Court's inquiry is substantiated, so the judgments testify, by various doctrinal arguments. Reliance upon prior case law, even in cases that concern at best analogous matters, is a well-tried argument for a novel reading of provisions whose scope can easily be seen as concerning predominantly or only the interests of the natural person. In referring to former judgments, whose reasoning is framed in a sufficiently open-ended way so as to include potentially new areas of law brought before the Court, the Court applies a sound approach to adjudication, effectively allaying whatever disquiet may arise at the sight of an infusion of collective elements into 'individual' rights and objective aspects of human rights protection.

The judgments demonstrate the Court's preoccupation with the principle of equal treatment as well as its refusal to be constrained by theoretical distinctions in its application of ECHR law. Additionally, it may be added, at least with regard to the approach taken to Arts 8 and 10, that the Court has thought it no great harm to open up the provisions to corporate actors in principle, at the applicability stage, since it has retained the possibility to modify the extent of protection afforded when it decides on the level of protection actually offered. The next chapter will demonstrate that the Court has decided, possibly as a means of 'curbing the enthusiasm' implied in its applicability approach, to adopt a lax standard of review when corporate interests under the provisions are balanced against other and sometimes conflicting concerns. As will be shown, the Court's pragmatism may mean that what are considered as unsuitable modes of interpretation in one context, may be regarded as viable approaches in another.

5

Lenient Standards of Review

If the Court finds that a provision applies to the corporate applicant, it must determine next whether the respondent State has in fact violated the applicant company's rights or freedoms. The answer to this question ultimately rests on the outcome of the Court's review of the opposing claims of the two parties of the dispute. This chapter considers the standard of review applied by the Court when it assesses the violability of governmental regulation that interferes with private business activity that in principle is entitled to ECHR protection. One purpose of this analysis is to complement the picture of the Convention as a liberal project.

The chapter discusses the norms for judicial scrutiny developed in contexts in which the scope and intensity of the review are informed by the business or corporate nature of the company petitioner's activities. The Court has articulated a system of low-intensity protection in two contexts—both of which were introduced in the preceding chapter—of pertinence for the present discussion. Deference to governmental regulation of commercial speech is an established doctrine in the case law under Art 10. A comparable deference to public needs is discernible in Art 8 practice, especially in circumstances in which corporate premises have been subjected to public interference in terms of searches and seizures. Although corporate case law remains foregrounded by the present discussion, it might be noted that the solutions adopted seem generally applicative to business actors regardless of corporate status. Specific company attributes, however, sometimes influence the standard adhered to. At any rate, the Court's assessment of the legitimacy of governmental regulation of business activity is too important an issue to ignore here simply because some of the conclusions may apply to other business actors as well: it is part and parcel of the overall pattern that can be discerned from the Court's response to corporate complaints.

The analysis does not cover the entire range of protective level granted to company-related claims under the Convention. In some instances, the Court does not appear to differentiate, in its review of governmental interference, between the nature or purpose of the applicant person. For instance, the right to a judicial process undertaken within a 'reasonable' period of time by an independent and impartial dispute-settling organ, as provided for in Art 6(1), is considered according to a universal standard in which the corporate or business nature of complaints is an insignificant factor.[1] In other instances, there is insufficient data to allow any firm conclusions to be drawn as to the probability of differentiation. This is clearly the case for corporate reliance upon Arts 9 and 11, provisions similar to Arts 8 and 10 in pattern.[2] Another example concerns corporate reliance upon the right to access to court in Art 6(1) to defy administrative authorities' regulatory power even if, in this particular context, there is sometimes a suggestion that recurrent features that pertain to corporate applicants may inform the scope of the right.[3]

Another group of related issues not analysed here concerns the lenient standard of review applied with regard to property right claims under Protocol 1 Art 1. The Court generally assumes that the assessment undertaken on the domestic plane remains within the boundaries of the provision unless it is 'manifestly without reasonable foundation'.[4] This might upset corporate Strasbourg strategies disproportionately because such claims tend to have a property dimension. The markedly reserved scrutiny of governmental interference with property rights has, however, a universal scope in that it is not as such a consequence of the status of the private applicant or the claim pursued. The Court's deference is based on the generally moderate status of property protection under the Convention and the reasons for public interference. Some aspects of leniency found in Protocol 1 Art 1 are included in the discussion below of possible factors that help justify the Court's approach with regard to Arts 8 and 10.

Part A familiarizes the reader with the tensions inherent to deliberations under Arts 8 and 10 to determine whether a specific case of interference amounts to a violation and the principal means by which the Court attempts to resolve these tensions. Part B introduces the Court's standards of relaxed scrutiny under the two provisions as they emerge from the case law. The Court's justification is characteristically brief. In fact, the Court's introduction

[1] On these aspects of art 6(1), see, eg, H Miehsler and T Vogler 'Artikel 6–Allgemeine Verfahrensgarantien' in H Golsong and others (eds) *Internationaler Kommentar zur Europäischen Menschenrechtskonvention* (Heymann Cologne, 1986) vol 1, 88.

[2] There is no evidence of differentiation in the few cases that do exist under art 11, see, eg, *AB Kurt Kellermann v Sweden* decision 11 July 2003 § 2. This is less immediately transparent with regard to corporate use of art 9, see App 19509/92 *Church of Scientology of Paris v France* (1995) § 1.

[3] *Fayed v UK* Series A No 294-B, (1994) 18 EHRR 393 §§ 75 and 81. *Delcourt v Belgium* Series A No 11, (1979) 1 EHRR 355 § 25(4) illustrates that differentiation is not applied as a rule.

[4] *James and Others v UK* Series A No 98, (1986) 8 EHRR 123 § 46(2) second sentence; see also, with regard to access to court of property claims of this kind, eg *Lithgow and Others v UK* Series A No 102, (1986) 8 EHRR 329 § 197; and *National & Provincial Building Society and Others v UK* Reports 1997-VII (1998) 25 EHRR 127 § 112.

of low-intensity protection standards in the business context is almost devoid of explanation. In lieu of justifications articulated by the Court, part C suggests a framework rationale that complements the Court's parsimonious reasoning and makes the adoption of lenient standards in Arts 8 and 10 appear reasonable on general structural and doctrinal grounds. Part D contains some summary observations.

A. Conflicting Interests and the 'Necessity' Criterion

The Court's low-intensity model of protection, to be discussed in this chapter, is applied in its interpretation of the so-called 'necessity' requirement in the second limb of Arts 8 and 10. The chapter first explains the structure of Arts 8(2) and 10(2) and how the Court's assessment of one criterion set forth there illustrates its handling of the tensions between private and public demands and national and international aspects of Convention protection. This description provides a background for the presentation in part C of the standards invoked by the Court.

As the Court stated in the *Belgian Linguistics Case* in 1968, the Convention implies a just balance between the protection of the general interest of the community and the respect due to fundamental human rights, while attaching particular importance to the latter.[5] As is the case with many ECHR provisions, Arts 8 and 10 rest on the ambiguity inherent in the Convention as such inasmuch as it aims at the reinforcement of the protection of individual persons belonging to the private sphere at the same time as it recognizes the exigencies of national and public interests (see also chapter 2).[6]

This ambiguity has two dimensions. One is the tension between public and private interests, the other the tension between national and international authority. The Court makes use of two interconnected principles of Convention interpretation to handle these respective tensions: the proportionality principle and the margin of appreciation doctrine.[7] They are considered in turn, since

[5] *Case relating to certain aspects of the laws on the use of languages in education in Belgium (Belgian Linguistics Case) (Merits)* Series A No 6, (1979) 1 EHRR 252 § 5.

[6] M Delmas-Marty and G Soulier 'Restraining or Legitimating the Reason of State?' in M Delmas-Marty (ed) *The European Convention for the Protection of Human Rights: International Protection Versus National Restrictions* (Martinus Nijhoff Dordrecht, 1992) 7, 7.

[7] P van Dijk and G J H van Hoof *Theory and Practice of the European Convention on Human Rights* (2nd edn Kluwer Hague, 1998) 80–97 introduces the two principles. On their interrelationship, see in particular Y Arai-Takahashi *The Margin of Appreciation Doctrine and the Principle of Proportionality in the Jurisprudence of the ECHR* (Intersentia Antwerp, 2002) 14–15.

familiarity with them is crucial for analysing the Court's lenient standards of review (which is done in parts B and C).

1 The Public-Private Tension: 'Necessity' and Proportionality

There is no doubt that the Convention is first and foremost a charter for the protection of the interests of private persons. As consistently held by the Court, the object and purpose of the treaty principally is 'the protection of individual human rights'.[8] Articles 8 and 10 provide safeguard for certain fundamental freedoms, liberties, against interference by the State in activities in which the applicants engage. The provisions embody the Convention's principal concern, also expressed in Art 1, notably the protection of fundamental private and/or individual concerns vis-à-vis governmental authority.

Recognition of the general needs of the public, as represented in a dispute by the government of the respondent State, is however also ingrained in the Convention structure. This is of course well known, but important enough to be briefly rehearsed. In the context under discussion here, consideration of public needs is expressed in the second limb of Arts 8 and 10, which are fairly similarly framed.[9] Article 10(2) proscribes:

> The exercise of these freedoms, since it carries with it duties and responsibilities, may be subject to such formalities, conditions, restrictions or penalties as are prescribed by law and are necessary in a democratic society, in the interests of national security, territorial integrity or public safety, for the prevention of disorder or crime, for the protection of health or morals, for the protection of the reputation or rights of others, for preventing the disclosure of information received in confidence, or for maintaining the authority and impartiality of the judiciary.

Article 8(2) contains the same essence, but is phrased slightly differently:

> There shall be no interference by a public authority with the exercise of this right except such as is in accordance with the law and is necessary in a democratic society in the interests of national security, public safety or the economic well-being of the country, for the prevention of disorder or crime, for the protection of health or morals, or for the protection of the rights and freedoms of others.

The two provisions establish a tripartite set of requirements the respondent State must meet for the Court to conclude that public interference does not amount to a Convention breach. They articulate the legitimacy of various policy aims (exhaustively, but not identically, listed in the two provisions), legislative power ('prescribed by law'/'in accordance with the law') and a

[8] *Soering v UK* Series A No 161, (1989) 11 EHRR 439 § 87.

[9] A number of other provisions subscribe to a similar pattern, see, eg, Arts 5(1), 9(2), 11(2) and Protocol 1 Art 1.

societal imperative ('necessary in a democratic society').[10] Even if they imply the fundamental ECHR tenet that governmental authority is subordinate to fundamental values such as non-arbitrariness, legality, and proportionality between ends and means,[11] they simultaneously represent a Convention acceptance of public interests.

(a) 'Necessity'

Only one of the three requirements is dealt with here, notably the condition that interference with private activity, which in principle is protected by Art 8 or Art 10, must be regarded as 'necessary in a democratic society'.[12] It is in the course of interpreting and applying this criterion that the Court has developed a lenient review of public regulation of business activity.

To understand how the Court's review is lenient, it is necessary to establish, in broad terms at least, how the criterion is normally understood when the Court's review is *not* lax. In *Silver and Others v UK*, a case unrelated to the matter under discussion here, the Court summed up the principles on the basis of which 'necessary in a democratic society' normally is to be assessed:

> On a number of occasions, the Court has stated its understanding of the phrase 'necessary in a democratic society', the nature of its functions in the examination of issues turning on that phrase and the manner in which it will perform those functions. It suffices here to summarise certain principles:
>
> (a) the adjective 'necessary' is not synonymous with 'indispensable', neither has it the flexibility of such expressions as 'admissible', 'ordinary', 'useful', 'reasonable' or 'desirable' . . .;
>
> (b) the Contracting States enjoy a certain but not unlimited margin of appreciation in the matter of the imposition of restrictions, but it is for the Court to give the final ruling on whether they are compatible with the Convention . . .;
>
> (c) the phrase 'necessary in a democratic society' means that, to be compatible with the Convention, the interference must, inter alia, correspond to a 'pressing social need' and be 'proportionate to the legitimate aim pursued' . . .;
>
> (d) those paragraphs of Articles of the Convention which provide for an exception to a right guaranteed are to be narrowly interpreted . . .[13]

The principle referred to in letter (b), the margin of appreciation doctrine, is for the sake of convenience considered separately in section 2 below. As for

[10] DJ Harris M O'Boyle and C Warbrick *Law of the European Convention on Human Rights* (Butterworths London, 1995) 283–301 gives a comprehensive introduction to the three requirements.

[11] M Delmas-Marty 'The Richness of Underlying Reasoning' in M Delmas-Marty (ed) *The European Convention for the Protection of Human Rights. International Protection versus National Restrictions* (Martinus Nijhoff Dordrecht, 1992) 319, 322–27.

[12] Harris O'Boyle and Warbrick (n 10) introduces the requirement with regard to arts 8 and 10 at 344–53 and 396–414 respectively.

[13] *Silver and Others v UK* Series A No 61, (1984) 5 EHRR 347 § 97; similarly, Arai-Takahashi (n 7) 63.

the three remaining principles, those expressed in (c) and (d) are the most important since they in essence elaborate what is meant by 'necessity'. They imply a fairly strict standard applied at Strasbourg for reviewing the legitimacy of public authority in light of the Convention standards. The *Silver* Court emphasised that the second limbs of the provisions are to be 'narrowly interpreted', that is, narrowly to the benefit of the private applicant. This interpretative approach is in accordance with the view generally held in Convention interpretation that it is 'necessary to seek the interpretation that is most appropriate in order to realise the aim and achieve the object of the treaty', ie the protection of human rights and fundamental freedoms, 'and not that which would restrict to the greatest possible degree the obligations undertaken by the parties'.[14]

The Court also says that the word 'necessary', found in Arts 8 and 10, implies that a governmental interference must correspond to a 'pressing social need', and, in particular,[15] that the interference must be 'proportionate to the legitimate aim pursued'. The Court consistently emphasizes the proportionality assessment of governmental means (the interference) and ends (the legitimate policy aim) in its case law, and it is fair to assume that balancing opposing considerations remains the central undertaking in all 'necessity' interpretation. As put by John Cremona:

> The essential argumentation is often in the sense that an interference is not proportionate to the legitimate aim pursued and *therefore* is not necessary in a democratic society.[16]

(b) *The Proportionality Assessment*

Proportionality is an elusive criterion which, besides, is variously applied according to the treaty environment in which it is used.[17] The Court's use of proportionality with regard to the 'necessity' requirement reflects one particular variant, namely:

> that a proportionate balance must be struck between the means employed and the aims pursued in order not to overburden the rights of individual persons in return for social goods.[18]

[14] *Wemhoff v Germany* Series A No 7, (1979) 1 EHRR 55 § 8 second sentence; and F Matscher 'Methods of Interpretation of the Convention' in R St John Macdonald F Matscher and H Petzold (eds) *The European System for the Protection of Human Rights* (Martinus Nijhoff Dordrecht, 1993) 63, 66.

[15] *Olsson v Sweden* Series A No 130, (1989) 11 EHRR 259 § 67.

[16] JJ Cremona 'The Proportionality Principle in the Jurisprudence of the European Court of Human Rights' in U Beyerlin and others (eds) *Recht zwischen Umbruch und Bewahrung: Völkerrecht, Europarecht, Staatsrecht. Festschrift für Rudolf Bernhardt*, (Springer Berlin, 1995) 323, 329.

[17] Matscher (n 14) 78–80; M-A Eissen 'The Principle of Proportionality in the Case-Law of the European Court of Human Rights' in R St John Macdonald F Matscher and H Petzold (eds) *The European System for the Protection of Human Rights* (Martinus Nijhoff Dordrecht, 1993) 125; and van Dijk and van Hoof (n 7) 81.

[18] Arai-Takahashi (n 7) 14.

This rendering of the principle, as Yutaka Arai-Takahashi points out, is a narrower and more specific meaning of proportionality than the general tenet sometimes proposed by the Court that 'a "fair balance" must be struck between the right of the individual applicants and the general interests of the public'.[19] Such nuances are not overly important here, since it is clear that both ultimately mean that the principle's function under Arts 8(2) and 10(2) is to balance the conflicting demands of the private and public interests at stake in the concrete dispute.[20] The public–private tension inherent in the determination of whether a violation has occurred is in other words primarily solved through the application of the principle of proportionality. Thus the usefulness of familiarize the reader with it here.

On the basis of what, exactly, is proportionality assessed, and how is that basis made to fit the business context? Clear answers cannot readily be given since the case law is far from helpful in this regard.[21] This dearth of material is of little consequence here. The lenient standard of scrutiny of governmental interference originates in the Court's application of the principle of proportionality, though it is not in its discussion of proportionality as such that the Court discloses its inclination to prefer the arguments of the respondent government over those of the applicant company. One needs to consider the margin of appreciation doctrine, and the place of proportionality within this doctrine, in order to draw nearer to the heart of the matter.

2 The Supranational Dimension: the Margin of Appreciation Doctrine

(a) The Margin of Appreciation Doctrine

The Convention builds on the equilibrium between national sovereignty concerns and the exercise of international authority in pursuit of human rights protection. Sovereign interests of the parties to the treaty are fixed in the structure of Convention protection,[22] and it is for the Court to relate, in its adjudication, to this tension between the national and the international.[23]

[19] ibid 193.

[20] ibid 14; and J McBride 'Proportionality and the European Convention on Human Rights' in E Ellis (ed) *The Principle of Proportionality in the Laws of Europe* (Hart Oxford, 1999) 23, 24.

[21] Arai-Takahashi (n 7) 87–91 (art 8) and 128–36 (art 10) analyses the meaning of proportionality.

[22] M Oreja 'Souverainité des Etats et respect des droits de l'homme' in F Matscher and H Petzold (eds) *Protecting Human Rights: The European Dimension. Studies in Honour of Gérard J Wiarda* (Heymann Cologne, 1988) 7; and H Petzold 'The Convention and the Principle of Subsidiarity' in R St John Macdonald F Matscher and H Petzold (eds) *The European System for the Protection of Human Rights* (Martinus Nijhoff Dordrecht, 1993) 41, 55.

[23] M Fordham and T de la Mare 'Identifying the Principles of Proportionality' in J Jowell and J Cooper (eds) *Understanding Human Rights Principles* (Hart Oxford, 2001) 27, 54.

In the 'necessity' requirement this dimension is handled by the margin of appreciation doctrine. As Eva Brems has observed:

> Very few international treaties interfere with the sovereignty of the contracting states to the same extent as the European Human Rights Convention and its protocols. In this perspective, the domestic margin of appreciation is used to counterbalance this interference, returning some control to the national authorities.[24]

The doctrine is not explained in detail here since it has been analysed extensively by others,[25] but a few comments are required because the relaxed standard of review becomes apparent in the Court's portrayal and application of this principle.

The margin of appreciation doctrine reflects the subsidiary nature of the Convention.[26] As a general matter the doctrine:

> refers to the latitude allowed to the member states in their observation of the Convention. The doctrine is one of judicial review which governs the extent to which ... the Court will scrutinize a complained-of practice.[27]

It serves the purpose of being an:

> interpretative tool ... needed to draw the line between what is properly a matter for each community to decide at a local level and what is so fundamental that it entails the same requirement for all countries whatever the variations in traditions and culture.[28]

This principle, too, has various functions under the Convention,[29] but here, only its role as an indispensable instrument for assessing 'necessity' under Arts 8(2) and 10(2) is of interest.

(b) Its Role in the Assessment of 'Necessity'

The above quotation from the *Silver* judgment shows that a margin of appreciation is permitted in domestic authorities' determination of whether a restriction of a protected Art 8 or 10 right was 'necessary' or not. But it is less

[24] E Brems 'The Margin of Appreciation Doctrine in the Case-Law of the European Court of Human Rights' (1996) 56 ZaöRV 240, 298; J Schoekkenbroek 'The Basis, Nature and Application of the Margin-of-Appreciation Doctrine in the Case-Law of the European Court of Human Rights. General Report' (1998) 19 HRLJ 30, 35; and R St John Macdonald 'The Margin of Appreciation' in R St John Macdonald F Matscher and H Petzold (eds) *The European System for the Protection of Human Rights* (Martinus Nijhoff Dordrecht, 1993) 83, 83, and 124.

[25] Major studies include Arai-Takahashi (n 7), Brems (n 24); HC Yourow *The Margin of Appreciation Doctrine in the Dynamics of European Human Rights Jurisprudence* (Kluwer Hague, 1996); and S Greer *The Margin of Appreciation: Interpretation and Discretion under the European Convention on Human Rights* (Council of Europe Publishing Strasbourg, 2000).

[26] Petzold (n 22) 55–59.

[27] TA O'Donnell 'The Margin of Appreciation Doctrine: Standards in the Jurisprudence of the European Court of Human Rights' (1982) 4 HRQ 474, 475.

[28] P Mahoney 'Marvellous Richness of Diversity or Invidious Cultural Relativism?' (1998) 19 HRLJ 1, 1.

[29] Brems (n 24) 242–56 gives a succinct overview.

evident to which elements of the 'necessity' assessment the margin relates. It would probably be fair to take it as saying, however, that domestic authorities are basically left to decide for themselves whether a 'pressing social need' exists and, in particular, whether 'proportionality' obtains between ends and means in the specific dispute. In other words, the application of the margin of appreciation with regard to the 'necessity' requirement concerns the proportionality assessment inherent in the criterion,[30] or, conversely (as some authors seem to prefer), the proportionality principle is a device at the Court's disposal to ascertain whether national authorities have overstepped their margin of appreciation.[31] The crucial feature of the doctrine for the purpose of the present discussion is that it is the instrument by which the Court handles the supranational dimension of the public–private tension referred to in the preceding section.

It remains to establish more precisely what the assessment implied in the margin of appreciation doctrine deals with, and how wide the margin is, in general and in more narrowly commercial matters. It would be an insurmountable task to consider these questions in detail. The relevant case law is inscrutable and the literature a veritable maze of abstractions,[32] and thus of little help in advancing our understanding of how the Court proceeds concretely in a given case.

As the Court observed in *Silver v United Kingdom*, the authorities of the respondent State will enjoy a 'certain but not unlimited' latitude in determining for themselves whether 'democratic necessity' exists. The flexibility inherent in this phrase brings us closer to the standards under consideration, since the discussion carried out below revolves exactly around the extent to which, and in which sense, the Court stretches this 'certain' latitude when corporate interests are at stake. At some juncture the Court superimposes its international supervisory power and scrutinizes the assessment of 'necessity' made at the domestic level.[33] But at which point does this occur? These issues are broadly touched on under the following discussion of the two standards of lenient scrutiny under Arts 8 and 10.

B. Introducing the Two Standards of Review

The problem of identifying in the literature (or in practice) the main tools applied by the Court when it discusses the place of the regulatory state in Arts 8 and 10 justifies this somewhat lengthy introduction to the 'necessity'

30 *Handyside v UK* Series A No 24, (1979) 1 EHRR 737§ 48(2) last sentence: 'it is for the national authorities to make the initial assessment of the reality of the pressing social need implied by the notion of "necessity" '.

31 Arai-Takahashi (n 7) 14–15; and Greer (n 25) 10.

32 A similar observation made in Macdonald (n 24) 85 remains true even if the theoretical attention given to the topic has virtually exploded since then.

33 *Handyside* (n 30) § 49.

assessment. Let us now examine the Court's understanding of 'necessity' in the context under consideration. Section 1 introduces the *markt intern* standard of leniency in Art 10(2); this standard is an established one. The suggestion that the Court adopts a special mode of self-restraint when it assesses the legitimacy of public intrusion of corporate premises is less well articulated, but the standard referred to in Art 8 case law, in particular in *Colas Est SA and Others v France*, suggests tendencies similar to those adopted under Art 10. This standard is considered in section 2. Circumstances that can help explain the Court's adoption of lenient standards are examined in part C, for the most part jointly for the standards in question.

1 Article 10(2): the *markt intern* Standard

(a) Introducing the Standard

The Court established its application of proportionality and margin of appreciation with regard to the 'necessity' of interfering with commercial speech in the case of *markt intern Verlag GmbH and Klaus Beermann v Germany* from 1989.[34] As will be remembered from the introduction of the judgment in chapter 4, the *markt intern* publishing company (and its editor whose position under Art 10 is of no consequence to the present discussion) sought Strasbourg invalidation of an injunction taken against its publication to prohibit the unqualified repetition of certain statements concerning a large distributor of beauty products. Its publication aimed at small and medium-sized retailers in the same sector. German authorities found the statements to contravene the German Competition Law. The status of the applicant company as an organ of the press suggests that the case might not be taken as evidence of 'pure' commercial statements,[35] but the Court majority considered the context as one involving typical commercial speech and this remains the prevailing doctrinal view. As already noted, the Court, in assessing the question of applicability, found the statements to fall within the concept of 'expression' in Art 10(1) despite their commercial nature.[36] The essence of the applicants' complaint was therefore discussed next in light of the 'necessity' criterion in Art 10(2).

On the deciding vote of the President of the Court after a tie, the majority ruled that there had been no breach of Art 10. The interference was in accordance with law, it pursued a legitimate aim ('the reputation or rights of others')

[34] *markt intern Verlag GmbH and Klaus Beermann v Germany* Series A No 165, (1990) 12 EHRR 161. It is controlling in the sense that it is still referred to, see RA Shiner *Freedom of Commercial Expression* (Oxford University Press Oxford, 2003) 97.

[35] As pointed out in *markt intern* (n 34) Dissenting Opinion of Judges Martens and Macdonald para 5.

[36] *markt intern* (n 34) § 26.

and it was 'necessary in a democratic society'. With regard to the standard of review to be applied concerning 'necessity', the Court majority observed as follows:

> The Court has consistently held that the Contracting States have a certain margin of appreciation in assessing the existence and extent of the necessity of an interference, but this margin is subject to a European supervision as regards both the legislation and the decisions applying it, even those given by an independent court.... Such a margin of appreciation is *essential in commercial matters and, in particular, in an area as complex and fluctuating as that of unfair competition.* Otherwise, the [Court] would have to undertake a re-examination of the facts and all the circumstances of each case. The Court must confine its review to the question whether the measures taken on the national level are *justifiable in principle and proportionate.*[37]

The majority also observed that it 'should not substitute its own evaluation for that of the national courts in the instant case, where those courts, *on reasonable grounds*, had considered the restrictions to be necessary'.[38]

These statements set out what will be referred to as the *markt intern* standard of lenient scrutiny of public regulation of commercial speech under Article 10.

(b) The Elements of Leniency

The *markt intern* majority's language is hardly transparent. The elements of deference to national authorities contained in the judgment are not immediately evident despite it being generally acknowledged that the statements imply a lenient standard of review.[39] The Court tends to be sparse in substantiating its application of the doctrine by showing which factors lead to the specific outcome. But obscurity is not a problem specific to the *markt intern* standard.[40] The Court's application of the margin of appreciation doctrine is generally difficult to reconstruct. As Ronald St John Macdonald has observed, it is 'not susceptible of definition in the abstract, as it is, by its very nature, context-dependent',[41] in the sense that the width of the margin is intimately related to the specific circumstances of each case.[42]

Be that as it may, the Court in the *markt intern* judgment observed that the margin of appreciation afforded to national authorities was 'essential' in commercial matters. By adding an adjective otherwise missing from its

[37] *markt intern* (n 34) § 33 (emphasis added). [38] ibid § 37 (emphasis added).

[39] There is wide agreement in this regard, eg, Harris O'Boyle and Warbrick (n 10) 405. In its report, the Commission observed that the level of protection must be less for commercial speech than that accorded to political speech in the sense that 'the principle according to which the test of "necessity"... can be less strict when applied to commercial advertising, see App 10572/83 *markt intern Verlag GmbH and Klaus Beermann v Germany* (report) (1987) § 231, citing *X and Church of Scientology v Sweden* Application 7805/77, (1979) 16 DR 68, 73 § 5(6) and (7).

[40] van Dijk and van Hoof (n 7) 93. [41] Macdonald (n 24) 85 and 123–25.

[42] Delmas-Marty (n 11) 337.

renditions of the margin of appreciation permitted, it may be inferred that the addition had a purpose. It is suggested here that the Court's use of the additional term 'essential' must imply a wide margin of appreciation in commercial matters. The conjecture that 'essential' means wide(r) is supported by the Court's most important doctrinal move in the *markt intern* case.[43] The Court retreated from the fundamental principle of leading freedom of speech cases that an interference with expression is 'necessary' only if is corresponds with a 'pressing social need', whether the reasons given by the respondent State to justify the interference are 'relevant and sufficient', and that the reasons given by the State must be 'convincingly established'.[44] The *markt intern* majority did not reiterate the 'pressing social need' criterion.[45] Nor did it speak of grounds marshalled by the government having to be 'convincingly established'; it merely noted that 'no breach of Article 10 has been established'.[46] The majority as a substitute introduced a test in which the Court's supervisory task was to ensure that national authorities 'on reasonable grounds' had considered that the interference was necessary,[47] and that its review of 'reasonableness' was confined to the determination whether the interference was 'justifiable *in principle* and proportionate'.[48]

The modus operandi inherent in these formulas has been established with considerable certainty. Christian Calliess, in one of the few detailed studies of the *markt intern* standard, fittingly distinguishes between formal and substantive judicial control with regard to the 'necessity' criterion.[49] Generally, or at least in the context of political speech, the Court tends to apply a substantive control of domestic authorities' assessment of 'necessity'. This control implies that the Court oversees the national appreciation of whether the interference was proportionate not only as a matter of principle but also in terms of the effects of the measure as felt by the applicant person. The Court, in other words, carries out an independent international assessment of proportionality of the case as a whole.[50]

In the *markt intern* judgment, the Court applies another form of control. Calliess describes this variant in the following words:

> [D]er Gerichtshof übt seine bereits beschränkte Kontrolle mittels Verhältnismässigkeitsprüfung und Abwägung noch zurückgehaltender aus, indem er grundsätzlich

[43] It is also indicated in *Hertel v Switzerland* Reports 1998-VI (1999) 28 EHRR 534 § 47.

[44] *Barthold v Germany* Series A No 90, (1985) 7 EHRR 383 § 58(2).

[45] Harris O'Boyle and Warbrick (n 10) 404.

[46] Eissen (n 17) 146.

[47] *markt intern* (n 34) § 37 (emphasis added). See also *Jacubowski v Germany* Series A No 291, (1995) 19 EHRR 64 § 26.

[48] *markt intern* (n 34) §§ 33 and 37 (emphasis added).

[49] C Calliess 'Zwischen staatlicher Souveränität und europäischer Effektivität: Zum Beurteilsungsspielraum der Vertragsstaaten im Rahmen des Art 10 EMRK. Zugleich eine Urteilsanmerkung zu den Entscheidungen des EGMR in den Fällen markt intern und Jacubowski' (1996) 23 EurGRZ 293.

[50] Calliess (n 49) 295.

nur überprüft, ob eine Abwägung der widerstreitenden Interessen durch die nationalen Gerichte in nachvollziehbarer Weise vorgenommen worden ist. Eine eigene inhaltliche Verhältnismässigkeitsprüfung nimmt der Gerichtshof also grundsätzlich nicht vor.[51]

In the *markt intern* case, the Court is, in other words, satisfied with exercising formal control only, in which it imposes its supranational supervision merely with regard to whether the proportionality assessment under the 'necessity' criterion has in fact been undertaken at the national level.[52] This obviously leaves much discretion to be decided on the national level. Without doubt, the *markt intern* approach contains a considerable element of deference to national authorities.

The departure from a full-fledged control of the substance of the proportionality between ends and means, and, implicitly, between private and public interests, is therefore the real impact of the *markt intern* majority's statements of an 'essential' margin of appreciation, and the criteria of 'principled justifiability' and 'reasonableness'.[53]

(c) The markt intern *Approach Prevails*

Before concluding this presentation of the *markt intern* standard, it is necessary to spell out its current scope and status. Recent development in the case law has helped clarify this issue to a considerable degree while at the same time, the literature on the Convention has not been able to pick this development up.

(i) **The Currency of the Standard**

An exploration of the vitality and scope of the standard is well deserved. A strong group of judges at the Court found much to criticize in the majority's choice of standard of review.[54] Separate opinions were issued by the dissenters that set out their concerns.[55] Several commentators have shared the dissenting judges' sense of disquiet concerning the leniency inherent in the Court's

[51] ibid 295–96. Roughly translated into English: By way of the principle of proportionality, the Court exercises its scrutiny in a more restrained manner than in other areas inasmuch as it only checks whether the national courts have in fact assessed the competing interests in an observable manner. It does not oversee whether the assessment substantively meets the Convention's requirements.

[52] Similarly, eg, U Prepeluh 'Die Entwicklung der Margin of Appreciation-Doktrin im Hinblick auf die Pressefreiheit' (2001) 61 ZaöRV 771, 806; and M de Merieux 'The German Competition Law and Article 10 ECHR' (1995) 20 ELR 388, 397.

[53] *markt intern* (n 34) Dissenting Opinion of Judges Gölücklü, Pettiti, Russo, Spielmann, de Meyer, Carillo Salcedo and Valticos paras I and II(2); see also AJ Dignam and D Allen *Company Law and the Human Rights Act 1998* (Butterworths London, 2000) 252; and Eissen (n 17) 146.

[54] *markt intern* (n 34) Dissenting Opinion of Judges Gölücklü, Pettiti, Russo, Spielmann, de Meyer, Carrillo Salcedo and Valticos, para II(1) and (2).

[55] *markt intern* (n 34) Dissenting Opinion of Judge Pettiti, paras 4–7; and Dissenting Opinion of Judges Martens and Macdonald.

approach.[56] One might, therefore, legitimately ask whether the standard has any force in contemporary Strasbourg jurisprudence.

Although some dissenting voices continued in decisions delivered in the period immediately following the judgment,[57] the Court majority persisted in applying the *markt intern* formula.[58] Today it constitutes the prevailing Strasbourg norm for scrutinizing governmental interference with commercial speech pursuant to domestic competition legislation.[59]As recently as in 2003, in *Krone Verlag GmbH & Co KG v Austria*, the Court reaffirmed the validity of the standard despite the widespread criticism made against it. Austrian authorities had issued a preliminary injunction at the instigation of one newspaper concern against the applicant company, its competitor, against the publication of an advertisement for subscriptions to the newspaper in which it compared its subscription rates with those of the applicant. In assessing the legitimacy of the interference under Art 10(2), the Court, finding that the statements at issue were of a commercial nature, reiterated the *markt intern* approach word by word,[60] and consequently found that no violation had occurred with respect to the applicant's Art 10 rights.

As the *markt intern* judgment was delivered in the context of the application of national competition law, its 'necessity' assessment essentially concerns the legitimacy under the Convention of public interference with market behaviour for the purpose of the common good.[61] The majority of decisions dealing with the level of protection afforded to commercial expression has in fact been delivered in this particular context.

There is however little evidence that the competition context has influenced the scope of the doctrine. In fact, one might venture that in the area of international review of the application of competition norms there exist (and existed also at the time of the *markt intern* affair) relatively uniform norms across Europe: this might justify lesser rather than greater deference to national

[56] Eissen (n 17) 145–46; A Lester 'Freedom of Expression' in R St John Macdonald F Matscher and H Petzold (eds) *The European System for the Protection of Human Rights* (Martinus Nijhoff Dordrecht, 1993) 465, 480; and Arai-Takahashi (n 7) 109.

[57] App 15450/89 *Casado Coca v Spain* (report) (1992) (1994) 18 EHRR 1 14–16 §§ 61, 54 and 55. Judges Vilhjálmsson and Palm issued a Dissenting Opinion in the judgment of the case, in which they stated their agreement with the views of the Commission in its report, see *Casado Coca v Spain* Series A No 285, (1994) 18 EHRR 1, Dissenting Opinion of Judges Vilhjálmsson and Palm. See also *Jacubowski* (n 47) Dissenting opinion of Judges Walsh, Macdonald and Wildhaber para 3.

[58] *Casado Coca* (n 57) § 50; and *Jacubowski* (n 47) § 26.

[59] App 16555/90 *R GmbH v Germany* (1990); App 18424/91 *Röda Korset Ungdomsförbund and Others v Sweden* (1993); App 16844/90 *Nederlandse Omroepprogramma Stichting v Netherlands* (1993), App 27388/95 *Grauso v Poland* (1997); App 18033/91 *Cable Music Europe Ltd v Netherlands* (1993); and App 21472/93 *X SA v Netherlands* (1994) 76 DR 129.

[60] *Krone Verlag GmbH & Co KG v Austria (No 3)* judgment 11 December 2003 Reports 2003-XII § 30.

[61] de Merieux (n 52) concerns herself with this.

authorities.[62] The standard is frequently invoked in connection with other commercial speech issues and in areas outside the stronghold of competition rules. In *Casado Coca v Spain*, for instance, the Court was asked to consider the legitimacy under the provision of a prohibition banning a lawyer from advertising his services. Judging the complaint as one concerning the climate for advertising services in light of the right to freedom of expression, the Court observed:

Under the Court's case law, the States parties to the Convention have a certain margin of appreciation in assessing the necessity of an interference, but this margin is subject to European supervision as regards both the relevant rules and the decisions applying them (See, inter alia, [*markt intern*] para. 33). Such a margin of appreciation is particularly essential in the complex and fluctuating area of unfair competition (ibid.). *The same applies to advertising.* In the instant case, the Court's task is therefore confined to ascertaining whether the measures taken at national level are justifiable in principle and proportionate.[63]

The standard also applies to the status under the provision of freedom for commercial broadcasting. For instance, the Court in *Groppera Radio AG v Switzerland*, which dealt with restrictions on commercial broadcasting, unanimously described the controlling standard of review in the field in the following words:

According to the Court's settled case-law, the Contracting States enjoy a certain margin of appreciation in assessing whether and to what extent an interference is necessary, but this margin goes hand in hand with European supervision covering both the legislation and the decisions applying it; when carrying out that supervision, the Court must ascertain whether the measures taken at the national level are justifiable in principle and proportionate.[64]

In a similar operation in *Demuth v Switzerland*, the Court examined the objectives of the applicant's television company, CAR TV AG, as an integral part of its 'necessity' interpretation. The Court majority found that it was:

a private enterprise which intended to broadcast on all aspects of automobiles, in particular news on cars and car accessories, and information on car mobility and the road traffic of private vehicles. Furthermore, it intended to deal with such matters as energy policies, traffic security, tourism and environmental issues. However, while it

[62] M Oesch *Standards of Review in WTO Dispute Resolution* (Oxford University Press Oxford, 2003) 53 makes a similar point with regard to the rationale for judicial restraint in the WTO as compared with the ECHR.

[63] *Casado Coca* (n 57) § 50 (emphasis added).

[64] *Groppera Radio and Others v Switzerland* Series A No 173, (1990) 12 EHRR 321 § 72, citing *markt intern* (n 34) § 33. See also *Casado Coca* (n 57); *Jacubowski* (n 47); and various screening decisions, including App 21554/93 *Janssen v Germany* (1994); and *Lindner v Germany* decision 9 March 1999.

could not be excluded that such aspects would have contributed to the ongoing, general debate on the various aspects of a motorised society, in the Court's opinion the purpose of CAR TV AG was primarily commercial in that it intended to promote cars and, hence, further car sales.[65]

Consequently, the speech was to be assessed according to *markt intern*'s doctrine by which 'the standards of scrutiny may be less severe' in that it 'must confine itself to the question whether the measures taken on the national level were justifiable in principle and proportionate'.[66]

(ii) Doubt as to Whether Statements Are 'Commercial'

The *markt intern* doctrine's status in situations involving 'commercial speech' is thus acknowledged in the Strasbourg jurisprudence. The discussion nowadays revolves instead around when statements are to be considered purely 'commercial' and thus subjected to the leniency of the *markt intern* standard and when they have elements to suggest retraction to the default standard of a more rigorous scrutiny.[67] This question may have been implied in judgments delivered prior to the *markt intern* case,[68] but it was not considered until well after 1989. While it does not as such concern the question of leniency, it is helpful to examine the main points in the discussion as they clarify the scope of the *markt intern* standard.

The guiding norm is the extent to which statements that, although they may be commercially motivated or otherwise commercial in their origin, concern the speaker's 'participation in a debate affecting the general interest'. This was the test introduced in the case of *Hertel v Switzerland*,[69] where the Court was asked to consider the appropriateness under Art 10(2) of court sanctioned injunctions sought by an association of manufacturers against the applicant, who had violated domestic competition laws by publishing statements of the alleged hazards involved in the use of microwave ovens. Since the statements concerned an ongoing debate of the effects of microwaves on human health, the *Hertel* claim was 'substantially different from ... *markt intern*' and it was therefore 'necessary to reduce the extent of the margin of application' implied in that judgment.[70]

The Court in 2001 elaborated on this distinguishing criterion in *VGT Verein gegen Tierfabriken v Switzerland*. A television commercial for the

[65] *Demuth v Switzerland* Reports 2002-IX (2004) 38 EHRR 20 § 41.

[66] ibid §§ 42–43. See also *Krone Verlag (No 3)* (n 60) § 30; and App 29473/95 *Grech and Montanaro v Malta* (1997).

[67] Shiner (n 34) 99.

[68] *Barthold* (n 44) § 55; *Autronic AG v Switzerland* Series A No 178, (1990) 12 EHRR 485 § 61; and *Informationsverein Lentia and Others v Austria* Series A No 276, (1994) 17 EHRR 93 § 35 in contrast to Apps 13914/88, 15401/89, 15717/89, 15779/89 and 17207/90 *Informationsverein Lentia and Others v Austria* (report) (1992) §§ 78–79.

[69] *Hertel* (n 43) § 47.

[70] ibid.

applicant, an animal rights association, which attacked aspects of the Swiss meat industry was prohibited on anti-competition grounds. The majority of the Court, having to determine whether the curtailment was 'necessary in a democratic society', observed that:

the Swiss authorities had a certain margin of appreciation to decide whether there was a 'pressing social need' to refuse the broadcast of the commercial. Such a margin of appreciation is particularly essential in commercial matters, especially in an area as complex and fluctuating as that of advertising [markt intern § 33].

However, the Court has found above that the applicant association's film fell outside the regular commercial context inciting the public to purchase a particular product. Rather, it reflected controversial opinions pertaining to modern society in general....

As a result, in the present case the extent of the margin of appreciation is reduced, since what is at stake is not a given individual's purely 'commercial' interests, but his participation in a debate affecting the general interest.[71]

There may be disagreement at the Court about its application in the case under discussion,[72] and in some cases, the Court may stretch the 'commercial' element far to the applicant's detriment.[73] But the Court does adhere on principal grounds to a distinction between 'pure' commercial speech and commercial speech with 'political' overtones and, significantly, accepts the consequence of this distinction for the purpose of the intensity of Strasbourg oversight of governmental interference with the two types of speech. The former remains subject to a lenient standard of review, while interference with the latter is scrutinized more rigorously. In this context, then, the Court is, perhaps for practical reasons, willing to rely on conceptual distinctions as means for its adjudication—a technique which it repudiates in, eg, the context of the interpretation of Art 10(1) and corporate commercial speech.

Whatever may inform the Court in this example of conceptual distinctions, the important point for the present discussion is that it is a means that helps the Court to adopt a lenient standard of judicial review in matters of practical significance for corporate actors. Suggested reasons of structure for the Court's approach will soon be elaborated. First, however, an introduction of a similar standard of review under Art 8 is called for.

[71] *VGT Verein gegen Tierfabriken v Switzerland* Reports 2001-VI (2002) 34 EHRR 4§§ 69–71 (footnotes omitted).

[72] *Demuth* (n 65) § 42 and *Demuth* (n 65) Dissenting Opinion of Judge Jörundsson §§ 5–6.

[73] *Krone Verlag GmbH and Mediaprint Zeitungs- und Zeitschriftenverlag GmbH & Co KG v Austria* decision 20 March 2003 §§ 5–7 (prohibition, on competition grounds, of publishing article attacking a competing newspaper's truthfulness on WW2 issues fell within the scope of the *markt intern* standard even if the 'topic of the article' in question 'was part of a journalistic debate on matter of public interest').

2 Article 8(2): the *Colas Est* Standard

The Court also proposes a lenient standard of review of governmental interference with business actors' privacy under Art 8. The low-tier protection approach developed by the Court in this context does not however enjoy the same status as the *markt intern* approach with regard to Art 10. The case law is less extensive and the Court's formulation of a deferential approach to governmental interference is characterized by an elusiveness absent in Art 10 jurisprudence. Yet the Court communicates a disposition for leniency which deserves attention, for what it is worth. This section explores the standard of leniency with regard to corporate privacy protection under Art 8. It also discusses its scope and impact.

(a) Introducing the Standard

In the context of corporate business claims, the strongest evidence of a relaxed judicial control is found in the Court's 2002 judgment in the case of *Colas Est SA and Others v France*.[74] This case was introduced in chapter 4 as a significant source for establishing the applicability of Art 8(1)—the 'home' alternative—to corporate premises. As may be recalled, the applicant companies petitioned the Court regarding the acceptance under French law of the searching of corporate premises and seizure of company documents by anti-competition authorities without a court warrant being required.

The Court agreed, as we know, that Art 8, which protects 'everyone's' right to 'respect for one's... home', covered corporate premises in the circumstances. The crucial question was therefore whether the three requirements for legitimate governmental interference with the applicant companies' 'home' were satisfied. The arrangement had an established legal basis and was therefore 'in accordance with the law' as required in Article 8(2).[75] It pursued two of the listed legitimate aims ('the economic well-being of the country' and 'the prevention of crime'). It remained to be determined whether the interference 'appear[ed] proportionate and... necessary for achieving those aims'.[76] The Court's rendition of this criterion has both strict and lenient elements.

(i) Elements of Strictness

With regard to the assessment of 'democratic necessity' in Art 8(2), a unanimous Court reiterated as a first step the main elements of the normal standard of measurement that apply to most matters of privacy interference.[77] This

[74] *Colas Est SA and Others v France* judgment 16 April 2002 Reports 2002-III.

[75] ibid § 43. [76] ibid § 44(1) and (2) respectively.

[77] On the Court's reasoning, see the more detailed presentation in M Emberland 'Protection against Unwarranted Searches and Seizures of Corporate Premises under Article 8 of the European Convention on Human Rights: The *Colas Est SA v France* Approach' (2003) 25 Mich J Intl L 77, 100–4.

standard must be described as fairly rigorous. The Court reiterated that the 'necessity' criterion was 'to be interpreted narrowly'.[78] Moreover, the need for interference in a given case 'must be convincingly established'.[79] Further, the Court recalled that it 'has consistently held that the Contracting States have a certain margin of appreciation in assessing the need for interference, but it goes hand in hand with European supervision'.[80] These formulas are well-known to the standard of scrutiny as it is normally applied under Art 8.

In the context of searches and seizures, however, additional safeguards were required, the Court believed and thus, seemingly, toughened the 'bite' of its review. It added the test developed in the *Funke, Crémieux*, and *Miailhe* judgments against France from 1993, where the private residences of businessmen had been subjected to investigatory measures of a similar kind as in the *Colas Est* case. The *Colas Est* Court thus recalled that 'relevant legislation and practice' providing for a legal basis for searches and seizures 'should [afford] adequate and effective safeguards against abuse',[81] and that operations must 'be regarded as strictly proportionate to the legitimate aim pursued'.[82] As the language plainly informs us, this test implies a fair amount of scrutiny to be applied. To say that the *Colas Est* standard is altogether relaxed cannot, therefore, be appropriate.

(ii) Elements of Leniency: the *Niemietz* Implication

In a second move, however, the Court introduced an element of leniency regardless of the apparently strict criteria otherwise in force in the applicants' case. While stating that the French legal arrangement under scrutiny did not satisfy the *Funke, Crémieux*, and *Miailhe* criterion and that the respondent State had therefore failed to meet the requirement of 'necessity', the *Colas Est* Court found that a violation had occurred '*even supposing that the entitlement to interfere may be more far-reaching where the business premises of a juristic person are concerned*'.[83]

The Court's supposition of a 'more far-reaching . . . entitlement to interfere' with corporate privacy must be seen in light of the parties' arguments before the Court. The French government argued that:

> while juristic persons could enjoy similar rights under the Convention to those afforded to natural persons, they could not claim a right to the protection of their

[78] *Colas Est* (n 74) § 47 second sentence, citing *Klass and Others v Germany* Series A No 28, (1980) 2 EHRR 214 § 42.

[79] *Colas Est* (n 74) § 47 second sentence citing *Funke v France* Series A No 256, (1993) 16 EHRR 297 § 55; *Crémieux v France* Series A No 256-B, (1993) 16 EHRR 357 § 38, and *Miailhe v France* Series A No 256-C, (1993) 16 EHRR 332 § 36.

[80] *Colas Est* (n 74) § 47 first sentence.

[81] ibid § 48 citing Funke (n 79) § 56; *Crémieux* (n 79) § 39; and *Miailhe* (n 79) § 37.

[82] *Colas Est* (n 74) § 49 fourth sentence citing Funke (n 79) § 57; *Crémieux* (n 79) § 40; and *Miailhe* (n 79) § 38.

[83] *Colas Est* (n 74) § 49 fourth sentence (emphasis added).

professional or business premises with as much force as an individual could in relation to his professional or business address.[84]

The government relied the Court's statements in the case of *Niemietz v Germany*, where the Court had conceded that a broad interpretation of Art 8(1)

> would not unduly hamper the Contracting States, for they would retain their entitlement to 'interfere' to the extent permitted by paragraph 2 of Article 8 . . .; that entitlement might well be more far-reaching where professional or business activities or premises were involved than would otherwise be the case.[85]

The government's argument did not meet with direct disapproval by the applicant companies, which rather suggested that a violation had occurred even supposing that the test implied in the *Niemetz* case were to apply.[86] As is evident, the Court chose to follow the same course. It conceded that the government may be right in applying the suggestion made in the *Niemietz* case but without directly deciding on its applicability ('even supposing') since it was not decisive for the outcome of the case.

(b) The Standard's Content and Scope

(i) Is There a *Colas Est* Standard?

The *Colas Est* judgment does not, therefore, determine whether there is in fact an element of leniency involved in assessing the 'necessary in a democratic society' requirement in Art 8(2) in the context of corporate premises.[87] The *Niemietz* judgment, on which basis the *Colas Est* Court built, is not helpful either, since in that case, too, the Court implied rather than decided the issue ('might well be more far-reaching') and merely suggested leniency as a rhetorical move for justifying a broad interpretation of Art 8(1); the *Niemietz* Court's assessment of 'necessity' in Art 8(2) contained no discussion of a standard of leniency.[88]

The Court's evasiveness in these judgments does not necessarily imply unwillingness to scrutinize when appropriate. In both cases the facts at hand suggest that

[84] *Colas Est* (n 74) § 30.

[85] ibid § 30 referring to *Niemietz v Germany* Series A No 251-B, (1993) 16 EHRR 97 (where the relevant passage is found in § 31).

[86] *Colas Est* (n 74) § 38 first sentence.

[87] The leniency was, however, adopted by the ECJ in Case C–94/00, *Roquette Frères SA v Directeur general de la concurrence, de la consummation et de la repression des fraudes* [2002] ECR I-9011 § 29; see further Emberland (n 77) 80 and 109–10.

[88] In some judgments, the Court cites *Niemietz* (n 85) as evidence of applicability of art 8 to various working place disputes. Such citations occasionally include § 31 of the judgment, where the leniency was implied. None of these judgments can, however, be interpreted farther than the implication in *Niemietz* itself. See, eg, *Halford v UK* Reports 1997-III (1997) 24 EHRR 523 § 44; *Kopp v Switzerland* Reports 1998-II (1999) 27 EHRR 91 § 50; and *Amann v Switzerland* Reports 2000-II (2000) 30 EHRR 843 § 65.

the contested governmental interferences were evidently in need of Strasbourg oversight: the *Colas Est* applicants were subjected to an anti-competitive investigation regime that provided insufficient safeguards against arbitrariness since a prior court warrant was not required according to French law.[89] In the *Niemietz* case, the given court warrant had been drawn in broad terms, in that it 'ordered a search for, and seizure of, "documents", without any limitation'.[90] Both matters go to the heart of important values built into the Convention, notably the absence of arbitrariness and intrusiveness (or, in other words, aspects of the rule of law).[91] The *Niemietz* investigation was besides carried out against the office of a member of a profession that enjoys a privileged Convention status thanks to its instrumental role in securing justice.[92]

In certain admissibility decisions, however, the Strasbourg organs have applied a lenient standard of review in the terms of the *Niemietz* implication. They concern facts that are not tied to the context of interference for the promotion of the idea of a regulated market and thus imply that deference to national authorities may apply in all areas in which the privacy aspects of corporate premises or business or professional activities are at stake. (The *Colas Est* judgment is yet too recent to have been cited in relevant cases.) In these cases, the Strasbourg authorities tend to apply the leniency in *Niemietz* with more conviction than in *Colas Est*.

A typical example is the case of *Verein Netzwerk v Austria* from 1999, where the Court was called to consider the admissibility of a complaint submitted by a non-profit-making association, whose premises had been subjected to searches for illegal aliens who, in the authorities' opinion, might have sought refuge there. The Court for a number of listed 'reasons' found the claim inadmissible. One of these reasons was the fact that the Court:

> recalls that the entitlement to 'interfere' might well be more far-reaching where professional or business activities or premises are involved than would otherwise be the case.[93]

The Court also omitted a reference to the elements of strict scrutiny normally found in Art 8(2) assessments. More directly than the *Colas Est* judgment, the Court here implied that a lenient standard of scrutiny was one of several reasons for there being no violation of Art 8.

[89] *Colas Est* (n 74) §§ 48–49.

[90] *Niemietz* (n 85) § 32.

[91] See, eg, Delmas-Marty (n 11) 322–27 on the impact of these values on assessments of the legitimacy of governmental interference.

[92] *Niemietz* (n 85) § 37(2).

[93] *Verein Netzwerk v Austria* decision 29 June 1999§ 1(4), citing *Niemietz* (n 85), § 31. Similarly, App 22287/93 *OL v Austria* (1993) § 3, and *Maini v France* decision 2 March 1999 § 3(2). Implicitly also App 20494/92 *G and G Ltd v Austria* (1994) § 1(3); *Reiss v Austria* Application 23953/94, (1995) 82 DR 51 (1995) 20 EHRR 90 §§ 3–4 and 6.

Some doubt should be attached to the assessment that the *Colas Est/ Niemietz* leniency applies to business activities and premises. At the same time, it is to be noted that no case law exists that proposes disposing with the standard in favour of rigorous scrutiny. The likelihood that a lenient standard is in force is in other words greater than the likelihood that it has no place in Strasbourg jurisprudence.

(ii) A Broader Margin of Appreciation

The standard should therefore be explored further, but this is by no means easy as the apparent *Colas Est* standard is even more vaguely articulated than the corresponding standard in Art 10. As the case law material is sparse, there are few reliable clues as to its substance. The *Colas Est* court only suggested that, with regard to the 'necessity' requirement, the 'entitlement to interfere' is 'more far-reaching' than would be the case with interference in activities or premises outside the corporate or business sphere. The Court applied in other words a standard the thrust of which is derivative of the standard normally in force. What the difference between the normal standard and the *Colas Est* standard consists of remains, however, difficult to ascertain since, as was shown above, *Colas Est* also included elements of strictness that characterize the standard normally applied.

Some guidance does nonetheless exist. In *Fontanesi v Austria*, from 2000, the Court in an admissibility decision which concerned an individual's privacy rights on business premises, referred to the leniency implied in the *Niemietz* case and expressed that standard in the following terms:

> The Court has to take into account that a margin of appreciation is left to the Contracting States which *may be broader* where professional or business activities are involved.[94]

That the leniency refers to a broader domestic latitude in assessing proportionality is supported, by implication, by the *Colas Est* judgment, where the Court's tentative discussion of the *Niemietz* standard was carried out as part of its assessment of the scope of the margin of appreciation, in assessing proportionality, afforded to French authorities in the case.[95]

Beyond this limited analysis, however, the standard remains obscure. It is, for instance, impossible to know whether the Court intends the standard to involve a formal rather than a substantial judicial control as is applied under the *markt intern* model of scrutiny with regard to Art 10. As long as the Court has not had the opportunity to expound its *Colas Est* approach, this reconstruction

[94] *Fontanesi v Austria* decision 8 February 2000 § 1(9). See similarly App 20062/92 *B Company and Others v Netherlands* (1993) (where *Niemietz* was not referred to).

[95] *Colas Est* (n 74) § 49 read in light of §§ 47 and 48.

of the suggestive leniency in Art 8 interpretations remains within the realm of speculation, which is an undertaking that extends beyond the scope of this book.

C. Leniency and the Court's Weighing of Competing Interests: A Suggested Rationale

1 An Approach in Need of Rationalization

The discussion has thus far not explored the rationale behind the Court's approach. In fact, the Court's motivation cannot be reconstructed with certainty since the case law contains few pointers in this regard. One form or another of rationalization is nonetheless desirable, for the following reasons.

The *markt intern* standard has been intensely criticized both by dissenters in the Strasbourg organs and by theorists observing the leniency from outside (the development under Art 8 remains largely uncommented). A significant element of this critique, espoused by the joint dissenting opinion in the *markt intern* case, is that the Court by adopting a low-tier standard of protection for the business community fails to heed the interests of that community vis-à-vis governmental authority.[96] That criticism reveals, perhaps, different ideologies among Strasbourg participants as to the areas of society that truly merit human rights protection.[97] Criticism of the *markt intern* judgment ranges sometimes wider than the business sphere, being directed more specifically at the overall effectiveness of Strasbourg supervision, in particular in the field of free speech, where the Court's leniency denotes a tendency to defer more of its power to national authorities.[98]

The main concern in the present discussion is not to assess the defensibility of the *markt intern* and the *Colas Est* standards along these lines. The observation that leniency in the case of Art 10 interpretation remains the law for 'pure' commercial expression provides the starting point for the following examination, along with the similar inclination with regard to Art 8 and the privacy of business actors. The Court carries out its activities in a framework where such tendencies presumptively are considered appropriate. Such are the realities of Strasbourg jurisprudence. What is rather sought here is an answer the following question: how may the standards of relaxed international oversight in Arts 8

[96] *markt intern* (n 34) Dissenting Opinion of Judges Gölücklü, Pettiti, Russo, Spielmann, de Meyer, Carrillo Salcedo and Valticos especially para II(1).

[97] JG Merrills *The Development of International Law by the European Court of Human Rights* (Manchester University Press Manchester, 1988) 207–29 (who does not discuss private enterprise).

[98] *markt intern* (n 34) Dissenting Opinion of Judges Gölücklü, Pettiti, Russo, Spielmann, de Meyer, Carrillo Salcedo and Valticos para II(2); and Dissenting Opinion of Judge Pettiti paras 4–6.

and 10 be justified? This is a question to which the critique thus far has given little consideration.

The present analysis does not aspire to map out every possible justificatory factor for judicial restraint in our context. This would in any event be futile since the margin of appreciation is a principle with an immense capacity for flexibility in which case-specific circumstances play a major part.[99] Studies of factors that recurrently inform the Court's application of the margin of appreciation tell us nonetheless that a variety of explanations related to the structure of ECHR protection could feasibly be assembled in favour of judicial restraint in the two contexts.[100]

The contentiousness of corporate complaints under Articles 8 and 10 may amplify, for instance, the Court's invariable concern with legitimizing its activities vis-à-vis its sponsors, the ECHR member States.[101] It is very likely, as also was intimated in the concluding observations in chapter 4, that the Court restrains its scrutinizing authority as a practical form of compensation to the respondent State for having to accept the broadened scope of applicability of the two provisions in the business context and thus uses the margin as an instrument for self-preservation. Evidence of the importance of this rationale is in fact found in the case law, at least as far as Article 8 is concerned. In *Niemietz v Germany*, the Court was in favour of an extension of the private life clause to the office of the applicant's office partly because:

> [s]uch an interpretation *would not unduly hamper the Contracting States, for they would retain their entitlement to 'interfere'* to the extent permitted by paragraph 2 of Article 8 . . .; that entitlement might well be more far-reaching where professional or business activities or premises were involved than would otherwise be the case.[102]

The nod to sovereignty exhibited by this statement says a great deal of the Court' sensibility towards the Convention's member States. It would be surprising if a similar rationale did not in part explain the lenient review under Art 10(2).

Leniency may also be a natural consequence of the subsidiary nature of Strasbourg protection: it reflects a practical allocation of authority since sometimes the Court is in fact not in the best position to assess all available facts and circumstances of a dispute. One underlying premise of the margin of

[99] *Buckley v UK* Reports 1996-IV (1997) 23 EHRR 101 § 74(2); and Greer (n 25) 32: '[I]t is questionable if it is really a 'doctrine' at all since it could be said to lack the minimum theoretical specificity and coherence which a viable doctrine requires.' This is also noted in Oesch (n 62) 54.

[100] Arai-Takahashi (n 7) 206–30; Brems (n 24) 256–93; and Harris O'Boyle and Warbrick (n 10) 290–301.

[101] Arai-Takahashi (n 7) 240; H Waldock 'The Effectiveness of the System Set up by the European Convention on Human Rights' (1980) 1 HRLJ 1, 9; Brems (n 24) 297–98; and Merrills (n 97) 71.

[102] *Niemietz* (n 85) § 31.

appreciation doctrine is simply that local institutions are better placed, functionally, to assess the issues of the kind requiring first-hand knowledge of national peculiarities, and that the Court is not intended to replace the primary role played by national authorities.[103]

Furthermore, it should be observed that the existence of a common European standard is an element which also informs the width of the margin permitted by the Court.[104] With regard to the low-tier standard of protection afforded to corporate privacy and commercial speech, the Convention system in fact occupies common ground with many other legal systems to which it is related. Thus, similar approaches, arguably for various reasons, are found, eg, in the jurisprudence of the German *Bundesverfassungsgericht* and the US Supreme Court.[105] The fact that the European Court of Justice tends to adopt the leniency standards established by the Strasbourg Court may testify to a European commonality in this area.[106]

The following discussion does not pursue these points further. By being inclined to judicial restraint, the Court evidently emphasizes public needs over the interests of the individual applicant, and possibly more so than is generally the case with Articles 8 and 10 jurisprudence. Deference to national authorities' own assessment of compliance may be at odds with the prevailing ideology of the Convention as a charter primarily intended for the protection of individual interests over those of the community, yet it highlights the treaty's structural incorporation of the interests and concerns of the member States. As may have been guessed by now, in this attempt to propose a rationale for the Court's approach the present discussion draws considerably on the structural framework which was introduced in chapters 1 and 2.

The public–private tension inherent in Arts 8 and 10 was described in part A above, while part B showed that the margin of appreciation relates to the supranational dimension of this tension. Rationalization of the *markt intern* and *Colas Est* approaches must at least relate to the Court's international handling of the intricate balance between individual rights and majoritarianism,[107] the search for which, says the Court, is inherent to the whole Convention.[108] The following discussion takes this balance as its point of departure since a certain amount of circumstantial evidence in the case law corroborates the plausibility that the standards of leniency can be justified in this context.

103 Schoekkenbroek (n 24) 31.

104 Arai-Takahashi (n 7) 215–16.

105 Emberland (n 77) 110–12 and Shiner (n 34) 55–57 with regard to the US approach to commercial speech and corporate 'home' protection. On the German approach to 'home' protection, see Emberland (n 77) 112–13. The status of commercial speech under the *Grundgesetz* is now determined by the Benetton case of 2000, see BVerfGE 102, 347 (this case was also mentioned in chapter 4).

106 On the development, Emberland (n 77) 107–10 (privacy protection); and Shiner (n 34) 103 (commercial expression).

107 Generally, Mahoney (n 28) 3.

108 *Sporrong and Lönnroth v Sweden* Series A No 52, (1983) 5 EHRR 35 § 69.

Section 1 focuses on the 'private side' aspect of this balance. It asserts that leniency is justified in part by a reverse application of the principle of teleological interpretation. The emphasis upon the object and purpose of Arts 8 and 10 cannot, however, fully justify the Court's approach. Section 2 directs its attention to the 'public side' aspects of the balancing exercise. It suggests that certain community interests take priority over the business claimants' interests, essentially because respect for national democratic processes plays such a crucial role in the Convention system, and that that role is augmented when the community's interference concerns interests that derive from property, since the Convention systematically shows deference to public authorities' regulation of activity connected with private property.

2 Lowering the Applicant's Convention Protection by Teleological Interpretation

(a) Emphasis upon the Object and Purpose of Convention Protection

The objectives of Convention protection are established with a fair amount of certainty with regard to Arts 8 and 10. It was argued in chapter 4 that freedom of speech deserves protection primarily because it promotes individual self-realization, is fundamental to democratic governance and is conducive to discovering truth through the exchange of ideas and opinions. Privacy protection is a cherished value primarily because it promotes the individual human being's right to be let alone and to enter into external relationships with other people.

Chapter 4 showed that corporate and for-profit interests do not completely match the objectives of Arts 8 and 10. They lie at the provisions' margins. The Court nonetheless includes them in the provisions' scope in the sense that the rights may apply, in principle, to these interests. The reasons for this may not be entirely known to us, but it must at least be assumed that certain factors outweigh the marginality of the interests pursued so that the corporate or business nature of the claims play no decisive role. As far as the question of an appropriate level of protection is concerned, however, we have just seen in the preceding section that the corporate or business features of a claim do play a decisive role in the sense that they entail a relaxed standard of Strasbourg review.

This apparent paradox can be explained in light of the importance in Convention interpretation of the principle of teleological interpretation. The Court's emphasis upon the object and purpose of Convention protection is primarily understood as a method which results in an improved status for the private applicant. The Court, it must be recalled, often speaks of the Convention's purpose in terms such as 'the protection of individual human beings'.[109] The

[109] *Soering* (n 8) § 87.

Court has added to the sentiment that teleology generally benefits the private applicant by pointing out the special character of the Convention as a human rights treaty as compared with the reciprocal nature of other treaties. As Franz Matscher observes:

> A . . . consequence of [the object and purpose] is that interpretation of a law-making treaty must depart from the theory of classic international law, which states that when there is doubt, preference should be given to the interpretation which restricts as far as possible the obligations entered into by a State in an international treaty. In reliance on the object and purpose of the Convention, the case-law has in part, however, actually reached the opposite conclusion: thus, the possible limitations on rights protected by the Convention, provided for in the second paragraphs of Articles 8 to 11, are in principle to be given a restrictive interpretation, which means a corresponding extension of the obligations of the Contracting States.[110]

In the case of the Court's assessment of the 'necessity' of interference with business actors' Art 8 and 10 rights, however, the principle of teleological interpretation, by virtue of the marginal nature of the claims, leads to the opposite conclusion than that otherwise proposed by the Court.

(b) *The Nearer the Provision's Core, the Narrower Is the Margin of Appreciation*

An inverse application of the ordinary rendition of teleological ECHR interpretation, however neglected it may be in relevant Strasbourg literature,[111] is consistent with the way in which the Court generally approaches the margin of appreciation doctrine. Studies of the doctrine have argued that the Court decides the scope of the margin having regard, inter alia, to the nature of the applicant's activities and the interests protected by the right under which the applicant seeks protection,[112] thus exposing an inclination at the Court to measure the legitimacy of governmental intervention with private enterprise by considering how closely the interests sought protected 'fit' the provisions' object and purpose. The fact that an applicant pursues business interests is thus likely to play a part in the Court's assessment of the latitude permitted.

Significantly, the consideration of interests protected by the provision corresponds in this context with the essential object and purpose of the right in question, since studies have shown that the nearer the applicant's activities approach the core of the provision under which protection is sought, the

[110] Matscher (n 24) 66, referring in particular to *Klass* (n 78) § 42.

[111] It is implied in the discussion in Yourow (n 25) 189–91; and in F Ost 'The Original Canons of Interpretation of the European Court of Human Rights' in M Delmas-Marty (ed) *The European Convention for the Protection of Human Rights. International Protection versus National Restrictions* (Martinus Nijhoff Dordrecht, 1992) 283, 294–302.

[112] Schoekkenbroek (n 24) 34.

narrower margin of appreciation is generally granted to national authorities in their assessment of proportionality. Typically, the margin permitted is likely to be very narrow when the State has interfered with the very substance of the right invoked.[113]

Thus, the Court will apply a narrow margin of appreciation when speech or privacy interests 'fit' the essential purpose, the underlying rationale, of Articles 10 and 8. If a complaint concerns the exchange of political ideas, the margin of appreciation plays a miniscule role in the Court's approach to the 'necessity' criterion.[114] For instance, the Court confirmed in *Handyside v UK* that political speech (broadly understood) constitutes the paradigm interest with which Art 10 is primarily concerned, and that the standard of review applied *accordingly* should be a strict one,[115] in which a substantive (as opposed to formal) Strasbourg control of proportionality was invoked.[116]

The Court has likewise said that Article 8 primarily aims to protect the 'individual against arbitrary interference by public authorities'.[117] This suggests a preference in Art 8 interpretation for matters that concern the individual's 'inner circle'.[118] With regard to Art 8(2) the Court is thus less likely to accept broad domestic discretion in assessing 'necessity' where a 'particularly important facet of an individual's existence or identity is in issue'.[119]

(c) Does Disassociation with the Core Purpose Suggest a Wider Margin?

It must be taken as a doctrinal fact that a 'fit' between the interests essentially pursued and interests primarily sought protected leads to a heightened concern at the Court for governmental interference. But does that necessarily entail that a reverse inference can be drawn: that absence of 'fit' with the core purpose would be tantamount to acceptance by the Court of a wider margin of appreciation?

The answer to this question is 'yes', but not in the sense that disassociation—which will be the case for certain business claims under both provisions—leads automatically to a margin of appreciation at the other extreme. The fact that the interests pursued do not match the core purpose of Art 10 or Art 8 cannot logically mean that a regime of *especially low* level of protection is therefore applied. Rather, the principle of teleological interpretation, as applied in the margin of appreciation context, merely informs us that the interests will not be subjected to an exceptionally *rigorous* standard of scrutiny. In this sense

[113] Brems (n 24) 289–90.

[114] S Prebensen 'The Margin of Appreciation and Articles 9, 10 and 11 of the Convention' (1998) 19 HRLJ 13, 14.

[115] *Handyside* (n 30) § 49(1) and (2).

[116] ibid § 50.

[117] *Niemietz* (n 85) § 31.

[118] The term is borrowed from *Niemietz* (n 85) § 29(1).

[119] C Ovey 'The Margin of Appreciation and Article 8 of the Convention' (1998) 19 HRLJ 10, 11.

corporate privacy and commercial expression, by virtue of the principle of teleological interpretation, will be subjected to a regime by which the Court applies a wide margin of appreciation: it is wide because it is wider than the narrow margin applied in the 'core' contexts.

The case law does suggest an approach along these lines. It intimates that the element of teleology plays a significant part in the Court's assessment of the margin's width and that absence of 'fit' will lead to a margin which is relatively wider than that accepted for 'core' interests. For instance, the Court in *Hertel v Switzerland* applied a strict scrutiny standard under Art 10(2) by reference to the form of speech in question—as we recall the Court considered the statements to represent 'participation in a debate affecting the general interest'—and explicitly distinguished the case from that of the *markt intern* dispute.[120]

Undoubtedly, the Court's careful assessment in the *Hertel* case of whether the speech was 'political' or purely 'commercial', and its emphasis on the objectives of Art 10 as part of this discussion, shows concern with the teleological element. But the case law does not suggest that an absence of 'fit' with the essential purpose leads to a departure from an 'average' margin of appreciation (if that indeed can be identified). Significantly, the Commission in the 1979 case of *X and Church of Scientology v Sweden*, when asked to consider the admissibility of a complaint filed by a religious society and its minister against a ban on certain phrases in an advertisement for an instrument for 'measuring the mental state of an individual', said that:

> the level of protection must be less [for commercial expression] *than that accorded to the expression of 'political ideas'*, in the broadest sense, with which the values underpinning the concept of freedom of expression are chiefly concerned.[121]

In the context of Art 8(2) and business claims, there is little direct evidence except from the fact that the Court, when advocating leniency in terms of a wide margin of appreciation, relates that discussion to a relativist margin approach pursuant to the principle of teleological interpretation. In the *Niemietz* case, the Court observed, as we recall:

> More generally, to interpret the words 'private life' and 'home' as including certain professional or business activities or premises would be consonant with the essential object and purpose of Article 8 . . ., namely to protect the individual against arbitrary interference by the public authorities. . . . Such an interpretation would not unduly hamper the Contracting States, for they would retain their entitlement to 'interfere' to the extent permitted by paragraph 2 of Article 8 . . .; that entitlement might well be

120 *Hertel* (n 43) §§ 46(i) and (ii) and 47.

121 *X and Church of Scientology* (n 39) 73 (emphasis added). See also J de Meyer 'Human Rights in a Commercial Context' (1984) 5 HRLJ 139, 157.

more far-reaching where professional or business activities or premises were involved *than would otherwise be the case.*[122]

The standard of review suggested by the Court in the *Niemietz* case was linked with, and indeed seen as a consequence of, its emphasis on the object and purpose for establishing a wide scope of the provision with regard to Art 8(1). But there is no evidence to suggest that the Court means to imply that the principle of teleological interpretation entails an *especially* wide margin of appreciation when there is absence of 'fit'. The statement that the margin 'might well be more far-reaching... than would otherwise be the case' can probably be read as 'than would be the case when interests are at stake *that are consistent with the essential object and purpose of the provision*'. But there is, arguably, room for other interpretations of this statement.

At any rate, there is no clear evidence to substantiate the contention that the principle of teleological interpretation under either provision can wholly rationalize the Court's especially deferential approach to governmental interference with business claims under the two provisions in question. It may in other words be supplemented. The present discussion now turns to an additional structural factor that helps make coherent the Court's proclivity for adopting a lenient regime for scrutinizing interferences with business complaints in the context of Arts 8 and 10.

3 Deference to Democratic Processes in the Economic Field

It has now been shown that the nature and purpose of the applicant's claim may play a role in determining the type of margin to apply in a particular circumstance. It has also been shown that the business nature of an applicant's claim pursuant to an inverse application of teleological interpretation in part helps rationalize the Art 8 and 10 leniency. Studies of the margin of appreciation have also revealed, however, that the Court's approach is influenced by the nature of the aim pursued by the contested measure and its policy context.[123] The public interest in regulating corporate activities that fall within the ambit of Arts 8 and 10 may therefore help explain the Court's proclivity to accept a wide margin of appreciation in such instances.

Two aspects of the public interest factor, intimately connected in the present context, stand out in relevant case law. The Convention's profound reverence for democratic processes is considered first (sections (a) and (b)). This actually represents an extension of the teleological approach dealt with in the preceding section, in the sense that the protection of a democracy is, as chapter 2 showed, a central objective of the whole of the Convention. It is asserted that a lenient

[122] *Niemietz* (n 85) § 31. [123] Schoekkenbroek (n 24) 34.

standard of review is plausible in light of the Court's respect for this central Convention value.

The second aspect of the public interest side of the Court's deliberations is considered in sections (c) and (d). In the received Convention tradition, plurality of opinion typically exists with regard to the implementation of economic policies in general and regulation of activities emanating from private property interests in particular. The Convention therefore generally takes a deferential view of governmental interference with private property, as seen with regard to various Convention provisions. It is not entirely unlikely that the same structural feature could help explain the Court's deference with regard to the margin of appreciation discussion in Arts 8 and 10 since business interests pursued under them emanate from property.

(a) Introducing the 'Complexity and Fluctuation' Rationale under Article 10

It should be re-emphasized that the rationale suggested here does not necessarily reflect the Court's motivation for adopting a low-tier protection approach. Certain circumstantial evidence in Art 10 case law does underpin, however, the importance of the democracy argument at least under this provision. Article 10 serves for the time being as a vehicle for the line of argument in question, since the Court's only open justification for permitting a wide margin of appreciation in the 'necessity' assessment is found in Art 10(2) case law (and not in Art 8(2)).

In the *markt intern* judgment, the Court majority observed, as we recall, that a margin of appreciation was 'essential in commercial matters and, in particular, in an area as *complex and fluctuating* as that of unfair competition'.[124] This statement, which is one of the most enigmatic expressions in Strasbourg opinion-writing, has been invoked in other Art 10 cases concerning the enforcement of competition laws.[125] The area is 'complex and fluctuating' in a manner that justifies, in the Court's opinion, a particular deference to national authorities' proportionality assessment. But 'complex and fluctuating' has also been used to describe other areas involving typical business claims under Art 10 and which are thus being tested according to standard of review in which the respondent State has a wide margin of appreciation. The Court and Commission have applied this enigmatic rationale to matters involving commercial radio and television broadcasting,[126] and advertising:[127] in fact,

124 *markt intern* (n 34) § 33 (emphasis added).

125 *Jacubowski* (n 47) § 26; *Hertel* (n 43) § 47(2); and *Krone Verlag and Mediaprint* (n 73) § 6.

126 *Demuth* (n 65) § 42. See also *Röda Korsets Ungdomsförbund and Others* (n 59) § 1(18); *Cable Music Europe* (n 59) § 1(17); and *X SA* (n 59) § 1(9).

127 *Casado Coca* (n 58) § 50; *VGT Verein gegen Tierfabriken* (n 71) § 69; and *Krone Verlag* (No 3) (n 60) § 30. See further *Lindner* (n 64) § 1(9); and *Janssen* (n 64) § 7.

the Court seems to justify any wide margin of appreciation with regard to 'pure' commercial activity sought protected under Article 10 with the 'complex and fluctuating' character of the field in question.

The Court does not explain why 'pure' commercial speech is more 'complex and fluctuating' than other forms of speech, or, for that matter, why 'complexity and fluctuation' as characteristics of a particular area suggest an especially wide margin of appreciation. It is submitted here that the phrase is indicative of the importance of democracy as an element of the Court's assessment of what is 'necessary' governmental interference and what is not.

(b) Democratic Legitimacy and the 'Necessity' Criterion

Articles 8(2) and 10(2) require that public interference with a right protected by these provisions must, to escape international censure, be regarded as 'necessary *in a democratic society*' (emphasis added). Appending a democratic imperative to the 'necessity' criterion, the requirement of democratic legitimacy of an interference with Arts 8–11 freedoms occurs frequently in the Court's assessment and is widely regarded as constituting the normative core of the margin of appreciation doctrine.[128] This is hardly surprising, as any interpretation of the Convention, the Court has said, must be consistent with 'the general spirit of the Convention itself, an instrument designed to maintain and promote the ideals and values of democratic society',[129] something that also applies to the application of the margin of appreciation doctrine and the weighing of the general interest of the community in interfering with Convention freedoms inherent in this assessment.[130]

The requirement that governmental interference must have a measure of democratic legitimacy may obviously restrain the respondent party's latitude in disputes in which the exercise of public authority suffers from a clear democratic deficit (which rarely has been a topic in Strasbourg case law). But the requirement also entails a treaty concession to the autonomy of democratic processes vis-à-vis international authority. Although indirectly democratically elected,[131] the members of the Court lack the democratic legitimacy for which the national authorities, and in particular its legislature, are cherished. In the majority of Convention member States democracy is an esteemed value in everyday governance, and, importantly, it is that type of governance that

[128] E Kastanas *Unité et diversité: notions autonome, et marge d'appréciation des Etats dans la jurisprudence de la Cour européenne des droits de l'homme* (Bruylant Bruxelles, 1996) 146; Arai-Takahashi (n 7) 242–43; Delmas-Marty (n 11) 332; and Mahoney (n 28) 3–4.

[129] *Kjeldsen, Busk Madsen and Pedersen v Denmark* Series A No 23, (1979) 1 EHRR 711 § 53.

[130] S Marks 'The European Convention and Its "Democratic Society" ' (1995) 66 BYIL 209, 219.

[131] ECHR Art 22(1) and Arts 10(1)(ii) and 25(a) of the Statute of the Council of Europe (adopted 5 May 1949, entered into force 3 August 1949) ETS 1. Further HG Schermers 'Election of Judges to the European Court of Human Rights' (1998) 23 ELR 568.

normally comes under scrutiny at Strasbourg. The Court does not extend the democracy argument as far as to cause the Convention rights to lose altogether their function as 'trumps'.[132] Democracy is, in other words, not synonymous with uncontrolled majoritarianism. But deference to democratic processes is frequent in the case law under Arts 8 and 10 and an application of this argument therefore tends to result in a wider domestic margin of appreciation with regard to the 'democratic necessity' of an interference.[133]

How is it that the democracy element supports the leniency applied in the context of regulating commercial speech under Art 10? Susan Marks has already paved the way for one answer in arguing that the adoption of a lower scrutiny under Art 10(2) can be explained on grounds of democracy. Public interference in the 'non-political' area of commercial relations does not engage democracy to the same extent as does governmental intrusion of public discourse. Free speech is protected to safeguard the public democratic discourse; interferences with it have a high priority for the Court as is shown in the weight it attaches to the provision's purpose. Governmental regulation with privatised discourse, however, does not engage democracy in the same manner. The Court's teleology would therefore suggest a less intense scrutiny in the commercial field.[134]

The pursuit for a viable explanation can be taken one step further. The *markt intern* case provides useful clues here. 'Complexity' and 'fluctuation' are both expressive of the difficulty or impossibility of achieving certainty in various matters. Of things complex and variable there will inevitably be different opinions. One element of democracy—the Convention's conception of it was introduced in chapter 2—which is consistently stressed by the Court is the value of pluralism.[135] As Paul Mahoney notes:

> In a pluralistic democratic society there will on many topics covered by the Convention be a spectrum of differing but acceptable opinions. As regards such topics it will be for each society to decide on its own policy and then, on the facts, to endeavour to do justice in individual cases. . . .
>
> Where societal values are still the subject of debate and controversy at the national level, they should not easily be converted by the Court into protected Convention values . . . .[136]

In its interpretation of a value judgment such as 'necessary in a democratic society', the Court needs to settle on one of several quite conceivable solutions, even more so when there is a genuine difference of opinion on the national plane. Where there tend to be different opinions in the democratic discourse,

[132] R Dworkin 'Rights as Trumps' (1981) 1 OJLS 177; and Mahoney (n 28) 3.
[133] Greer (n 25) 17 and 24–25. [134] Marks (n 129) 233. [135] *Handyside* (n 30) § 49.
[136] Mahoney (n 28) 3.

the Court is not the organ to superimpose a particular set of opinions since doing so could be seen as an expression of the judges' own convictions. This calls for particular vigilance at the Court to avoid the appearance of interfering in domestic debates.[137]

In this manner, then, can the Court's allegiance to democracy as a Convention value justify the lenient standard in Art 10 (if not in Art 8).

(c) The Special Status of Property Protection under the Convention

The impact of the democracy argument in a determination of the width of the margin of appreciation permitted is strong in the area of private enterprise. The Convention builds on the presumption that opinions in the public and among Convention member States differ extensively over the appropriate policy choices in the economic field, at least relatively more so than with regard to the question of the limits to governmental interference with physical and mental integrity of the human person or the core elements of political discourse.[138]

Unlike what is the case with regulation of political discourse, the Convention therefore permits a measure of ambiguity concerning the conditions of private enterprise in the regulatory state.[139] This is an approach that enjoys a long Convention history. As was mentioned in chapter 2, the treaty drafters were divided as to whether a provision for the protection of private property should enjoy Convention status at all. Those opposing its inclusion, a largely ideologically motivated stance, succeeded in postponing the adoption of the guarantee now laid down in Protocol 1 Art 1.[140] Although an integral part of the Convention today, some eminent ECHR observers remain ideologically opposed to an extensive protection of private property rights under Protocol 1 Art 1.[141] Such dissension remains a gauge of 'the difficulty that even western democracies find themselves in when trying to formulate' a right to property as a fundamental right.[142]

The protection of private property under the Convention is discussed in somewhat more detail in section (d). For the time being, suffice it to observe that the Court subscribes to the truism that interference with private property is an area in which opinions differ widely. *James and Others v UK* typifies the Court's sentiment even today. In a case which concerned a challenge brought

137 Mahoney (n 28) 2–3. 138 ibid 2 and 5. 139 Marks (n 130) 219–20.

140 eg, L Serment *The European Convention on Human Rights and Property Protection* (Council of Europe Publishing Strasbourg, 1992) 7.

141 eg, HG Schermers 'The International Protection of the Right of Property' in F Matscher and H Petzold (eds) *Protecting Human Rights: The European Dimension. Studies in Honour of Gérard J Wiarda* (Heymann Cologne, 1988) 565, 574–75.

142 J Kingston 'Rich People Have Human Rights Too? The Status of Property as a Fundamental Right' in L Heffernan and J Kingston (eds) *Human Rights: A European Perspective* (Dublin Round Hall Press, 1994) 284, 290.

by a major private landowner in metropolitan London against legislation aimed at controlling the market for lease of residential property by enabling the tenants to buy their flats, the Court, in one of its landmark cases in its attempt to arbitrate between free enterprise and the regulatory state, observed that:

> the notion of 'public interest' is necessarily extensive. In particular, as the Commission noted, the decision to enact laws expropriating property will commonly involve consideration of political, economic and social *issues on which opinions within a democratic society may reasonably differ widely*. The Court, finding it natural that the margin of appreciation available to the legislature in implementing social and economic policies *should be a wide one*, will respect the legislature's judgment as to what is "in the public interest" unless that judgment be manifestly without reasonable foundation.[143]

In his study of the margin of appreciation, Elias Kastanas leaves no doubt that the Court's deference to domestic authorities' proportionality assessment under Protocol 1 Art 1 is based on the democracy argument's underlying respect for plurality of opinion.[144]

Commercial expression is closely linked with the property interests of the speaker. The very purpose of 'pure' commercial speech such as advertising is to incite the listener to purchase the speaker's goods or services, transactions whose main purpose is to make profit for the enterprise in question.[145] It is highly likely that the considerations that apply to permit interference with the main property right clause in the Convention can also be applied in the context in Article 10 as far as commercial expression is concerned. Against this background, the *markt intern* judgment's 'complex and fluctuating' phrase is a sensible result of the Court's general regard for national democratic discourse.

(d) The Social Function of Property

Yet the argument from democracy is not the only rationale on which the *markt intern* approach can be defended. There is at least one additional dimension of the Convention's consideration of private property that merits our attention, especially since it can provide an additional justification also for the suggestive leniency approach taken to corporate privacy under Art 8 by the Court in *Colas Est SA v France*.

The argument requires familiarity with the protection of private property under the Convention.

[143] *James and Others* (n 4) § 46(2) (emphasis added). [144] Kastanas (n 128) 145–53.

[145] F Ossenbühl 'Die Freiheiten des Unternehmers nach dem Grundgesetz' (1990) 115 AöR 1, 22 (with regard to German constitutional law).

(i) Protocol 1 Article 1 and Property Protection

The protection of private property is primarily undertaken through the application of Protocol 1 Art 1. It states:

> Every natural or legal person is entitled to the peaceful enjoyment of his possessions. No one shall be deprived of his possessions except in the public interest and subject to the conditions provided for by law and by the general principles of international law.
>
> The preceding provisions shall not, however, in any way impair the right of a State to enforce such laws as it deems necessary to control the use of property in accordance with the general interest or to secure the payment of taxes or other contributions or penalties.

Several theorists have discussed the provision at length in works more suitable for such analyses.[146] It is important, nonetheless, to reiterate here that 'possessions' more or less equal the concept of (private) property as is generally understood in most liberal constitutional systems.[147] The concept 'possessions' includes income derived from capital and from business undertakings regardless of personal labour, involvement and use; it is not restricted to property necessary to facilitate private life and income and savings derived from work. The provision is a safeguard for property already in the applicant person's possession against governmental regulation,[148] and thus not, for instance, guarantees a right to acquire possessions.

As the Court has repeatedly stated, the provision consists of three distinct, yet interconnected, 'rules':[149] the first proclaims the principle of peaceful enjoyment of possessions (property) in areas not covered by the two other rules (first sentence); the second protects against deprivation of property (second sentence); and the third covers various forms of public control of property in the course of everyday governance (third sentence). The first rule is an overarching rule in light of which the two other rules should be construed.[150]

None of the three rules proclaims unconditional property protection but it requires the fulfilment of certain conditions for a governmental interference

[146] See among many authorities AR Çoban *Protection of Property Rights within the European Convention on Human Rights* (Ashgate Aldershot, 2004); M Frigo 'Peaceful Enjoyment of Possessions, Expropriation and Control of the Use of Property in the System of the European Convention on Human Rights' (2001) 10 It Ybk Intl L 45; M Pellonpää 'Reflections on the Notion of "Deprivation of Possessions" in Article 1 of the First Protocol to the European Convention on Human Rights' in P Mahoney and others (eds) *Protecting Human Rights: The European Perspective: Studies in Memory of Rolv Ryssdal* (Heymann Cologne, 2000) 1087; and Serment (n 140).

[147] *Gasus Dosier- und Fördertechnik GmbH v Netherlands* Series A No 306-B, (1995) 20 EHRR 403 § 53; and *Marckx v Belgium* Series A No 31, (1980) 2 EHRR 330 § 63(3), where the Court explicitly stated that 'Article 1 is in substance guaranteeing the right of property'.

[148] *Pressos Compania Naviera SA and Others v Belgium* judgment 20 November 1995 Series A 332 § 31; and Serment (n 130) 11.

[149] *Sporrong and Lönnroth* (n 108) § 61.

[150] *James and Others* (n 4) § 37.

with private property to be legitimate. The third rule shows deference to the public interest in speaking of legitimate control 'in the general interest'; the second allows for the taking of property when in 'the public interest' and provided that compensation is afforded to the proprietor. A similar criterion is implied, so the Court says, in the first rule.[151]

The tension between individual and collective demands and between international and national interests is taken up in particular in the devices which provide for an overall assessment of the appropriateness of governmental interference with property. The rule proclaiming 'peaceful enjoyment' of property and its role as 'meta-rule' mean that 'the principle of proportionality is inherent in Article 1 of the Protocol, regardless of which rule is applied'.[152] Proportionality is reflected independently in the requirement of 'necessity' in the third sentence.[153] The principle serves an integral function in the interpretation of the two other rules;[154] the standard of proportionality applicable to the third sentence is often set at a lower level than under the two other rules.[155]

The Court's task, when assessing proportionality under Protocol 1 Art 1, is to:

> determine whether a fair balance was struck between the demands of the general interest of the community and the requirements of the protection of the individual's fundamental rights.[156]

The Court has found that the margin of appreciation also applies to this assessment, as it does with regard to the 'necessity' assessment under Arts 8 and 10.

It is important to appreciate that the Court accepts a very wide margin of appreciation under Protocol 1 Art 1. Naturally, the Court's review is not entirely toothless.[157] But the Court assumes that the assessment undertaken on the domestic plane remains within the boundaries of discretion unless it is manifestly without reasonable foundation.[158] The margin of appreciation is

151 Çoban (n 146) 199–204. 152 Pellonpää (n 146) 1088.

153 *Mellacher and Others v Austria* Series A No 169, (1990) 12 EHRR 391§ 56 was a turning point in the Court's case law in this respect.

154 As regards the second rule, see *James and Others* (n 4) § 54(2). With respect to the first rule, see *Sporrong and Lönnroth* (n 108) §§ 69 and 73.

155 App 9063/80 *Gillow v UK* (report) (1984) §§ 148 and 154; and Arai-Takahashi (n 7) 151.

156 *Sporrong and Lönnroth* (n 108) § 69(2) (first sentence); *Holy Monasteries v Greece* Series A No 301, (1995) 20 EHRR 1 § 70 (first sentence); and *Velosa Barreto v Portugal* judgment 21 November 1995 Series A 334 § 36 (first sentence).

157 In *SA Dangeville v France* Reports 2002-III (2004) 38 EHRR 32 §§ 52–62 for instance, the Court found that the national authorities had failed to strike a fair balance between the regulatory needs and the interests of the applicant company despite the application of the proportionality principle enunciated in *Sporrong and Lönnroth* (the case concerned inability to obtain refund of paid VAT for an insurance broker firm).

158 *James and Others* (n 4) § 46(2) (second sentence); *Mellacher and Others* (n 153) § 45(3) (third sentence); and *Sporrong and Lönnroth* (n 108) § 69(4) (first sentence). See further Arai-Takahashi (n 7) 152–54.

thus wider already at the outset under Protocol 1 Art 1 than under, say, Arts 8 and 10.[159] This may have ramifications, however, for the interpretation of Arts 8 and 10.

(ii) A Systematically Wide Margin in the Implementation of Economic Policies

The Court with regard to its weighing of considerations in Protocol 1 Art 1 is thus generally deferential to the respondent State's needs,[160] that is, regardless of who pursues the private complaint. One might say that the Court's deferential stance is nearly tantamount to the inclusion of a 'right to regulate' within the right to property protection under the Convention.[161] All Protocol 1 Art 1 complaints concern the status of private property in the face of governmental regulation of it. The case law is therefore suggestive of the Convention's general regard for private property vis-à-vis the general interests of the public. The Court consistently says that 'in areas of social, financial or economic policy', national authorities enjoy a wide margin of appreciation 'in implementation of laws regulating property and contractual relationships'.[162] Lenient scrutiny of governmental interference with property rights is therefore not explained solely by the existence of plurality of opinion in the member States in the fields of implementing economic or financial policies: acceptance of the member States entitlement to regulate their respective economies is embedded in the Convention's structure.

This generally deferential stance towards public regulation of private property is doubtless amenable to many angles of analysis. One of them is the general observation that Protocol 1 Art 1 case law proves that the concept of private property enjoys limited protective status in Strasbourg because the Convention system acknowledges property's social function. The Court accepts the legitimacy of public regulation of private economic activity for the benefit of the common good. It cannot be denied that the right to property, in the words of van Dijk and van Hoof, 'has actually lost a good deal of its inviolability [under the Convention] under the influence of modern social policy'.[163] This is not unique to the law of the ECHR: the social function of private property, and its implied legitimacy of extensive governmental regulation, is acknowledged in the national constitutions of the Council of

[159] Arai-Takahashi (n 7) 151–52.

[160] ibid 151–54; and R Bernhardt 'Einwirkungen der Europäischen Menschenrechts-Konvention auf das Staatliche Wirtschaftsrecht' in R Briner and others (eds) *Law of International Business and Dispute Settlement. Liber Amicorum Karl-Heinz Böckstiegel* (Heymann Cologne, 2001) 67, 69.

[161] The 'right to regulate' discourse was introduced in chapter 1.

[162] *Stretch v UK* (2004) 38 EHRR 12 § 37 (rejection of application for an extension of permission to erect buildings for industrial use).

[163] van Dijk and van Hoof (n 7) 618.

Europe area.[164] It is also part and parcel of the approach taken to private property in the EU,[165] and indeed in what may be established as general international law in this area.[166]

Finally, the crucial point for the purpose of the present discussion. The dimension now fleshed out extends beyond the context of Protocol 1 Art 1, since property protection may be pursued also under other provisions. 'Especially in the economic sphere', Eva Brems has noted in her overall study of the margin of appreciation, the Court 'recognises that the member states need some breathing space to realise their policy'.[167] Her observation applies to all aspects of Convention protection where private economic activity is measured against the needs of the regulatory state, including Arts 8 and 10 as applied in the economic context. As is the case with Art 10 (noted above), Art 8 may also represent a means for the protection of private property. A company's freedom from public intrusion on its premises is a condition for the smooth running of business and thus to generate income. Claims for the protection of the privacy of business activities activate a property dimension of Art 8 which should be seen in light of the Convention's overall conception of private property vis-à-vis the public interest.

Through the Court's application of the margin of appreciation doctrine in balancing competing private and public interests, national authorities are therefore systematically permitted to regulate economic activity in pursuit of the common good. This systemic feature of the Convention, its acknowledgement of the regulatory state's rightful and necessary place in a capitalist society, is a significant justificatory factor underlying the *markt intern* and *Colas Est* approaches.

D. Summary Observations

The discussion above reflects the Court's acceptance of the principle of the *raison d'état*—the principle that says that public interests sometimes must override the interests of the individual—as a legitimate factor when it interprets

164 Including principal constitutional regimes as those in France and Germany, eg, W Veelken 'Wirtschaftsverfassung im Systemvergleich' (1991) 55 RZaiP 463, 488–99.

165 Case 4/73 *Firma J Nold KG v Commission* [1974] ECR 491 § 14. See further JA Usher *General Principles of EC Law* (Longman Harlow, 1998) 88–99; and B de Witte 'The Past and Future Role of the European Court of Justice in the Protection of Human Rights' in P Alston (ed) *The EU and Human Rights* (Oxford University Press Oxford, 1999) 859, 878–80.

166 I Seidl-Hohenveldern 'The Social Function of Property and Property Protection in Present-Day International Law' in F Kalshoven PJ Kuyper and JG Lammers (eds) *Essays on the Development of the International Legal Order: in Memory of Haro F van Panhuys* (Sijthoff & Noordhoff Alphen aan den Rijn, 1980) 77.

167 Brems (n 24) 274–75.

provisions that permit a balanced assessment of a variety of interests.[168] The low-intensity approach adhered to by the Court with regard to Arts 8 and 10 protection deviates from the standard of scrutiny in force at the Court when most non-business or non-corporate applicants' complaints are interfered with. It would perhaps be misguided to say that the protection of the general interest or a consideration of national exigencies is part and parcel of the Convention's object and purpose, at least when that general interest conflicts with the rights of individual persons. The Convention is, after all, a treaty for the protection of human rights and fundamental freedoms. Introductions to the Court's teleological approach generally suggest that the teleology normally widens the member States' obligations more than is the point of departure in general international law.[169] But this assumption requires us to ask what teleology actually means in terms of the ECHR. This book is not the place for a detailed consideration of this matter, although it will be revisited in the final chapter.

The Court's approach in the *markt intern* and *Colas Est* cases can be rationalized in terms of the framework within which the Court works, but whether the suggested structures in fact motivated the Court to adopt these standards is unclear. The Convention is to a large extent primarily intended for the protection of interests the characteristics of which do not readily correspond with those pursued by corporate and other business applicants before the Court. A lenient standard of scrutiny may therefore simply be the result of the Court's general emphasis upon the object and purpose of Convention protection. The Convention is additionally conceived in a reality in which the roles of state and market have been clearly defined by the regulatory model and the acknowledgement of the social function of property. The Court would unlikely depart from this conception.

Naturally, there might be room for criticism of the Court's lenient approach, and criticism has indeed been marshalled by others. The joint dissenting opinion in the *markt intern* case was at pains to record its strong objections to what it conceived as the business-unfriendly approach taken by the Court majority. In their opinion:

> [i]t is just as important to guarantee the freedom of expression in relation to the practices of a commercial undertaking as it is in relation to the conduct of a head of

[168] JC Soyer 'Retour discret de la raison d'état dans ces états soumis à la raison du droit (La fonction publique nationale)' in J-L Aujol (ed) *Mélanges en hommage à Louis-Edmond Pettiti* (Bruylant Bruxelles, 1998) 661, 661: defines the reason of state principle in the Convention context as 'la considération de l'intérêt public au nom duquel une decision se trouve justifiée'.

[169] Matscher (n 24) 66; and H Golsong 'Interpreting the European Convention on Human Rights Beyond the Confines of the Vienna Convention on the Law of Treaties?' in R St John Macdonald F Matscher and H Petzold (eds) *The European System for the Protection of Human Rights* (Martinus Nijhoff Dordrecht, 1993) 147, 148.

government, which was at issue in the Lingens case [concerning political speech]. Similarly the right thereto must be able to be exercised as much in the interests of the purchasers of beauty products as in those of the owners of sick animals, the interests at stake in the Barthold case. In fact, freedom of expression serves, above all, the general interest.

The fact that a person defends a given interest, whether it is an economic interest or any other interest, does not, moreover, deprive him of the benefit of freedom of expression.

In order to ensure the openness of business activities . . ., it must be possible to disseminate freely information and ideas concerning the products and services proposed to consumers. Consumers, who are exposed to highly effective distribution techniques and to advertising which is frequently less than objective, deserve, for their part too, to be protected, as indeed do retailers.[170]

The interest pursued by the applicant company was, however, in the Court majority's opinion property related and therefore subjected to a less rigorous scrutiny than that afforded to political speech. The public interest carried more weight in this context. The general interest that, in the context of Articles 8 and 10, often weighs more than the interests of the applicant company or business actor whose claim emanates from property, cannot be defined here as its nature will depend on the circumstances of each case.

It should be recalled, by way of a conclusion, that the *markt intern* and *Colas Est* judgments both concerned governmental regulation of anti-competitive behaviour. Action against anti-competitive behaviour is undertaken by the State to secure equal opportunities in the various markets. In the case of *markt intern*, for instance, the Court was well aware of its instrumental role in securing the market in the beauty product sector.[171] The granting of a wide margin of appreciation under the Convention for the implementation of competition laws benefits public interests since a functioning market presumptively generates economic surplus to the advantage of the common good. Significantly, the Court in the *Colas Est* case found the competition authorities' searches and seizures to pursue the legitimate aim of restricting the privacy right for the purpose of 'the economic well-being of the country'.[172]

Considerable deference to governmental authority in the sphere of competition is advantageous for the business community, in the sense that the Convention thereby accepts a disadvantaged position in the market as a legitimate concern the pursuance of which is permissible for the respondent state. This element, too, finds support in the case law. The *markt intern* Court, for instance, found

[170] *markt intern* (n 34) Dissenting Opinion of Judges Gölücklü, Pettiti, Russo, Spielmann, de Meyer, Carillo Salcedo and Valticos paras 1(7)–(9).

[171] *markt intern* (n 34) § 35. See similarly, eg, *Jacubowski* (n 47) §§ 27–29 (the news market); and *Krone Verlag (No 3)* (n 60) §§ 31–34 (the newspaper market).

[172] *Colas Est* (n 74) § 44.

the prohibitions against the applicant company's statements to protect the 'rights of others' as provided for in Art 10(2).[173] The competition context, as noted previously, does not seem to have informed the lenient standards of scrutiny as such. But the context of competition reveals that governmental interference in the name of the public good, although detrimental to the individual applicant whose claim does not succeed in Strasbourg, may in fact benefit the business sphere as a whole. Once again, we observe (as we did in chapter 3) that Convention protection has significant instrumental aspects and that this instrumentalism may have various shades and entail different consequences for an applicant company and the business sector as a whole.

Whatever the right way of looking at the Court's case law in which lenient standards of review have been developed may be, it remains a fact that the standards of review applied by the Court are conveyed to us in a very uninformative way. The Court has generally been criticized for its failure to articulate the reasons for its views on the margin of appreciation doctrine.[174] This is a reproach which applies also to the context under discussion here.

[173] *markt intern* (n 34) § 31(2); criticized by de Merieux (n 52) 393.
[174] Macdonald (n 24) 124.

6

Retrospect and Prospect

The time has come to bring this study to a close. This chapter sums up the book's themes and findings (part A); suggests certain issues, highlighted in part by this book, that warrant further research (part B); and finally, offers some concluding observations on the corporate usage of the Convention in light of the recent effort to restructure anew the enforcement machinery in Strasbourg (part C).

A. Retrospect

This book has considered certain aspects of corporate actors' utilization of the system for private application under the European Convention on Human Rights. More concretely, it has described and explored the manner in which the European Court of Human Rights, as the internationally authorized arbiter of claims arising under the Convention, responds to corporate complaints in its decisions in cases which have represented difficult issues of treaty interpretation. Important in its own right, since the topic has not been the subject of comprehensive analysis before, the study has also sought, by using the Court's approach to contentious corporate cases as an analytical vehicle, to reveal certain structures of ECHR law and adjudication, the significance of which extends beyond the business context. It is to be hoped that its findings may help widen our understanding of the ECHR and how we think of it.

1 The Framework That Shapes the Court's Response

Corporate use of the right of application in Art 34 is not favourably received in all corners, and it challenges commonly held perceptions of what human rights are about. Chapter 2 submitted examples of the sense of impropriety, particularly evident in the British-based ECHR discourse, concerning the putative ill-use by for-profit entities of a system of fundamental norms primarily intended to safeguard basic civil and political rights of individual human beings. The grounds offered vary, as chapter 2 has demonstrated, but they are often normatively laden.

The book has probed exclusively the doctrinal responses of the Court to corporate litigation in light of the structures within which the Court is situated. In this perspective, the Court is empowered, but also constrained, by the legal framework that is the Convention and its right of private application. It is, we must not forget, the only parameter that is able to shape the Court's doctrinal manifestations unless the Convention is altered by the member States of the Council of Europe. The members of the Court cannot be guided by anecdote, assumptions or historical or current examples of abuse in other legal systems, or by their personal convictions of the place of private business enterprise in a system for human rights protection.

The Court's methodology is essentially teleological: its reasoning is significantly shaped by what it perceives as the object and purpose of ECHR law. The Court's identification of the Convention's object and purpose is naturally inspired by the treaty text, its drafting history, the value system on which it builds, and other aspects of the nature of human rights protection that find their expression in the treaty or follow by implication from it. Chapters 1 and 2 sought to identify the elements of the Convention that inspire the Court's teleological jurisprudence and which function as essential guidelines for the Court's reasoning.

From a standpoint *de lege lata*, the criticism of corporate human rights protection can largely be rebutted. Thus, it was argued that the treaty text, read in isolation and in light of the preparatory works, entitles for-profit business entities to seek ECHR protection. It was also submitted that the Convention's underlying value system, as expressed in the treaty's Preamble, which in short comprises respect for individual dignity, democracy, the rule of law, and European liberalism, suggests that companies' concerns are largely compatible with the treaty's ideology. The treaty has, besides, collective and economic features that moderate the impression that the treaty is an instrument only for the protection of individual civil and political rights. There is further support for the view that corporate interests are principally welcomed in ECHR law in the system's instrumental and objective aspects, even if, sometimes, the nature of the corporate entity, when compared with basic functions of human rights may render corporate complaints doctrinally problematic and require a particular adjudicatory response.

2 The Court's Response

Chapters 3, 4, and 5 explored on the basis of this structural background the Court's response to certain corporate complaints. It was a dual investigation that sought first to identify the main lines in the Court's approach, as found in relevant case law, and second to rationalize the Court's response in light of the structural framework laid down in chapters 1 and 2. It was suggested how the Court's reasoning might be made structurally coherent, since the judgments and decisions themselves intimate only vaguely their underlying rationale.

(a) The Court's Response Identified

Chapters 3 through 5 dealt with three issues regarded as doctrinally unsettled or contentious by the Court. They were the question of whether corporate shareholders may legitimately seek 'victim' status, pursuant to Art 34, for matters that have formally befallen the companies in which they own shares; whether corporate entities may successfully rely on rights-provisions that traditionally have been reserved, or believed to be reserved, for individual human beings outside the business context; and whether governmental interference with for-profit entities' interests, once protected by rights-provisions, should be subject to a lower standard of judicial scrutiny than that applied for interferences with individuals outside the for-profit setting.

In all three contexts, the Court's response was described in detail, since comprehensive analyses of this kind have not been undertaken before. For instance, chapter 3 presented the Court's point of departure when responding to shareholders' claims to be identified with their company for the purpose of Convention protection. Following the reasoning of *Agrotexim Hellas SA and Others v Greece*, the Court in principle said that shareholders cannot be 'victims' for matters that formally concern the company in which they own shares.[1] But the Court was inclined to allow shareholder complaints of this form when it is 'impossible' for the company itself to apply to the Court and when the company is merely a 'vehicle' for the individual shareholder's business activities.[2] The *Agrotexim* approach has been criticized for being too rigid in upholding the corporate veil. Chapter 3 sought to show that the Court's doctrinal response rested on a balanced assessment of a host of factors, the starting point and two acknowledged exceptions of which merely served as guiding principles for a holistic and pragmatic reasoning, while at the same time heeding the structural framework on the basis of which it operates.

Chapter 4 introduced the Court's response to hard cases of applicability, that is, when corporate entities pursuing economic goals have sought refuge under aspects of provisions that for various reasons have been conceived of as means for the protection of individuals' civil and political concerns. It could be argued that the object and purpose of select aspects of Art 8(1), 10(1), and 41 suggest

1 *Agrotexim Hellas and Others v Greece* Series A No 330, (1996) 21 EHRR 250.

2 ibid § 66; and *Pine Valley Developments Ltd and Others v Ireland* Series A No 222, (1992) 16 EHRR 379 § 42.

that companies and their characteristic interests are quite outside the scope and thrust of the provisions. The Court nonetheless concluded that companies in principle are capable of relying on the provisions. The chapter identified how the Court reasoned in the context of each provision, on the basis of the landmark judgments in each field: the *Autronic AG v Switzerland* judgment with regard to corporate commercial protection under Art 10(1);[3] the *Comingersoll SA v Portugal* judgment with regard to corporate entitlement to monetary compensation for immaterial loss pursuant to Art 41;[4] and the *Colas Est SA and Others v France* judgment, which decided that corporate business premises may be regarded as a 'home' within the meaning of Art 8(1) in cases concerning searches and seizures.[5]

Chapter 5 dealt with instances where the Court assesses the legitimacy of governmental regulation of business activity in light of the Convention's standards. At this juncture of the Court's handling of cases, where a provision is found to be applicable to the corporate person, the tension between private and public needs crystallizes in an overall proportionality assessment at the Court in which a variety of considerations must be weighed against each other. This delicate balance of conflicting interests is tackled by the Court through its formulation of the appropriate intensity of its review of national governmental regulation. This standard of review is predominantly expressed through the principle of proportionality and the margin of appreciation doctrine. The chapter introduced the lenient standard of review adopted by the Court through its application of the margin of appreciation: the lenient standard of scrutiny adopted with regard to interference with commercial expression in Article 10(2), as established in *markt intern Verlag GmbH and Klaus Beermann v Germany*;[6] and the tentative standard of relaxed judicial review of public authorities' searches and seizures of business premises, as suggested in *Colas Est SA and Others v France*, pursuant to Art 8(2).[7]

(b) *Justifying the Court's Response*

The study has also been preoccupied with deciphering the Court's reasoning in its response to these three instances of treaty interpretation. This has been important because the Court's views in some cases have been remarkably 'business-friendly' while in others, the Court has retracted to a formalistic or restrained reasoning that has not been supportive of the individual business applicant's claims. In all instances, the Court's generally brief and enigmatically phrased reasoning leaves us largely ignorant of its motivations.

[3] *Autronic AG v Switzerland* judgment Series A No 178, (1990) 12 EHRR 485.

[4] *Comingersoll SA v Portugal* Reports 2000-IV (2001) 31 EHRR 772.

[5] *Colas Est SA and Others v France* judgment 16 April 2002 Reports 2002-III.

[6] *markt intern Verlag GmbH and Klaus Beermann v Germany* Series A No 165, (1990) 12 EHRR 161.

[7] *Colas Est* (n 5).

It was argued that while we cannot discern every factor that shapes the Court's response in a given case, its reasoning can at least be rationalized and made coherent from a structural viewpoint. More concretely, it was explained how the Court's responses can be justified in light of the underlying factors that were introduced in chapters 1 and 2.

Chapter 3 suggested in consequence that the upholding of the corporate veil in some, and its disregard in other cases, reflect a pragmatic application of the principle of effectiveness, which again derives from the Court's teleological methodology. The preservation of the corporate veil at the level of international law is justified in terms of the Convention's due regard for national interests as exemplified by domestic legislative arrangements. Reverence for the construct of separate corporate personhood is, besides, in a broader perspective, beneficial for the business sector and for society in general as it preserves a fruitful climate for private business investment. The Court's occasional disregard for the constraints presented by separate corporate personality demonstrates, on the other hand, a pragmatic disdain for conceptually inspired jurisprudence when it hampers the effectiveness of human rights protection in individual cases.

Chapter 4 observed that the Court's response to hard cases of applicability represents an *avant-garde* jurisprudence compared to comparable fundamental rights regimes. It was argued that the Court's business-friendly approach can be explained as a reflection of its teleological approach. A reconsideration of what constitutes the 'object and purpose' of Convention protection tells us that the question of applicability need not depend on the degree of harmonization between personal status and interests of the individual applicant and the core purpose of ECHR protection. Rather, the Court is enabled to inquire whether the complaint at hand should be discussed inasmuch as values other than those entailed by the actual dispute are worth protecting. The Court's consideration of the principle of equality, the rule of law implications of a given case, and the effects on political democracy for the public at large should the corporate complaint not be subject to the Court's decision are examples of such objective values that also fall within the meaning of the Convention's object and purpose.

Chapter 5 argued that the Court's lenient standard of scrutiny is partly a consequence of the Court's teleological approach: in Art 10 and Art 8, the safeguard of the civil and political rights of the individual human being remain the primary objective for the Court. The acceptance of corporate reliance on the provisions essentially means that the provisions also include collective and economic components, which, while not necessarily in contravention with the provisions' objective, are removed from the core purpose of the provisions. The adoption of a less intense judicial review of governmental interference is, in this respect, merely a reflection of the fact that corporate concerns lie closer to the perimeter of the provisions' objective than its heart. The Court's leniency can also be justified in terms of the prominence of political democracy under the Convention and structurally justified in that it demonstrates deference to governmental regulation of the private economy, and is thus in line with another Convention objective, notably to secure the common liberal values shared in the Council of Europe area, where a regulated market economy remains important.

B. Questions of Wider Significance

Several scholars and practitioners have studied aspects of the status of companies and other persons belonging to the business community under the European Convention on Human Rights. Despite such efforts, a number of issues pertaining to the interpretation of the Convention in a corporate context remain obscure. This book has attempted to compile and clarify some, but far from all, of these issues.

At bottom, however, this is a structural study of the Court's response to corporate litigation. The Court's reasoning, and the framework within which it is developed, has remained the main focus of attention. By applying this perspective, the study has sought to disentangle in some measure the debate on companies' (and shareholders') appropriate status in the Convention system, and locate the interests of private business enterprise within the Convention landscape. It is to be hoped that the present work may provide a fruitful platform for normative studies of this form of human rights law.

By exploring difficult questions of treaty interpretation in a context likely to upset mainstream human rights perceptions, the book has also sought to improve our understanding of the Court's reasoning in areas beyond the corporate business context. It has intended to map broader themes pertaining to the Convention and its system of private application and has made certain discoveries in this regard. It has revealed aspects of the Court's reasoning and areas of ECHR law which are deserving of further studies. Three of them are now enumerated.

1 A Many-Sided Teleology

The Court adheres to the main principles of treaty interpretation as found in Art 31(1) of the Vienna Convention on the Law of Treaties, where the treaty text as read in light of the treaty's object and purpose represent significant devices for judicial reasoning. The Court arguably applies several techniques and principles in its interpretation. This book has revealed the pervasiveness of teleology in the Court's reasoning, typically through its application of the effectiveness principle and the principle of dynamic interpretation in addition to its direct reference to teleology in its case law.

It is no new discovery that the Court applies a teleological method, but its study, and the Convention's object and purpose, have yet to be undertaken on a general basis. This book has taken a preliminary step in its demonstration of the pervasiveness of teleology and by attaching the principle of teleological interpretation directly to the underlying values of the Convention as they can be perceived in the Preamble. Doubtless further studies would be required outside the business context to determine the full measure of the Convention's object and purpose and which instruments the Court has at its disposal in pursuing a teleological approach.[8]

In particular, it is significant for our perception of human rights protection in the Convention system to explore further what has been referred to in the present book as the aspects of instrumentality and objectiveness in Convention protection, where the Convention's regime is considered from the broader perspective of the law of the Convention and the European public order to which it contributes, as opposed to the subjective approach whereby the regime is seen in terms of the legal interests of the individual applicant. The Convention, says the Court, represents 'a constitutional instrument of European public order (*ordre public*)',[9] which, among other things, permits detachment from the specific concerns of the individual applicant pursuing a complaint before the Court. In our context, this objectiveness allows the Court to hear corporate complaints since the protection of their concerns is sometimes instrumental to the protection of others' interests.[10] The treaty as an objective value system, while sometimes referred to in the Court's practice and in the literature,[11] is

[8] Preoccupation with teleology in international law has increased in recent years, see, eg, A Albors-Lorens 'The European Court of Justice, More than a Teleological Court' (2000) 2 Cambridge Ybk Eur Leg Stud 373; I Buffard and K Zemanek 'The "Object" and "Purpose" of a Treaty: An Enigma?' (1998) 3 Austrian Rev Intl & Eur L 311; V Crnic-Grotic 'Object and Purpose of Treaties in the Vienna Convention on the Law of Treaties' (1997) 7 Asian Ybk Intl L 141; and J Klabbers 'Some Problems Regarding the Object and Purpose of Treaties' (1997) 8 Finnish Ybk Intl L 138.

[9] *Loizidou v Turkey (Preliminary Objections)* Series A No 310, (1995) 20 EHRR 99 § 75(2); further EA Alkema 'The European Convention as a Constitution and its Court as a Constitutional Court' in P Mahoney and others (eds) *Protecting Human Rights: The European Perspective: Studies in Memory of Rolv Ryssdal* (Heymann Cologne 2000) 41, 41; and J-P Costa 'La Cour européenne des droits de l'homme: vers un ordre juridique européen?' in J-A Aujol (ed) *Mélanges en hommage à Louis-Edmond Pettiti* (Bruylant Bruxelles, 1998) 197.

[10] G Ress 'Schmerzengeld für juristische Personen?' in G Lüke T Mikami and H Prütting (eds) *Festschrift für Akira Ishikawa zum 70. Geburtstag am 27. November 2001* (de Gruyter Berlin, 2001) 429, 441–42.

[11] *Ireland v UK* (1980) 2 EHRR 25 § 239; and W Kälin 'Menschenrechtsverträge als Gewährleistung einer objektiven Ordnung' in W Kälin and others (eds) *Aktuelle Probleme des Menschenrechtsschutzes: Referate und Thesen mit Diskussion* (Müller Heidelberg, 1994) 9.

a suitable object of further research in a comparative perspective,[12] and also from the viewpoint of the Court's teleological methodology. It is important since it helps us to understand that human rights teleology, as human rights themselves, is a many-sided and complex thing.

2 Economic and Collective Aspects of Civil and Political Rights

As was observed in chapter 2, international human rights law rests, at least conceptually and pedagogically, on a distinction between civil and political rights on one hand and economic and social (and cultural) rights on the others. The system for human rights protection at the Council of Europe relies fundamentally on this distinction since civil and political rights constitute the realm of the Convention, while economic and social rights are the domain of the European Social Charter.

The former group of rights aims primarily to protect the individual natural person from the arbitrary and excessive interference of public authorities—in other words, the protection of individual integrity and other traditional values of a liberal democracy. Economic and social rights, tailored to meet challenges posed by the modern welfare state, are collective rather than individual, and economic rights in particular have a natural affinity with economic life even if the economic activity sought protected primarily relates to labour contracts and not for-profit businesses as such. The elements of property protection often found in civil and political rights treaties do not overshadow the general sentiment that civil and political rights predominantly concern other spheres of life than that concerning economic activity.

It has long been held that the two groups are not water-tight compartments, and the rights belonging to one sometimes share propensities met with in the other. This study has revealed the complex nature of the civil and political rights found in the Convention. The treaty contains rights and freedoms that have a collective and economic bearing in addition to their predominantly individual and non-economic properties. The vast scholarly literature on economic and collective aspects of international human rights rarely lends space for an ECHR perspective.[13] Conversely, ECHR discourse is rarely coupled with a discourse on collective and economic rights. The ICCPR and ACHR systems are facing increasing corporate use of their respective civil and political

[12] On the development from a subjective to an objective approach to rights protection in the German constitutional context, see C Starck 'Artikel 2' in H von Mangoldt F Klein and C Starck (eds) *Das Bonner Grundgesetz. Kommentar* (4th edn Vahlen Munich, 1999) vol 1, 186, 188.

[13] Except, perhaps, with regard to studies on the protection of minorities offered under the Convention, see in this respect G Gilbert 'The Burgeoning Minority Rights Jurisprudence of the European Court of Human Rights' (2002) 24 HRQ 736.

rights;[14] here, too, there is room for exploration of the collective and economic features of civil and political human rights. Given the importance of collective and economic activity in contemporary society, it behoves us to study these aspects of modern life in treaties on civil and political rights more thoroughly. It is highly likely that ECHR discourse and related human rights discourses could reinforce each other in this regard.

3 A Liberal Project

As has been observed throughout, the book's focus on the company, and occasionally corporate shareholders, has rested on a concern to paint a broader picture of the regard of the Court to the business sector's rights and concerns in a human rights setting. The overall conclusion is that the Court is sympathetic to corporate complaints, at least as far as the treaty text and its interpretative modes permit it to be so, and as long as conflicting interests do not suggest a tempered response.

It was noted in chapter 2 that the Convention text and preparatory history provide a welcoming atmosphere, at least when business needs and the nature of the rights protection are evidently compatible. We have also seen that the Court is largely sympathetic to the needs of private businesses even in less obvious situations, typically in its response to the hard cases of applicability dealt with in chapter 4. The study has, at the same time, demonstrated how acutely sensitive the Court is to public authorities' regulation of private enterprise and to the conflicting interests of other private persons or individuals than those companies being applicants before the Court in a given case. Typically, as was shown in chapter 5, the Court adopts a generally lax standard of review when it scrutinises intervention with private economic activity unless the interference obviously lacks a rational basis and a societal purpose.

The coupling of human rights and business in ECHR law is a complex matter. The Court's reticent approach to individual business applicants' specific concerns—for instance in its application of a wide margin of appreciation in Art 10(2), or in showing reverence for the maxim of the corporate veil for the purpose of Art 34—while being perceived as business unfriendly from the individual corporate applicant's viewpoint, can actually benefit the business community as a whole. Reluctance to intervene in national authorities' regulation of competition laws can, as was observed in chapter 5, be taken as evidence that the Court believes in the values of the (regulated) market. The preservation of

[14] eg, M Emberland 'The Corporate Veil in the Jurisprudence of the Human Rights Committee and the Inter-American Court and Commission of Human Rights' (2004) 4 HRLR 257; and M Nowak *CCPR Commentary. UN Covenant on Civil and Political Rights* (2nd edn Engel Kehl am Rhein, 2005) 829–32.

separate legal personality for corporate entities with regard to the 'victim' requirement in Art 34, likewise tells us that the Convention, as interpreted by the Court, is supportive of private business investment (see chapter 3).

It would be unfeasible to instance every occasion on which the Court exposes its views on the place of private enterprise in the Convention system. What is certain, is that the Court's handling of complaints from persons pursing common enough business community interests, or, for that matter, any actor claiming protection for economic activity under the Convention, reveals to us parts of the nature of the Convention as a liberal project of Europe.[15] This liberal project cannot, however, be regarded separately from those parts of ECHR law and the Court's case law that concern other interests than that typical for the business community. It is also a project the nature of which must be considered within a greater Council of Europe context, where other instruments and initiatives—the European Social Charter being one of these—also have a prominent place.

C. Whither Corporate ECHR Protection?

This book has been limited by the Convention's structural framework and content *de lege lata*. It has sought to describe and justify—within present ECHR structures—the Court's response to some difficult issues of Convention interpretation arising from corporate Strasbourg applications. In this respect, it has sought to emulate the pragmatic approach of the Court itself. While it is to be hoped that the book may encourage further research, also of a normative nature, it has not been its intention to engage with current normative debates on the issue.

Having said that, the soundness of the Court's response to corporate litigation, from a pragmatic viewpoint, does not outweigh the importance of ideological, political or other informed critique of the very notion that a company may 'have' human rights—views that were introduced in chapter 2. Let us therefore end this book with a few words on a topic of normative significance, the corporate utilization of ECHR standards in light of the Court's widely perceived excessive workload. It cannot be denied that the Court's approach to corporate complaints, in particular its accommodating interpretation of provisions that, on the face of it, seem to lie beyond the reach of companies or other business entities, is evidence of the internal workings of a system the effect of which is to

[15] A Moravcsik 'The Origins of Human Rights Regimes: Democratic Delegation in Postwar Europe' (2000) 54 IO 217 provides a social science view on the liberalism of the Convention.

widen the Convention's scope and expand its application into new areas of social life, providing more opportunities for new groups to press their complaints at Strasbourg.[16]

The workload of the Court is overwhelming. In 1993, a mere 9,759 applications were lodged with the European Commission of Human Rights. In 2003, the Court's Registry received a total of 38,435 applications.[17] The annual figures seem to be escalating at a tremendous speed.[18] The restructuring of the control machinery presently in force, which was established by Protocol 11 in 1998, providing for a single Court with new functions, was aimed at tackling this escalating workload.[19] But the accession to the Convention and its supervisory system by new Council of Europe member States has greatly challenged the restructured Court's ability to work speedily and effectively thanks to the new wave of private applications, including from persons of the business sector, widened membership brought with it.[20] Reliance on the Convention's supervisory system by new social groups, or by groups making use of it in novel ways, surely does not help diminish the workload at the Court.

As we know, corporate Strasbourg complaints do not dominate the institution of private application. But any group of human rights litigants at variance with the system's main focus of attention—and that is undeniably the individual's civil and political rights in a classical sense—is likely to be in delicate position as soon as the future of the system of private application is discussed. One might, therefore, ask whether Protocol 14, adopted 13 May 2004, and which entails considerable changes in the supervisory mechanism, including the admissibility criteria, as solutions to the problems of a swamped Court, envisage the future of corporate human rights litigation as an issue worthy of discussion.[21]

[16] M Emberland 'Compensating Companies for Non-Pecuniary Damage: *Comingersoll v Portugal* before the European Court of Human Rights and the Ambivalent Expansion of the ECHR Scope' (2003) 74 BYIL 409, 431–32 also discusses this.

[17] Figures from *Survey of Activities 2003* (Strasbourg: European Court of Human Rights 2004) 34.

[18] See figures presented in Council of Europe Directorate of Human Rights (ed): *Guaranteeing the Effectiveness of the European Convention on Human Rights. Collected Texts* (Strasbourg: Council of Europe 2004).

[19] This follows indirectly from the Preamble of Protocol 11 and explicitly in Explanatory Report to Protocol No 11 to the Convention for the Protection of Human Rights and Fundamental Freedoms restructuring the control machinery established thereby (Protocol 11 Explanatory Report), available at <http://conventions.coe.int/Treaty/en/Reports/Html/155.htm> (15 April 2003) §§ 19–25.

[20] A number of business-related disputes derive from the new Council of Europe member states of the former East Bloc. This is not surprising, given the challenges posed to states that have undergone a rapid transition from a planning to a market economy. Notable cases include *Credit and Industrial Bank v Czech Republic* judgment 21 October 2003; *Veeber v Estonia (No 1)* judgment 7 November 2002; and *Sovtransavto Holding v Ukraine* judgment 25 July 2002 Reports 2002-VII.

[21] Protocol No 14 to the Convention for the Protection of Human Rights and Fundamental Freedoms, amending the control system of the Convention (adopted 13 May 2004, not in force) ETS 194 (Protocol 14).

Protocol 14 Art 12 introduces, significantly, the following change to Art 35(3) of the Convention:

The Court shall declare inadmissible any individual application submitted under Art 34 if it considers that:

(*a*) the application incompatible with the provisions of the Convention or the Protocols thereto, manifestly ill-founded, or an abuse of the right of application; *or*

(*b*) *the applicant has not suffered a significant disadvantage, unless respect for human rights as defined in the Convention and the Protocols thereto requires an examination of the application on the merits and provided that no case may be rejected on this ground which has not been duly considered by a domestic tribunal.*[22]

The purpose of this additional admissibility criterion is to:

provide the Court with an additional tool which should assist it in its filtering work and allow it to devote more time to cases which warrant examination on the merits, whether seen from the perspective of the legal interest of the individual applicant or considered from the broader perspective of the law of the Convention and the European public order to which it contributes.[23]

Cases that, according to the drafters, do not 'warrant examination on the merits' are referred to in the Protocol 14 Explanatory Report as 'unmeritorious' and 'trivial'.[24]

Business-related Strasbourg complaints are not specifically addressed in the Explanatory Report or in the drafting process as a whole as examples of trivial forms of human rights litigation that ought not to hamper the Court's adjudicatory activities. But the criterion, when coming into effect, may create an ambience in which corporate human rights under the Convention might face a new hurdle. Corporate human rights issues may be judged trivial when compared with alleged violations of an individual human being's dignity, security, or participation in political life.

It remains to be seen how the Court develops its jurisprudence in consideration of this reconstruction of the system of private application. Thus far, the status of companies under the Convention has not been seriously questioned or challenged. Only time will show whether the company, as the protagonist of private business enterprise, will continue to be favourably received in Strasbourg.

[22] The proposed changes are italicized here.

[23] Explanatory Report to Protocol No 14 to the Convention for the Protection of Human Rights and Fundamental Freedoms, amending the control system of the Convention (Protocol 14 Explanatory Report) Protocol 14 Explanatory Report), available at <http://conventions.coe.int/Treaty/EN/Reports/Html/1194.htm> (16 June 2005) § 77.

[24] Protocol 14 Explanatory Report §§ 79 and 82.

Bibliography

MONOGRAPHS

Al-Shawi, KA *The Role of the Corporate Entity in International Law* (Overbeck Ann Arbor MI, 1957).

Amerasinghe, CF *Local Remedies in International Law* (2nd edn Cambridge University Press Cambridge, 2004).

Amerasinghe, CF *Local Remedies in International Law* (Grotius Cambridge, 1990).

Arai-Takahashi, Y *The Margin of Appreciation Doctrine and the Principle of Proportionality in the Jurisprudence of the ECHR* (Intersentia Antwerp, 2002).

Arnardóttir, OM *Equality and Non-Discrimination under the European Convention on Human Rights* (Martinus Nijhoff Hague, 2003).

Barendt, E *Freedom of Speech* (Clarendon Press Oxford, 1987).

Beyer, S *Der diplomatische Schutz der Aktionäre im Völkerrecht* (Nomos Baden-Baden, 1977).

Bleckmann, A *Staatsrecht. Die Grundrechte* (4th edn Heymann Cologne, 1997).

Brower, CN and Brueschke, JD *The Iran-United States Claims Tribunal* (Martinus Nijhoff Hague, 1998).

Burgstaller, M *Theories of Compliance with International Law* (Martinus Nijhoff Leiden, 2005).

Caflisch, L *La protection des sociétés commerciales et des interêts indirects en droit international public* (Martinus Nijhoff Hague, 1969).

Cançado Trindade, AA *The Application of the Rule of Exhaustion of Local Remedies in International Law. Its Rationale in the International Protection of Human Rights* (Cambridge University Press Cambridge, 1983).

Clapham, A *Human Rights in the Private Sphere* (Clarendon Press Oxford, 1993).

Çoban, AR *Protection of Property Rights within the European Convention on Human Rights* (Ashgate Aldershot, 2004).

Cotterrell, R *The Sociology of Law. An Introduction* (2nd edn Butterworths London, 1992).

Crawford, J *The International Law Commission's Articles on State Responsibility. Introduction, Text and Commentaries* (Cambridge University Press Cambridge, 2002).

Dan-Cohen, M *Rights, Persons, and Organizations* (University of California Press Berkeley Ca, 1986).

Dannemann, G *Schadenersatz bei Verletzung der Europäischen Menschenrechtskonvention. Eine rechtsvergleichende Untersuchung zur Haftung nach Art. 50 EMRK* (Heymann Cologne, 1994).

Davies, PL *Gower's Principles of Modern Company Law* (6th edn Sweet & Maxwell London, 1997).

Dignam, AJ and Allen, D *Company Law and the Human Rights Act 1998* (Butterworths London, 2000).

Dine, J *Companies, International Trade and Human Rights* (Cambridge University Press Cambridge, 2005).

van Dijk, P and van Hoof, GJH *Theory and Practice of the European Convention on Human Rights* (2nd edn Kluwer Hague, 1998).

Donnelly, J *International Human Rights* (2nd edn Westview Boulder Col, 1998).

Donnelly, J *Universal Human Rights in Theory and Practice* (2nd edn Cornell University Press Ithaca NY, 2003).

Dröge, C *Positive Verpflichtungen der Staaten in der Europäischen Menschenrechtskonvention* (Springer Berlin, 2003).

Drzemczewski, AZ *European Human Rights Convention in Domestic Law: A Comparative Study* (Clarendon Press Oxford, 1983).

Dworkin, R *Law's Empire* (Belknap Press Cambridge Mass, 1986).

Dworkin, R *Taking Rights Seriously* (Harvard University Press Cambridge Mass, 1977).

Fawcett, JES *The Application of The European Convention on Human Rights* (2nd edn Clarendon Press Oxford, 1987).

Fernández Esteban, ML *The Rule of Law in the European Constitution* (Kluwer Hague, 1999).

Friedmann, W *The Changing Structures of International Law* (University of Columbia Press New York, 1964).

Frowein, JA and Peukert, W *Europäische Menschenrechtskonvention. EMRK-Kommentar* (2nd edn Engel Kehl am Rhein, 1996).

Glendon, MA *Rights Talk. The Impoverishment of Political Discourse* (Free Press New York, 1991).

Gomien, D Harris, DJ and Zwaak, L *Law and Practice of the European Convention on Human Rights and the European Social Charter* (Council of Europe Publishing Strasbourg, 1996).

Greer, S *The Margin of Appreciation: Interpretation and Discretion under the European Convention on Human Rights* (Council of Europe Publishing Strasbourg, 2000).

Guradze, H *Die Europäische Menschenrechtskonvention. Konvention zum Schutze der Menschenrechte und Grundfreiheiten nebst Zusatsprotokollen. Kommentar* (Vahlen Berlin, 1968).

Hallis, F *Corporate Personality. A Study in Jurisprudence* (Oxford University Press Oxford, 1930).

Harris, DJ and Darcy, J *The European Social Charter* (2nd edn Transnational Ardsley, NY 2001).

Harris, DJ, O'Boyle, M and Warbrick, C *Law of the European Convention on Human Rights* (Butterworths London, 1995).

Harris, JW *Property and Justice* (Clarendon Press Oxford, 1996).

Hartmann, T *Unequal Protection: the Rise of Corporate Dominance and the Theft of Human Rights* (Rodale Press Erasmus PA, 2002).

Held, D *Models of Democracy* (3rd edn Stanford University Press Stanford Ca, 2004).

Henkin, L *The Age of Rights* (Columbia University Press New York, 1990).

de Hochepied, J-P *La protection diplomatique des sociétés et des actionnaires* (Pedone Paris, 1965).

Hondius, F *Emerging Data Protection in Europe* (North-Holland Amsterdam, 1975).

Janis, M, Kay, R and Bradley, A *European Human Rights Law. Text and Materials* (2nd edn Oxford University Press Oxford, 2000).

Jennings, R and Watts, A *Oppenheim's International Law* (9th edn Longman London, 1992) vols 1 and 2.

Joseph, S *Corporations and Transnational Human Rights Litigation* (Hart Oxford, 2004).

Kaegi, W *Die Verfassung als rechtliche Grundordnung des Staates. Untersuchungen über die Entwicklungen im modernen Verfassungsrecht* (Polygraphischer Verlag Zürich, 1945).

Kastanas, E *Unité et diversité: notions autonomes et marge d'appréciation des Etats dans la jurisprudence de la Cour européenne des droits de l'homme* (Bruylant Bruxelles, 1996).

Klug, F (ed) *A People's Charter: Liberty's Bill of Rights: A Consultation Paper* (National Council for Civil Liberties London, 1991).

Jägers, N *Corporate Human Rights Obligations: In Search of Accountability* (Intersentia Antwerp, 2002).

Laski, H *The Rise of European Liberalism: An Essay in Interpretation* (Allen & Unwin London, 1936).

Macpherson, CB *The Life and Times of Liberal Democracy* (Oxford University Press Oxford, 1977).

Malanczuk, P *Akehurst's Modern Introduction to International Law* (7th edn Routledge London, 1997).

Marks, S *The Riddle of All Constitutions. International Law, Democracy, and the Critique of Ideology* (Oxford University Press Oxford, 2000).

Meiklejohn, A *Free Speech and Its Relation to Self-Government* (Harper New York, 1948).

Merrills, JG and Robertson, AH *Human Rights in Europe. A Study of the European Convention on Human Rights* (4th edn Manchester University Press Manchester, 2001).

Merrills, JG *The Development of International Law by the European Court of Human Rights* (2nd edn Manchester University Press Manchester, 1988).

Mikaelsen, L *European Protection of Human Rights: the Practice and Procedure of the European Commission of Human Rights on the Admissibility of Applications from Individuals and States* (Sijthoff & Noordhoff Alphen aan den Rijn, 1980).

Morsink, J *The Universal Declaration of Human Rights. Origins, Drafting and Intent* (University of Pennsylvania Press Philadelphia, 1999).

Mowbray, A 'The Development of Positive Obligations under the European Convention on Human Rights by the European Court of Human Rights (Hart Oxford, 2004).

Muchlinski, PT *Multinational Enterprises and the Law* (2nd edn Blackwell Oxford, 1999).

Nowak, M *CCPR Commentary. UN Covenant on Civil and Political Rights* (2nd edn Engel Kehl am Rhein, 2005).

Oesch, M *Standards of Review in WTO Dispute Resolution* (Oxford University Press Oxford, 2003).

Ovey, C and White, RCA *Jacobs and White The European Convention on Human Rights* (3rd edn Oxford University Press Oxford, 2002).

Personnaz, J *La réparation du préjudice en droit international public* (Sirey Paris, 1939).

Posner, RA *Law, Pragmatism, and Democracy* (Harvard University Press Cambridge Mass, 2003).

Samuel, L *Fundamental Social Rights: Case Law of the European Social Charter* (Council of Europe Publishing Strasbourg, 2002).

Schauer, F *Free Speech: A Philosophical Enquiry* (Cambridge University Press Cambridge, 1982).

Schlaich, K *Das Bundesverfassungsgericht: Stellung, Verfahren, Entscheidungen: Ein Studienbuch* (4th edn Beck Munich, 1997).

Schreuer, C *The ICSID Convention: A Commentary on the Convention on the Settlement of Investment Disputes between States and Nationals of Other States* (Cambridge University Press Cambridge, 2001).

Seidl-Hohenveldern, I *Corporations in and under International Law* (Grotius Cambridge, 1987).

Sen, AK *Development as Freedom* (Oxford University Press Oxford, 1999).

Serment, L *The European Convention on Human Rights and Property Rights* (Council of Europe Press Strasbourg, 1992).

Shelton, D *Remedies in International Human Rights Law* (2nd edn Oxford University Press Oxford, 2005).

Shiner, RA *Freedom of Commercial Expression* (Oxford University Press Oxford, 2003).

Sicilianos, L-A *L'ONU et la démocratisation de l'état. Systèmes régionaux et ordre juridique universel* (Pedone Paris, 2000).

Siegan, BH *Economic Liberties and the Constitution* (University of Chicago Press Chicago, 1980).

Simpson, AWB *Human Rights and the End of Empire. Britain and the Genesis of the European Convention* (Oxford University Press Oxford, 2001).

Smyth, M *Business and the Human Rights Act 1998* (Jordans Bristol, 2000).

Steiner, HJ *Diverse Partners: Non-Governmental Organizations in the Human Rights Movement: The Report of a Retreat of Human Rights Activists* (Harvard Law School Human Rights Program Cambridge Mass, 1991).

Tavares Da Costa, C and de Meester Bilreiro, A *The European Company Statute* (Kluwer Hague, 2003).

Thorgeirsdóttir, H *Journalism Worthy of the Name. Freedom Within the Press and the Affirmative Side of Article 10 of the European Convention on Human Rights* (Martinus Nijhoff Leiden, 2005).

Tschentscher, A *The Basic Law (Grundgesetz). The Constitution of the Federal Republic of Germany (May 23, 1949)* (Jurisprudentia Würzburg, 2002).

UNCTAD: *Scope and Definition. UNCTAD Series on issues of international investment agreements* (United Nations Conference on Trade and Development New York/Geneva, 1999).

UNCTAD: *World Investment Report 2003. FDI Policies for Development: National and International Perspectives* (United Nations Conference on Trade and Development New York/Geneva, 2003).

Usher, JA *General Principles of EC Law* (Longman Harlow, 1998).

Velu, J and Ergec, R *La Convention européenne des droits de l'homme* (Bruylant Bruxelles, 1990).
Yourow, HC *The Margin of Appreciation Doctrine in the Dynamics of European Human Rights Jurisprudence* (Kluwer Hague, 1996).
Waldron, J *The Right to Private Property* (Clarendon Press Oxford, 1988).
Zander, M *A Bill of Rights?* (4th edn Sweet & Maxwell London, 1997).
Zurcher, AJ *The Struggle to Unite Europe, 1940–1958: An Historical Account of the Development of the Contemporary European Movement from its Origin in the Pan-European Union to the Drafting of the Treaties for Euratom and the European Common Market* (New York University Press New York, 1958).
Zwart, T *The Admissibility of Human Rights Petitions. The Case Law of the European Commission of Human Rights and the Human Rights Committee* (Martinus Nijhoff Dordrecht, 1994).

EDITED BOOKS

Addo, MK (ed) *Human Rights Standards and the Responsibility of Transnational Corporations* (Kluwer Hague, 1999).
Bannock, G (ed) *The Promotion of Small and Medium-Sized Enterprises in Europe* (Council of Europe Press Strasbourg, 1994).
Horton, WV (ed) *Damages for Non-Pecuniary Loss in a Comparative Perspective* (Springer Vienna, 2001).
International Commission of Jurists (ed) *The Rule of Law and Human Rights. Principles and Definitions as Elaborated at the Congresses and Conferences held under the auspices of the International Commission of Jurists, 1955–1966* (International Commission of Jurists Geneva, 1966).
Kamminga, MT and Zia-Zarifi, S (eds) *Liability of Multinational Corporations under International Law* (Kluwer Hague, 2000).
Knowles, E (ed) *The Oxford Dictionary of Quotations* (6th edn Oxford University Press Oxford, 2004).
Morris, W (ed) *American Heritage Dictionary of the English Language* (3rd edn Houghton Mifflin Boston, 1992).
Robertson, AH (ed) *Collected Editions of the 'Travaux Préparatoires' of the European Convention on Human Rights* (Martinus Nijhoff Dordrecht, 1975–1985) vols 1–9.
UNCTAD: *Scope and Definition. UNCTAD Series on issues of international investment agreements* (United Nations Conference on Trade and Development New York/Geneva, 1999).
UNCTAD: *World Investment Report 2003. FDI Policies for Development: National and International Perspectives* (United Nations Conference on Trade and Development New York/Geneva, 2003).
United Nations Development Programme (ed) *Human Development Report 2000* (Oxford University Press New York, 2000).

CHAPTERS IN BOOKS

Addo, MK 'The Corporation as a Victim of Human Rights Violations' in Addo, AK (ed) *Human Rights Standards and the Responsibility of Transnational Corporations* (Kluwer Hague, 1999) 187.

Alkema, EA 'Freedom of Association and Civil Society' in Council of Europe (ed) *Freedom of Association. Proceedings. Seminar organised by the Secretariat-General of the Council of Europe in collaboration with the Ministry of Justice of Iceland (Reykjavik, 26–28 August 1998* (Council of Europe Press Strasbourg, 1994) 55.

Alkema, EA 'The European Convention as a Constitution and its Court as a Constitutional Court' in Mahoney, P and others (eds) *Protecting Human Rights: The European Perspective: Studies in Memory of Rolv Ryssdal* (Heymann Cologne, 2000) 41.

Baehr, PR 'Mobilization of the Conscience of Mankind: Conditions of Effectiveness of Human Rights NGOs' in Denters, E and Schrijver, N (eds) *Reflections on International Law from the Low Countries in Honour of Paul de Waart* (Martinus Nijhoff Hague, 1998) 135.

Barendt, E 'Introduction' in Barendt, E (ed) *Privacy* (Ashgate Dartmouth Aldershot, 2001) i.

Barendt, E 'Privacy as a Constitutional Right and Value' in Birks, P (ed) *Privacy and Loyalty* (Clarendon Press Oxford, 1997) 1.

Bernhardt, R 'Comparative Law in the Interpretation and Application of the European Convention on Human Rights' in Busuttil, S (ed) *Mainly Human Rights. Studies in Honour of JJ Cremona* (Fondation Internationale Malte Valletta, 1999) 33.

Bernhardt, R 'Einwirkungen der Europäischen Menschenrechts-Konvention auf das Staatliche Wirtschaftsrecht' in Briner, R and others (eds) *Law of International Business and Dispute Settlement. Liber Amicorum Karl-Heinz Böckstiegel* (Heymann Cologne, 2001) 67.

Bernhardt, R 'Thoughts on the Interpretation of Human-Rights Treaties' in Matscher, F and Petzold, H (eds) *Protecting Human Rights: The European Dimension. Studies in Honour of Gérard J Wiarda* (Heymann Cologne, 1988) 65.

Blackburn, R 'The United Kingdom' in Blackburn, R and Polakiewicz, J (eds) *Fundamental Rights in Europe. The ECHR and Its Member States, 1950–2000* (Oxford University Press Oxford, 2001) 935.

de Blois, M 'The Fundamental Freedom of the European Court of Human Rights' in Lawson, R and de Blois, M (eds) *The Dynamics of the Protection of Human Rights in Europe. Essays in Honour of Henry G Schermers* (Martinus Nijhoff Dordrecht, 1994) vol 3, 35.

Bottomley, S 'Corporations and Human Rights' in Bottomley, S and Kinley, D (eds) *Commercial Law and Human Rights* (Dartmouth Ashgate Aldershot, 2002) 61.

de Búrca, G 'The Language of Rights and European Integration' in Shaw, J and More, G (eds) *New Legal Dynamics of European Union* (Clarendon Press Oxford, 1995) 29.

Byrnes, A 'An Effective Complaints Procedure in the Context of International Human Rights Law' in Bayefsky, AF (ed) *The UN Human Rights Treaty System in the 21st* Century (Kluwer Hague, 2000) 139.

Cançado Trindade, AA 'The Procedural Capacity of the Individual as Subject of International Human Rights Law: Recent Developments' in *Human Rights at the Dawn of the Twenty-First Century. Karel Vasak Amicorum Liber* (Bruylant Brussels, 1999) 521.

Carrillo Salcedo, JA 'The Place of the European Convention in International Law' in Macdonald, R St John, Matscher, F and Petzold, H (eds) *The European System for the Protection of Human Rights* (Martinus Nijhoff Dordrecht, 1993) 15.

Chayes, A 'The Modern Corporation and the Rule of Law' in Mason, ES (ed) *The Corporation in Modern Society* (Harvard University Press Cambridge Mass, 1959) 41.

Cohen-Jonathan, G 'Transparence, démocratie et effectivité des droits fondamenteaux dans la Convention européenne des droits de l'homme' in Mahoney, P and others (eds) *Protecting Human Rights: The European Perspective: Studies in Memory of Rolv Ryssdal* (Heymann Cologne, 2000) 245.

Collins, AM 'Commercial Speech and the Free Movement of Goods and Services at Community Law' in O'Reilly, J (ed) *Human Rights and Constitutional Law. Essays in Honour of Brian Walsh* (Round Hall Press Dublin, 1992) 319.

Costa, J-P 'La Cour européenne des droits de l'homme: vers un ordre juridique européen?' in Aujol, J-A (ed) *Mélanges en hommage à Louis-Edmond Pettiti* (Bruylant Bruxelles, 1998) 197.

Cremona, JJ 'The Proportionality Principle in the Jurisprudence of the European Court of Human Rights' in Beyerlin, U and others (eds) *Recht zwischen Umbruch und Bewahrung: Völkerrecht, Europarecht, Staatsrecht. Festschrift für Rudolf Bernhardt* (Springer Berlin, 1995) 323.

Decaux, E 'Les Etats parties et leurs engagements' in Pettiti, L-E, Decaux, E and Imbert, P-H (eds) *La Convention européenne des droits de l'homme. Commentaire article par article* (Economica Paris, 1995) 3.

Delmas-Marty, M 'General Introduction' in Delmas-Marty, M (ed) *The European Convention for the Protection of Human Rights: International Protection Versus National Restrictions* (Martinus Nijhoff Dordrecht, 1992) 1.

Delmas-Marty, M 'The Richness of Underlying Reasoning' in Delmas-Marty, M (ed) *The European Convention for the Protection of Human Rights. International Protection versus National Restrictions* (Martinus Nijhoff Dordrecht, 1992) 319.

Delmas-Marty, M and Soulier, G 'Restraining or Legitimating the Reason of State?' in Delmas-Marty, M (ed) *The European Convention for the Protection of Human Rights: International Protection Versus National Restrictions* (Martinus Nijhoff Dordrecht, 1992) 7.

Dicke, K 'The Founding Function of Human Dignity' in Kretzmer, D and Klein, E (eds) *The Concept of Dignity in Human Rights Discourse* (Kluwer Hague, 2002) 111.

van Dijk, P ' "Positive Obligations" Implied in the European Convention on Human Rights: Are the States Still the "Masters" of the Convention?' in Castermans-Holleman, M, van Hoof, F and Smith, J (eds) *The Role of the Nation-State in the 21st Century: Human Rights, International Organisations, and Foreign Policy. Essays in Honour of Peter Baer* (Kluwer Hague, 1998) 17.

Drzemczewski, AZ 'Decisions on the Merits: By the Committee of Ministers' in Macdonald, R St John Matscher, F and Petzold, H (eds) *The European System for the Protection of Human Rights* (Martinus Nijhoff Dordrecht, 1993) 733.

Duffy, PJ 'The Protection of Commercial Interests under the European Convention on Human Rights' in Cranston, R (ed) *Making Commercial Law. Essays in Honour of Roy Goode* (Clarendon Press Oxford, 1997) 525.

Dürig, G 'Artikel 19' in Maunz, T and Dürig, G (eds) *Grundgesetz: Kommentar* (2nd edn Beck Munich, 1985) vol 2.

Dworkin, R and Lukes, S 'The Political Culture of Liberalism and the Prospects for Eastern and Central Europe. Panel Discussion' (1993-II) 2 AEL 273.

Eissen, M-A 'The Principle of Proportionality in the Case-Law of the European Court of Human Rights' in Macdonald, R St John, Matscher, F and Petzold, H (eds) *The European System for the Protection of Human Rights* (Martinus Nijhoff Dordrecht, 1993) 125.

Evrigenis, D 'L'interaction entre la dimension internationale et la dimension nationale de la Convention européenne des Droits de l'homme: notions autonomes et effet direct' in Bernhardt, R and others (eds) *Völkerrecht als Rechtordnung, Internationale Gerichtbarkeit, Menschenrechte: Festschrift für Hermann Mosler* (Springer Berlin, 1983) 193.

Feldman, D 'Privacy-related Rights: Their Social Value' in Birks, P (ed) *Privacy and Loyalty* (Clarendon Press Oxford, 1997) 15.

Flinterman, C 'The Protection of Economic, Social and Cultural Rights and the European Convention on Human Rights' in Lawson, R and de Blois, M (eds) *The Dynamics of the Protection of Human Rights in Europe. Essays in Honour of Henry G Schermers* (Martinus Nijhoff Dordrecht, 1994) vol 3, 165.

Fordham, M and de la Mare, T 'Identifying the Principles of Proportionality' in Jowell, J and Cooper, J (eds) *Understanding Human Rights Principles* (Hart Oxford, 2001) 27.

Friedbergh, E and Villiger, ME 'The European Commission of Human Rights' in Macdonald, R St John Matscher, F and Petzold, H (eds) *The European System for the Protection of Human Rights* (Martinus Nijhoff Dordrecht, 1993) 605.

Frowein, JA 'Fundamental Human Rights as a Vehicle of Legal Integration in Europe' in Cappelletti, M Seccombe, M and Weiler, J (eds) *Integration Through Law. Vol 1 Methods, Tools and Institutions* (de Gruyter Berlin, 1986) 300.

Frowein, JA Schulhofer, S and Shapiro, M 'Fundamental Human Rights as a Vehicle of Legal Integration in Europe' in Cappelletti, M Seccombe, M and Weiler, J (eds) *Integration Through Law. Vol 1 Methods, Tools and Institutions* (de Gruyter Berlin, 1986) 230.

Frowein, JA 'Human Dignity in International Law' in Kretzmer, D and Klein, E (eds) *The Concept of Dignity in Human Rights Discourse* (Kluwer Hague, 2002) 121.

Frowein, JA 'La notion de victime dans la Convention européenne des Droits de l'homme' in *Studi in onore di Giuseppe Sperduti: fonti internazionali e rapporti fra ordinamenti, l'individuo nel diritto internazionale, altri contribute* (Giuffrè Milano, 1984) 585.

Frowein, JA 'Präambel' in JA Frowein and W Peukert *Europäische Menschenrechtskonvention. EMRK-Kommentar* (2nd edn Engel Kehl am Rhein, 1996) 13.

Frowein, JA 'The Protection of Property' in Macdonald, R St John Matscher, M and Petzold, H (eds) *The European System for the Protection of Human Rights* (Martinus Nijhoff Dordrecht, 1993) 515.

Ganshof van der Meersch, WJ 'Le caractère "autonome" des termes et la "marge d'appréciation" des gouvernements dans l'interprétation de la Convention européenne des Droits de l'Homme' in Matscher, F and Petzold, P (eds) *Protecting Human Rights: The European Dimension. Studies in Honour of Gérard J Wiarda* (Heymann Cologne, 1988) 201.

Gawron, T and Rogowski, R 'Implementation von Bundesverfassungsgerichtsentscheidungen' in Blankenburg, E and others (eds) *Implementation von Gerichtentscheidungen* (Westdeutsches Verlag Opladen, 1987) 352.

Geck, WK 'Diplomatic Protection' in Bernhardt, R (ed) *Encyclopedia of Public International Law* (North-Holland Amsterdam, 1992) vol 1, 1045.

Golsong, H 'Interpreting the European Convention on Human Rights Beyond the Confines of the Vienna Convention on the Law of Treaties?' in Macdonald, R St John, Matscher, F and Petzold, H (eds) *The European System for the Protection of Human Rights* (Martinus Nijhoff Dordrecht, 1993) 147.

Golsong, H, Karl, W and Miehsler, H 'Artikel 25' in H Golsong and Others (eds) *Internationaler Kommentar zur Europäischen Menschenrechtskonvention* (Heymann Cologne, 1986) vol 2.

Häberle, P 'Grundprobleme der Verfassungsgerichtbarkeit' in Häberle, P (ed) *Verfassungsgerichtbarkeit* (Wissenschaftlichers Buchgesellschaft Darmstadt, 1976) 15.

Harlow, C 'Access to Justice as a Human Right: The European Convention and the European Union' in Alston, P (ed) *The EU and Human Rights* (Oxford University Press Oxford, 1999) 187.

Harlow, C 'Access to Justice as a Human Right: The European Convention and the European Union' in Alston, P (ed) *The EU and Human Rights* (Oxford University Press Oxford, 1999) 187.

Harris, DJ 'The Collective Complaints Procedure' in Council of Europe (ed) *The Social Charter of the 21st Century. Colloquy organised by the Secretariat of the Council of Europe* (Council of Europe Publishing Strasbourg, 1997) 100.

Henkin, L 'Constitutionalism and Human Rights' in Henkin, L and Rosenthal, AJ (eds) *Constitutionalism and Rights. The Influence of the United States Constitution Abroad* (Columbia University Press New York, 1990) 383.

van Hoof, GJH 'The Legal Nature of Economic, Social and Cultural Rights: A Rebuttal of Some Traditional Views' in Alston, P and Tomasevski, K (eds) *The Right to Food* (Martinus Nijhoff Hague, 1984) 97.

Huber, PM 'Artikel 19' in von Mangoldt, H, Klein, F and Starck, C (eds) *Das Bonner Grundgesetz. Kommentar* (4th edn Vahlen Munich, 1999) vol 1, 2174.

Jennings, R 'International Law Reform and Progressive Development' in Hafner, G and Böckstiegel, K-H (eds) *Liber Amicorum Professor Ignaz Seidl-Hohenveldern in Honour of His 80th Birthday* (Kluwer Hague, 1998) 325.

Jacot-Guillarmod, O 'Règles, méthods et principes d'interprétation dans la jurisprudence de la Cour européenne des droits de l'homme' in Pettiti, L-E, Decaux, E and Imbert, P-H (eds) *La Convention européenne des droits de l'homme. Commentaire article par article* (Economica Paris, 1995) 41.

Jacot-Guillarmod, O 'The Relationship Between Democracy and Human Rights' in Council of Europe (ed) *Democracy and Human Rights, Proceedings of a Colloquy organized by the Government of Greece and the Council of Europe, Thessaloniki, 24–26 September 1987* (Engel Kehl am Rhein, 1990) 43.

Jörundsson, G 'The Case-Law of the Commission as Regards the Freedom of Assembly and Association' in de Salvia, M and Villiger, ME (eds) *The Birth of European Human Rights Law. Liber Amicorum Carl Aage Nørgaard* (Nomos Baden-Baden, 1998) 101.

Kälin, W 'Menschenrechtsverträge als Gewährleistung einer objektiven Ordnung' in Kälin, W and others (eds) *Aktuelle Probleme des Menschenrechtsschutzes: Referate und Thesen mit Diskussion* (Müller Heidelberg, 1994) 9.

Kentridge, S 'The Incorporation of the European Convention on Human Rights' in Beatson, J (ed) *Constitutional Reform in the United Kingdom: Practice and Principles* (Hart Oxford, 1998) 69.

Kingston, J 'Rich People Have Human Rights Too? The Status of Property as a Fundamental Right' in Heffernan, L and Kingston, J (eds) *Human Rights: A European Perspective* (Dublin Round Hall Press, 1994) 284.

Kiss, A 'La protection diplomatique des actionnaires dans la jurisprudence et la pratique internationales' in Bastid, S and others (eds) *La personnalité morale et ses limites* (Pichon et Durand-Auzias Paris, 1960) 179.

Koskenniemi, M 'The Preamble of the UDHR' in Alfredsson, G and Eide, A (eds) *The Universal Declaration of Human Rights. A Common Standard of Achievement* (Martinus Nijhoff Hague, 1999) 27.

Klein, E and Kretzmer, D 'Foreword' in Kretzmer, D and Klein, E (eds) *The Concept of Dignity in Human Rights Discourse* (Kluwer Hague, 2002) i.

Krause, C 'The Right to Property' in Eide, A, Krause, C and Rosas, A (eds) *Economic, Social and Cultural Rights. A Textbook* (2nd edn Martinus Nijhoff Dordrecht, 2001) 191.

Krause, C and Alfredsson, G 'Article 17' in Alfredsson, G and Eide, A (eds) *The Universal Declaration of Human Rights. A Common Standard of Achievement* (Kluwer Hague, 1999) 359.

Krüger, HC and Nørgaard, CA 'The Right of Application' in Macdonald, R St John, Matscher, F and Petzold, H (eds) *The European System for the Protection of Human Rights* (Martinus Nijhoff Dordrecht, 1993) 657.

Leben, C 'Is There a European Approach to Human Rights?' in Alston, P (ed) *The EU and Human Rights* (Oxford University Press Oxford, 1999) 69.

Lester, A 'Amici Curiae: Third-Party Interventions before the European Court of Human Rights' in Matscher, F and Petzold, H (eds) *Protecting Human Rights: The*

European Dimension. Studies in Honour of Gérard J Wiarda (Heymann Cologne, 1988) 341.

Lester, A 'Freedom of Expression' in Macdonald, R St John, Matscher, M and Petzold, H (eds) *The European System for the Protection of Human Rights* (Martinus Nijhoff Dordrecht, 1993) 465.

Leuprecht, P 'The Execution of Judgments and Decisions' in Macdonald, R St John, Matscher, F and Petzold, H (eds) *The European System for the Protection of Human Rights* (Martinus Nijhoff Dordrecht, 1993) 791.

Lowe, V 'Shareholders' Rights to Control and Manage: From Barcelona Traction to ELSI' in Ando, N, McWhinney, E and Wolfrum, R (eds) *Liber Amicorum Judge Shigeru Oda* (Kluwer Hague, 2002) vol 1, 269.

Lutter, M 'Limited Liability Companies and Private Companies' in Vagts, D (ed) *International Encyclopedia of Comparative Law: Business and Private Organizations* (Mohr Siebeck Tübingen, 1998) vol 13.

Macdonald, R St John 'The Margin of Appreciation' in Macdonald, R St John, Matscher, F and Petzold, H (eds) *The European System for the Protection of Human Rights* (Martinus Nijhoff Dordrecht, 1993) 83.

Mahoney, P 'The Status of the Registry of the European Court of Human Rights: Past, Present and Future' in Mahoney, P and others (eds) *Protecting Human Rights: The European Perspective: Studies in Memory of Rolv Ryssdal* (Heymann Cologne, 2000) 845.

Maitland, FW 'Moral Personality and Legal Personality' in Fisher, HAL (ed) *Collected Papers* (London University Press London, 1911) vol 3, 307.

Marsh, NS 'The Rule of Law as a Supra-National Concept' in Guest, A (ed) *Oxford Essays on Jurisprudence. First Series* (Clarendon Press Oxford, 1961) 223.

Matscher, F 'Methods of Interpretation of the Convention' in Macdonald, R St John, Matscher, F and Petzold, H (eds) *The European System for the Protection of Human Rights* (Martinus Nijhoff Dordrecht, 1993) 63.

Matscher, F 'Vertragsauslegung durch Vertragsrechtsvergleichung in der Judikatur internationaler Gerichte, vornemlich vor den Organen der EMRK' in Bernhardt, R and others (eds) *Völkerrecht als Rechtsordnung, Internationale Gerichtbarkeit, Menschenrechte Festschrift für Hermann Mosler* (Springer Berlin, 1983) 545.

Maunz, T and Papier, H-J 'Artikel 13' in Maunz, R and Dürig, G (eds) *Grundgesetz. Kommentar* (Beck Munich, 1999) [10 ff].

McBride, J 'Proportionality and the European Convention on Human Rights' in Ellis, E (ed) *The Principle of Proportionality in the Laws of Europe* (Hart Oxford, 1999) 23.

de Meyer, J 'Electoral Rights' in Macdonald, R St John, Matscher, F and Petzold, H (eds) *The European System for the Protection of Human Rights* (Martinus Nijhoff Dordrecht, 1993) 553.

Miehsler, H and Vogler, T 'Artikel 6–Allgemeine Verfahrensgarantien' in Golsong, H and others (eds) *Internationaler Kommentar zur Europäischen Menschenrechtskonvention* (Heymann Cologne, 1986) vol 1, 88.

Møse, E 'New Rights for a New Court?' in Mahoney, P and others (eds) *Protecting Human Rights: The European Perspective: Studies in Memory of Rolv Ryssdal* (Heymann Cologne, 2000) 943.

von Mutius, A 'Artikel 19 Abs. 3' in Dolzer, R and others (eds) *Kommentar zum Bonner Grundgesetz* (2nd edn Müller Heidelberg, 1975) vol 2, [26 ff].

Nowak, M 'Human Rights "Conditionality" in Relation to Entry to, and Full Participation in, the EU' in Alston, P (ed) *The EU and Human Rights* (Oxford University Press Oxford, 1999) 687.

Nowicki, MA 'Non-Governmental Organisations (NGOs) before the European Commission of Human Rights' in de Salvia, M and Villiger, ME (eds) *The Birth of European Human Rights Law. Liber Amicorum Carl Aage Nørgaard* (Nomos Baden-Baden, 1998) 267.

Ogus, A 'Property Rights and Freedom of Economic Activity' in Henkin, L and Rosenthal, AJ (eds) *Constitutionalism and Rights. The Influence of the United States Constitution Abroad* (Columbia University Press New York, 1990) 125.

Oreja, M 'Souverainité des Etats et respect des droits de l'homme' in Matscher, F and Petzold, H (eds) *Protecting Human Rights: The European Dimension. Studies in Honour of Gérard J Wiarda* (Heymann Cologne, 1988) 7.

Ost, F 'The Original Canons of Interpretation of the European Court of Human Rights' in Delmas-Marty, F (ed) *The European Convention for the Protection of Human Rights. International Protection versus National Restrictions* (Martinus Nijhoff Dordrecht, 1992) 283.

Partsch, KJ 'Die Rechte und Freiheiten der europäischen Menschenrechtskonvention' in Bettermann, KA Neumann, FL and Nipperdey, HC (eds) *Die Grundrechte. Handbuch der Theorie und Praxis der Grundrechte* (Duncker & Humblot Berlin, 1966) vol 1, 237.

Pellonpää, M 'Compensable Claims before the Tribunal: Expropriation Claims' in Lillich, RB and Magraw, DB (eds) *The Iran-United States Claims Tribunal: Its Contribution to the Law of State Responsibility* (Transnational Irvington NY, 1998) 185.

Pellonpää, M 'Reflections on the notion of "deprivation of possessions" in Article 1 of the First Protocol to the European Convention on Human Rights' in Mahoney, P and others (eds) *Protecting Human Rights: The European Perspective: Studies in Memory of Rolv Ryssdal* (Heymann Cologne, 2000) 1087.

Pettiti, L-E 'Réflexions sur les principes et les mécanismes de la Convention. De l'idéal de 1950 à l'humble réalité d'aujourd'hui' in Pettiti, L-E Decaux, E and Imbert, P-H (ed) *La Convention européenne des droits de l'homme. Commentaire article par article* (Economica Paris, 1995) 27.

Petzold, H 'The Convention and the Principle of Subsidiarity' in Macdonald, R St John Matscher, M and Petzold, H (eds) *The European System for the Protection of Human Rights* (Martinus Nijhoff Dordrecht, 1993) 41.

Peukert, W 'Artikel 25 (Individualbeschwerde)' in Frowein, JA and Peukert, W *Europäische Menschenrechtskonvention. EMRK-Kommentar* (2nd edn Engel Kehl am Rhein, 1996) 523.

Peukert, W 'Artikel 50' in Frowein, JA and Peukert, W *Europäische Menschenrechts-Konvention. EMRK-Kommentar* (2nd edn Engel Kehl am Rhein, 1996) 667.

Rehof, LA 'Article 12' in Alfredsson, G and Eide, E (eds) *The Universal Declaration of Human Rights. A Common Standard of Achievement* (Martinus Nijhoff Hague, 1999) 251.

Ress, G 'Schmerzengeld für juristische Personen?' in Lüke, G Mikami, T and Prütting, H (eds) *Festschrift für Akira Ishikawa zum 70. Geburtstag am 27. November 2001* (de Gruyter Berlin, 2001) 429.

Rogge, K 'The "Victim" Requirement in Article 25 of the European Convention on Human Rights' in Matscher, F and Petzold, H (eds) *Protecting Human Rights: The European Dimension. Studies in Honour of Gérard J Wiarda* (Heymann Cologne, 1988) 539.

Ryssdal, R 'The Enforcement System Set up under the European Convention on Human Rights' in Bulterman, MK and Kuijer, M (eds) *Compliance with Judgments of International Courts: Symposium in Honour of Henry G Schermers* (Martinus Nijhoff Hague, 1996) 49.

de Salvia, M 'L'élaboration d'un "ius commune" des droits de l'homme et des libertés fondamentales dans la perspective de l'unitè européenne: l'oeuvre accomplie par la Commission et la Cour européenne des droits de l'homme' in Matscher, F and Petzold, H (eds) *Protecting Human Rights: The European Dimension. Studies in Honour of Gérard J Wiarda* (Cologne Heymann, 1988) 555.

Samnøy, Å 'The Origins of the Universal Declaration of Human Rights' in Alfredsson, G and Eide, E (eds) *The Universal Declaration of Human Rights. A Common Standard of Achievement* (Martinus Nijhoff Hague, 1999) 3.

Sansonetis, N 'Costs and Expenses' in Macdonald, R St John, Matscher, F and Petzold, H (eds) (*The European System for the Protection of Human Rights* (Martinus Nijhoff Dordrecht, 1993) 755.

Schermers, HG 'Exhaustion of Domestic Remedies' in Ando, N McWhinney, E and Wolfrum, R (eds) *Liber Amicorum Judge Shigeru Oda* (Kluwer Hague, 2002) vol 2, 947.

Schermers, HG 'The International Protection of the Right to Property' in Matscher, F and Petzold, H (eds) *Protecting Human Rights: The European Dimension. Studies in Honour of Gérard J Wiarda* (Heymann Cologne, 1988) 565.

de Schutter, O 'L'accès des personnes morales à la Cour européenne des droits de l'homme' in *Mélanges offerts à Silvio Marcus Helmons, Avancées et confines actuels des droits de l'homme aux niveaux international, européen et national* (Bruylant Bruxelles, 2003) 83.

Schwaighofer, C 'Legal Persons, Organisations, Shareholders as Applicants (Article 25 of the Convention)' in de Salvia, M and Villiger, ME (eds) *The Birth of European Human Rights Law: Liber Amicorum: Studies in Honour of Carl Aage Nørgaard* (Nomos Baden-Baden, 1998) 321.

Seidl-Hohenveldern, I 'The Social Function of Property and Property Protection in Present-Day International Law' in Kalshoven, F, Kuyper, PJ and Lammers, JG (eds) *Essays on the Development of the International Legal Order: in Memory of Haro F van Panhuys* (Sijthoff & Noordhoff Alphen aan den Rijn, 1980) 77.

Skouteris, T 'Customary Rules of Interpretation of Public International Law and Interpretative Practices in the WTO Dispute Settlement System' in Mengozzi, P (ed) *International Trade Law on the 50th Anniversary of the Multilateral Trade System* (Giuffrè Milan, 1999) 113.

Soyer, JC 'Retour discret de la raison d'état dans ces états soumis à la raison du droit (La fonction publique nationale)' in Aujol, J-L (ed) *Mélanges en hommage à Louis-Edmond Pettiti* (Bruylant Bruxelles, 1998) 661.

Smith, J 'A Citizens' Democracy' in R Blackburn (ed) *Towards a Constitutional Bill of Rights for the United Kingdom. Commentary and Documents* (Pinter London, 1999) 932.

Starck, C 'Artikel 1' in von Mangoldt, H, Klein, F and Starck, C (eds) *Das Bonner Grundgesetz* (4th edn Vahlen Munich, 1999) vol 1, [17 ff].

Starck, C 'Artikel 2' in von Mangoldt, H Klein, F and Starck, C (eds) *Das Bonner Grundgesetz. Kommentar* (4th edn Vahlen Munich, 1999) vol 1, 186.

Stavenhagen, R 'Cultural Rights: A Social Science Perspective' in Eide, A Krause, C and Rosas, A (eds) *Economic, Social and Cultural Rights. A Textbook* (2nd edn Martinus Nijhoff Dordrecht, 2001) 85.

Strachan, J 'The Human Rights Act 1998 and Commercial Law in the United Kingdom' in Bottomley, S and D Kinley (eds) *Commercial Law and Human Rights* (Dartmouth Ashgate Aldershot, 2002) 161.

Sudre, F 'Le recours aux "notions autonomes" ' in Sudre, F (ed) *L'interprétation de la Convention européenne des droits de l'homme. Actues du colloque des 13 et 14 mars 1998* (Bruylant Bruxelles, 1998) 93.

Teitgen, P-H 'Introduction to the European Convention on Human Rights' in Macdonald, R St John Matscher, F and Petzold, H (eds) *The European System for the Protection of Human Rights* (Martinus Nijhoff Dordrecht, 1993) 3.

Tomuschat, C 'Freedom of Association' in Macdonald, R St John Matscher, F and Petzold, H (eds) *The European System for the Protection of Human Rights* (Martinus Nijhoff Dordrecht, 1993) 493.

Tomuschat, C 'International Courts and Tribunals with Regionally Restricted and/or Specialized Jurisdiction' in *Judicial Settlement of International Disputes: International Court of Justice, other Courts and Tribunals, Arbitration and Conciliation: An International Symposium* (Max-Planck-Institut für ausländisches öffentliches Recht und Völkerrecht Heidelberg, 1987) 285.

Toth, A 'The Concept of Damage and Causality as Elements of Non-Contractual Liability' in Heukels, T and MacDonnell, A (eds) *The Action for Damages in Community Law* (Kluwer Hague, 1997) 179.

Twomey, PM 'Freedom of Expression for Commercial Actors' in NA Neuwahl and A Rosas (eds) *The European Union and Human Rights* (Martinus Nijhoff Hague, 1995) 265.

Vasak, K 'Analytical Examination of Civil and Political Rights' in Vasak, K and Alston, P (eds) *The International Dimensions of Human Rights* (UNESCO Paris, 1982) vol 1, 142.

Vosskuhle, A 'Artikel 93' in Dreier, H (ed) *Grundgesetz. Kommentar* (Mohr Siebeck Tübingen, 2000) 1077.

Wachsmann, P 'L'interprétation de la Convention européenne des droits de l'homme' in Sudre, F (ed) *L'interprétation de la Convention européenne des droits de l'homme. Actues du colloque des 13 et 14 mars 1998* (Bruylant Bruxelles, 1998) 335.

Wadham, J 'Why Incorporation of the European Convention on Human Rights Is Not Enough' in Gordon, R and Wilmot-Smith, R (eds) *Human Rights in the United Kingdom* (Oxford University Press Oxford, 1996) 25.

Weiler, JHH 'Fundamental Rights and Fundamental Boundaries: On the Conflict of Standards and Values in the Protection of Human Rights in the European Legal Space' in Weiler, JHH *The Constitution of Europe. 'Do the New Clothes Have an Emperor?' and Other Essays on European Integration* (Cambridge University Press Cambridge, 2000) 102.

Wildhaber, L 'Precedent in the European Court of Human Rights' in Mahoney, P and others (eds) *Protecting Human Rights: The European Perspective: Studies in Memory of Rolv Ryssdal* (Heymann Cologne, 2000) 1529.

de Witte, B 'The Past and Future Role of the European Court of Justice in the Protection of Human Rights' in Alston, P (ed) *The EU and Human Rights* (Oxford University Press Oxford, 1999) 859.

Wymeersch, E 'A Status Report on Corporate Governance Rules and Practices in Some Continental European States' in Hopt, KJ and others (eds) *Comparative Corporate Governance: The State of the Art and Emerging Research* (Clarendon Press Oxford, 1998) 1045.

Zwart, T 'Standing to Sue in Human Rights Litigation: Abstract and Hypothetical Cases' in Lawson, R and de Blois, M (eds) *The Dynamics of the Protection of Human Rights in Europe. Essays in Honour of Henry G Schermers* (Martinus Nijhoff Dordrecht, 1994) vol 3, 361.

ARTICLES

—— 'Company Law: Victim—Shareholders in Company—Lifting the Corporate Veil' [1996] EHRLR 191.

Alber, S and Widmaier, U 'Die EU-Charta der Grundrechte und ihre Auswirkungen auf die Rechtsprechung' (2000) 27 EuGRZ 497.

Albors-Lorens, A 'The European Court of Justice, More Than a Teleological Court' (2000) 2 Cambridge Ybk Eur Leg Stud 373.

Alston, P 'Resisting the Merger and Acquisition of Human Rights by Trade Law: A Reply to Petersmann' (2002) 13 EJIL 815.

Andriantsimbazovina, J ' "Chronique droits de l'homme": 1988–1995: L'élaboration progressive d'un ordre public européen des droits de l'homme' (1997) 33 CDE 655.

Aronovitz, AM 'Notes on the Current Status of the Rule of Exhaustion of Local Remedies in the European Convention on Human Rights' (1995) 25 Israel Ybk HR 73.

Blumberg, P 'The Corporate Entity in an Era of Multinational Corporations' (1990) 14 Delaware J Corp L 283.

Boisson de Chazournes, L 'Publicité commerciale et liberté d'expression dans la cadre du Conseil de l'Europe' (1988) 92 RGDIP 929.

Bratza, N 'The Implications of the Human Rights Act 1998 for Commercial Practice' [2000] EHRLR 1.

Brems, E 'The Margin of Appreciation Doctrine in the Case-Law of the European Court of Human Rights' (1996) 56 ZaöRV 240.

Brillat, R 'A New Protocol to the European Social Charter Providing for Collective Complaints' [1996] EHRLR 52.

Buffard, I and Zemanek, K 'The "Object" and "Purpose" of a Treaty: An Enigma?' (1998) 3 Austrian Rev Intl & Eur L 311.

Caflisch, L 'The Protection of Corporate Investments Abroad in the Light of the Barcelona Traction Case' (1971) 31 ZaöRV 162.

Calliess, C 'Zwischen staatlicher Souveränität und europäischer Effektivität: Zum Beurteilsungsspielraum der Vertragsstaaten im Rahmen des Art. 10 EMRK. Zugleich eine Urteilsanmerkung zu den Entscheidungen des EGMR in den Fällen markt intern und Jacubowski' (1996) 23 EurGRZ 293.

Carozza, PG 'Uses and Misuses of Comparative Law in International Human Rights: Some Reflections on the Jurisprudence of the European Court of Human Rights' (1998) 73 Notre Dame L Rev 1217.

Chayes, A 'The Role of the Judge in Public Law Litigation' (1976) 89 Harv L Rev 1281.

Cohn, J and Simitis, S ' "Lifting the Veil" in the Company Laws of the European Continent' (1963) 12 ICLQ 189.

Conforti, B 'Reflections on State Responsibility for the Breach of Positive Obligations: the Case-law of the European Court of Human Rights' (2003) 13 It YB Intl L 3.

Connelly, AM 'Problems of Interpretation of Article 8 of the European Convention on Human Rights' (1986) 35 ICLQ 567.

Copp, SR 'A Dignam and D Allen *Company Law and the Human Rights Act 1998* and M Smyth *Business and the Human Rights Act 1998*' (book review) (2001) 12 ICCLR 287.

Coppel, J and O'Neill, A 'The European Court of Justice: Taking Rights Seriously?' (1992) 29 CMLR 669.

Craig, PP 'Formal and Substantive Conceptions of the Rule of Law' (1995) 1 Diritto Pubblico 35.

Craven, M 'Legal Differentiation and the Concept of the Human Rights Treaty in International Law' (2000) 11 EJIL 489.

Crnic-Grotic, V 'Object and Purpose of Treaties in the Vienna Convention on the Law of Treaties' (1997) 7 Asian Ybk Intl L 141.

Cunningham, LA 'Commonalities and Prescriptions in the Vertical Dimensions of Global Corporate Governance' (1999) 84 Cornell L Rev 1133.

Diéz de Velasco Vallejo, M 'La protection diplomatique des sociétés et des actionnaires' (1974-I) 141 Receuil de Cours de l'Académie de Droit International 87.

Doswald-Beck, L 'The Meaning of the "Right to Respect for Private Life" under the European Convention on Human Rights' (1983) 4 HRLJ 283.

Douraki, T 'Les associations devant la Commission et la Cour européenne des Droits de l'Homme' (1989) 2 Hague Ybk Intl L 139.

Drzemczewski, AZ 'A Major Overhaul of the European Human Rights Convention Control Mechanism: Protocol No 11' (1997-II) 6 AEL 121.

Duffy, PJ 'The Protection of Privacy, Family Life and Other Rights under Article 8 of the European Convention on Human Rights' (1982) 2 YEL 191.

Dworkin, R 'Rights as Trumps' (1981) 1 OJLS 177.

Ely, JH 'Flag Desecration: A Case Study' (1975) 88 Harv L Rev 1482.

Emberland, M 'Case Comment: McElhinney v Ireland, Fogarty v United Kingdom, Al-Adsani v United Kingdom' (2002) 96 AJIL 699.

Emberland, M 'Compensating Companies for Non-Pecuniary Damage: *Comingersoll v Portugal* before the European Court of Human Rights and the Ambivalent Expansion of the ECHR Scope' (2003) 74 BYIL 409.

Emberland, M 'The Corporate Veil in the Case Law of the European Court of Human Rights' (2003) 63 ZaöRV 945.

Emberland, M 'The Corporate Veil in the Jurisprudence of the Human Rights Committee and the Inter-American Court and Commission of Human Rights' (2004) 4 HRLR 257.

Emberland, M 'Protection against Unwarranted Searches and Seizures of Corporate Premises under Article 8 of the European Convention on Human Rights: The *Colas Est SA v France* Approach' (2003) 25 Mich J Intl L 77.

Ermacora, F 'L'accès aux mécanismes jurisdictionnels de protection des personnes privée dans la Convention européenne des droits de l'homme' (1973) 6 HRJ 645.

Ewing, K 'The Human Rights Act and Parliamentary Democracy' (1999) 62 MLR 79.

Ewing, K and Gearty, C 'Rocky Foundations for Labour's New Rights' [1997] EHRLR 146.

Feliciano, FP 'Legal Problems of Private International Business Enterprises: An Introduction to the International Law of Private Business Associations and Economic Development' (1966-II) 118 Receuil de Cours de l'Académie de Droit International 209.

Franck, T 'The Emerging Right to Democratic Governance' (1992) 86 AJIL 46.

Frigo, M 'Peaceful Enjoyment of Possessions, Expropriation and Control of the Use of Property in the System of the European Convention on Human Rights' (2001) 10 It Ybk Intl L 45.

Ganshof van der Meersch, WJ 'Reliance, in the Case-Law of the European Court of Human Rights, on the Domestic Law of the States' (1980) 1 HRLJ 13.

Gilbert, G 'The Burgeoning Minority Rights of the European Court of Human Rights' (2002) 24 HRQ 736.

Goodman, R and Jinks, D 'Measuring the Effects of Human Rights Treaties' (2003) 14 EJIL 171.

Grewe, C 'Vergleich zwischen den Interpretationsmethoden europäischer Verfassungsgerichte und des Europäische Gerichtshof für Menschenrechte' (2001) 61 ZaöRV 459.

Hathaway, O 'Testing Conventional Wisdom' (2003) 13 EJIL 185.

Hathaway, O 'Do Human Rights Treaties Make a Difference?' (2002) 111 YLJ 1935.

Helfer, L 'Consensus, Coherence and the European Convention on Human Rights' (1993) 26 Cornell Intl L J 133.

Helfer, L and Slaughter, A-M 'Toward a Theory of Effective Supranational Adjudication' (1992) 107 YLJ 273.

Higgins, R 'Aspects Concerning the Barcelona Traction Light and Power Company, Ltd' (1970–71) 11 VJIL 327.

Jiménez de Aréchaga, E 'Diplomatic Protection of Shareholders in International Law' (1965) 4 Phil Intl L J 71.

Kennedy, D 'The International Human Rights Movement: Part of the Problem?' (2002) 15 Harv HR J 101.

Kingsbury, B 'Claims by Non-State Groups in International Law' (1992) 25 Cornell Intl L J 481.

Klabbers, J 'Some Problems Regarding the Object and Purpose of Treaties' (1997) 8 Finnish Ybk Intl L 138.

Kozinski, A and Banner, S 'Who's Afraid of Commercial Speech?' (1990) 76 Va L Rev 627.

Krohn, M 'Minority Squeeze-outs and the European Convention on Human Rights' (2003) 10 Tidsskrift for forretningsjus 394.

Lester, A 'The United Kingdom Acceptance of the Statutory Jurisdiction: What Went on in Whitehall in 1965' [1998] PL 237.

Lillich, RB 'Two Perspectives on the Barcelona Traction Case: The Rigidity of Barcelona' (1971) 65 AJIL 522.

Loucaides, L 'Personality and Privacy under the European Convention on Human Rights' (1991) 61 BYIL 175.

Mahoney, P 'Judicial Activism and Judicial Self-Restraint in the European Court of Human Rights: Two Sides of the Same Coin' (1990) 11 HRLJ 57.

Mahoney, P 'Marvellous Richness of Diversity or Invidious Cultural Relativism?' (1998) 19 HRLJ 1.

Marcus Helmons, S 'L'applicabilité de la Convention européenne des droits de l'homme aux personnes morales' (1996) 4 JdT 150.

Marks, S 'The European Convention on Human Rights and Its "Democratic Society" ' (1996) 66 BYIL 209.

Marston, G 'The United Kingdom's Part in the Preparation of the European Convention on Human Rights, 1950' (1993) 42 ICLQ 796.

Mattli, W and Slaughter, A-M 'Revisiting the European Court of Justice' (1998) 52 IO 177.

Maupain, F 'The Settlement of Disputes within the International Labour Organization' (1999) 2 JIEL 273.

Mayer, CJ 'Personalizing the Impersonal: Corporations and the Bill of Rights' (1990) 41 Hastings L J 577.

McCloskey, RG 'Economic Due Process and the Supreme Court' [1962] S Ct Rev 34.

McCrudden, C 'The Future of the EU Charter for Fundamental Rights' (Jean Monnet Working Paper 2001:10).

de Merieux, M 'The German Competition Law and Article 10 ECHR' (1995) 20 ELR 388.

de Meyer, J 'Human Rights in a Commercial Context' (1984) 5 HRLJ 139.

Miles, J 'Standing under the Human Rights Act 1998. Theories of Rights Enforcement and the Nature of Public Law Adjudication' (2000) 59 CLJ 133.

Miller, SK 'Piercing the Corporate Veil among Affiliated Companies in the European Community and in the US: A Comparative Analysis of US, German, and UK Veilpiercing Approaches' (1998) 36 Am Bus L J 73.

Moravcsik, A 'The Origins of Human Rights Regimes: Democratic Delegation in Postwar Europe' (2000) 54 IO 217.

Negley, G 'Philosophical Views on the Value of Privacy' (1966) 31 L & Contemp Probs 319.

Nissenbaum, H 'Protecting Privacy in an Information Age: The Problem of Privacy in Public' (1998) 17 L & Phil 559.

O'Donnell, TA 'The Margin of Appreciation Doctrine: Standards in the Jurisprudence of the European Court of Human Rights' (1982) 4 HRQ 474.

Orrego Vicuña, F 'Changing Approaches to the Nationality of Claims in the Context of Diplomatic Protection and International Dispute Settlement' (2000) 15 ICSID Rev 340.

Ossenbühl, F 'State and Market in the Constitutional Order' (2000) 53 SMU L Rev 561.

Ovey, C 'The Margin of Appreciation and Article 8 of the Convention' (1998) 19 HRLJ 10.

Petersmann, E-U 'Human Rights and International Economic Law in the 21st Century. The Need to Clarify Their Interrelationships' (2001) 4 JIEL 3.

Pietzcker, J 'The US Commercial Speech Doctrine' (1999) 59 ZaöRV 1.

Posner, RA 'The Right to Privacy' (1978) 12 Ga L Rev 393.

Prebensen, S 'The Margin of Appreciation and Articles 9, 10 and 11 of the Convention' (1998) 19 HRLJ 13.

Prepeluh, U 'Die Entwicklung der Margin of Appreciation-Doktrin im Hinblick auf die Pressefreiheit' (2001) 61 ZaöRV 771.

Rachels, J 'Why Privacy Is Important' (1975) 4 Phil & Pub Aff 323.

Ratner, SR 'Corporations and Human Rights: A Theory of Legal Responsibility' (2001) 111 YLJ 443.

Redish, MH 'The First Amendment in the Marketplace: Commercial Speech and the Values of Free Expression' (1971) 39 Geo Wash L Rev 429.

Said, T and Wadham, J 'What Price the Right of Individual Petition: Report of the Evaluation Group to the Committee of Ministers on the European Court of Human Rights' [2002] EHRLR 169.

Schachter, O 'Human Dignity as a Normative Concept' (1983) 77 AJIL 848.

Schermers, HG 'Election of Judges to the European Court of Human Rights' (1998) 23 ELR 568.

Schoekkenbroek, J 'The Basis, Nature and Application of the Margin-of-Appreciation Doctrine in the Case-Law of the European Court of Human Rights General Report' (1998) 19 HRLJ 30.

de Schutter, O 'L'interpretation de la Convention européenne des droits de l'homme: un essai en démolition' (1992) 70 RDISPPS 83.

Sedley, S 'Opinion: A Bill of Rights for Britain' [1997] EHRLR 458.

Sevecke, T ' "Schockwerbung" der Firma Benetton verstösst nicht gegen 1 UWG. Zugleich eine Anmerkung zum Urteil des Bundesverfassungsgerichts vom 12.12.2000' (2001) 32 AfP 179.

Shestack, JJ 'The Philosophic Foundations of Human Rights' (1998) 20 HRQ 201.
Smith, C 'More Disagreement over Human Dignity: Federal Constitutional Court's Most Recent Benetton Advertising Decision' (2003) 4 German L J 533.
Temple Lang, J and Rizza, C 'The Ste Colas Est and Others v. France Case: European Court of Human Rights Judgment of April 16, 2002' (2002) 23 Eur Comp L Rev 413.
Vasak, K 'Le droit international des droits de l'homme' (1974) 140 Receuil des Cours de l'Académie de Droit International 333.
Walden, IN and Savage, RN 'Data Protection and Privacy Laws: Should Organisations Be Protected?' (1988) 37 ICLQ 337.
Waldock, H 'The Effectiveness of the System Set up by the European Convention on Human Rights' (1980) 1 HRLJ 1.
Warren, SD and Brandeis, LD 'The Right to Privacy' (1890) 4 Harv L Rev 193.
Wood, SG and Scharffs, BG 'Applicability of Human Rights Standards to Private Corporations: An American Perspective' (2002) 50 Am J Comp L 531, 531–32.
Wright, J 'The Protection of Corporate Privacy' (1983) 11 Intl Bus Lawyer 119.
Yannaca-Small, C '"Indirect Expropriation and the "Right to Regulate" in *International Investment Law*' (OECD Directorate for Financial and Enterprise Affairs Working Paper on International Investment 4:2004).

MISCELLANEOUS

—— *Survey of Activities 2003* (Strasbourg European Court of Human Rights 2004).
Council of Europe Directorate of Human Rights (ed): *Guaranteeing the Effectiveness of the European Convention on Human Rights. Collected Texts* (Strasbourg: Council of Europe 2004).
Explanatory Report to Protocol No 11 to the Convention for the Protection of Human Rights and Fundamental Freedoms restructuring the control machinery established thereby (Protocol 11 Explanatory Report), available at <http://conventions.coe.int/Treaty/en/Reports/Html/155.htm>.
Explanatory Report to Protocol No 14 to the Convention for the Protection of Human Rights and Fundamental Freedoms, amending the control system of the Convention (Protocol 14 Explanatory Report), available at <http://conventions.coe.int/Treaty/en/Reports/Html/1194.htm>.
International Law Commission's Draft Articles on the Responsibility of States for Internationally Wrongful Acts, UN GAOR 56th Session Supp No 10 Un Doc A/56/10, chapter IV.E.1, UNGA Res 56/83 (28 January 2002) UN Doc A/RES/56/83.

Index

Please note that ECHR stands for European Convention on Human Rights

The manufacturer's authorised representative in the EU for product safety is Oxford University Press España S.A. of el Parque Empresarial San Fernando de Henares, Avenida de Castilla, 2 – 28830 Madrid (www.oup.es/en or product.safety@oup.com). OUP España S.A. also acts as importer into Spain of products made by the manufacturer.

www.ingramcontent.com/pod-product-compliance
Lightning Source LLC
LaVergne TN
LVHW011754200926
848484LV00003B/702
* 9 7 8 0 1 9 9 2 8 9 8 3 7 *